UPHILL ALL
THE WAY

UPHILL ALL THE WAY

A Documentary History of Women in Australia

Compiled and introduced by
Kay Daniels and Mary Murnane

 University of Queensland Press

Typeset by Press Etching Pty Ltd, Brisbane.
Printed and bound by Southwood Press Pty Ltd, Sydney.

Distributed in the United Kingdom, Europe, the Middle East, Africa, and the Caribbean by Prentice-Hall International, International Book Distributors Ltd, 66 Wood Lane End, Hemel Hempstead, Herts., England.

National Library of Australia
Cataloguing-in-Publication data

Daniels, Kay.
  Uphill all the way.

  Index
  ISBN 0 7022 1345 4

  1. Women — Australia — History — Sources. I. Murnane, Mary, joint comp. II. Title.

301.412'0994

Contents

Illustrations

Note

The numbers in square brackets in the introductions apply to document numbers. When full names have been removed they are acknowledged in the text of the document in the form Ann [B ——] and the person referred to elsewhere as Ann B. Original spelling has been retained. Omissions are signified in the usual way (. . .) and our interpolations are placed in square brackets. The term *sic* to signify an error in the text of the original document only appears on those few occasions when its omission would lead to misinterpretation.

Acknowledgments

We are grateful to the following people and institutions whose co-operation and kindness made possible the publication of the material contained in this collection: Mr Jack Beynon for permission to print an extract from the writing of Bee Miles; and Mr P.M. Drake-Brockman for correspondence of Dr Roberta Jull; Comndr. J.S. Horn for correspondence of Penelope Belt; Mrs Clarice McNamara for an extract from her article "The 'New' Married Woman"; Sir Laurence Street for letters and addresses of Jessie Street; Mr Ric Throssell for Katharine Susannah Prichard's "Notes on the Modern Women's Club"; Sigmund Freud Copyrights Ltd for correspondence from Sigmund Freud to Marion Piddington; the Estate of Stella Maria Sarah Miles Franklin for permission to print in part a short story by Miles Franklin; Mrs Evelyn Wood for extracts from the writing of Jean Beadle; the United Associations of Women for permission to print documents contained in their collection of papers in the Mitchell Library; the Tasmanian Aboriginal Centre, Hobart, for correspondence in their possession; Mr Shadrak Munisi for his assistance and the International Planned Parenthood Federation, London, for permission to use material from their archives; Ms Judith McLean and the Family Planning Association of N.S.W. for permission to reprint material from the records of the Racial Hygiene Association. The extract from *Tell Morning This* by Kylie Tennant is reprinted by permission of Angus & Robertson Publishers. We thank the Tasmanian Historical Research Association and N.J.B. Plomley for permission to reprint extracts from *Friendly Mission;* Mrs Patricia Hurd for permission to reprint extracts from the work of Jean Devanny; Melbourne University Press for an extract from F.W. Eggleston et al, *Australian Standards of Living;* the University of Sydney for extracts from the writing of Dr Norman Haire; the Communist Party of Australia for permission to reprint extracts from journals and pamphlets including the *Working Woman.* For permission to reprint extracts from the press we thank the *Sunday Telegraph,* John Fairfax & Sons Ltd, West Australian Newspapers Ltd, Queensland Newspapers Pty Ltd.

We are very grateful to Patricia Hurd, Irene Greenwood, Nell McLeod, Jenny Prohaska and the other women who did not wish their names to be published, for their permission to print tape recorded interviews, and to Jean Daniels, Eva Bacon and to the Union of Australian Women, Brisbane, for helping us to record some of these interviews.

We would like to thank the following libraries and archives for their assistance and, where they were able to do so, for giving us permission to print material from their records: the Archives Offices of Tasmania, South Australia, Queensland, New South Wales and the Public Record Office of Victoria; the J.S. Battye Library of Western Australian History, the Tasmanian Collection in the State Library of Tasmania, the La Trobe Library, the Mitchell Library, the

John Oxley Library, the National Library of Australia, the British Library, London and the Fawcett Library in the City of London Polytechnic. Photographs reproduced are from the State Archives of South Australia and Western Australia, the Mitchell Library, the La Trobe Library and the Sir John Ferguson Collection, Manuscript Section, the National Library of Australia. We are grateful to them and to the Family Planning Association of N.S.W. who allowed us to reproduce photographic material published by the Racial Hygiene Association. We would also like to thank Miss Margaret Medcalf of the Battye Library and Miss Suzanne Mourot of the Mitchell Library for their help in locating holders of copyright. Although we have attempted to trace copyright holders we have not always been successful. We would like to apologize to anyone to whom this applies.

Our thanks also go to Denise Hare for helping with the proof reading, Amanda Lohrey for her work on the index, Kati Griffiths for typing much of the correspondence associated with the collection, and to Annie Bickford, Bob Debus, John Lonie, Susan Magarey, Ian North, Mrs Ruth Goble and Anne Picot for their help. We are grateful, too, to our editor, Bridget Everett, and at the University of Queensland Press, to Merril Yule and Ailsa Andersen. Kay Daniels would like to thank the University of Tasmania for assistance and for leave.

Finally, we acknowledge our debt to the National Research Programme funded during International Women's Year and to its publication *Women in Australia: An Annotated Guide to Records* which we edited with Anne Picot in 1977 and which pointed us in the direction of many of the documents printed here.

Introduction

This book is intended to bring the reader into an active relationship with the past. The problem in compiling it has been to put together a collection of documents that does not create a false relationship between reader and compiler.

Books of historical documents often give the reader the illusion of acting as a historian, by presenting a selection of documents as if they are raw material waiting to be turned into new and exciting history. The compiler pretends not to press upon the reader an historical interpretation. Documents are left to speak for themselves, a surrogate archives in which the reader is invited to wander. But collections of documents are not substitutes for libraries and archives, and instead of generating new ideas, often the effect of the documentary collection is to direct the reader backwards into the already known. History, in its polished state, is disguised as documents. There remains little chance for the reader to become more than a passive consumer.

We hope that this collection does not do these things, but raises new ideas and encourages the reader to participate by moving beyond our selection of documents and our interpretation. With that in mind, we have tried throughout to retain the sense that these are historical documents that, examined internally and in relation to each other, can help to reveal the way that history is written and therefore help to make both our past and our present more intelligible. But documents, even in aggregation, give only a partial picture and need to be seen as part of the social history of the period and the themes pursued and tested in the broader context.

As compilers, we have not tried to remain invisible behind the documents. We have been intrusive rather than self-effacing, and the collection is structured in such a way as to express our own ideas about the position of women in Australia and the way that the study of women's history can be approached. The documents have been introduced in such a way that they can be seen not only in relation to each other — sometimes confirming, sometimes antagonistic — but are also given the coherence of a continuing commentary.

The selection is large and covers a diverse range of women's experiences. It includes women from different classes, ages and races, over a wide area of Australia from the early days of settlement until the beginning of the 1950s. We have used a variety of different kinds of records, many of them unpublished — government reports, comments by eminent visitors, the pencilled notes of ordinary women, minutes of organizations, pamphlets, speeches, letters, depositions, radio talks, police reports. Most are written records; but the past also resides in the memories of the living and we have supplemented the written personal testimonies with some tape-recorded interviews. We do not wish to assert the paramountcy of one kind of record over another and we hope that the collection demonstrates that our knowledge of the past is enriched by assessing different types of historical evidence.

The documents are divided into four sections and into subgroups in three of those sections. Each section is concerned with themes over a broad period of time. We have also made use of clusters of documents relating to an episode; for example, in the case of Biloela Industrial School, a number of documents expressing the attitudes of different people at a point of crisis in the institution together provide a picture of one aspect of social relations in Sydney, as well as illustrating the movement in welfare away from untrained and often uneducated officers to the professional. Similar clusters around the themes of prostitution, birth control and eugenics offer some indication of the importance of these themes in the history of women in Australian society.

Two other major themes are explored in documents scattered throughout the book: the active response of women to their conditions and the class relationship between women.

Because ordinary women most often found a place in recorded history when they were criminal, poor or prostitutes, this book has a number of documents that describe those experiences. When women's involvement with the authorities was not a matter of public notice, we have usually omitted names.

While we have attempted to show ways in which women were oppressed and exploited, we have not always shown them as passive victims whose responses are left to the imagination of the reader instructed by observers from a different social class. On many occasions, women and even very young girls fought back against individuals who were the representatives of the structures that oppressed them, sometimes using traditional pre-political forms of rebellion such as arson. This militancy is again evident during the Great Depression, amongst unemployed women and the wives of workers who interpreted their individual experiences within the framework of an analysis of the broader society.

Amongst bourgeois women, the rebellion took a more sedate form, as they too protested against the position of women in society and attempted to gain a share in the privileges of their class. Not excluded from "womanliness" by coarsening work nor by the defeminizing processes of material hardship, they were unwilling to relinquish the stereotype in the battle for political influence. Their ideas remained confined both by received ideas about femininity and by liberal political conventions.

These two groups of women, separated by class and politics — rebels against exclusion from privilege on the one hand and against exploitation on the other — cannot be regarded separately by historians. Only in their relationship to each other, as part of a wider relationship between classes, can they be understood.

This book is also about the women's movement: its continuing dilemmas and its ability to respond to the problems of women in Australia. What is striking is the repetition of problems and responses and the repeated loss of the knowledge gained from women's experiences over time. This is not the result of something timeless in the condition of women that can be made accessible through ahistorical analysis, but seems instead to lie in the unity of the period from the end of the nineteenth century to the present. In many ways, we are still in that period in which progressive women as a group within the bourgeoisie began to fight for a wider sphere of action for themselves. Their philosophy of feminism, allied with welfare reformism and a rejection of the concept of a class-divided society, was projected on to all women. Success for them waxed and waned according to the degree of influence progressive views in general gained in the broader community and ultimately depended on factors beyond their control : population policy, workforce requirements, the economy. Armed only with this philosophy, the movement was either immobilized by the transparency of conflicts it could not acknowledge, as in times of economic crisis, or met with limited success on single issues and considerably more success in winning new niches in the community for its activists. Many of these continuing problems of the women's movement, we think, can be approached through the historical documents included here.

KAY DANIELS
MARY MURNANE
Hobart, 1 January 1979

PART 1

Outcasts of Society

Introduction

Within this section, we look at the lives and circumstances of some of the women and girls who could be described as "outcasts" of Australian society. We begin with the convict institutions; but female convicts are not the only women to fall into this category, and while all convict women were outcasts of the old society, not all were thought to be irreclaimable in the new. Women who were destitute or were unable to support themselves and did not have the protection of a man, women who were both poor and old or infirm or insane, children who were neglected or criminal or thought to be in "moral danger", all could be described as outcasts, in the sense that they did not or were not able to comply with society's expectations of them, with the result that they were often incarcerated in asylums and other institutions and generally regarded as not contributing to the general well-being of society. But whereas for men of the working classes, conformity to a work ethic was the keynote of their social role, the relationship between these women and society's expectations is more ambiguous.

Raymond Evans, in looking at Queensland, has suggested that inside the colonial community, "the dominant group concensus imposed the exacting regimen of regular, productive, responsible work as the basis of all social utility and good", and that, cast out from society were the idle and the useless.[1] For women, however, there were a variety of ways in which they could be productive, beyond paid work. Their contribution to society could be made through unpaid work in the family, which helped to make the working-class family a viable and efficient unit, or alternatively, they could contribute through procreation. Women were expected to perform a variety of roles in society, some of which were contradictory, and the expectations placed upon women in general are reflected in the following documents, which describe the lives of women and girls commonly thought to be on its peripheries.

What emerges immediately is the vulnerability of women. In the first years of the settlement, the sexual vulnerability of the convict women, combined with the difficulties they faced in achieving economic independence, gave the institutions erected to house them and to punish colonial offenders a dual role that institutions for the male able-bodied seldom possessed: they were both refuges and places of punishment. This dual character persisted in later institutions erected by both government and private charitable organizations and contributed to the problem of classification of inmates, which was a continuing issue for administrators whose job it was to divide the reclaimable from the lost, and to aid reform of some while punishing others. One function of these institutions, beginning with the Female Factory at Parramatta, was to find the women who could be "made useful" and returned to ordinary society — that is, who would be able to become, within their own social station, good wives and mothers, or who could be trained to become efficient (usually domestic) workers. While good training for service also fitted a woman for married life, the tendency for servant girls to marry was one of the causes of the shortage of servants. Both roles were therefore intimately connected with the survival of the family — that is, of two different families at two different levels of society. They were complementary roles, but they also could be antagonistic.

What then dominates these institutions is the implicit belief that the problems of middle- and upper-class women requiring servants to sustain a particular style of life and the problems of lower-class women and girls who were destitute, or neglected or criminal, could be resolved within the same institution. Reformation is given a precise social meaning within this context of sustaining and supporting "the family". More illustrations of the "servant question" are given in later sections. Here the main emphasis is on the role of the institutions.

The widespread belief that among convict women, few were able to be reformed is placed in perspective when what was expected of them is considered. The Committee of Inquiry that looked into female convict discipline in Van Diemen's Land [18] pointed out that a greater degree of reformation was expected of women than men, and less attainable standards were held out to them. This in part derived from the double standard of morality observed by society, but also from the fact that servants provided part of the support system for the family. More hope, however, was held out for the children of convicts and the institutions set up to train and care for girls reveal even more clearly the same processes and expectations.

The convict origins of the early settlements, the high incidence of illegitimacy and the visible failure of ticket-of-leave and poor families to imbue their children with moral rectitude and a willingness to work hard, induced the government to intervene early to make good these deficiencies. From the early nineteenth century, colonial authorities were aided in these efforts by the work of philanthropic women.[2] In 1826, Lady Darling established the Female School of Industry in Sydney, which trained girls to be domestic servants and apprenticed them out to a "subscriber", one of the women who contributed to the upkeep of the institution, thus beginning a tradition of reciprocity continued in later establishments. [19] The family influence was considered to be such a threat to the girls, that they were allowed to see their parents only once a year, and then only in the presence of an officer of the institution. Insulated from the "vices" of the lower classes, the girls were to be taught skills and, more importantly, taught attitudes consistent with a life of respectability conferred by hard work, honesty and a willingness to tolerate a life on the threshold of poverty. In 1867, industrial schools for destitute children were set up in New South Wales and Tasmania, and reformatories or training schools for children who had come before the courts. Particular emphasis was placed on female juveniles who were thought to be exposed to greater temptations. The industrial schools in Hobart and Launceston were subsidized by the State, supervised by a male board of governors and run by ladies' committees. The records of the Hobart Girls' Industrial School show that many girls were apprenticed to members of the ladies' committee.

While in Tasmania and New South Wales there existed the hope that problems of institutional care and punishment would diminish or wither away with the demise of the old convict class, institutions for children and the necessity of establishing institutions to house women in the non-convict colonies belied this. The difficulties entailed in disposing of free female labour, especially among the Irish girls who had few of the required skills, had led to the setting up of servant homes and emigrant depots in ports and country areas. The mobility of the male labour force, as well as changes in regional employment, meant that the numbers of women without support were frequently swelled by those who were deserted or whose husbands had left in search of work. The extreme hardships of pioneering life, the shock of unfamiliar conditions left casualties too, as the records of asylums show. Moreover, the areas of employment open to women, especially to women with children, who formed the bulk of recipients of relief, were few, overcrowded and poorly paid. The crucial question asked of women seeking support was not whether or not work was available (although women with children were more frequently expected to be able to support themselves in the early period than they were later), but whether there was a man to support them. Their sexual behaviour and relationships therefore were always relevant to an enquiry into their material circumstances and this made the enquiry more personal, more open to hearsay and opinion. In this way, the productive and useful function of these women was recognized; the problem was, who was to pay for it — the community or the individual? The dilemma faced by governments from the earliest period in both convict and free settlements was to resolve this difficulty so that the reproduction of the family in the working classes could proceed in a structured way that would relieve the authorities of the economic burdens entailed. This is reflected in the early legislative attempts to make members of the family responsible for each other (usually to make husbands responsible for the support of their wives). The almost complete failure of this legislation was by the 1890s a matter of urgent concern to the private charity organizations, who were aware of the high incidence of female pauperization. Documents in this section reveal the economic precariousness of women and the consequences of this.

In many female trades, the failure of earnings to be sufficient to support one or more persons, and low wages as a continuing cause of destitution, are illustrated here and in the later section on "Working Women". What is striking is that an increase in the female wage does not immediately present itself as a solution to the problems of these women, even though charitable institutions were aware that their aid often supplemented low wages. It was left to others to argue, however, that these payments allowed some women, particularly in the sweated trades, to undercut others and reduce rates by taking less than subsistence pay. Similarly, the needlewoman who was made more efficient by the gift of a sewing-machine was likely to be replaced as a recipient of charity by the woman who could not now compete with her. In this way, the charities inserted themselves into the economic lives of their beneficiaries, but in solving the individual problem they left the broader question of low pay and competition in the female trades untouched. Furthermore, within the institutions themselves, the wish that institutions should be as nearly as possible self-supporting, led to them being firmly placed within the economic structure of society. Not only were they involved in training labour, they were also employers, and allegations were made that officers benefited personally from the labour of inmates and that the training and allocating of inmates were determined on the basis of the financial needs of the institution. Just as important, many of these institutions entered into the female trades (particularly washing), and with the advantages of mechanized equipment and exemption from factory legislation regulating hours and pay, they were often formidable competitors. Pauperization of women in these trades was the result.

The emphasis on delineating between deserving and undeserving applicants for relief, and the aim of bringing about a personal reformation, illustrate the stress placed on the individual and her control over her circumstances. But, as the documents show, the institutions had no control over the world into which their inmates were released. Girls taught to be submissive and to hope for marriage were not necessarily equipped to protect themselves, and "recidivism" in actuality often meant simply that a girl who had been admitted to an industrial school to "protect" her from the sexual advances of a man (who was himself unpunished) was on release seduced, made pregnant and launched on another journey through the institutions. [See 41.]

The documents include a series of descriptions of spectacular riots and escapes, not because the institutions were in a continual state of uproar — Alice Henry, a well-known Melbourne journalist with a special interest in health and welfare pointed out that life in these institutions tended rather to be monotonous and repressive — but because documentation of these occasions is revealing of the institution, its life and the relationships within it. While many reasons were given at the time for such disturbances, the behaviour and suitability of staff was always mentioned. In 1873, Rosamond Hill told the Royal Commission into Public Charities in New South Wales that the operation of industrial schools should be supervised by voluntary committees of wealthy people with philanthropic interests. [32] In 1899, Alice Henry argued that the State could no longer afford to leave the supervision of industrial schools to people who had no scientific training. [37] A number of the documents in this section are concerned with the women who worked in the institutions as matrons, teachers, turnkeys, midwives. Some things about their backgrounds emerge: they were often from poor families, sometimes in the early period they were convicts, sometimes their families also worked in institutions. Mrs Hutchinson, the matron at Cascades, whose life is better documented than most, was the daughter of a super-intendent of the Parramatta Female Factory. The matron at the Perth lunatic asylum, who lost her job when her husband died and who later became a recipient of poor relief, is a more extreme example of the precariousness of this sort of employment than any of the women described here, whose lives outside the job remain sketchy. Nevertheless, officers were clearly subjected to scrutiny in their private lives and subject to pre-emptory dismissal. Distinguished from the voluntary ladies' committees by their social station and from later welfare workers by their lack of training, these women present a neglected group of female workers. Their social position is suggested in a passage from Tasma's *Uncle Piper of Piper's Hill*, when George is forced to reveal to his pedigreed fiance that his mother was the matron on a convict ship, one "of the very few *respectable* females in Hobart", and Sara's reaction is thus:

> He need not have despoiled her so ruthlessly of the last vestige of an illusion. There have been great and noble ladies who have undertaken missions to savage countries and who have been reformers of prisons, too. Why should not the former Mrs Piper have been allowed the benefit of the legitimate doubt that might have rested upon the nature of her calling? ... After all, the matron of the convicts *might* have been a lady. In all cases she was buried out of sight, and the actual prospects of buying a trousseau that would realise the most ecstatic day-dreams might be accepted as a set-off against the doubtful antecedents of a deceased mother-in-law.[3]

Clearly, too, outside the relationships of the institution, many of the people employed in these institutions were as powerless as their charges, and the phrase "outcasts of Society", when used in one of the documents, is in fact used by George Lucas, who was Superintendent in charge of the Newcastle Industrial School, to describe not the inmates, but he and his fellow officers. [21]

Notes

1.   Raymond Evans, "The Hidden Colonists: Deviance and Social Control in Colonial Queensland", in *Social Policy in Australia: Some Perspectives, 1901-1975*, ed. Jill Roe (Melbourne: Cassell, 1976), p. 94.

2.   Elizabeth Windschuttle has examined the role of these women in "Evangelicalism and Philanthropy: The Public Role of Ruling-class Women in Colonial Australia, 1788-1850", a paper presented at the Women and Labour Conference, Sydney, May 1978.

3.   Tasma, *Uncle Piper of Piper's Hill* (Melbourne: Nelson, 1969), p. 214.

Convict Institutions

1. "Unhappy Exiles"

The Reverend Samuel Marsden was not always compassionate in his attitude to convicts, but in this essay, written in 1807, his strong feelings about the corruption and depravity of life in the Sydney settlement led him to view the vulnerability of newly arrived convict women with some perception, and to propose the building of a "Place of Accommodation" to give them refuge on arrival.

... tho the Settlement in N.S.W. has been established almost twenty years, yet no serious Attempts for the Reformation of the Female Convicts, sent out from time to time, have hithertoo been made ...

One great Inconvenience they suffer, is for the want of a public Building for their Reception out of the transport Ships, where they might be decently accommodated and provided for till their respective Characters and Qualifications were ascertained, and suitable Situations and Employments found for them. On their first arrival for the want of a public Place of Accommodation, many of them are much distressed, and from that distress are urged to form such Connections as preclude all human Probability of their future Reformation. It has been a common Custom (a Custom that reflects the highest Disgrace upon the British Government in that Colony) that shortly after a Ship has anchored in the Cove with female Convicts, Settlers, Soldiers and Prisoners have been permitted to go on Board, and make their respective Selections amongst them and to induce these poor unfortunate women, some by threats and some by Promises, to accompany them to their habitations and to become their mistresses and to make room for them a former wife or mistress with their children are not unfrequently turned out into the Street in the utmost want and distress. These women having never set foot in N.S. Wales and being totally ignorant of the Circumstances, Characters and Dispositions of their Admirers, are not likely to derive any happiness from their new Connections but almost certain accumulated misery and wretchedness. These abandoned men will keep them as long as it is agreeable or convenient or until some other female object strikes their fancy when they are immediately turned off with perhaps one or more natural Children to struggle with ... These unhappy Exiles, by suffering every hardship that nature can bear, and by living in habitual vice to procure a precarious Subsistance, lose every Idea of Propriety, Morality, and Religion and exist merely to increase their own wretchedness and to corrupt Society by their vicious Examples ... was there a public Place of Accomodation provided for the reception of the female Convicts, on their first arrival, where they might be usefully employed, till they had learned the local situation of the Settlement; this would give them an opportunity of consulting their own Interest and Happiness; and of forming such *lawful Connections* as might not only tend to their future welfare, but also to that of their children ...

Samuel Marsden, "Essays: A Few Observations on the Situation of Female Convicts in New South Wales" (1807).

2. Building the Female Factory

The Female Factory at Parramatta was one of the many public buildings erected during Macquarie's administration. The Colonial Office saw the absence of any systematic distribution of the female convicts as a threat to order and authority in the colony. One dispatch to Macquarie, in 1809, described the colony as "little better than an extensive brothel". Macquarie's solution was a female factory for the reception and employment of the convict women. Work on the factory began in 1819. Macquarie describes it as:

A Large Commodious handsome stone Built Barrack and Factory, three Stories high, with Wings of one Story each for the accomodation and residence of 300 Female Convicts, with all the requisite Out-offices including Carding, Weaving and Loom Rooms, Work-Shops, Stores for Wool, Flax etc. etc.; Quarters for the Superintendant, and also a large Kitchen Garden for the use of the Female Convicts, and Bleaching Ground for Bleaching the Cloth and Linen Manufactured; the whole of the Buildings and said Grounds, consisting of about Four acres, being enclosed with a high Stone Wall and Moat *or Wet Ditch*. N.B. — This important and highly useful as well as necessary Building was erected by Contract.

"Description of Public Works Undertaken", Macquarie to Lord Bathurst, 27 July 1822.

3. The Treatment of Female Convicts

The following letter from the English prison reformer Elizabeth Fry gives her views on the treatment of female convicts. Lord Bathurst sent a copy of the letter to Sir Thomas Brisbane and a duplicate to Colonel George Arthur, commenting that the papers seemed to him "to contain many valuable Suggestions" and recommended them "to your attentive consideration with the view of carrying them into practical operation, as occasion may require".

Respected Friend,
    In compliance with thy obliging proposal, I take the liberty to state in writing our views relative to the Female Convicts in Van Diemen's Land, in order that they may be submitted to the consideration of Lord Bathurst, as we cannot but feel anxious that the care we extend to this degraded class of the Community, not only in the different Prisons but also on the Voyage, should be rendered permanently beneficial through the co-operation of Government in the Colonies. In the first place, we deem it expedient that a Building be erected at Hobart Town for the reception of Female Convicts. That a respectable and judicious matron be there stationed, to superintend the whole Establishment under the direction of the Governor or some magistrate appointed by him for that service. That part of the building be appropriated to the use of an adult and girls' school, and that School Mistresses be selected by the Matron from among the reformed Prisoners, provided they be sufficiently qualified for the office.
    That immediately on the arrival of a ship, after it has been visited either by the Governor or by some person appointed by him for the purpose of inspecting into its general condition, the convicts shall be quietly (and as privately as possible) conducted from the ship to the said building, where the deportment of every prisoner

shall be scrutinized with exactness; that those, who merit a favourable report, be selected and allowed to be taken into service by the respectable inhabitants under such restraints and regulations as may be considered needful. The others to remain confined, receiving at the same time suitable instruction and employment until they evince sufficient amendment in habits and disposition to warrant the grant of similar indulgence; and we conceive that much benefit might result, if some of the regulations mentioned in the new act of Parliament relative to prisons were enforced in this Colony and in New South Wales. We would also propose that a sufficient supply of strong and decent clothing (not parti-coloured) be provided for them during the Voyage, to be put on when they enter the ship in exchange for their own, of which an Inventory shall be immediately taken by a female officer and given with the clothes to the Surgeon (in the presence of their respective owners), who shall carefully keep them in reserve and deliver them to the Matron of the prison, to which they are destined, who shall receive the same in presence of the prisoners, and shall at the same time see if they tally correctly with the inventories; and upon their discharge from prison but not before, she shall restore them to their proper owners; and we consider that it would be a great advantage, on the voyage and more especially whilst lying in the river, that the women should wear a simple uniform dress; and we think it *indispensable* for establishing of order and for enforcing the needful regulations on board the ship that a Matron be stationed constantly therein, while they remain in the river, to attend to their clothing and to search their female visitors, in order that no spirituous liquors or anything else that is improper be introduced; and, could a person in that capacity accompany them during the voyage, it would no doubt be highly useful.

We are pleased to understand that the Factory in Parramatta has more than cleared its expences during the last year, as the interest we feel in the welfare of the colonies induces us not only to desire the religous and moral improvement of the population at large, but in all our plans we wish to keep in view such a system as shall eventually prove the most economical to Government as well as the most beneficial to the Colonial States.

In consequence of thy friendly encouragement, I have ventured thus freely to offer with submission our sentiments; we are fully aware that much has been accomplished, that many of our requests have been granted with obliging readiness; and we shall feel our sense of gratitude much increased, if Lord Bathurst will condescend to peruse these remarks and to act in compliance as far as his judgement can approve and his authority enforce.

Elizabeth Fry to Under-Secretary Horton, in Bathurst to Sir Thomas Brisbane, 30 August 1823.

4. Report of the Board

In sending this report on the operation of the Female Factory to Sir George Murray in February 1829, Governor Darling asked that no women be sent out for twelve months, in the hope that during that time some of the 537 women who remained in the Factory at the end of 1828 would have been "disposed of". He pointed out that the numbers of women sent out in the previous two years had been well beyond the demand of the settlers and that the Female Factory was the only place in the colony in which the women could be kept. In addition to transported women and the seventy-one children in the establishment, there were also free women who had been sentenced in the colony, so that the building served a number of purposes. He made particular point of asking that no more "Women from Ireland" be sent out for some time, "the inhabitants appearing to have a strong objection to receiving them". He also recommended the granting of tickets-of-leave to "the well behaved women", who he believed to be few in number, but who would then to given an opportunity "of marrying or settling in some line of Business".

[Enclosure.]

REPORT of the Board of Management of the Female Factory for the Half Year ending the 31st December, 1828.

1st. The number of Convict Women in the different Classes of the Establishment is:

First Class	208	
Second do	107	
Third do	173	
Hospital	49	including 6 nurses.
Total	537	

Crown Prisoners, which, with 36 free Persons, committed as to House of Correction, make 573 Women and 71 children, Total 644 persons, showing an increase during the Half Year of 63 Crown Prisoners, 19 free persons, and 12 children, as per Statement No. 1 accompanying.

2nd. The number of Crown Prisoners received into the Establishment and discharged from it during the Half Year is, Viz.:—

Receipts.

From Ship *Competitor* not being assigned	19	
City of Edinburgh	39	
Private Service to 1st Class	210	
do to 2nd do	5	
do to 3rd do	275	
		548

Discharged.

Assigned to Service	381	
Returned to do	38	
" Husbands	33	
Original Sentences expired	10	
Married	12	
Dead	9	
Absconded and not returned	2	
		485
Increase of Crown Prisoners		63

3rd. The accompanying Statement No. 2 exhibits the number of Free Persons sentenced as to House of Correction:

Remained 1st July	17	
Received	81	
		98
Discharged Fines expired		62
Remains 31st Decr. 1828		36

Showing an increase of 19 free persons.

The comparison of the years 1827 and 1828, as shewn in Statement No. 1. proves an increase to the Establishment of 171 Crown Prisoners.

4. There are now in the first class from which the Assignments take place, 107 available for Service; the remaining 101, from causes subjoined, cannot be considered as eligible, Vizt.:

Monitresses	6
Cooks and other Servants	30
Old and infirm	5
Advanced in pregnancy	6
Having young children	54
	101
Available for Service	107
Total of the Class	208

5th. The Board would here call the attention of the Government to the fact of the great increase, which appears to take place by Women coming to the Establishment to lye in, and would suggest that some measure might be adopted to oblige the Fathers to provide for their illegitimate offspring by the payment of a sum of money, or a weekly rate for its support; and they could hope such a measure might tend to induce parties to marry, who now never think of such an ordinance; but a serious difficulty presents itself to such a measure, from the belief they are obliged to entertain that many of the Women are so bad that, to gratify any purpose they might form, they would not hesitate to swear their children to any one; and, in the case of a Master turning away servants, it is not improbable, as a means of revenge, they might not infrequently accuse him of being the father of their children.

6th. A Legislative enactment also appears to be called for to oblige Husbands to withdraw from this Establishment their wives, who are sent to it for a limited punishment, when such has expired; in several instances now in the Establishment, the committing Magistrates have ordered, on sending married Women, that their husbands are to pay the Expenses.

The Board are at a loss to know how to charge and levy this sum. Other cases occur in which the Wives being Prisoners, and married to free or Ticket of Leave men, are kept in the Establishment after their fine or punishment has expired; and, in all such cases, the Board would recommend that a Law be passed, authorizing by summary process that *three shillings* a day be levied on the Husband to provide for the maintenance of the Wife. It is true this sum will much more than pay the actual expenses of the Women; but the measure carries with it a second object, that of preventing Numbers accumulating in this Establishment.

7. The general health of the Establishment continues undiminished, though for some short time past "Ophthalmia" has spread among the Women and prevails as an Epidemic, increasing the numbers in the Hospital to an extent beyond the means of the Establishment to provide. In consequence, one of the sleeping Wards of the Second Class has been appropriated in aid of the Hospital Establishment.

The Number of Deaths (9) of Women belonging to the Establishment exceeds by one only those of last Half Year, the particulars of which are detailed in the Surgeon's Report No. 4 accompanying.

It may perhaps be necessary to observe that this Establishment is the receptacle (with the exception of a single Ward, appropriated to Females in Sydney) for all the Females in the Colony who require medical aid.

8. The conduct of the Women during the Half Year has been good with a few exceptions; some two or three of the most troublesome having been obliged to be punished as often as six times. Punishment has however decreased notwithstanding the increased number in the Establishment; the accompanying Return No. 5 Contains but 261 cases of Punishment during the Half Year, shewing a diminution of 59 cases on that of the preceding, proving most satisfactorily the advantages arising from the improved order and discipline of the Establishment. The crimes are of an ordinary character, and therefore do not appear to call for any particular observation from the Board, further than was noted in their last report, being of the same character, vizt., Drunkenness, insolence and obscene Language.

9th. The Board find the Regulations of the Establishment duly observed; the books required by the Establishment are in good order, and are neatly kept by the parties having charge of them. The Matron states that Morning and Evening Prayers are read by herself to the Protestants, and by one of the Monitresses to the Catholics, and that good order and attention is observed.

10th. It is pleasing to the Board to have it in their power to report their continued satisfaction at the cleanliness, order, and regularity observable in the Establishment, and their approbation of the manner in which the Matron, Mrs. Gordon, performs the arduous duties of her Office; the Assistant Monitresses of the different Classes, who are selected from among the Prisoners of the first Class, give satisfaction in their appointments. Mrs Gordon however complains that she does not receive such assistance, as she might do from the Free Women appointed Matrons of the Classes, a source of difficulty to the Board and Managing Committee, who have had much trouble in procuring them, and are at a loss to know where to obtain others to replace them.

11th. The Board had occasion to observe in their last Report, under the recommendation of the Surgeon, that the Diet allowed to the children of the Establishment might with advantage be altered, and their recommendation met with Your Excellency's ready sanction. The Surgeon now reports that the result of the measure has not turned out so favourably as was anticipated. The Board therefore again solicit Your Excellency's sanction to its change, substituting the following as the scale of diet for the children. Vizt.:—

Under one year — Six ounces bread and eight ounces or one half pint of milk.

From 1 to 3 yrs. old — Twelve ounces bread. sixteen ounces or 1 pint of milk and 4 ounces of beef or mutton.

12th. The employment of the Women of the Establishment is attended to as far as possible in the present state of the Building. The late alterations and additions by no means contemplated the possibility of the present numbers being thrown upon the Establishment; and it is apparent to the Board, unless some effectual steps are taken either to restrain importations, or otherwise devise means by which the Women may be more distributed, additional Buildings must be erected to provide for the growing necessities. As it is, with the view of giving more employment, the Board have to suggest that an additional Room may be added to the Penitentiary for the purpose of carrying on the Weaving, whereby it is hoped that additional labour for the Women will be obtained. The factory will have then within its Walls the means of Spinning, Weaving, and making up the whole of the clothing required by Government for the Convicts in their employ. To this end, the Board beg to forward a plan of the Building required, together with as Estimate, which amount to the sum of £42 13s. 8½d. as a money Expense, and £103 9s. 8d. for Convict Labour. The Board are reluctantly obliged to press the necessity of this Building. It is however a satisfaction to think it will prove a measure of economy to Government by enabling the present Weaving Establishment to be broke up, thereby causing a saving in the amount equal to the expense of that Establishment.

13th. The Board, while thus under the necessity of adding buildings to the Factory, beg to point out the importance of shading the front of the Hospital with a Verandah. The Surgeon considers it essential, as a place where he can receive the cases which daily apply for admittance.

The Committee also, during the time they are employed assigning the Prisoners, experience the want of a similar shade, and therefore again urge Your Excellency to sanction this trifling Work, and Expense of which, as shewn in the Accompanying Estimate, will be but £12 17s. 10d. money Expense, and £24 1s. 6d. for Convict Labour.

14th. From the Accompanying Statement of the Expenses of the Establishment for the Half Year, shewing also the Value of the Labour performed, it appears that the Total Expenses have been £3,298 9s. 6½d., that the Value of Labour is £1,210 10s. 8d., leaving a Balance of £2,087 18s. 10½d. against the Establishment, being less than the proceeding Half Year by £371 3s. 9½d., although, on a daily average of Numbers, there has been 17 Women and 9 Children more maintained.

15. The result of each half Year proving that the Establishment is encreasing owing to the importations exceeding the demand for Female Labour, it is with feelings of some satisfaction, the attention of the Board has been directed to the subject of a modification of the present system of granting Tickets of Leave and Indulgencies to the more meritorious of this Class of Females, as called for by the Colonial Secretary's Letter of the 16th January, 1829. The Board are as much disposed to believe, as to hope, a measure of this nature may be attended with beneficial results. In considering the subject, they have to propose their opinion that Tickets of Leave might be granted as follows, Vizt.:—

To Women under Sentence for Seven Years, for continued good
    Conduct in Service, or in the Married State .... 2 Years
14 Years' Sentence 3   do
Life 4   do

As the first Class of this Establishment is considered as an Asylum and not a place of Punishment for the unappropriated Female Prisoners, Women returned to the first Class will not be considered as having forfeited their Claim to a Ticket of Leave, as it must be inferred that they have committed no offence in their Service, or they would have been punished by being sent to the third Class. The same Indulgence might also be extended to Monitresses in the Estt., who retain their Situations for the periods specified, such employment being considered as a Service. Women, who have been permitted to Marry, should their Husbands die or absent themselves, if they have lived two, three or four Years, according to the period of their Sentence, without being complained of or becoming known to the Police, to be equally eligible to have Tickets of Leave.

16th. In reviewing generally the state of the Establishment, its operation and progress during the Half Year, the Board are pleased to have it in their power to report favourably on all its branches, with the exception of the encrease to its Numbers, over which, arising as it has done from the extent of the importations, they can have no control; Punishments have diminished, and, although the Labour of the Women has not been pushed so far as could be wished, its value has encreased sufficient to diminish the Expense of Maintenance below what it was calculated at the last Half Year. In concluding their Report, the Board have much pleasure in adverting to the circumstance of the formation and introduction into the Establishment of a Ladies' Committee, composed of the principal Ladies in the Neighbourhood, actively encouraged and patronized by Mrs. Darling, the object of which is, by the adoption of an Evening School, to inculcate moral Instruction, and excite and raise into being a better feeling for their condition, and a desire to improve (by becoming good Servants) their Stations in Society. The Ladies also hold out encouragement to Work during their leisure time, intending from the proceeds of their Labour to form a fund from which to reward those who have remained long in their Services with good Characters.

The Board need hardly remark that they anticipate much good to result from the interest taken in the Establishment by the Ladies' Committee.

ALEXR. MCLEAY.   T. DE LA CONDAMINE.
S. MARSDEN.   M. ANDERSON.
W. LITHGOW.   A. C. INNIS.
W. DUMARESQ.

Female Factory, Parramatta, 19th January, 1829.

Darling to Sir George Murray, 18 February 1829.

5. Woman Power

The recurring problems of the Female Factory are listed in this report of the proceedings of the all-male Board of Management. Not the least of these was the difficulty of finding employment for the women that was profitable, time-consuming and in harmony with the economic requirements of the colony.

No. 1 The Board having inspected the Several Buildings belonging to the Establishment, beg to report the very bad state of the Drains, Wash houses, Privies etc. representations and circumstantial reports have been repeatedly made in the proper quarters, but without success. The Building in consequence is suffering materially and unless early attention be paid to these Reports, the expense of repairs must ultimately be very great.

No 2. The Board beg to recommend that the 3rd Class be divided into Two Divisions for the purpose of Classification, which the Board thinks can be done at no great expense, this arrangement the Board are of opinion will obviate the necessity of Building Cells.

No 3. As the present state of the Wool Market is such that sufficient quantity cannot be procured to keep the women constantly employed in spinning etc. the Board would respectfully suggest the construction of a Mill capable of being worked by the power of 30 Women the machinery being so placed and contrived, as to prevent any access thereto by the Prisoners, in order to preserve the works from damage, a precaution without which Mills for grinding grain could not safely be introduced into the Establishment.

No 4. The Board recommend in consequence of the crowded and unhealthy state of that portion of the Building allotted to the Children, that some measures to be taken to reduce their numbers, in order to effect this the Board suggest that a certain sum be offered to small settlers or others to take the children out to nurse, this expense would not be so great as the present one, that of maintaining the women acting as nurses and the children also.

No 5. The Board in consequence of great inconvenience having arisen in distributing the women to their several assignees, at all hours of the day, recommend that
in future the women be only distributed at the following hours daily, viz
    From Eleven to One O'Clock
    and
    From Two to Three O'Clock
and that this Regulation be painted on a Board, and placed upon the Entrance Gate of
the Establishment.

Minute of the Proceedings of the Board of Management, Female Factory, Parramatta, 1 April 1834.

6. Employment at the Factory

It was not unusual for two or more members of one family to be employed in colonial
institutions such as the Female Factory. In this case, the parents of the new teacher
were both turnkeys at Parramatta.

On referring to my instructions I find his Excellency the Governor has been
pleased to order a School to be formed on this establishment.
    I have the honor to propose for his Excellency's approval Miss Elizabeth Snape,
as teacher, whose parents are employed on the establishment. She being highly
recommended by the Chaplain, and approved of by the Bishop of Australia. She is
employed as teacher at the Sunday School in Parramatta where she is very much
approved of. I have further the honor to state Miss Snape has taken charge of the
School since the fifth inst. and the Matron considers her competent.

Thomas Bell, Keeper at the Female Factory, Parramatta, to the Colonial Secretary, 20 September 1836.

7. Factory Midwife

The difficulty of finding suitable free women to take up positions at the Female
Factory was balanced by the cheapness of the convict labour. A free woman employed
as a midwife had to be paid £50 a year; a convict, one shilling a day. At this time,
there were employed at Parramatta three male turnkeys (£60 a year), four female
turnkeys (£50 a year), a midwife and a laundress (each paid a shilling a day — indicating they were not free), and an overseer in the needle-room (8d. a day). Apart
from this, selected prisoners performed all the duties of servants.

I have the honour to propose for the consideration of his Excellency the Governor that the Prisoner named in the margin [Elizabeth Donohoe] may be appointed
Midwife in the room of Elizabeth Scott, who has resigned.
    I beg to enclose a certificate from the visiting Surgeon of her being capable to
fill the situation.
    She has been a length of time employed in the Lying in Ward and has success-
fully done the duty of the two last midwives in their absence.
    I have reason to think she will suit as well as any free woman that can be pro-
cured as they only come here for a short time to establish themselves.

Salary to commence the 1st Inst. at the rate of 1s. per day the usual gratuity allowed to prisoners she not yet being entitled to a Ticket of leave.

Thomas Bell to the Colonial Secretary, 7 February 1839.

8. Debacle

In July 1836, the Factory Committee, headed by Samuel Marsden, inquired into incidents involving staff at the Female Factory at Parramatta. The midwife, Mrs Neale, had "claimed their protection", alleging indecent conduct on the part of the matron's husband. The committee barred Mr Gordon from the Factory and concluded that the Matron's daughters as well as her husband, were "highly immoral", the eldest having at that time "two illegitimate children living in the Factory". In her statement to the Board, Mrs Neale describes the climax of the affray.

July 4th   Mr Gordon told me in the hearing of the First Class Women, that I was in the habit of receiving and concealing Government Property — at the same time his daughter Maria flew at me like a fury, calling me all the nasty cats she could think of; when I checked her by saying she had illused many, and for every act towards me, she should be made accountable — Maria then crying with passion, turned towards the women, and said, how can you bear to see me used so. The women shouted at me one and all, some said you old thief, and some you old whore . . .

Mary Anne Neale, statement to the Factory Committee, Parramatta Female Factory, 15 July 1836.

9. "More a Gaol than an Asylum"

If the incidents involving the Matron's family were a prelude to the reorganization of the Parramatta Factory rather than the reason for it, the Matron herself ultimately lost most. In this memo from the Colonial Secretary, attached to reports of the inquiry, there is no mention of recompense to Mrs Gordon for loss of her position, although she had been Matron for some years and performed her "arduous" tasks satisfactorily. A different opinion of Mrs Gordon was given by James Mudie to the Molesworth Committee in 1837.

Independently however of the former occurrences to which I refer and the recent representation of the Committee, I am now satisfied that it is necessary to place the Factory at Parramatta upon an entirely new footing. The numbers of Women now confined there under sentence have rendered the place much more a Gaol than an Asylum, and it requires in consequence the government of a Prison. A Matron alone is not sufficient to the task of controlling and superintending so large a number of Prisoners. I propose therefore to place a Man and his wife at the head of the Establishment the one as Keeper the other as Matron with a sufficient number of Male and Female Turnkeys — and to have the Prison Rules . . . as far as they apply, carried into effect in the management of the Factory . . . Let Mrs Gordon be informed that at the close of this month her services will no longer be required as it is proposed to place the Factory upon a footing which will not admit of retaining her in employment.

Memo from the Colonial Secretary, 4 August 1836.

10. Reform

In 1837, before leaving England to take up his appointment as Governor in New South Wales, Sir George Gipps investigated English innovations in prison organization. The idea of separate cells for prisoners had been dismissed earlier on the grounds of expense.

Having by your Lordship's desire perused the instructions which have been drawn up for the guidance of Mrs Leach and Mr & Mrs Clapham, who are now on the point of proceeding to New South Wales, for the purpose of introducing an improved system of Discipline into the Female Factory at Parramatta, I think it right to submit to your Lordship, that these instructions appear to be framed on the supposition that each prisoner, is confined in a separate cell, whereas according to the most authentic information I can obtain, the very reverse of this is the case, the women being simply divided into three classes, and occupying large rooms, in which sometimes even as many as fifty are congregated by night and by day — The necessity of separation in an Establishment of the nature of that at Parramatta, is now so fully admitted, that I think it unnecessary to trouble your Lordship with any arguments to prove its advantage . . . I cannot but feel, that much of the success to be hoped for from the appointment of Mrs Leach and Mr Clapham, will depend on their being able at once, to enter in the system, which they have been instructed to follow . . .

Gipps to Lord Glenelg, 19 September 1837.

. . . a supply should in my opinion be sent from this Country, of articles required to fit up solitary cells, in the mode recommended by the Inspectors of Prisons for the Home District, and which is now being put in execution, in the Millbank Penitentiary, under the Sanction of Lord John Russell; the articles in question being required for the purposes of venitilation, and for the preservation of cleanliness — I beg to state to your Lordship, that I have personally inspected what is going on in the Millbank Penitentiary, and here also conferred upon the subject with Messrs. Crawford and Russell, the Inspectors of prisons for the Home District, both of whom concur with me in thinking that a supply of the articles in question, and particularly the Apparatus for water closets, should be sent out sufficient for about fifty cells . . .

Ibid., 9 October 1837.

11. Refractory Girls

Although the female factories were increasingly "more gaols than asylums", some women preferred factory life to life outside. The two women referred to by the Keeper at the Parramatta Factory in this letter were removed from the Factory by "the Steamboat to be embarked for Port McQuarie".

In consequence of the repeated disorderly conduct of Eliza Reynolds, and Margaret Campbell /Sisters by the Lady Rowena, Prisoners for life/ in this Establishment, and their endeavours to create disturbance among the Women;
I have the honor to recommend to His Excellancy the Governors consideration, the absolute necessity of having them removed to some distant Settlement; they have

been several times provided with situations but will not remain in them, and from the length of time they have been in the Colony they have contracted such connections in Parramatta, that they prefer the Factory to private service; should his Excellency be pleased to order their removals, the example would be of the utmost benefit to the remaining part of the Establishment.

Thomas Bell, Keeper at the Female Factory, Parramatta, to the Colonial Secretary, 7 June 1837.

12. Mrs Ajax and the Amazons

Lieutenant-Colonel Godfrey Charles Mundy, soldier and writer, who was stationed in Australia from 1846 to 1851, recorded his impressions of the Female Factories at Parramatta and Cascades in Hobart. In Van Diemen's Land, he was most impressed by the work done, the "squads" of women washing, "displaying their thick ankles as they spread the linen over the drying lines", and the young girls, "debauched ere the pith had hardened in their little bones". In *Our Antipodes*, he gives an extravagant picture of a riot at the Parramatta Factory.

In the towns of New South Wales, the first object upon which the stranger's eye falls, is some grand building devoted to the custody and coercion of convicts; — in civiler terms, to the accommodation of its original white population; or to their protection, when age and disease, mental and bodily, may have overtaken them, — gaols, in short, hospitals, lunatic asylums, and the like.

At Parramatta, the most prominent of these establishments — a handsome solid stone edifice, a "stone-jug" well calculated to contain the most ardent and effervescent spirits — is the Female Factory, where prisoners of that sex, sanely or insanely unruly, are incarcerated. I had an opportunity of visiting it with the Governor, and have no wish either to repeat the visit, or to dwell on the details thereof. The numbers of the tenants of this establishment are, since the cessation of transportation, much diminished; but it is not many years ago that the Amazonian inmates, amounting to seven or eight hundred, and headed by a ferocious giantess (by all accounts, a regular she-Ajax), rose upon the guards and turnkeys, and made a desperate attempt at escape by burning the building. The officer commanding the troops then occupying the stockade, who gave me this account, sent a subaltern with a hundred men, half of them armed only with sticks, and an effort was made to drive the fair insurgents within one of the yards, in order to secure them. This manoeuvre, however, failed. They laughed at the cane-carrying soldiers, refuting their *argumentum baculinum* by a furious charge upon the gates, in which one man was knocked over by a brickbat from Mrs. Ajax. The military were reinforced; the magistrate made them load with ball-cartridge, and the desperadas were eventually subdued.

This unladylike ebullition was considered, as I am assured, the most formidable convict outbreak that ever occurred in the colony, not even excepting that of Castle Hill, in the year 1804! I believe the periodical close-cropping of the women's hair was the prime cause of the outbreak. From Samson downwards it has been a dangerous trick to play man or woman. I have known many a good soldier rendered disaffected by the harassing warfare waged against his whiskers and side-locks by martinet officers. In the case of the Parramatta factory, the Governor was diplomatic enough to relax the depilatory laws.

G.C. Mundy, *Our Antipodes* (1852).

13. A Riot at the Launceston Factory

Another picture of rioting at the female factories is given in this report of a riot at the Female Factory at Launceston in 1841.

On the morning of that day Catherine Owen represents that she is unwell and demanded upon that ground to be released from solitary confinement. The Colonial Assistant Surgeon visited the same morning but did not find her in any way indisposed and her confinement therefore continued. In the afternoon the Sub Matron visited her and immediately upon the cell being unlocked a number of the females in the crime class yard seized and held the Sub Matron whilst others conveyed Owen from the cells to the Mess Room, and then bid defiance to the authorities in the factory. One and all stating they would not allow her to serve the remainder of her sentence in the Cells.

The Superintendent ordered the Ringleaders of this disturbance to be brought before him, this order the whole class resisted and having (85 in number) barricaded themselves in the Ward, it became necessary to procure some Constables to take the parties into Custody, but upon this being attempted the police were beaten off by the women who had armed themselves with the spindle, and leg, from the spinning wheels, bricks taken from the floors and walls of the building, knives, forks etc and also Quart Bottles in which some of them had received medicine. From the great excitement the women were in the Superintendent thought it advisable to leave them to themselves for a time giving directions to the Keeper of the House of Correction not to supply them with food or water.

In the evening the women expressed a wish to see the Superintendent who therefore proceeded to the Factory and was told by them, that if he would give them their Rations and promise not to send the prisoner who had been rescued from the Cells again to punishment and also not try the Ringleaders of the women who took her out of the Cells they would submit. The Superintendent of course refused to enter into such conditions, but required the immediate submission of the whole party at the same time every effort in his power was used by remonstrance and persuasion to induce them to submit but without effect.

On the following morning at daylight the prisoners became very outrageous breaking the Furniture and windows and attempting to burn the Building. The Superintendent then determined to temporise no longer and ordered about fifty men from the prisoners' Barracks to proceed to the female House of Correction and having been sworn in special Constables and furnished with sledge Hammers and Crow bars with the assistance of some constables, the Crime Class ward was forced, the most refractory and violent of the female prisoners were captured and removed to Cells in the Male House of Correction and Gaol. The utmost resistance was offered and every description of Missile that could be procured was brought into operation by the females nothing but the extreme forbearance and proper Conduct of the Men employed prevented in the opinion of the Superintendent very serious results.

The Ringleaders of this riot were subsequently brought to trial and punished by sentences of hard labour to the House of Correction at Hobart Town. These offenders even upon their trial exhibited the most outrageous Conduct abusing and threatening the Magistrates to their face.

Appendix to "Report . . . of the Committee Inquiring into Female Convict Discipline, 1841-43".

14. The Flash Mob

This description of the Female Factory at Cascades in Hobart, and its most striking occupants, the "Flash Mob", emphasizes the easy life and lack of discipline widely thought to be prevalent at the establishment. The "Flash Mob" were "old hands" who wore earrings and silk scarves, and wielded more power over the other women than the *Colonial Times* was aware of, though some of the details were to emerge later during a government inquiry into female convict discipline.

There is a class of persons in this Colony, the management of which produces more trouble to the Prison Disciplinarians than that of any other class. We refer to the Female Prisoners of the Crown, whose tricks, manoeuvres, and misconduct, have baffled the exertions of every person, appointed to control and correct them. We have ascertained that there is what is termed a "mob", always in the Factory, and that this mob has assumed the title of "The Flash Mob". Now it is very clear, that "female women" can never be punished like men; for it would be wrong to flog them, wrong, also, to put them on the tread wheel, and very wrong, to subject them to many punishments, which are inflicted upon their superiors, the "Lords of Creation". But it strikes us very forcibly, that there is no adequate system of correction, (we do not say punishment,) for any of the ladies sentenced to "durance vile" at the Factory. We have seen, with our own eyes, and heard with out own hears, several insolent hussies say, that they could "bowl off" their three or four months with the greatest ease; laugh at the Magistrate, and skip out of the office with the utmost *nonchalance*.

The system, with regard to the management of Female Prisoners, is decidedly and most radically wrong: they are subjected to no punishment, they are exposed to no, or at least but to few, hardships. The wash tub affords an opportunity for the merry laugh, the song and the joke, and this punishment is laughed at, absolutely laughed at. Then there are the cells; these *are* rather uncomfortable; for the rats run over the inmates, and *that*, they do not like. But the whole system of punishment is not properly arranged; nor is it adequately apportioned. We know for a positive fact, that the female servants shout out in derision, and perfect ridicule, the state of punishment inflicted upon them at the Factory. Oh! but the *Crime Class!* What is it? Why, it inflicts upon the poor females, subjected to its operations, the quiet picking of a little wool — and the almost unrestrained indulgence in telling funny stories, and occasionally in singing funny songs.

The plain and simple fact is, that over the heads of female prisoners, there is not sufficient power held; the Principal Superintendent having his attention chiefly directed to the male prisoners, very naturally considers the "softer sex", of a much softer description, and not amenable to harsh correction. But, in the meantime, the public suffer; several persons have been applying lately for female servants — but none are to be had. Why? Because their characters are so bad, that they have been ordered to the country. Could not some means be taken to amend this conduct? Are the women less liable to favourable impressions, as regards reformation, than the men? We should think not; and a little trouble — some small pains, on the part of the proper authorities, might effect a change in this respect, not only beneficial to the public, but advantageous and favourable to themselves.

We must close these observations with the following anecdote: — A lady in this town charged her servant with being . . . , as ladies are, "who love not wisely, but too well;" telling Mary, at the same time, that she need not deny it. Mary acknowledged the truth of this charge, and coolly asked, "what of it?" The woman's mistress said, she, Mary, to wit, ought to be ashamed of her conduct; enquiring, at the same time, who was the father of the expected bantling? One George was named as the progenitor; when the mistress, a good creature, in every respect, asked if this George would marry Mary? Mary said, he would; but *she*, high-minded lady as she was, would not have *him*! "Not have him?" exclaims Mrs. —, with indignant surprise — 'Why not? would you rather cast disgrace upon your poor child, and go to the Factory?" "Indeed would I, Missus; for I know that George can't keep me, comfortably, like a lady; and as to *going to the Factory*, we think no more of *that*, than we do of going for a white loaf!"

And *this* is Prison Discipline! What shall we have next?

"Female Servants", *Colonial Times*, 18 February 1840.

15. Gross and Disorderly

The severity of punishment rather than the lack of it is illustrated by the fact that the women involved in the escapade described below were each given twelve months' hard labour, with the recommendation that during that period they be placed in separate confinement. Here John Hutchinson, Superintendent of the Hobart Female Factory, gives evidence at the trial of the five women, who were charged with gross disorderly conduct in the wards of the Factory.

John Hutchinson being sworn states I am Superintendent of this Establishment,

bout eight o'clock last night it was reported to me that there was a noise. I took the keys and went to the ward in question and allowing myself some time to identify if possible by their voices those who were disorderly and looking in at the window I saw five Prisoners now present dancing perfectly naked, and making obscene attitudes towards each other, they were also singing and shouting and making use of most disgusting language, there was a sixth woman but I could not positively swear to her, the disgusting attitudes towards each other were in imitation of men and women together.

What the women now say about their washing themselves is quite untrue, they had no right to have the tubs in the rooms when I went in there were none there, I was observing the women before I spoke or made myself known, the language they used and the attitudes they made use of corresponded in obscenity so that no mistake could be made by me as to the nature of both — "Smith" states that the matter arose from a mere joke but it was a dirty beastly action.

John Hutchinson, evidence given at hearing of charges against inmates of the Cascades Female Factory, Hobart, 24 March 1842, in "Report . . . of the Committee Inquiring into Female Convict Discipline, 1841-43".

18. "A Higher Degree of Reformation"

The Committee of Inquiry that, between 1841 and 1843, looked into female convict discipline in Van Diemen's Land observed in its Report that it was aware that "the question as to the best mode of managing the Females in the Factories had long been regarded by the Local Government as one of which a satisfactory solution was rather to be hoped for than confidently expected". But of the behaviour of the female convicts and the expectations of society about women in general, the Committee had some perceptive comments to make. In doing so, it described precisely the problem faced by these women.

. . . a corresponding degree of *success* had not by any means been experienced in the management of the Convicts of the opposite sex [female] confined in the Factories. It had, we know well, often been remarked that the consequences were but too apparent; of its being impossible to apply, in the case of the latter, these *summary punishments*, which were found to *repress so effectually* violent or *improper conduct* in that of the former. Neither were we ignorant that a degree of coarseness of character which might not unfit a man for labouring in a field would completely disqualify a female for being an attendant upon a family, that Society had fixed the standard of the average moral excellence required of women much higher than that which it had erected for men, and that crime was regarded with less allowance when committed by a woman than if perpetrated by a man, not because the absolute amount of guilt was supposed to be greater in the one case than in the other, but because the offender was deemed to have receded further from the average proprieties of her sex. Even therefore had the female convict discipline of the Colony produced equal effects with that which has been devised for Males, we should still have been ready to confess, that it had not accomplished the desired end, not that it had not equally succeeded in its action upon character, but that a higher degree of reformation is required in the case of a female, before society will concede to her that she has reformed at all . . .

"Report . . . of the Committee Inquiring into Female Convict Discipline, 1841-43".

Girls' Industrial Schools

19. Servants for Protestant Ladies

The Female School of Industry was established in Sydney in 1826 by Lady Darling, wife of the governor, to train girls from poor families to be reliable domestic servants. When the girls turned fourteen, they were apprenticed to "subscribers", ladies who contributed to the upkeep of the School. This institution is particularly interesting because, for a century, it managed to sustain considerable continuity in policy and management.

That at the age of fourteen years the girls to be eligible to go out of the School as servants to Subscribers in the order in which the names stand in the Secretary's book; the Subscriber being of good moral character and a member of the Church of England.

Female School of Industry, *Annual Report*, 1862, Rule 8.

That after the age of 15 years, the girls will be eligible to be engaged (subscribers having the preference) as house servants, at the current rate of exchange. The Subscriber being of good moral character and a Protestant.

Female School of Industry, *Annual Report*, 1893, Rule 8.

After the age of 16 years, the girls will be eligible to be engaged (subscriber having the preference) as house servants at the current rate of wages; the subscribers being of good moral character and Protestants.

Female School of Industry, *Annual Report*, 1926, Rule 12.

20. Industrial Schools

In the late 1860s, most of the colonial legislatures, following the British example, introduced Industrial and Training Schools Acts. The institutions established under these Acts were designed to rescue deserted, neglected and criminal children from a life of poverty and crime. In the case of girls, they aimed to produce well-behaved servants, thereby reducing the incidence of pauperization and relieving the acute shortage of domestic labour in that area. In 1873, Rosamond and Florence Hill, who were actively involved in many areas of welfare work in England, visited Australia and inspected institutions where the destitute and criminal were incarcerated. Their observations, not always accurate, on Biloela Industrial School in Sydney were included in their book, What We Saw in Australia.

Quitting the "Vernon" [a floating reformatory for boys], we rowed two or three miles eastward to Cockatoo Island, where the Industrial School for girls is established, enjoying on our way a variety of lovely views, which deepened our impression of the extent and beauty of both the city and the harbour. Every now and then we crossed the entrance to a bay or an inlet often running many miles inland, while the coast was exquisitely varied. Villas and gardens contrasted with bold rocks of rich yellow, or red, or deep grey, and these again with masses of dark foliage, where "primeval forest and snakes," said Mr Parkes, "had it all their own way." The sky was bright blue, and the water sparkled under the fresh breeze. The scene recalled the Cove of Cork, when, several years ago, under not unsimilar circumstances, we rowed from point to point, to visit the different convict prisons upon its shores.

Cockatoo Island, nearly square in form, measuring perhaps a quarter of a mile in each direction, lies across the entrance to the gulf which receives the Paramatta River. The school was originally established in old military barracks, close to the town of Newcastle, at the mouth of the Hunter River, sixty miles north-east of Sydney. There, however, it had been a failure. The character of the building, and its position, where the inmates could be overlooked from the adjacent streets, rendered the maintenance of discipline impossible. Riots even occurred, and removal was considered the only remedy. Cockatoo Island was chosen as the new location; but this site was really no better than the old one. The building allotted to the school had obtained a terrible notoriety as a convict gaol. The home influences essential to the wholesome training of girls, the very lack of which had brought them to the school, are impossible of attainment within the gloomy walls of a prison. Doubts, indeed, of the suitableness of the place were entertained at the time even of removal, but no better one was immediately available, and proximity to a town, at least, would be avoided. It was hoped, too, that by abandoning a name connected in the public mind with all that is evil in gaol-life, and resuming the aboriginal appellation of the island, — Biloela — prison associations would be forgotten, and the girls would escape the dreaded reproach of having "been at Cockatoo".

Not only, however, did the evils already described attach to the locality, but the Government dock, bringing necessarily large numbers of sailors to the spot, is upon this island. Three hundred men, we heard, had been there a few days before our visit. The school premises are on high ground overlooking the dock, from which they are divided by a low wall or fence, and the presence of a policeman is necessary to prevent sailors and school-girls from crossing the boundary.

Landing at a minute stone pier, a steep rocky path led us to a heavy door, which was unlocked for our admission. Passing through it, we found ourselves among the old prison buildings, scattered over a wide space, but singularly devoid of the neatness and order which usually somewhat relieve the gloom of a gaol. The girls, some of whom were enjoying an interval of play between school and dinner, looked healthy, and the younger ones were tolerably neat in their dress, but the expression of their countenances struck us as inferior to that of the boys we had seen on the "Vernon". The appearance of the older girls was in all respects most discreditable to the school.

The work of the institution, including the care of two or three cows, is performed by the inmates, but no washing or employment of any kind is taken in, and it was evident to us that the elder girls had not hard work enough to do. The diet is abundant — excessive, indeed, to our English ideas, but we were told that a proposal to limit the food of these children to what would be considered enough for them at home, would upset a ministry in New South Wales!

The girls never attend public worship; there is no church, either Catholic or Protestant, on the island, and no measures have been taken to convey them on shore. Ministers of both denominations visit the school occasionally, and conduct services there for their respective flocks; but the humanizing influence of joining a congregation in worship is entirely wanting.

The New South Wales Act of 1867, wisely permits the retention, until the age of eighteen, of girls or boys committed to Industrial Schools. For want, however, of the means of classifying, which three or four small institutions would afford, the effect of this provision is, as regards the girls, disastrous, by bringing those together who should never be intermingled. Thus we found that of the ninety-eight present to-day, some are little children whose sole qualification for admission consisted in their destitution, while others are almost young women whose loose conduct has led to their committal. All are mixed together, without classification or efficient supervision.

At half-past six in the evening the girls are locked up in the dormitories, "essentially gaol-like and cheerless. Stone floors, hewn from the solid rock — all worn away by the tread of the countless criminals, who for years occupied the island — grated iron doors, with massive locks and heavy bolts; instead of windows, grated apertures high in the blank walls, allowing no outlook upon the scene beyond — all must constantly impress upon the minds of the children the prison-like character of their life."*

These gloomy chambers are at so great a distance from the houses inhabited by the sub-matrons, that they can hear nothing that goes on among the girls. None come near them; but at nine o'clock it is the duty of the head matron to extinguish a lamp which till then burns in a small lobby forming the entrance to each pair of dormitories. The light penetrates but a very little way into the gloomy interior, and these young creatures, we were told, huddle and press against the bars of which their prison doors are made, to get as near to it as they can. Thus left to themselves for hours together, with neither supervision or occupation, good and bad intermingled, their outrageous conduct gave us no surprise. Last night ten among their number, first barricading their door, tore the straw out of their mattresses, and set it alight in the middle of the floor.

Yesterday evening we were admiring from our balcony the brilliancy of the moon as it glittered upon the harbour, little imagining the wild insubordination among these miserable girls it was revealing. The smoke, made visible by the moonlight, issuing through the shingle roof, gave notice of what was going on, and the superintendent (who, strange to say, is a man), in terror lest the building should be burnt, had to implore the girls to let him enter the dormitory to extinguish the fire. Outbreaks of a similar or worse description have not been infrequent. To-day we saw the culprits imprisoned in their dormitories, some half-dressed, others wrapped in blankets, awaiting judgment for their offence.

It is the intention of the Government to thoroughly reorganise the school, removing it at the same time to a more fitting place, as soon as one can be found. We believe (April 1875), however, that as yet this intention has not been carried into effect.

It will be a happy augury for the institution if, in its contemplated reorganisation, it be found possible to place it under the care of *voluntary* managers, subject, of course, to Government inspection. Then the school may enjoy the advantage of being directed by persons undertaking the duty from love of the work, and not

* Public Charities Commission Report.

merely because it falls within their official capacity. Thus also the institution would be removed from the disturbing influence of politics.

Within the precincts of the prison, separated from the Industrial School, there is a Reformatory for girls. It occupies a small cottage, and to-day has but eight inmates. The windows unfortunately look on the space frequented by the pupils of the Industrial School, whose turbulence is consequently well-known to these children, and the accommodation is insufficient; but the frank countenances and affectionate manner of the girls afforded a striking contrast to the bearing of those we had just left. The number is small enough to promote a real family feeling, and the superintendent appeared to exercise a motherly influence over her young charges. Here, as on the "Vernon", and in the Biloela Industrial School, the terms for which the children are sentenced are far too short, and until a change be effected in this important respect, besides the radical reform indispensable in the Industrial School, the beneficent aim of the law under which these institutions were established will not be attained.

Rosamond and Florence Hill, *What We Saw in Australia* (1875).

21. "Outcasts of Society"

George Lucas was criticized while he was the Superintendent of the Newcastle Industrial School because of his inability to command respect and obedience. The same situation was to confront him at Biloela.

The inmates of this institution are still in a very refractory state, being very riotous and disorderly and destroying Government property by tearing the bedding and breaking the bedsteads and window-frames; a reason can be given to account for such conduct by their having being taught that we are the outcasts of Society and should not be respected . . .

George Lucas, Superintendent of the Industrial School, Newcastle, to the Colonial Secretary, 28 March 1871.

22. Disruption at Newcastle

Riots were as frequent in industrial schools as they had been in the earlier female factories. This report describes the classic progress of such a riot at the Newcastle Industrial School and suggests that the Superintendent had lost charge of the institution and that new officers should be appointed.

. . . I then confined three girls in the cells, we shortly afterwards locked up five others for mis-conduct. The other girls were soon locked in their dormitories for the night and No 1. Ward commenced such a scene of riot and disorder I never witnessed before or during my ten years on Cockatoo Island with the worst of Criminals. Some of these young children employed themselves in Singing obscene songs others cursing swearing, others cutting up their Beds and Bedding and throwing it out of the windows, others were breaking the Iron bedsteads and with the end torn off forcing out the window sashes that were already broken and throwing them on the ground, they also destroyed the chamber utensils scattering the contents on the floor, this conduct was carried on until 9½. o'clock, p.m. when they seemed fairly hoarse and exhausted and they went to sleep — in another ward No. 3. some girls stripped naked and danced in the middle of the room the Gas burning at the windows being broken and blinds torn down they were in view of persons passing in the Street but being immediately reported by the Constable on duty the Superintendent turned the Gas off. I would wish to add that the Supt. has at all times acted in the most kind and indulgent manner towards these girls . . .

Senior Sergeant John Lane, Industrial School, Newcastle, to the Inspector of Police, Sydney, 28 March 1871.

23. A Period of Calm

This report by George Lucas, now the Superintendent of Biloela Industrial School, describes the daily work of the girls. While the girls washed the clothes of their male counterparts on the *Vernon*, the boys reciprocated by making boots for the girls.

Sir,
        I have the honor to report for the information of the Hon'ble The Colonial Secretary
1st   That the number of inmates is 104.
2nd   The health of the inmates is good.
3.   The two girls named in the Margin were discharged as apprentices.
4.   The girl named in the margin was confined in No 3 Dormitory on bread and water, for breaking the Fence and going beyond the enclosure on the 28th Ultimo.
5.   The quantity of sewing completed as in the margin.
        [8 Pinafores, 8 Chemise, 2 nightdresses, 2 check Frocks, 1 jacket, 3 Petticoats]
6.   The washing named in the margin was done for the H.S.S. Vernon.
        [14 doz. Trousers and Jumpers]
7.   On Sunday last the 1st Instant 31 girls attended religious service conducted by the Rev. Frank Firth Weslyan Minister of Balmain; and 49 Girls attended religious instruction given by the Teacher, Roman Catholic. There was a larger number of Boats than on previous Sundays, causing considerable trouble and annoyance.
8.   The Teacher has applied for the two girls named in the margin as Monitors.
9.   The Teacher's report is attached.

George Lucas, Superintendent, Industrial School for Girls, Biloela, to the Colonial Secretary, 2 October 1871.

24. A Contaminating Exhibition

On this occasion, the officers from the boy's floating reformatory, the *Vernon*, had to be called in to control the girls.

I have the honor to report for the information of the Hon the Colonial Secretary, that, last evening at 4.40 pm the ship was hailed from Cockatoo Island, for assistance at the Industrial School of Biloela. I immediately sent Mr Waller [the schoolmaster] with the Carpenter and three others on shore, to render what assistance they could.

While they were on shore, three of the girls came down abreast of the ship, in a semi-nude state, throwing stones at the windows in the workshops — blaspheming frightfully and conducting themselves more like fiends than human beings, I was compelled to send all our boys on the lower deck, to prevent them from viewing such a contaminating exhibition . . .

Captain J.S.V. Mien, Superintendent of the *Vernon*, to the Colonial Secretary, 17 October 1871.

25. American Sailors' Invasion of Cockatoo Island

Both the Royal Commission into Public Charities in New South Wales of 1873 and the Hill sisters found that Biloela was an unsuitable site for an industrial school because of, among other reasons, its closeness to the docks.

Sir,
I have the honor to report, for the information of the Hon'ble The Colonial Secretary.

That during last week some Sailors caps were found within the Institution, and in consequence of information received the Police were kept on the grounds.

On Friday evening at 9.30 the 15th Instant, two men were seen at the windows of one of the Dormitories, when followed by the Police, they took to the water and were captured outside the Institution, by the Officers of the St Marys, American Ship of War, now in the Fitzroy Dock, part of whose crew the men were.

On Saturday Evening the 16th Instant a number of sailors rushed the School, constable Turner attempted to stop them outside the Gate they got thro' the holes of the Fence, seven were captured, and the others returned to the Ship.

The Officers of the Ship followed the men and captured them.

The girls named in the margin, Four having been generally insubordinate during the week more particularly on Saturday night, Mr Charles Cowper Water Police Magistrate ordered them to be put in the Cells.

George Lucas, Superintendent, Industrial School for Girls, Biloela, to the Colonial Secretary, 18 December 1871.

26. Dormitory Blaze

In her evidence before the inquiry into the Biloela riots, the Matron describes the fire viewed across the water by Rosamond and Florence Hill.

Mary Ann Lucas states: I am the Matron of the Biloela Industrial School for Girls — On Monday 3rd November 1873 in consequence of what my daughter Georgiana told

me I went to the dining room and found no 3 Dormitory in a blaze — I came back for
Mr Lucas, Mr Lucas got a ladder and got up to the window to see what it was. We
found that the door was barricaded with bedsteads and that we could not open it. I
begged of them to open the door and Mr Lucas entreated them for the sake of the
other children as the place would be burnt down. The smoke was streaming out of the
room. They then opened the door and I opened the baths and the girls got water and
put out the fire. They then removed the bedsteads and cleared the dormitory out.
After some little while they went back into the dormitory and were locked up for the
night. I inquired who done it. They all said, "We all done it".

Deposition of Mary Ann Lucas, in the report of Charles Cowper, Water Police Magistrate, on the riots at
the Biloela Industrial School for Girls, to the Colonial Secretary, 25 November 1873.

27. War Songs

George Lucas, probably correctly, believed that these riots at Biloela were the result
of a concerted assault on his administration rather than of individual and impetuous
acts of defiance. The girls continued their disturbance and eventually were straight-
jacketed and one of the girls gagged.

... That on Tuesday the 30th of January four girls named in the margin, marched
down to the Beach, singing certain songs, which I always look upon as war songs, such
having ever proved the sign of disturbance.

George Lucas, Superintendent, Bileola Industrial School for Girls to the Colonial Secretary, 18 March
1872.

28. Balmain Regatta Day

This day in November 1873 was particularly hectic for the police, not only because of
the presence of many boats in the vicinity of Biloela, but because it was the occasion
of a spectacular escape attempt by the inmates, during which Senior Sergeant Ferris
of the Water Police reported taking from them "a tomahawk, a marling spike, a
chisel" and other articles, with which the girls had cut down the door and were
attempting to make their escape.

Senior Sergt. Ferris
Respectfully reports for the information of the Water Police Magistrate that
according to instructions he called at "Cockatoo" Island on Saturday last the 8th inst.
in reference to arrangements for "Balmain Regatta" whilst receiving instructions it
was reported to him by one of the police that the girls on "Biloela" were smashing the
windows and destroying other Government property. The Senior Sergt. with his boats
crew accompanied the police stationed on the island into the institution where they
found the girls all running about in the greatest disorder and state of excitement. A
number of the windows were broken also a large number of the mugs crockery etc.
which the girls use at their meals. The refractory girls were all locked up in one apartment where they commenced yelling and shouting making use of most filthy and disgusting language. Two of the girls got up to the window holding on by the iron bars

making use of most filthy language, one of these girls had no dress on nothing but her Chemise her neck and bosom all exposed, all this time a number of the other girls big and small were coming round under the window listening to the foul and obscene language made use of. A number of stones were thrown at the police by the girls some of the smallest throwing stones following the example of the big ones. The Senior Sergt. afterwards accompanied Mr & Mrs Lucas to the apartment the refractory girls were confined in for the purpose of supplying them with bread & water they still in the presence of Mr & Mrs Lucas continued screaching and yelling making use of most filthy language.

It appeared to the Senior Sergt. that these girls do just as they like the persons in charge seemed to have no control over them for when spoken to they took no notice.

Senior Sergeant Ferris, Water Police Station, to the Water Police Magistrate, 11 November 1873.

29. Sectarian Antagonism?

Lucas attempted to divert the attention of a committee inquiring into the riots at Biloela away from his incompetence to the issue of sectarian rivalry, which he claimed was incited by the schoolteacher.

... By a careful questioning of both the officers and the girls we have been unable to discover that any Sectarian influences have been employed. Although the majority of the elder girls are Catholics, and have been most prominent, the protestants have joined with them in all the riots. Party Sectarian Songs have been sung; but this did not occur until after the late Superintendent, Mr Lucas, had most improperly called the girls "Fenians", and the protestant girls would seem to have joined in the Songs and calling him an "Orange dog".

Public Charities Commission to the Minister of Justice and Public Instruction, 9 December 1873.

30. The Marks of Violence

This handwritten testimony confirms the charges of ill-temper and lack of control made against George Lucas.

... One of these girls having requested permission to make a statement to the Commission was called in and examined. She complained of ill treatment on the part of Mr & Mrs Lucas stating that both these officers had beaten her and ill treated other girls named by knocking them down striking them with their fists, a cane and a broomstick and by knocking their heads against a wall on which some caricature of Mr & Mrs Lucas had been drawn. She exhibited the marks of blows recently inflicted in support of her statement. The other girls named by her were called in and examined, every precaution being taken to prevent collusion between them. Every one of these girls bore marks of violence and corroborated the account given by the first witness of the ill usage to which they had been subjected. One girl was found with discoloured bruises on her arms, shoulders and bosom and asserted, as did the other girls, that they were the effects of blows inflicted by Mr Lucas.

These girls who were from 14 to 18 years of age though closely cross-examined by members of the Commission were consistent in their account of the proceedings connected with the treatment they had received . . .

William Charles Windeyer, President of the Public Charities Commission, to the Colonial Secretary, 25 November 1873.

31. "Their Superiors"

The Public Charities Commission, in its examination of the situation at Biloela, was critical of the school's management and found Mr Lucas to have been an unsuitable person to fill the position of superintendent.

Shortly before the removal of the School from Newcastle, Mr George Lucas, the Superintendent in charge at the time of our inquiry, was appointed, and though he has since resigned, on being called upon to show cause why he should not be dismissed on account of the proceedings disclosed in our minutes of the 25th November, we cannot avoid pronouncing an opinion on his management, inasmuch as public interests require that your Excellency should be fully informed of the causes contributing to the comparative failure of an institution established by the Legislature in furtherance of a philanthropic scheme of social reform worthy of the Country.

Previous to his appointment, Mr. Lucas appears to have been known as a citizen of Sydney taking considerable interest in the destitute classes of the city. Of a kindly disposition, he devoted a considerable portion of his time to the management of a night refuge for the homeless poor, and enjoyed the consequent popularity arising from his charitable conduct. On the removal of Mr. Clarke from the office of Superintendent, the Government of the day, in consequence of representations from numerous persons that Mr. Lucas was, by his disposition suited for the office, appointed him to the vacant post, at the same time giving the office of Matron to his wife. Mere kindliness of disposition, however, does not necessarily imply the possession of abilities requisite in the efficient administrator of an Industrial School. Beyond the possession of good intentions, Mr. Lucas appears to have possessed no qualifications for a post requiring a singular combination of natural and acquired attainments for the successful discharge of its duties, and it was soon discovered that a mistake had been made in his appointment. At the time of his nomination to the office no one seems to have been aware of the fact that Mr. Lucas was unable to write the simplest report in grammatical English, and, since his first attempt, all his official documents seem to have been drawn up by the clerk and storekeeper of the institution. Besides his deficiency of education, there was soon exhibited a disregard of appearance, and a slovenliness of attire very much calculated to destroy the respect of young people, quick in associating roughness of manner and appearance with want of culture and refinement. Experience seems to prove that probably no class so absolutely require for their successful management persons placed over them as instructors whom they at once distinctly recognize as their superiors, intellectually, morally, and socially, as the children to be found in a female Industrial School.

. . . The facts, however, which came to our knowledge on the 25th November . . . conclusively prove how dangerous it is to trust well-meaning but weak and ignorant people with uncontrolled power over the helpless and defenceless, and how quickly the best of such natures drift into a course of action which when unspoilt by the exercise of absolute authority they would shudder at adopting. Though we believe that the power to inflict corporal punishment should be allowed in the institution, it should only be exercised by a woman, as the infliction of the punishment by a man must necessarily degrade the character of young women subjected to such an outrage, whilst it must inevitably lower the dignity and blunt the moral sense of the man allowing himself to violate one of the first instincts of a manly nature.

It would appear from the evidence given by several witnesses as to the violence used towards the girls, that the treatment to which they were subjected was little calculated to impress them with a reverence for authority, but rather to perpetuate in their minds familiarity with scenes of domestic quarrel and violence, frequent indeed amongst the classes from which neglected vagrant children spring, and which furnish the wife-beaters of our Police Courts, but hardly to be expected in a reformatory home provided by the State for the children whom it seeks to reclaim from misery and neglect.

Public Charities Commission, *Second Report of the Commissioners Appointed to Inquire into and Report upon the Working and Management of the Public Charities of the Colony* (May 1874).

32. "We are Dealing with Children"

In her evidence to the 1873 Royal Commission into Public Charities in New South Wales, Rosamond Hill clearly separated the functions of an industrial school from those of a prison, and stressed that the purpose of an industrial school was to instill social virtues in children who had suffered the neglect or desertion of their parents. She also stressed the importance of voluntary assistance from members of the "leisure class".

A SUMMARY of the Principles of Reformatory Treatment, with especial reference to Girls.

IT is the lack of good home influence which, in the great majority of cases, brings girls into the condition necessitating reformatory training. In order to change them into respectable members of society, *i.e.*, to *re*-form them, we must as far as possible supply to them that wholesome family life which they have not before enjoyed; therefore, a prison with its bolts and bars should never be used for their dwelling-place.

The numbers of girls in a Reformatory or Industrial School must be small, or they must be subdivided into distinct groups, each group resembling a real family as nearly as possible, and occupying a dwelling to itself. This arrangement would facilitate the separation of Catholics from Protestants, and the placing them under the care of persons of their respective faiths. But a number of these groups living in small houses near each other might unite for purposes of secular instruction in a common schoolroom.

It is, above all, essential to imbue the children with a *love* of work. Therefore, care must be taken to prevent their labour from being either beyond their strength or too monotonous, creating in them in either case, a distaste for work.

A sufficient amount of recreation must be allowed — it must never be forgotten that we are dealing with children.

The members of each group or family should as far as possible do the whole work of their own house — baking, washing, and ironing, and the making of their own clothes, household linen, mattresses and pillows, inclusive. It is also essential that the children should frequently go beyond the boundaries of the institution, especially that they should go to a place of public worship.

The girls should also be employed — as it is found they can be trusted — to do errands for the household; they should be trained gradually to market and to shop, in order that when they leave the school and go to service, they should know how to purchase for their employers and to buy their own clothes — in fact, how to manage their wages with economy.

It must always be borne in mind that the training the girls receive in the institution is a means to an end — not an end in itself; and that therefore, however perfect the order and discipline of the school may be, unless the girls are allowed a certain amount of voluntary action and power of self-government, it will not prepare them for life after they have quitted its roof.

When the girls enter the school, they are idle, dirty, and very probably untruthful and dishonest. The aim of the managers is to render them industrious, cleanly, and honest. As the training gradually improves them, they will require less supervision, which should diminish by degrees as they become more and more able to govern themselves, until, when the time comes for their quitting the Institution they shall be able to fight the battle of life successfully for themselves.

Rewards and punishments, indispensable in Reformatory and Industrial Schools, should be, whenever possible, the natural consequence of the girls' conduct, — not on the one side an indulgence, or on the other an infliction of pain arbitrarily awarded by the managers. Good conduct should better the position of the girls in the school; and, on the other hand, bad conduct should worsen it.

This end will be most easily attained by allowing the girls to earn their privileges by their own efforts, and to lose them by bad conduct.

The best means of registering their behaviour is by the use of the mark system.

A certain number of marks gained by industry and good conduct should raise the girls in rank in the school. Bad conduct and idleness should take away their marks, and deprive them of the privileges they had earned, with the power of re-earning the marks and of regaining their position by their subsequent good conduct.

Thus, on entering the school a girl would necessarily possess no marks, and would therefore be at its bottom. A certain number of marks earned would raise her a stage, and would entitle her to certain privileges; a further number of marks would raise her to a second stage and entitle her to more privileges, and so on until she has reached the highest stage of all. In the course of climbing to the highest stage, the girl would gradually acquire that perseverence and self-control essential to her well-doing when she quits the school. The strict discipline under which she had been placed on admission would slacken by degrees until, as the time of her departure approached, she would almost govern herself.

By this time she would have become trustworthy, and would be accorded a certain degree of liberty. For instance, she might be permitted to go out on errands with a companion of similar rank in the school, and might have an allowance for the purchase of some part at least of her clothing.

Great care must be taken to prevent the ascent from being too difficult, and it must be made more easy to rise in the lower stages than in the higher, because the first efforts at self-control are always the hardest. The girl must not on the one side be disheartened by the too great steepness of the ascent, nor on the other must the privileges lose in value by the too great facility of their attainment. The advance from stage to stage should be so arranged that the girls should be able to reach the highest at least six months before the term of her detention expires.

The foregoing remarks are founded on practical experience, and no plan is suggested which has not been in successful operation.

They apply specially to schools in which girls enter at an early age and where they remain for some years. Those committed above twelve years old should be dealt with in separate institutions, and for these of course the plan described would require modification. For instance, the shorter term of detention would probably necessitate either fewer stages or a more rapid transition from one to another. There would be less school instruction and more industrial work, and the privileges would be different — adapted to the more advanced ages of the girls.

In order that the management of Reformatory and Industrial Schools should be successful, it is essential to secure voluntary, *i.e.* unpaid assistance.

In England the voluntary managers of these schools attest their interest in them by subscribing towards their funds; but as the power of legally detaining the pupils, and pecuniary aid from the State, are indispensable, justice demands that the managers should submit to Government inspection.

A Committee of ladies and gentlemen should be formed to direct the management, which should be carried on under their auspices by paid officials. The volunteer manager acquires an influence over the inmates of these schools distinct in character from that of the paid official, and very beneficial to the children. The leisure class, from which necessarily the volunteers must be drawn, possess the mental culture and training necessary for surmounting the difficulties inherent in the application of reformatory science — under their guidance the hard-working, conscientious, paid official will be able to carry the undertaking to a successful issue.

But the work of the managers is not complete when their pupils quit the Industrial School. They will require, when put out into the world, friendly supervision, which may be found necessary for some years.

Public Charities Commission, *First Report of the Commissioners Appointed to Inquire into and Report upon the Working and Management of the Public Charities of the Colony* (September 1873); Appendix V, evidence of Rosamond Hill.

33. Education at the Hobart Industrial School for Girls

Although most industrial schools made some attempt to provide elementary education for the inmates, it was considered far more important to give the girls vocational training in washing and sewing. In her report, the teacher at the Hobart Industrial School, Miss Sinclair, observed that "owing to the irregular periods at which the girls are able to come into the school, it is impossible to work from a timetable." The reasons for irregular attendance are explained by the Honorary Secretary, Mrs Salier.

Sir,

I beg to enclose Miss Sinclair's report of the system of Education adopted by her in teaching the girls at the Industrial School, Barracks. It must however be borne in mind that the School is of an industrial character, partly self supporting, and that the chief object of the Ladies Committee is to train the girls for useful service. It would be almost impossible to include a timetable, showing at what hours instruction is given, the elder girls go to their lessons when they can be spared from their washing, mangling etc. The younger ones are taught regularly from 9 till 12 and from 2 to ½ past 4 daily. With the exception of the girls who were received from the Queens Asylum in 1879 scarcely any could read or write, on entering the school many not even knowing the alphabet, and those children who had been previously boarded out were particularly ignorant.

Harriet Salier, Honorary Secretary, Girls' Industrial School, Hobart, to the Colonial Secretary, 14 January 1884.

34. Self-Supporting at Sixteen

At the age of sixteen, girls in Hobart institutions were considered adults, at least economically, and were expected to support themselves.

Madam,

I have the honour to acknowledge the receipt of your letter of the 14th instant, enclosing Miss Sinclair's report on the system of Education adopted in the Girl's Industrial School, and giving the names and ages of the children.

I observe that in Class IV there are two girls of nearly 16 years of age and one nearly 15. — In Class III, division 1, one girl is nearly 16 and one nearly 15. In Class II one girl is nearly 16 and in Class I one girl will be 16 next August.

While I am not desirous, at the present time, to call in question the advantages derived by the children from the training they receive in the School, I feel bound to point out that the girls of the ages specified ought, when not physically incapacitated, to be able to earn their own living after so long a residence in the Institution, and thus cease to be a burthen on Public Funds.

I shall feel obliged by your bringing the subject under the notice of the Governors of the School, with the view of these girls being discharged or apprenticed.

William Moore, Colonial Secretary, to Harriet Salier, 18 January 1884.

35. The Profits from Washing

Apart from training the girls for their future work, their employment in washing was necessary for the upkeep of the institution. For their labours, they received only an occasional reward for good behaviour. In 1887, at the Girls' Training School Reformatory in Hobart, the total amount expended on rewards came to £2.

Girls' Training School Reformatory Report for 1886

Sir

The Ladies Committee of the Girls Training School Reformatory are glad to report that the work of the Institution has gone on quietly and steadily throughout the past year.

The Institution continues to be self-supporting and has now a sum of £288.8.1. towards a Building or Reserve Fund.

The average number of inmates for the year has been ten and their behaviour on the whole good. Four girls were admitted during the year, and two left for situations.

The girls are employed in washing, housework, cooking and needlework and receive Bible Lessons and Instruction in reading writing & Arithmetic.

The amount earned during the year by washing is £329.17.4.

The Committee desire again to record their appreciation of the Matron's untiring energy and devotion which so materially helps towards the success of the Institution.

Mary Wright, Honorary Secretary, Girls' Training School Reformatory, Hobart, to the Colonial Secretary, 21 February 1887.

36. Allegations of Cruelty

In the late nineteenth century, there were many allegations made about the harsh and inhumane treatment of girls in industrial schools. In this report, a Victorian police constable describes conditions at Brookside Reformatory as told to him by seven escapees. The report is noteworthy for the constable's readiness to treat the girls' testimony as reliable. The Superintendent of Police at Ballarat agreed with Constable Clifford and observed that, "If the girls are treated in the manner described, it is no wonder that many cases of absconding are reported from there." The reformatory was run by Mrs Elizabeth Rowe, who was described as "a lady of fortune with large philanthropic aspirations".

I have to report that on the evening of 13th inst Const Stephens, of Napoleons, brought seven girls whose ages ranged from 12 to 17 years to the Lockup.

These girls had absconded from the Brookside Reformatory on the 11th inst and after wandering in the bush fell into his hands at Enfield, their condition when found was pitiable, being hatless and very poorly clothed. They were returned to the institution, under escort of Constable Shaw by the 11.25 am train on this date.

At the watchhouse they collectively complained of the tasks and treatment meted out to them, and stated that they had to fell, saw, and split trees, and afterwards with the aid of a horse cart the wood home, dig post-holes and erect fencing, load and cart gravel from a neighboring gravel heap (to repair roads and footpaths), plough, harrow, assist in harvesting operations etc as well as to do the washing and other domestic duties.

The slightest neglect or indolence on their part in performing any of those multifarious duties earns the delinquent a flogging with a heavy leather strap, (portion of a discarded belly band) and two of the girls had marks on their arms corroborative of the severity of a whipping which they said had been administered a few days previously.

It was also stated that a 12 year old girl is now confined to her bed at the Reformatory, her hands tied, and her body covered with black and blue bruises, the result of a flogging given her by the matron, the alleged offence being that she (the girl) had torn or destroyed a portion of her clothing.

They expressed a lively apprehension of the consequences that would follow on their return to the Reformatory asserting that their hair would be cut off, that they would be fed on bread and water for at least a month, with liberal applications of the belly-band, and further that they would have to follow their tree felling and gravel carting labours without boots or stockings. Considering the nature of the work, and the severity of this climate, this last seems to me, to be, if true very cruel indeed.

Constable Clifford, Victoria Police, Ballarat Station, to the Superintendent of Police, Ballarat, 14 July 1899.

37. Repression Not Reform

Following the escapes from Brookside, the Melbourne *Argus* sent Alice Henry to report on the situation at this reformatory. She was highly critical of the private reformatory system whereby the government gave ten shillings per week for the maintenance of each child and surrendered all control in matters in policy and day-to-day running to the superintendent. Her report also indicates the increasing criticism that was being made of large portions of the welfare system being administered by ladies with only philanthropic aspirations and religious zeal to qualify them.
Mrs Rowe was the founder and superintendent of the institution and Miss King and Miss Hamilton her subordinates.

Miss King is doubtless actuated by the best of motives and tries to act up to the texts on the walls, but what are her training and qualifications for a post demanding the scientific treatment of such girls as come under her supervision? Twelve as a machinist in a shop in Ballarat and 18 years spent as Bible woman under the Wesleyan mission constitutes her record. I was unable to discover that Miss King or Mrs Rowe either had the remotest conception of the psychological aspect of their work, of the long preparation, of the thorough training necessary, of the breadth of view to which she must attain who would venture into a field like this. The matron's personal standpoint may be judged from an entry in her own handwriting, copied verbatim: — "Nov. 8 1897 — Punished A. Stevenson for tearing and destroying her Bible. She said the devil told her to do it; gave her a whipping, isolated her for a short time, told her that was the devils pay for serving him so well."

Miss Hamilton, who has charge of the other cottage, though also untrained is in every way a better stamp of woman; at once more intelligent and more kindly. Miss King's assistant is supposed to be the teacher of the establishment. I have shown that the amount of teaching the girls receive can't hurt the pupils very much. Let us now examine into its quality as judged by the status of the instructress. Her history is this. At the age of 16 Mrs Rowe undertook to keep her under her eye as a private case. That is nine years ago. She has overcome her peculiarities and has for some time been acting as assistant to the matron. She holds a sixth class state school certificate: has had no education beyond this and no training in the art of teaching.

On the one hand, there is no evidence to prove that the Brookside girls are either half starved or insufficiently clothed, nor that they are cruelly overworked or beaten black and blue. But quite apart from any such unproved charges the system and methods savour of the dark ages. We will grant all that has been said regarding the exceedingly low character of the inmates. They probably include the department's very hardest cases. Some are criminal, almost all are grossly immoral. But all are young, and some, it is admitted by the ladies themselves, are mentally deficient. According to their own showing, the sole idea the officers have of dealing with their difficult charges is repression. A girl is mischievous, idle, careless, untruthful, and she is housed in a bare, ugly place; she is put to monotonous, resultless toil; her instincts for fun, her harmless vanities are all starved. She must not wear a pretty dress even if she has earned it when out at service, because she is a wicked girl, and must never be allowed to forget it. Sankey's hymns are all the music that is permitted, and that generally without the support of instrumental harmonies. Reckless, devil-may-care creatures as some of them are, a wholesome book of Clark Russell's or the absurdities of "Three Men in a Boat" would help to absorb some of their animal spirits, but no, that would never do. They must be limited to the ineffable insipidities of Pansy and her sister twaddlers. Fancy three years of Pansy relieved only by an un-comprehended Bible and badly-rendered Sankey's hymns. Why not have a dance of an evening, or the steadying influence of a march, or a turn with dumb bells and clubs? This would cost nothing, nothing at all except expert management. One doesn't require to know much of human nature to forecast the result of all this re-pression. One girl tears her clothes, another fights with her fellows or uses filthy language. Yet another runs away, driven to aimless and stupid rebellion by the ghastly monotony of her life. No merely negative means will banish sensual images and criminal impulses from the mind of the youthful offender. . .

If the authorities are slow to see how to prevent outbreaks, they are swift and sure to punish them. Since 1897 the punishment book has been kept with great irre-gularity, so for actual data one is mostly thrown back to the earlier period. It is a sickening record; none the less so because, possibly no excessive physical pain may have been inflicted. For absconding, a recognized offence, the penalty has been to have their hair cut off, boots and stockings taken away, and sometimes isolation as well. Canings appear so frequently that one would think their futility with such big girls would have suggested itself by now. Occasional gleams of a grim, if accidental, humour lights it pages. "Absconding without provocation", prompts the query as to what combination of circumstances might, in this lady's opinion, be supposed to amount to provocation. For eating green apples one culprit received a dose of castor oil; one may charitably hope with some remedial end in view, but it is recorded as a punishment. One girl was isolated both Christmas Day and Boxing Day. Another entry is of three hours exercise (walking around the house in sight of all) tied up in a strait-jacket. About as sensible as the obsolete treadmill. With so much reliance placed on mere physical restraint for evil passions of every sort, what chance of reform has the weakwilled girl when left to her own devices in the comparative freedom of service on a distant farm? This brings up the question of the conditions under which girls can be sent out with safety to others and with benefit to themselves. The impression left on the mind of the investigator is of a very happy-go-lucky system indeed. As far as I can discover the department gives carte blanche to the superintendent of the reformatory, and she sends them out at her discretion. The sooner they can be sent out the better. It is one child less for the state to pay for. But she admits that they are frequently quite unfit for domestic work under family con-ditions, and the perpetual returns to the home which the roll-book shows are not en-couraging reading . . .

It is not merely Mrs Rowe's forty that are in this coil. In the private reforma-tories alone are 205 children, costing £6,514 a year, existing without supervision, and it's lucky if none of them are not worse treated. It isn't the department's fault if they are not. The money is paid over, the superintendent has full authority over the child, and the department practically washes its hands of him or her. Once a year Mr Millar [secretary and inspector of the Department for Neglected Children and Re-formatory Schools] makes an inspection, but of independent, expert investigation into accounts, teaching, recreation, reform where is the record? My conclusions then are that the authorities at Brookside are untrained and unsuited for their difficult task; that the system pursued is antiquated and non-reformatory in its effects; and that the inspection is so inefficient and casual as to be practically a negligible quantity.

"Reformatories and Reform" by a "A Special Reporter" (Alice Henry), *Argus*, 2 August 1899.

38. "Rough and Unsexing Work"

In the same article from the *Argus,* Alice Henry argues that the work assigned to the inmates of Brookside was not chosen with the future employment of the girls in mind.

... There is no timetable only a sort of understanding that the morning shall be spent in house and outdoor work, and the afternoon in sewing, and a little desultory teaching for the younger ones. From teatime till 8 o'clock I was told they were at liberty to amuse themselves reading or playing games. An occasional night of games with sweets forms the extreme of dissipation, and at long intervals a picnic is given by Mrs Rowe. The question of the outdoor work of which so much has been made resolves itself into this. In the absence of a proper timetable and tabulated results it is impossible to decide with any degree of accuracy of what it consists. The matron admits that girls have to saw and chop wood, cart gravel, and empty nightpans. To these local rumour adds well and dam sinking and fencing, but as to that I cannot speak. It is clear, however, that there must be a fair amount of this rough and unsexing work done, for the girls have to be kept employed, and so poorly appointed an establishment cannot furnish "feminine" employment for 13, not to mention 40 inmates. It is argued that the girls prefer outdoor work, and that hard exercise in the open air is the best occupation they can have. Making all due allowance, the fact remains that wood-chopping etc is of no use in qualifying them to earn their living, still less is such experience needful in the training of a wife and mother. Their youth is passing and it is not being employed, as the Government ought to insist it should be be employed, in fitting them for the future.

"Reformatories and Reform" by "A Special Reporter" (Alice Henry), *Argus,* 2 August 1899.

39. "A Very Humble Sphere of Life"

Norman Dowling, a doctor, was sent by the Department for Neglected Children and Reformatory Schools to investigate the health of St Ann's inmates. In his report, he defended the sort of work imposed on the girls at Brookside and St Ann's Reformatory, on the grounds that it was consistent with what should be their social and economic aspirations.

... So far as the criticism [in the press] might be also applied to St Ann's, I crave permission to add an expression of opinion on the subject. I dissent entirely from the view that the work the girls have to do is unnecessarily rough, unsexing, and ill-calculated to fit them for the spheres of work that may possibly lie before them as domestic servants or even the wives of farmers and labourers. On the contrary having due regard to the defective conditions, physical, mental, and moral, under which they labour (almost without exception) the employment is wholly suitable, if viewed in the threefold aspect of occupation, discipline, and education. These poor girls can never expect to attain to any but a very humble sphere of life or duty, and it is wise and right to train them accordingly for country homes and farms where this kind of work will fall to their lot.

Norman Dowling, report on the administration of St Ann's Reformatory, Heywood, "a branch of Mrs Rowe's Home", to the Secretary, Department for Neglected Children and Reformatory Schools, Melbourne, 26 August 1899.

40. "Impulses of Goodness"

Leading suffragist Rose Scott, like many well-meaning and sympathetic women, was puzzled when the girl apprenticed to her family slipped out of the confines of respectability.

I remember with a bitter pang, a hopeless feeling the girl we had from the Industrial School who was apprenticed to us for so many years — we *made* her love us, we loved her, and yet the day her engagement was over she left us and went on the streets and we could do *nothing* to save her. These girls seem to have mere impulses of goodness, wickedness was an excitement to them.

Rose Scott, Journal, 1 June 1890.

41. Casualities of the Double Standard

Frequently, girls were charged under the New South Wales Industrial Schools Act of 1866 for being in moral danger. In the cases documented below, one girl, Ellen B., was admitted to Parramatta Industrial School for her protection while the man who sexually assaulted her was discharged. The other girl, Lily F., was apprenticed as a domestic servant from the same institution, only to have her career abruptly halted when she became pregnant to a lodger in the house where she was employed.

Ellen [B——] was arrested at the instance of her mother and was brought before the Water Police Court on 20th July 1888. She was 12 years old.
The charge brought against her was that of living in a brothel and associating with reputed thieves. The charge further states that —
A man named Patrick [M——] was charged at the same court on the same day with assaulting with intent to carnally know, the girl, he was discharged owing to insufficient evidence. According to medical evidence an attempt had been made to carnally know her, but a doubt existed as to the end being attained. The Presiding Magistrate suggested that she should be charged under the Industrial Schools Act.
   I am of the opinion that this girl will not, if she be treated kindly, abscond. Apart from the ordinary faults of girls of her age she has not shown any vicious tendency, nor has she given any more than ordinary trouble to the officer here.

Report on Ellen B., C. H. Spier, Superintendent, Parramatta Industrial School for Girls, 21 February 1893.

Lily [F——'s] statement.
I was 16 years old on 31st July last. I came here [to be apprenticed as a servant to Mr Edward Badgery] on 16 June 1892. Mr [B——, a school teacher] was staying here. Shortly after I came Mr [B——] began to pull me about. I told him to stop or I would tell Mrs Badgery, he went out of the kitchen. This occurred many times early in the morning when I came down from my room. After I had been there a short time he had connection with me. I was in a little room with a bed in it; I was fixing up my hair. Mr [B——] came in and pulled me onto the bed. It was before my birthday on a Sunday morning; he frequently had connection with me afterwards until the Christmas holidays. No one else ever took liberties of any kind with me, no one else ever pulled me about or kissed me. I did not tell Mrs Badgery until quite recently; I was afraid she would tell my father. Mrs Badgery accused me of being stout but I denied

it. I told her that I used to get stout like that when I was in the Institution, and was given medicine for it by Dr Violette. I never was so treated, I told Mrs Badgery so to deceive her. Mrs Badgery never left me alone, she used to take me with her when she went to M [illegible] or any other place around the district. Only once did Mr [B——] have connection with me at night. Mrs Badgery was then in another part of the house. It always, with these exceptions, occurred in·the mornings about half past six or seven.

Included in Report on Lily F., C. H. Spier, Superintendent, Parramatta Industrial School for Girls, 22 May 1893.

42. "Not Without Her Good Points"

This report by the Superintendent of the Industrial School for Girls at Parramatta gives an unusual importance to the connection between the class origins of the girls and their present circumstances.

Our girls are largely drawn from the poorer classes, who are not given to habits of reflection or foresight. They live in the present and enjoy to the full any passing pleasure.

Their education (taking the word education in its widest sense) being usually poor, and their mental horizon in consequence small, their scale of interests and pleasures is very limited. This is amply reflected in the letters which pass between our inmates and their parents, and which almost invariably are confined to the great events of life — birth, death, marriage, accidents, and such enjoyments as dancing, singing and feasting. As regards the higher moral qualities, and particularly what may be referred to as "Social Morality", we are inclined to expect too much of them . . . We should make the path of virtue somewhat easier, and those of us that are happily circumstanced as regards the material comforts of life, should remember how much these conduce to our being able to lead good lives . . . The Industrial School type of girl is not without her good points. In many cases it is the presence in a high degree of those very emotions which, under proper control, produce the best woman that cause her downfall, and it is by acting as fully as possible on these same emotions that any permanent success is due.

Industrial School for Girls, Parramatta, Superintendent's Report for 1908.

43. Victims of Heredity

The numbers of people that were a charge against the welfare system of the State, particularly the incidence of different generations of the one family in various institutions, led some welfare and health administrators to regard the heredity factor as insurmountable and to advocate the breeding out of such stock. No legislation was passed to implement these recommendations, although these beliefs, as this report shows, resulted in some inmates of institutions being written off as an irredeemable residuum.

The child being the victim not merely of its environment but of its heredity, we find that to effect the results we desire we must struggle not only against its want of opportunities and its want of training, but against what must mainly prove an impossible task, namely, an evil heredity. This compels the struggle to be therefore carried into fresh territory against the causes responsible for the production of evil or defective types of humanity, a question of such magnitude as to at present defy our best efforts. The only hope for success in this direction lies in a determined educational propaganda which will awaken the whole nation to an intelligent comprehension of the modern science of eugenics . . . An examination of our civilised social systems shows that we have as yet made only the feeblest attempts to prevent the unfits and the undesirable human stocks from propagating their like, . . . Hope, which springs eternal in the human breast, also prompts us, like the philosophers and alchemists of old in their search for perpetual motion and the elixir of life, to ceaselessly pursue "will o' the wisps", to imagine that environment and training can do everything, and that heredity may be reduced to a factor of inferior dimensions, if not neglected altogether. The girls of this institution continuously show just the very divisions one would expect, namely: —

(a) Those whose innate disposition is good, but have had an evil environment, and lack training. These may include perhaps 20 to 30 per cent.

(b) Those whose innate disposition is good but who are somewhat unbalanced, or whose emotions are undisciplined, and are lacking in will power. These may include perhaps 50 per cent.

(c) Those whose innate disposition is evil, because it is abnormal, callous, or unbalanced, and whose mentality may be fairly good, or of very low grade. With these may be included also those who are of deficient intellect, abnormally dull intelligence, or are semi-imbeciles. These comprise 20 to 25 per cent of admissions.

In most cases the mentality is deficient to some degree or other, but not more so than we would expect to find among the lower ranks of the industrial classes. Rarely could we say that girls give evidence of any high-class ability — such ability, for example, as would enable them to attain to a high standard of scholarship. Capacity for original thought is generally wanting, and there is little reflection or foresight.

Industrial School for Girls, Parramatta, Superintendent's Report for 1915.

Destitute Women and Benevolence

44. "A Small Sum from Government"

This letter, written in a large, ornate hand, possibly by a professional letter-writer, asks directly for aid for a widow with young children to support, to supplement her earnings from sewing and washing. Women in similar circumstances who were unable to support themselves and their children in such trades frequently became recipients of aid or inmates of destitute institutions from the early colonial period.

Mr Viveash Esq

Sir I hope your Honour will be so Kind as to lay my case before His Exelency The Governor. I have five Small children one girl nine years of age four Boys Their ages are six four & two years and one sickly child six months old And as I cannot get sufficient work to support them I hope your Honour will recommend me to His Exelency The Governor to allow me a small sum weekly as I have rent to pay. A few shillings per week would Keep me from breaking up my home and becoming destitute** There are some Ladies in Guildford promised to give me a little sewing and washing to do and this with a small sum from Government will Keep me from want And becoming a burden to Government. And I hope and trust that you will do all in your Powr for me as Necessity alone compels me to ask for ade and give you this trouble.

I remain your Humble Servant

Mrs [M——]

Mrs M., Guildford, to Mr Viveash, Resident Magistrate, 27 January 1865.

45. "Brought Up Respectable"

When a woman applied for relief, an enquiry was made, usually by the local police, into her character, background and sexual relationships. In this case, the woman was lucky.

MEMORANDUM

Sergt Snook begs to inform Mr Stone that he has made inquiries as requested by him, in the case of Mrs [T——] wife of a Ticket holder lately reconvicted, and am able to report that she is and has been since her arrival in the Colony a respectable woman. She is reported to be a good needle woman but at present unable to obtain but little work. The child she has to support is her husbands by another woman he lived with previous to the arrival of his wife in the Colony, this woman has since died. Mrs [T—

——] was married to [T——] in England and came out to him. She appears to have been brought up respectable.

N. Snook, Sergeant of Police, to John Stone, Officer-in-Charge, Perth Poor House, 11 August 1864.

46. Buying a Mangle

Well-wishers and charitable organizations persisted in the belief that in giving items of equipment such as mangles and later sewing-machines to needy women, the recipients were not degraded and self-reliance was encouraged. At best, each woman was given a chance to compete more successfully in trades that were overcrowded and underpaid.

Sir,

I have the honor to again request your attention to the case of the Widow [G——], as it appears that you have henceforth to withhold the allowance so judiciously and charitably granted up to this time.

The poor woman, [G——], tries to maintain her family, as a Washerwoman. She is unable to do so now, but all who can judge best of her circumstances agree that with the help of a Mangle she would be certain of being able to procure a sufficient livelihood. Hence endeavours have been made to get a Mangle for her. Several subscriptions are promised for that purpose, but at present one cannot be had. Mr S. Cooke, of Perth, who makes such things, replied to my inquiry, that he had not one for sale, but that he would in a short time be making others, and then would duly inform me of the price etc.

Meanwhile what is Mrs [G——] to do? When this little machine can be placed at her disposal she will be able to do for herself, but until that time she cannot maintain herself and family without support from others.

Mrs [G——] has conducted herself with propriety in every respect since her husband's death, and as support from Government will be required only for the short time above indicated, I beg to request that your influence will be used for the continuance of the support hitherto granted, until Mrs [G——] can have the Mangle and thus be left in a position to maintain herself and children without being a burden to any person . . .

A. B [illegible], York (W.A.), to Mr Cowan, Resident Magistrate, 16 September 1865.

47. Getting into the Poor House

An institution such as the Perth Poor House was seen by some women as a place to be "threatened with" when they requested outdoor relief. To others, it was a refuge. In his letter to the Colonial Secretary, John Stone, Officer-in-Charge, gives reasons for his unwillingness to admit two women to the Poor House. The admission of Mary C. was refused, with the proviso that "if she be really destitute, she may be supplied with such food as is necessary to prevent starvation".

A woman named Margaret [R——] has applied for admission into the Poor

House for a short time, and from inquiries I have made, I have ascertained that she seeks admission merely for the purpose of being properly attended to during her confinement shortly expected, that her husband is in gaol, and that she is living with a man named [S———], who either has not the means, or declines procuring a Midwife to attend her —

Mrs [R———] was admitted into the Poor House some 18 months since for a similar purpose as the above, and was, while there, I am informed, very unruly in her conduct, and in fact had to be forcibly expelled — to prevent a repetition of that conduct (which would no doubt be the case if admitted) I would request to be informed whether I will meet with the approval of His Excellency, if I direct the Poor House Midwife, Mrs Gaunt, to attend the woman at her own house, which is no doubt all that is required; or, on the other hand, if I inform her that no assistance whatever can be given her by the Government.

Another woman named Mary [C———] has also applied for admission into the Poor House being unable to support herself and two children — I had the honour to report her case to you on the 23rd May last, and received the sanction of His Excellency to outdoor relief at the rate of 2/6 per week being given her which has been continued up to a short time since — Mrs [C———] has repeatedly asked for admission into the Poor House, stating that she cannot possibly get any needlework or washing wherewith to support herself honestly, and I have ascertained that this is the case, and for the simple reason that she is not a fit person to be trusted, being one of the worst prostitutes in the Town — under these circumstances I wish to be informed whether His Excellency will think fit to sanction this woman's admission —

John Stone, Officer-in-Charge, Perth Poor House, to the Colonial Secretary, 31 August 1864.

Margaret [R———] is the person mentioned in my letter of the 31st August last and is one of the very *worst characters* in the Town — she is, I am informed by the police living with a man well able to support her during her confinement, and I do not therefore see any reason why she should be admitted into the Poor House. Were she admitted, I feel certain that she would behave in a similar manner to what she did when there on a former occasion.

Ibid., 16 September 1864.

48. "Not a Lucretia"

Character references and commendations from sympathizers sometimes supported requests for aid and, as in this case, gave a different view of the applicant and circumstances. Margaret R. is again the subject.

My dear Sir,

A young woman named [R———] — not a Lucretia — is within a day or two of her confinement and has no place of abode.

I do not like to ask Stone to take her into the House, for even if he has not refused already, I feel sure he would.

Would you object to ask the Governor to desire her reception till she has recovered.

I know this is a difficult matter to deal with: but I know that distress and misery among the mothers of this Class is a fertile source of infanticide . . .

G.W. Leake to the Colonial Secretary, 16 September 1864.

49. Entry by Force

In this memorandum, John Stone not only describes the events leading up to the admission of Margaret R. to the Poor House, but reasserts one of the reasons for his refusal to admit her: that there was a man capable of supporting her.

In addition to my memorandum of yesterday's date, I have the honor to inform you that Margaret [R——] came to my house last night, and stated that "she had determined to remain there until I took her into the House, as Mr Leake told her I was to do so". As I could not possibly get rid of the woman, I obtained two police-men, who after a period of two hours, managed with great difficulty, to carry her away on a stretcher; but not before she had twice assaulted me, threatened my life, and the lives of all in my house, made use of many other like threats, and screamed the most filthy and disgusting language the whole time she was there, in fact roused the whole neighbourhood —

On the Police removing the woman to the Lockup, I believe it was found that in all probability she would be confined during the night, and as admittance to the Hos-pital was on application refused, she was conveyed to the House, and I afterwards informed of the fact — As labour pains had then commenced there was no other alternative but to admit her, which I did most reluctantly; the police taking all respon-sibility in the matter, and considering her still a Prisoner.

I still maintain that from the information I received from the Police, and which is most undoubtedly correct, that the man [S——] is in a position to support the woman, and that she is not therefore a person for the Public to maintain.

John Stone, Officer-in-Charge, Perth Poor House, to the Colonial Secretary, 17 September 1864.

50. Inmates of the Poor House

Inside the Poor House, women with young children were a prominent group. The problem of how to occupy the women was solved, as in other institutions, by applying them to the sort of work that many of them had done outside. Insufficient earnings from this work frequently had been the cause of their destitution.

There are at present in the Poor House 12 women, 3 Boys under 12, 6 children under ten, 15 under 6, and 6 under 2 years of age.

Of the women 4 are imbecile, three of whom are unfit to be trusted with any work other than cleaning their rooms and occasionally a little needle work. Another of the women is over 70 years of age, and unfit to perform any hard work such as washing, she is however very willing and does as much needlework as her failing sight will permit.

Of the remaining 7, 6 have very young children in arms, requiring a great deal of attention from the mothers.

The work at present performed by the Poor House women is the Hospital washing, the private washing of Hospital assistant (about 170 pieces weekly exclusive of their own washing), occasionally washing [illegible] from Government House, and making and mending all their own clothes. They have also picked a quantity of coir.

The women have not sufficient to keep them employed throughout the whole day. it would be a great satisfaction to me if they had, but the amount of washing required for the Perth Prison is I am confident quite sufficient to keep 8 women constantly employed for that sole purpose. It would therefore be absurd for this work to be undertaken when it is evident one third of it could not be accomplished, and I think if some lighter work were named, and one which can be increased at the event of more women being admitted, it would be more advisable.

John Stone, Officer-in-Charge, Perth Poor House, to the Colonial Secretary, 6 August 1864.

51. Responsibility for Support

Who was responsible for the support of a lone woman with children? This was a question posed by government authorities and charitable institutions. In the case of Mrs M., the government was seen to have no responsibility for her maintenance.

Sir,

I have the honour to enclose herewith a petition on behalf of Mrs Adele C. [M——], a widow, aged 44, and 4 children aged respectively 11, 8, 5, and 1, together with various enquiries respecting her. Mrs [M——] has well to do relatives who should assist her in a start in life, and she being young and educated should make an effort to maintain herself and family as very many others have to do even without assistance from friends.

Mrs [M——] and children reside with her mother who will provide them with food, and it is but natural to surmise that her other relations will also assist her, if she will make an effort to assist herself.

Under the circumstances disclosed in the attached reports I do not consider it a case for Government interference and recommend that the petition be not acceded to.

F. R. Seager, Administrator of Charitable Grants, Charitable Grants Department, New Town (Tas.), to the Chief Secretary, Hobart, 17 April 1900.

52. Off to the Goldfields

The problem of women deserted and left to support their children was exacerbated by changes in mining fortunes. When mines closed, local magistrates observed an increase in female and child paupers. During the gold-rushes, government agencies and private charities in Adelaide, Melbourne and throughout Tasmania commented on the increase in destitute and deserted women.

Previous to the gold discoveries the crime of desertion was of infrequent occurrence, which however I regret to say is not now the case. The scattered nature of the population, and the number of gold fields and central towns, renders it a difficult task to trace a person's locality, thus the mother of a family may in vain seek the father, who in the eager pursuit of his vocation forgets the ties of nature.

The increase to our population has been attended by a worse than a proportionate number of idle and dissolute persons who regardless of all social bonds, become familiar but with crime, drunkenness and the Watch House.

To these causes may be attributed the many instances of desertion, and the painful cases of distress that so frequently come under my notice . . . I assure you Sir, that a Magistrate cannot but feel at a loss how to act, when the degraded mother of a squalid family is again brought up as an habitual drunkard, being well aware that any punishment inflicted on her falls on the unhappy children, who must either follow her to gaol, or seek a miserable existence by theft or the charity of others.

Magistrate of the City Police Court, Melbourne, to the Chief Secretary of Victoria, letter dated 14 June 1856.

53. Desertion and Poverty

The problem of deserting husbands and the pauperization of their families attracted particular attention at the First Australasian Conference on Charity, convened under the auspices of the Charity Organization Society in Melbourne in 1890. T. H. Atkinson, describing the situation in South Australia, showed how difficult it was to track down a deserting husband.

The question of wife desertion has attracted considerable notice at this Conference, and a committee, as you are aware, has been asked to consider the matter, with a view of suggesting some practical means whereby the evils resulting from this offence may be lessened. In South Australia, in the Destitute Persons Amendment Act of 1886, clauses exist which read as follows:—

"In addition to the remedies provided by section 9 of the Destitute Persons Act 1881, whenever any husband unlawfully deserts his wife, or leaves her without or fails to provide her with adequate means of support, or when any father or mother deserts his or her child under the age of fourteen years, or leaves them without or fails to provide them with adequate means of support, and goes to reside beyond the province of South Australia, either temporarily or permanently, such husband, father, or mother shall be deemed to be guilty of a misdemeanour, punishable with hard labour for any term not exceeding twelve months.

"In any of the cases specified in the last preceding section if complaint be made on oath to any justice of the peace by any respectable person, such justice, upon the production of a certificate under the hand of the Chairman of the Destitute Board that such complaint is well founded, may, if satisfied that an offence has been committed within the meaning of the said section, but not otherwise, issue his warrant for the apprehension of the person against whom such complaint has been made."

Misdemeanours are provided for in the Fugitive Offenders Act, which now applies to all our colonies. We have, therefore, the power to bring any wife-deserter back to South Australia.

In my experience, however, no case has occurred in which the law has been put in operation by our department.

The difficulties in the way of doing so are great.

Firstly, it is necessary that the husband's exact whereabouts should be known.

Secondly, a constable who can identify the offender must be sent after him in charge of the warrant. When the man is brought back his defence might be such that a conviction would not follow. If the offence be proved, and the twelve months' sentence follows, the family has still to be supported by the Government during his incarceration. Many men leave their wives and families in the first instance with an honest intention to procure employment, with the idea of returning to or sending for their families as soon as such is possible. Absence, however, instead of strengthening the ties of affection has the contrary effect, and with some men of vicious natures new associations are formed, and those who should rightly claim their support are neglected. In the crowded cities of our colonies a man's identity can soon be lost, and if he leaves home for the purpose of avoiding his responsibilities he can very easily baffle inquiries by changing his name. By the desertion of some men their wives and families have been distinctly benefited.

A drunkard who deserts his family is an instance. The evil influence of his presence is removed, and his absence secures relief for his family, which would not otherwise be eligible for assistance.

When a man deserts his wife, and is known to be in our colony, the issue of a warrant for his arrest is insisted upon before relief is granted.

The wife is always made the complainant, as, without her evidence, a prosecution would be useless. Many cases have occurred where the wife has refused to appear against her husband when arrested. Thus the provisions of the law have often no other effect than the bringing of husband and wife together again. If the man is known to have money when he returns, the department has power to recover from him the value of the relief issued to his family. If the charge of desertion be substantiated, an order for a weekly payment is made, and in the event of non-compliance therewith the man is committed to gaol for a period which is left to the discretion of the magistrate.

T. H. Atkinson, "The Destitute Poor Department of South Australia", in *Proceedings of the First Australasian Conference on Charity* (1890).

54. Legislative Remedies

The resolution by the First Australasian Conference, to press for the enforcement of interstate maintenance orders, reflects an interest in desertion as a cause of poverty rather than a concern with finding the causes of desertion.

DISCUSSION.

DESERTING HUSBANDS.

THE HONORARY SECRETARY introduced the question of deserting husbands. He said that at the First Conference all the delegates who spoke on the question were unanimous in pointing out the misery caused by the ease with which legal and natural responsibilities could be evaded, by merely changing the place of residence from one colony to another. The most carefully considered suggestion (No. 5) adopted at that Conference had reference to this subject. It ran thus —

"5. This Conference suggests to the legislative bodies in each colony that maintenance orders, made in any one colony against deserting husbands or fathers of families or putative fathers of illegitimate children, be enforceable in any other colony on the original order; and that power should be given to issue maintenance orders where intention to desert is shown, or in defendant's absence if he have left the colony; and that power should be given for the issue and enforcement of maintenance orders against deserting mothers."

Proceedings of the Second Australasian Conference on Charity (1891).

55. "The Responsibilities of Relatives"

The Second Australasian Conference on Charity in 1891 showed the same interest as the first in the wife desertion question and its relationship to female poverty.

I have been requested to prepare a minute on the responsibilities of relatives, by which is understood their liability to support, in one form or other, those allied to them by ties of kindred who may need help.

The only legislation upon this matter in New South Wales compels a husband or parent to support a wife or legal infant, whether they be inmates or not of the public asylums, but there is no provision for compelling any person to contribute, either wholly or in part, towards the maintenance of other relatives in the charitable institutions of the country, no matter how close the tie of kinship may be. Several other colonies represented at this Conference are precisely in the same position in this respect as New South Wales; and it would be well, therefore, to consider how this peculiarly discreditable abuse of charity is to be remedied.

In my colony the abuse complained of had become so great that I considered it a public duty to publish some of the cases in detail, suppressing names only, in my last annual report on the charitable institutions of the colony; and the particulars disclosed a degree of heartlessness among a number of well-to-do persons that would have been quite incredible if the official records had not afforded such undoubted proof of it. (The speaker here quoted a number of very gross cases in illustration. All these were from official and undeniable records.)

The matter of wife and child desertion, as you all know, unfortunately prevails to a large extent in all the colonies. New legislation should be made sufficiently comprehensive to deal more effectually with this phase of the matter than it does at present. It is true it is possible, under a very cumbersome legal process, to follow up deserters of these classes; but there is no method of tracing them, and they need now only cross the border or the sea in order to secure immunity from punishment, after leaving wives and families to the mercy of the world. I heard a gentleman at this Conference yesterday remark that so far as child-deserters were concerned he had had no difficulty — that no matter in which colony the offender might be he has been arrested and brought back. I regret to say that the experience of my own department is quite contrary to this, and of the many warrants which have been issued from it during the past ten years not 5 per cent. have been executed. Legislation should make registration at some central point (indeed this might be a branch of charity organization work) compulsory on the part of any person removing without his family from one colony to another, and also with regard to his change of residence after such removal, say for a period of one year. Again, the penalty upon deserters should be more severe than it is now. It is really, apart from the degradation, which counts for very little with such persons, no punishment to offenders of this class to go to gaol. In my colony the penalty is merely imprisonment. There is no hard labour attached to it, so that the State usually has to keep the parent in comparative idleness, at a cost, perhaps, of £40 a year, in addition to supporting his family.

S. Maxted, "The Responsibilities of Relatives", in *Proceedings of the Second Australasian Conference on Charity* (1891).

56. "Acknowledging Guilt in the Sight of God"

Often, the primary concern of private charities was with moral reclamation. George Washington Walker, a prominent Hobart Quaker and philanthropist, illustrates in this letter the beginning of such a charitable organization, run by men but directed to and sustained by women.

In conformity with our appointment we have communicated with the Young Woman desirous to avail herself of the Society's protection, and have acquainted ourselves with the particulars of her case. Her real name is Mary Ann [N——] though she has passed under that of [F——]. She was brought from the Mother Country to this Colony, when only five years of age, by her mother, who, as well as her father, is deceased. After some years abode in the Orphan School she went into service; and was last at place with a Dressmaker, from whence she was unhappily seduced by a young man, who shortly afterwards abandoned her & went to Sydney. Since that period M.A. [N——] has lived a dissolute life, along with another woman with whom she has been associated in housekeeping, & who according to the statement of the former, is also disposed to abandon her present evil course of life. The house they have occupied is stated to belong to a publican named Tilly and is situated at the upper end of Murray St.

We closely questioned the present applicant as to the motives of her application. She signified that they originated from an anxious desire to break off from her past habits of which she was both "wearied & ashamed" to use her own expressions, and of which she acknowledged she saw the guilt and offensiveness in the sight of God, as well as before man.

Under the belief that she was sincere in her profession of determination to amend could she be put in the way of obtaining an honest livelihood by her own exertions; we set about obtaining a place for her in some family, the Mistress of which more especially, should be of a character in whom the Committee might confide in regard to the exercise of that judicious restraint, & considerate treatment which would be especially requisite in reference to a young woman under such circumstances. We are happy to state that after several fruitless efforts a situation was at length obtained for your applicant with Mrs & Mary Jane Warham, who are kindly disposed to go hand in hand with the Committee in promotion of the objects contemplated by the Society in extending the arm of aid and protection to the Young Woman in question.

Mary Ann [N——] has been only a few days in her new situation, but during that interval she has shewne a disposition to exert herself, and also to conform to the duties and restraints that devolve upon her. She has entered upon her present engagement with a distinct undertaking both on her part & on that of her Employers, that she is to be subject to the counsel & direction of the Committee in all future movements of importance, until through the fostering aid and protection of the Society she shall have been favoured to establish her character as a virtuous & industrious member of society.

George Washington Walker, to the Society for the Suppression of Vice, Hobart Town, 13 May 1842.

57. "Unhappy Females of the Town"

The aims and rules of this institution reveal an attempt to rescue and reform women, and teach them self-discipline, thrift and repentance. Opium is thought to be sufficient enough a temptation to women for it to be mentioned, along with alcohol and smoking.

THE FEMALE REFORMATORY HOME,

Under the auspices of the "Melbourne City Court Missionary Society".

This Institution is designed as an Asylum for Unfortunate and Destitute Females, who may be found desirous of abandoning their vicious, degrading, and ruinous way of life.

RULES.

1. Females admitted into this Reformatory will be required to conform to all the prescribed Rules.
2. The Inmates shall engage to remain in the Institution, until the "Mission Council Board" shall be justified by their indications of sincere reformation, in recommending them to suitable situations.
3. When the Inmates walk out, they shall always be accompanied by the Matron, or some other authorized person.
4. The Inmates shall be required to devote an appointed portion of each day to some useful occupation. For work done, wages shall be awarded by the Board, according to their several capacities. The surplus of wages due to each inmate, above what may be required for maintenance, shall be deposited in the Savings' Bank to her credit, to be drawn from the Bank at her option, after leaving the Institution.
5. Portions of every day shall be appointed for moral, religious, and mental improvement. Devotional services shall be performed morning and evening.
6. Breakfast at half-past eight; Dinner at one; and Tea at six o'clock. Rising, not later than seven; retiring at ten; and lights extinguished at half-past ten.
7. The Inmates shall give special attention to personal cleanliness. Their dress shall be characterized by neatness and simplicity. Every approximation to gaudy display to be studiously avoided. — *See* 1 Timothy, ii. 9 and 10; and 1 Peter, iii. 3 and 4.
8. All intoxicating liquors, smoking, and the use of opium are strictly prohibited. Every one connected with the establishment must be a Total Abstainer from the use of all strong drinks. Steps shall be immediately taken against any person introducing alcoholic liquors into any of the departments of the Reformatory.
9. When Applicants are received into the Reformatory, an inventory shall be taken of every article brought in with them; and when other articles are procured, they shall be added to the inventory. No one, on leaving the Institution, shall remove any article not found in her inventory.
10. The Inmates must be careful, at all times, duly to regard the directions of the Matron; to be kind and courteous in their language and deportment toward one another; and respectful and amiable toward all connected with the Institution. The Matron will report all cases of delinquency to the Managing

Director, who will, when necessary, report them to the Mission Council Board.

11. For persistence in refractory conduct any Inmate may be expelled by the Board, after the third admonition.

12. Although the Inmates will be rigidly required to deport themselves in accordance with the Rules, yet they will be uniformly treated with the greatest possible kindness; the purpose of the institution not being to punish those who may avail themselves of this proffered Refuge, but to elevate them from their depths of degradation; to lead them to repentance — to the foot of the Cross — to the feet of Jesus, that they may be useful and happy here, and eventually obtain the life eternal.

"One word of kindness, such as said, 'Go sin
"No more,' will sooner reach a Peter's heart,
"Than thunderbolts of reckless wrath."

13. All Applicants, on being received, shall be required to sign the Rules.
14. The Rules may be revised by the Board whenever it may be deemed necessary.

Melbourne City Court Mission House and Female Reformatory,
        77, Spring Street, Nov. 12, 1856.

*Name*_____

*Age*_____

When Admitted_____

Female Reformatory Home, Melbourne, *Rules*, 1856.

58. The Ladies' Committee

By the 1890s, the involvement of ladies in philanthropic work was an established social activity, as this paper by Lady Hamilton, wife of Tasmania's Governor, on the Anchorage Refuge Home at Hobart shows. The idea that institutions should be as nearly self-supporting as possible led to the inmates' employment at work such as washing.

Of all the classes of society with which we are brought in contact, and which appeals to womanly charity, none is so difficult to deal fairly by as the "fallen woman." We use the word "fairly" because there are two duties that create the difficulty.

One is the duty we owe to the "fallen," the other is the duty we owe to society, and also to the future generation. For to ease our own present difficulties by burdening posterity is not the highest form of charity by any means; and, in fact, the question is raised as to its being true charity at all when it is absolutely irresponsible as to future results.

These ideas naturally crossed our minds in considering the question of refuges, and the following is an account of how we arrived at our Anchorage Refuge Home, which has now been established for more than twelve months, and about which we should by happy to receive further suggestions of improvement. The committee, composed entirely of ladies of all denominations, has worked *con amore*, and without any member having before been engaged on such work, so that each step has been gained by experience, not bought very dearly, fortunately for us.

The scheme is as follows:—

Only those who have once fallen are admitted into the Anchorage, and, again, only after the expiration of the ten days after confinement. When the government institution for that purpose ceases to keep them they are taken in, so that things should not be made too easy for them.

Prior to this, the committee visit and instruct the girls, and ask them to come into the Anchorage Home with their child.

Here they are encouraged to nurse their infant, and look after him or her thoroughly; and the love of the mother for her child is made the motive power by which she shall keep good and straight when she leaves the Home. She signs a paper consenting to remain twelve months in the Anchorage.

After this period has elapsed, a situation is found for her, if possible, with the child; or, if that is quite out of the question, the child is boarded at the Home, at the rate of five shillings a week, or boarded close to the mother's place of work.

Those who have led these girls astray are, if possible, found — obliged to pay something for the child as compensation; and that sum or sums are placed in the hands of trustees, to be used for the child's benefit when he shall require to be educated or apprenticed, but not for his maintenance as long as his mother can work for him.

A record is kept of each one passing through the Home, and it is hoped that no mother nor child will ever be lost sight of by the Anchorage committee, and that it will thus not only help the present but the future generation.

Whenever one of these cases is met with, the clergyman, minister, or priest of the parish is communicated with, and it then rests with him to decide for or against his parishioner being taken into the Anchorage.

The committee and the matron give the Anchorage girls all the instruction they can, and once a week a service is given at the Home by some clergyman or minister, and they attend some place of worship on Sundays.

Every effort is being made to humanize these children of sorrow, and as they become more and more loving to their babies, to each other, and to their matron, it is felt that God's love will come to them.

To teach them to be Christian members of society is the main object of our work.

It may be interesting to some of our listeners to have the annual report of our work, and to inspect the balance-sheet.

As we do not approve of going into debt, we have necessarily to limit our number of boarders. In the first twelve months the whole work has not cost two hundred pounds, furnishing and everything else; but the Hobart citizens have been most liberal with their donations in kind.

Washing is taken in, but with six mothers', six babies', and the matron's washing, cooking, and house-work to be attended to, it does not leave a large margin of time for much money to be earned in that line.

The rules are *few*, the bolts and bars *none*. If loving care can teach them to be a law unto themselves always, and also teach them that in their right up-bringing of their little child their womanly dignity is restored, surely a place of not only repentance but of regeneration has been found for them in this life and in the great hereafter.

Our committee would like to know how other places deal with those who have gone astray three or four times, and with their children?

Also, those who are found half silly, or wanting in wit or intelligence, who have fallen? Is there any provision made, or restraint for them, to prevent such a class being replenished by such-like children in the next generation?

Lady Hamilton, "The Anchorage Refuge Home, Hobart, Tasmania", in *Proceedings of the First Australasian Conference on Charity* (1890).

59. Mrs Drew's Home

The process by which the Queensland government became involved in the provision of a refuge for women is described in this report on what was known familiarly in Brisbane as "Mrs Drew's Home".

The Female Refuge in Brisbane was first opened in a hired house, in 1871, by a widow lady, Mrs R. L. Drew, who, in her visits to the hospital, gaol and other places of suffering, had become impressed with the need of some home being provided for young women who had forfeited their character and were anxious to reform. It was supported by the foundress and private friends for the first year and a half, by which time its public usefulness was so manifest that the Government recognized it by granting a subsidy of £100, increased in 1878 to £200 a year. In addition, at that time, a grant of land was made on which stands the present building, erected at a cost of nearly £3000, £1200 being Government grant, the rest by public subscription. This was for 10 years the only refuge of the kind in Queensland, and women were and are sent from all parts of the Colony — no religious distinctions being made. The sole claim for admission is the distress of the applicants and their willingness to conform to the rules of the place. It was found that a large proportion were newly arrived immigrant girls, who had left their old homes for fear of disgrace.

The infants belonging to the inmates, and some others (orphan and neglected) are maintained in the home up to the age of 12 months, and the care of these children, together with needle and laundry work, occupies the women and affords them training for service, as well as helping towards their maintenance. All the work of the home is done by them, under the superintendence of the Matron & Nurse, paid officers of the Institution. The management, excepting during her absence of 18 months in England, has rested with the Lady Superintendent & foundress, Mrs Drew, whose service is purely honorary.

The weekly average of inmates may be taken as 23 women and 18 infants. The women remain for 6 months or longer, till they can be sent to suitable situations and — as far as may be — supervision is kept up afterwards, on the whole with very satisfactory results.

Many are happily married and otherwise provided for, and they are always free to come to the Matron or Lady-Superintendent for help or advice. The total number of women who have passed thro the refuge during these 21 years is 725, children 736.

Report of the Brisbane Female Refuge and Infants' Home, July 1892, unsigned.

60. Autocrat

Criticism of the Brisbane Female Refuge led to a government investigation, which revealed the way in which government-funded institutions sometimes remained

resistant to government control. By 1901, Mrs Drew's institution had become so profitable that the government subsidy was withdrawn.

Mrs Drew is 78 years of age: she has been the acknowledged autocrat of the institution for 30 years, and has admittedly done a large amount of useful philanthropic work. She has no Committee to advise her, and consequently her methods have perhaps become somewhat out of touch with modern ideas. By means of shrewd business methods she has succeeded in making the institution financially sound, a by no means easy task, and she has besides gained in the post the goodwill and gratitude of very numerous inmates.

Her position at present, however, is unique. She regards herself as the *proprietor* of the institution, because, as she says, she collected the money for it, built it, and has managed it, without reference to trustees, committee or government. She even draws whatever salary she thinks fit for herself, although it must be said in fairness, that she has always erred on the side of economy in this respect.

That a charity, for which public subscriptions are collected and which is also in part supported by government money, should be so governed, is, I submit, quite inconsistant with the spirit of the age.

Inspector F. E. Hare, Charitable Institutions Office, Brisbane, to the Home Secretary, 11 October 1900.

61. Help for the Lost and Erring

The Woman's Crusade, a group of Christian women affiliated with the Sydney Rescue Society and the temperance movement, visited lock-ups, hospitals and what they regarded as scenes of vice, to reclaim souls and dispense comfort in the form of food. This extract from the report of their work for 1893 shows some aspects of their work amongst destitute women.

POLICE STATIONS.

Each Sunday morning, and on Christmas Day and Good Friday, the cells of the City and Suburban Police Courts have been visited by various members of the Crusade, who have taken with them gifts of tea and bread and butter, and on special occasions, cake and fruit. Each man and woman locked up in the various Police Stations — the Central, No. 2, Clarence Street, Woolloomooloo, Darlinghurst, Newtown and Redfern — has been supplied with some provisions, and many expressions of thankfulness have been heard by the workers. The numbers thus provided during the year have been as follows:—

Police Stations.	Women.	Men.	Total.
Central	128	203	331
No. 2	273	461	734
Clarence Street	82	235	317
Woolloomooloo	103	99	202
Darlinghurst	101	194	295
Redfern	82	194	276
Newtown	25	77	102
	794	1,463	2,257

The opportunity has been taken to warn the victims of intemperance against a return to the intoxicating cup, and as many as possible induced to sign the pledge. During the year 247 pledges were taken in the police cells. As far as time would permit a kindly word of warning was spoken to each person, and the way of salvation and deliverance by faith in Christ Jesus set before them. Illustrated books and gospel tracts have been distributed, and some portion of God's Word read to them. We would take this means of thanking the officers of police in charge of the various police stations for their uniform and continued kindness to our visitors. They have in every possible way facilitated our visits, which have indeed seemed as welcome to them as they have been to those under their charge for offences against the law.

POLICE COURTS.

On special occasions, Mrs. Walker, one of our voluntary and most valuable helpers, has attended at the Central and Water Police Courts to receive young women, on remand to the Home of Hope, who would otherwise have been committed to gaol. Much more might have been done in this direction but for the fact that the Home of Hope has been taxed to its utmost limits during most of the year. The several Stipendiary Magistrates welcome the attendance at the Courts of our visitor, and invariably accede to her requests for the remand of young women instead of committing them to gaol.

HOSPITAL VISITATION.

Each Tuesday and Friday afternoons Miss Fuller and Mrs Walker have continued to visit the Sydney Hospital, carrying the message of pardon and deliverance to the poor victims of disease and suffering. Bouquets of flowers and illustrated leaflets have been freely distributed. The Lock Ward has been specially attended to, as there are found those who come from the number of lost women whose sins have found them out. Many of the inmates of this ward were mere children in years, and perhaps the saddest of all the sights were the very young children who were in the ward with their mothers, bearing the traces of their mother's transgression. Many of the women spoken to appeared to be seriously impressed. Some of them, having been informed of the Open All Night Refuge and Home of Hope, have, on their discharge from the Hospital, sought shelter at these institutions.

Special visits have been paid to Newington Asylum and the Coast Hospital. The inmates expressed much gratification at the ministrations of our workers.

HOUSE TO HOUSE VISITATION.

During the year the visitation of the haunts of vice has been continued and the work considerably extended. The Sunday afternoon presents a fitting opportunity for this effort and therefore has been chosen for it. A cordial welcome has been given to the workers, who have thus cast bread upon the waters in confidence that it shall be seen, if even after many days.

STREET AND PARK VISITATION.

Some of our workers have from time to time visited the various parades of the lost and erring, and by kindly words have sought to win them to forsake their evil courses. In every case they have been well received and several have confessed their desire to escape from the thraldom of the life of shame. To each a card of invitation, containing the addresses of the Homes of the Society, has been given.

WEXFORD STREET MISSION.

The principal event of the year has been the opening of the Mission House, 36 Wexford street. A house was secured in the centre of the street, and on 22nd March last, formally opened. Up till that date we had continued to hold our meetings on Sunday afternoon, in the house of one of the women resident in the street. We now hold meetings for women only on Sunday afternoons and Thursday evenings; a Band of Hope and Mercy on Tuesday evenings; and on Friday evenings the Rev. Soo Hoo Ten conducts a service for Chinese; then on Saturday evenings we have an openair Meeting in front of the Mission House; and, for the children, a Sunday School — Morning, 11 o'clock and afternoon at 2 o'clock. All the meetings have been well attended, the utmost capacity of the room oftentimes being taxed.

FURTHER HELPERS NEEDED.

To accomplish what is in our hearts to do we need our membership largely augmented, and the number of actual workers considerably increased. Surely the deep and pressing needs of so many hundreds of lost women in our city should be sufficient incentive to arouse the activity latent in some of the churches of our land.

Surely in the membership of the Christian Endeavour Societies there are some who from love to the Lord Jesus Christ will give themselves to His work amongst their lost sisters. Voluntary helpers will be gladly welcomed, and service at convenient times accepted.

We want to undertake the visitation of every lock-up in the city and suburbs during the present year.

Pending the opening of Mission Rooms in other centres, we want Christian women to consent to join in the visitation of the poor lost ones in their own homes. Every fallen woman should have some Christian woman who will visit her, until she is induced to forsake her evil course.

When writing of the opening of our Mission House the *Australian Christian World* said:— "The Woman's Crusade are engaged in a Christlike mission, and they deserve the support of all who believe in God and righteousness. How are these plague spots to be removed if we all fold up our robes and stand aloof from our fallen brothers and sisters? As was remarked by Mr. ARDILL, the Churches and Evangelistic Missions cannot reach such classes; they can only be reached — if reached at all — by men and women who will go to them, and in the spirit of the Master attempt to lift them up, and teach them what is still possible to them. *It has often appeared strange to us that so many should be willing to go to the heart of China, Africa, and other countries and live among the degraded for Christ's sake, and that so few are willing to do the same work among the degraded in our great cities.*"

Christian women resident in Woolloomooloo, Surry Hills, Waterloo, Chippendale, Glebe, Paddington, Balmain, North Sydney, Newtown, etc., etc., or elsewhere, desirous to assist in the work of the Woman's Crusade, should communicate with Miss Williams, Hon. Secretary, Woman's Crusade, Temperance Hall, Pitt Street, Sydney.

Woman's Crusade, *Our Erring Sisters* (1893).

62. Teaching Self-Reliance

While the refuges and institutions continued to train, discipline and reform their inmates, other charitable organizations, such as the Melbourne Ladies' Benevolent Society and the organization described here, encouraged women to support themselves. Ascertaining that the necessary conjuncture between good moral character on the one hand and poor material circumstances on the other had in fact occurred, entailed efficient enquiry and documentation. The Queen's Jubilee Fund mark, branded on tubs and mangles, was essential not only to prevent the bailiffs' seizure (as was suggested during the discussion of the paper) if the material circumstances proved to be worse than anticipated, but to prevent these items from being sold, if a similar miscalculation was made about the moral character of the recipient.

The second annual report of the Queen's Jubilee Fund contains an account of the work accomplished during the year 1890. The details must necessarily be the same year after year, varied only by the number of applications for relief. The amounts expended for the relief of applicants will increase as the income increases; at present, it is only possible to give small sums to each applicant, and since the first distribution in May, 1889, no sums have been voted under £1, nor exceeding £10. It is the wish of every member of the council to be in a position to vote a sum of money, say, £15 to £20, to a case where it is apparent that the money would entirely relieve the distress, and would be the means of enabling the applicant to earn her own livelihood. In voting money to applicants, the council have always endeavoured that the help given shall put the woman in the way of earning her own living; for instance, if a woman has been left suddenly destitute by the death of her husband, with a family to support, and thinks she could earn a living by washing, but has no mangle, or tubs, &c., the council would vote money for that object, which would be given either to some one in the district who recommended the case, or to a member of the council who would see that the money was properly expended. If a woman is desirous of earning her living by taking in needlework, a sewing machine is bought in the same way; or, again, if a woman wishes to open a small shop, is in great distress, and has no money for outlay, the council will vote money for that object, care being taken that the money is used for the specific purpose mentioned. Machines and mangles are branded with a distinguishing mark, and a nominal rent of one shilling a year is imposed, to provide, so far as the law will allow, against seizure of goods under a bill of sale, &c. In addition to the above-mentioned cases, money has been voted in payment of arrears of rent; in payment of debt, where an article has been purchased on the time-payment system, and through falling into arrears with the payments the woman is liable to lose the article, and, of course, the money already paid. Assistance in a case like this is directed towards putting a woman in full possession of the article in question. Assistance has also been given towards passage-money, and where the amount required is larger than can be given from the fund, a sum of money is voted to be paid, provided that the remainder is collected by the applicant or otherwise. Assistance has been given for the purpose of buying goods and clothes, though this is an instance of a case hardly coming within the province of the fund, and has only been entertained on account of extreme distress. It is, of course, necessary that careful investigation should be made into every case coming before the council, and to this end great assistance is rendered by Mr. Sidney, Secretary of the Charity Organization Society, who personally investigates all applications from in or around Sydney. To all other applicants a printed form is sent, which has to be returned with full information respecting the case, and signed by one or more prominent local persons to whom the money is forwarded, if voted. When an application is rejected, a printed letter is sent to that effect, giving no reason for such refusal.

Miss Martin, "The Queen's Jubilee Fund", in *Proceedings of the Second Australasian Conference on Charity* (1891).

63. "Our Common Womanhood"

Apart from her suffragist concerns, Rose Scott was also involved in campaigning to improve the conditions of working girls and women prisoners, through legislative change and through voluntary organizations such as the Prisoners' Aid Association, of which she was Lady President. In this address on the Factory Girls' Club, she looks more deeply than most reformers at the relationship between the helper and the helped, and suggests that such benevolent work is "paying back" rather than "giving". She poses the problem in her first sentence:

Was this a charity only for the gratification of the Rich and the deterioration of the Poor — or had it real grounds for support?

Give me the letters the Factory Girls have written to you . . . "How much I miss those evenings" writes one girl "which brought us together in the presence of God!" and it was these letters which convinced me that many girls found in this Club — Help, Courage & Sympathy — and that Mrs Edwards had power to help them since her letters show they regard her as a friend . . . These letters believe me — I felt the sacredness of, since they were "side lights into souls" — convinced me more than any printed Report could do that this Club has been, and is, much to many Girls, whose life is hard, and whose homes are often very unsatisfactory.

This alone appears to me a reason for the continuance and wider outlook of this Club that it may be enlarged and placed where it will do most good — and be, where the girls (after their day's work) may find it easy to go — not far from their homes. There what an inestimable advantage it is, that the girls should be taught sewing, dressmaking, dress cutting, cookery etc. and that they should feel there are women who care for them enough to leave their comfortable homes and journey to the Club at night to help them and teach them all these things. What can be greater work than to unite women and girls in love and sympathy? And if I may venture to say so — how much better economically, socially — and financially to have the one club where all can unite and share the work and build up a really good and useful Institution, instead of scattering time, money and energy in 2 or 3 directions.

For girls who have no homes or bad homes — surely nothing could be better than to enlarge the usefulness of this Club and make it as large a measure as possible Residential — so that girls may sleep in pure, fresh surroundings and acquire a taste and love for that decency and order in home life which is the best foundation upon which to build up "a noble national life". Then that it should be made more and more self supporting so that the girls may feel that the Club is their own possession — and take a pride, a responsible pride, in its being and growth.

If anything of this sort is to do real work — we must feel that we are not so much giving to others as paying back to them something we owe them. I went through the Central Police Cells the other night. How could I help feeling ashamed,

ashamed not so much to witness the degradation of our common womanhood, as to feel — how little we women in better circumstances have ever done for such as these! How little we concern ourselves about them, and how disgracefully we think our duty done when we are content to make our homes comfortable . . .

Rose Scott, address on the Factory Girls' Club (*c.* 1900).

64. The Depression

Many of the features familiar in cases of destitution and outdoor relief are evident in this report dealing with the wife of a worker during the Depression of the 1930s: the mixture of voluntary and government agencies, the combination of cash payment and rations, the detailed investigation of circumstances (this time by a woman police officer).

1.   With Policewoman Clarey I interviewed Mrs. [L——] of Secombe Street, North Fitzroy, today.

2.   Mrs. [L——] advises that her husband returned from Briagolong on Tuesday evening (2nd inst.) in response to letters from herself and her son, aged 11 years, in which they stated that things were very bad at home, and that he left her this morning (4th inst) to go back to his work at Briagolong by the 8 a.m. train today.

3.   Mrs. [L——] advises that her husband gave her 10/- which he said was all he had.

4.   The family consists of Mr. and Mrs. [L——], and five children ranging in ages from seven months to eleven years.

5.   Mr. [L——] applied for sustenance from the Unemployed Relief Committee, Fitzroy, and on the 19th November 1930 he received sustenance to the extent of 11/- (representing 5/- for the parents and 1/- per child). Sustenance Card was produced to us. Since then Mr. [L——] has not called at the Fitzroy Town Hall for sustenance, but Mrs. [L——] advises that she had obtained from Mrs. Richardson, J.P., of Rae Street, North Fitzroy, two emergency orders, one for 5/- and the other for 6/-. Mrs. [L——] is regularly receiving milk free from her own milkman, and today is to receive one loaf of bread from St. Bridget's Church, but other than that she had no food in the house, and the only cash she had at the time of our visit was sixpence.

6.   Mrs. [L——] produced her rent book showing a rental of 13/- per week dating from 27th September 1930, and the rent is paid to 1st November. This book is in the name of J. D. Jones, owing to the family having received notice to quit their previous residence at Dickens Street, North Carlton.

7.   I have rung Mrs. Richardson, J.P., Rae Street, North Fitzroy, re the case; her husband stated she was at an Executive Meeting at the Trades Hall, but he took particulars and promised to inform Mrs. Richardson on her return and assured me she would help the family. I have also rung the Rev. Rae, 89 Alfred Crescent, Fitzroy, and he also is familiar with the case.

8.   Owing to Mrs. [L——] bad eye sight and the fact that she has so large a family of small children, she finds it difficult to attend the Town Hall for relief, and she would be glad if arrangements could be made for her to receive an order for sustenance without the necessity of her personally having to come such a distance. As mentioned in the preceding paragraph, we have communicated with the Members of the Relief Committee.

M. C. Cox, Woman Police Constable 7710, Fitzroy Station, to the Superintendent of Police, Melbourne District, 4 December 1930.

65. Intermediaries

At a time when many women were faced with the problem of trying to feed their families on inadequate rations, the Unemployed Relief Council in Adelaide considered reducing expenditure by reducing rations. It interviewed the wife of an unemployed worker and the wife of a pensioner with this in mind. Ultimately, however, the Council concentrated on making it more difficult for applicants to receive rations rather than cutting down the rations themselves.

Mrs [E——] of Brompton Park, a recipient of relief was seen by the Council in reference to the ration list.
She stated that her husband had been unemployed three years and made the following remarks:—

> The groceries were inadequate but there was too much bread and she could manage with one loaf Bread a ration less.
> The Wood allowance could be reduced by one-half in summer but the present allowance would not be too much in winter.
> Suggested that cheese be added to the list and that vegetables be granted in lieu of some of the bread.
> She spent 6d. per week on onions and potatoes. Had not heard of any impositions.
> Fish would be very much availed of if obtainable.
> Mutton went further but she would like some Beef.
> There was no call for Sago and Rice.

Mrs [J——] of Jervois Avenue, Hindmarsh was then seen. She stated she had ten children, four of whom were under 14 years.

> Husband had been out of work nine years on account of defective eye-sight. Son employed 2 years. Husband an Invalid Pensioner.
> She stated she would like less bread and more meat.
> She had received 5lbs. Meat the previous day and the Butcher had deducted a ¼lb. not giving any reason.
> They grow beans. Receives 4/- per fortnight from the Benevolent Society.
> Her bread allowance from the Children's Welfare and Public Relief Department was reduced from 48 to 42 loaves but nothing was substituted in lieu of bread.
> She receives 17/6 per week cash in addition to the rations.
> She could manage on the groceries but was four days short in Meat in 28 days.
> Would like Beef twice a week. Obtains tinned milk but would like fresh. The husband consumed portion of the rations but he was not on relief.
>   Consideration deferred.

Minutes of the Unemployed Relief Council, Adelaide, 7 January 1930.

66. Single Women

Single women and girls, particularly, found it difficult to obtain relief. Authorities stressed the role of women within the family and single women were expected to seek refuge within it rather than ask for aid for themselves. It was often left to groups of private citizens to attempt to cope with the problems of women outside the family. Prominent on the Perth committee for the relief of unemployed girls and women were members of feminist groups.

The citizens' committee for the relief of unemployed girls and women is in need of funds. Indeed if financial help is not forthcoming in the immediate future the committee will have to suspend its labours and go into recess. This will mean the loss of a very necessary facility at the present time. Only last week a typical case occurred when three girls from Fremantle who had failed to get work at the port and had no fares, walked from Fremantle to consult the committee's representative (Mrs Frank Orgill), at her office at the headquarters of the Young Women's Christian Association, St George's-terrace. They told a sad story of need, and one of the committee members determined to visit the homes and see what could be done. She found that the cases were absolutely genuine ones and the stories told had been entirely correct. The girls in question thanked her for her kindness in coming to make the visit. One of these girls was so ill, that she had to be taken to hospital.

The committee is one worthy of the complete trust of the community and includes the following:— Miss Wylie (late of the Education Department, president); Mrs Jean Beadle, J.P., and Mrs H. B. Semmens (vice-president); Mrs Frank Orgill (honorary secretary); Mr L. Elsegood (honorary treasurer); Mr Ben Carter (auditor); committee, Professor Cameron, Mr E. Needham, M.L.A., Miss M. Godlee (general secretary of the Y.W.C.A.), Mr J. Lynch (of the Technical School), Dr Roberta Jull, Mr Dillon Smith, Mrs M. Driver (of the W.C.T.U.), Mrs C. Richardson and Mrs Cherry (two representatives of the Women's Service Guilds), and Mrs R. Robertson.

During the time that Mrs B. M. Rischbieth was president of the committee, the following resolution was passed on December 17, 1934:— "That the committee be increased by the addition of other members and that a fresh objective should be the establishment of a household management centre". The following scheme was outlined:— The obtaining of suitable rooms; a training course of 12 weeks — 10 weeks for classes and two weeks for revision and examination with a competent teacher. Girls were to be taught to cook a good plain dinner and serve it with correct table setting, the use and care of linen, etc; waiting and clearing away; washing up of dishes and utensils; all laundry work, correct methods of cleaning and care of the house, polishing, etc.; bedmaking and household mending. At the end of three months it was proposed that each girl should be examined by a competent examiner appointed by the Government, given a certificate of efficiency and placed in a suitable position by the committee. The employers were to be communicated with and progress reports to be asked for. Girls were to be trained from the age of 14 years. This scheme was to be on probation for 12 months, and every effort was to be made to raise the standard of domestic work.

The Government offered to make available rooms at the old university buildings for the scheme, and city firms signified their willingness to furnish the centre, but the committee has no money to carry on the work.

The Government was approached but the reply was that the Government could not finance the scheme. The Lotteries Commission was also communicated with unavailingly.

The record of the committee covering the past five years tells its own story which shows that the public generally, and individuals in particular, have every reason to be grateful to this body for tiding so many girls and women over the extremely difficult years of the depression.

The following is a list of significant figures:— Positions filled, 3,774; number of rents paid during the first period, 8,166; number of girls and women on books, 5,089; amount of money raised, £4,274/1/4½; Government subsidy, £2,248.

Officers and members naturally feel that they have gained an experience by the actual doing of this work of helping unemployed single girls and women to become self-supporting, which would be invaluable in the carrying to fruition of the scheme which the past five years of anxious work has proved to be the only solution to the problem of a very large number of West Australian girls.

They therefore have every confidence in appealing to the public for financial help at the present moment and the honorary secretary (Mrs Frank Orgill) will be grateful to receive on behalf of the committee any donations which the friends of unemployed girls may wish to send to enable the committee's work to continue.

"Workless Girls: An Appeal for Aid" by "Adrienne", *West Australian*, 5 July 1935.

67. Awaiting a Response

In Perth, the committee set up to look after the needs of unemployed single women found that there were also other women outside the family in urgent need of assistance. The two members of the committee who signed a letter to the press on this issue were Bessie Rischbieth, the president of the feminist organization, the Women's Service Guilds, and Miss E. Hooten, who was prominent in the labour movement in Western Australia.

Sir, — The citizens' committee for the relief of unemployed girls, which was formed on July 8, 1930, and has since struggled with very inadequate resources to solve the many problems, financial and otherwise, arising from the unemployment of several thousand girls, has now had a new trouble thrust upon it. The position of married women on maintenance orders and otherwise separated from their husbands, and unable to find work, is becoming a scandal in Western Australia and calls for immediate action. It need scarcely be pointed out that, owing to the men concerned being workless, a large number of women to whom the Courts have granted maintenance orders are receiving nothing, and because of the existence of these orders, they cannot claim sustenance. It is a fact that some of these women are being allowed a few shillings for food by the Welfare Department, but it is nobody's business to see that they are housed, and obviously seven shillings' worth of groceries is not much use to a person who has nowhere to live, and no means of getting necessary clothing; there are young children also concerned in the problems. In their misery, these unfortunate women are flocking to members of our committee, begging for help, which owing to the scope of our funds collected for single unemployed women, we are unable to give financially. We are however, trying earnestly to put their case before those who can help. A sub-committee of our members has already appealed to the Unemployment Board and to three relief institutions without any definite result. The pressure of the women is daily becoming more painful, and we suggest that this work is awaiting the response of some generous persons or organisations who can give it time and attention. Our committee will give all possible help and co-operation to such a move. A ring (B4764) will be welcomed.

> Bessie M. Rischbieth, Acting Pres.
>
> E. Hooten, Hon. Sec., Citizen's Committee for the Relief of Unemployed Single Girls and Women

Letter to the Editor, *West Australian*, 22 April 1932.

68. "She Greatly Needs a Pair of Boots"

Like the female factories before them, the prisons were seen to perform a variety of functions. The lives of the women described in these reports from the State Reformatory for Women at Long Bay were plotted between institutions, suggesting that such women were not ":reformed" or given a "new start", but instead became enmeshed in an institutional cycle.

As directed by you, by telephone, I have the honor to forward the description cards of the prisoners named in the margin who have long lists of previous convictions recorded against them but who have not been declared "inebriates". Persons of this class come here so frequently in most wretched conditions from drink and neglect they receive every possible attention during their short sentences but they hardly get over the drunken bouts before they are discharged to return in a few days time in the usual condition, and so the process is repeated.

Officer-in-Charge, State Reformatory for Women, Long Bay, to the Deputy Comptroller of Prisons, 20 November 1909.

I have the honor to report that prisoner Mary [E——] — who was detained in the Lock Hospital under the provisions of the Prisoners' Detention Act, and who was certified by the visiting surgeon to be free from contagious disease — was in accordance with your directives by telephone released from custody at noon today.

As the prisoner was quite destitute — neither money nor friends she was sent in care of a female officer in plain clothing to the Central Methodist Mission Depot 41 George Street with the view to her admission to one of the Methodist Homes at Burwood.

Ibid., 15 January 1910.

This woman's age on the books of the Reformatory appears as 50, she looks much older, she is feeble minded was brought up in the orphan's school at Parramatta and has spent a great part of her time since she left the school either in prison or Newington Asylum. Her conduct in prison is good and she works fairly well, she greatly needs a pair of boots on discharge, she has only 3d private cash, and is not entitled to any gratuity. She was wearing an old pair of men's boots on reception. She intends to apply for admission to Newington Asylum on discharge.

Ibid., 13 July 1910.

69. How Is She to Live?

The need for shelters and refuges for girls and women in a variety of circumstances is rediscovered at intervals, right up to the present day. In this radio talk, given in 1944 in support of a feminist organization campaign, A. E. Bennett draws on his experience at the Sydney Children's Court to describe the processes by which young women are precipitated into "lives of vice". What emerges incidentally is a clear picture of the consequences for women of existing legal restraints and low rates of pay.

Within the past few weeks, there was a press statement that a Special Conference of Women's and other organisations, convened by the United Associations of Women, had decided to bring about the launching of an appeal to raise an amount of £25,000 to establish Residential Clubs or Hostels for young women. Investigation by those working in the field in contact with young women has shown that there are different kinds of such Hostels needed to cope with the many problems. Some aim at the cure of certain social ills and the rescue and rehabilitation of young women; while others aim at providing conditions of living which are preventive, which would lessen the numbers against whom living conditions are too adverse, and who succumb to the pressure of such and fall into a life of vice. The more of such places there are in existence, then the more there can be of classification and segregation, and adaptation to the needs of the different women. The more such classification, then the greater will be the success achieved. It would enable circumstances of living to be adapted to the psychological, medical or other needs of individuals, instead of their having to be moulded to whatever accommodation is within their reach, as prevails at present.

Let me be more precise, and specify some of the residential clubs that are needed.

First, let us prevent recruitment into the ranks of those girls and young women who fall into immorality and perhaps enter on a life of vice, of vagrancy and imprisonment. Examination of hundreds of such cases shows that the causes are many and varied, in any individual case. Probed to its roots, the causes lie in the home training, and later school training with all their defects. Training and education should be to develop character, and the habit of righteous living, which should be learned from earliest childhood, and learned from the example of the parents and elders, and later from companions, when they reach adolescence. Where the training has been right, then that girl would not come into our consideration. But we find in most cases of girls who fall that they come from broken homes, due to the death of one or both of the parents, due to divorce or marital separation, due to quarrelling and discord in the home, due to moral laxity on the part of one or both of the parents. There are many girls who are homeless and have to live in rooms and keep and fend for themselves for the above reasons, or they may come from the country to work in the city, or they may have quarrelled with their parents . . . alone they cannot pay their way. A study of wages awards shows that the average wage for girls in factory work is at 15 years about 25/- and at 18 years about £2 and for adults over 21 years up to £3. That is generally the maximum. How can they live decently and respectably on these wages? They cannot.

If a girl of 15 earning 25/- a week has to depend on herself and pay a rent for a room in a residential of 20/- to 25/-, then she may take the easier road, and earn plenty of money the easier, but the immoral way, rather than starve to death. Her position is impossible. The only alternative for such a girl is to take work as a domestic where she will have a roof over her head, but, while many such girls do this, and while many of such an age are placed by Manpower authorities in domestic work, there are girls who are not suited for domestic service or who will not take up that life.

Even if the girl is 18 years old and earns about £2 weekly, after paying room rent, she has insufficient for food, clothes, medical and other requisites, amusements etc. She may roam the streets with another girl similarly placed. They will before long accept an invitation from some sailor to go to the pictures and have a meal or two, then have a drink and the rest follows. Before long, she succumbs to pressure; she cannot repell the advances made because she has been accepting entertainment and gifts, and things go further than she thought. Having once started, the way is easier the next time.

Even when a young woman earns £3 a week and has no home or guidance, the same thing happens, and the ranks of the fallen are recruited. These girls can have and have an easier time living this life at the start, they neglect their jobs and ultimately leave them; they just don't go to work. Then they are picked up by the Vice Squad of the police in a residential with some man; they admit they have no position and no money, and that they have accepted food etc. from the man; they are arrested as vagrants and lodged in the cells at the Central Police Court, where they meet others further advanced in this life than they were. They get all kinds of advice what to do etc. Henceforth, they are branded and known to the police. In the Court next day, they are remanded for 14 days to the Women's Reformatory inside Long Bay gaol for medical observation. There was no one at the Court to befriend the girl. If there had, the friend could have given an undertaking to care for the girl, to have her medically examined and attended to so that she would not be a menace to society. She would then not have been sent to Long Bay. Once inside Long Bay, the girl mixes with the worst of her type, and learns all the ways of evil; she contacts acquaintances who know the haunts and ways of immorality, and who will henceforth claim her as one of them and help to drag her down further. She may have been sentenced to a few months in gaol at the end of the 14 days' remand as a vagrant. Or she may have disease and be ordered to remain in gaol until cured, in which case she may be there a year or more.

In the end, she is discharged, with hardly a penny in her pocket, not having a job, not knowing how to earn enough to keep body and soul together, temperamentally and psychologically unfitted to face life alone, and suffering the drawback of having been shut off from life for a year. . . She is hungry, poorly clothed. When she was arrested before she went to gaol, all her clothes were at the residential; when arrested, she was taken to the cells at Central Police Court in what she stood up in. If she is sent from Court straight into gaol, the police do not go hunting for her clothes and minding them. They are not called for and are lost. So she has nothing. . .

. . . Remember that there are hundreds of these homeless girls in just this situation. Those who meet them and know all about it know that there is only one way to prevent it and that is by provision of Hostels where the girls will receive accomodation like that in a residential club or a home, with organised recreation, guidance and supervision under modern methods. They are not all hopeless by any means and scores could be saved and made good mothers and citizens. . .

We want hostels of this kind.
1.   Places for girls who are homeless and who earn too little, to live with assistance and supervision as a means of prevention.
2.   A Shelter where young girls arrested can be taken instead of to the Police cells.
3.   A place where girls on their discharge from Long Bay may be lodged until they are restored in health of body and mind and placed in work and settled down to a steady life.
4.   A place for young unmarried mothers who need to go out to work, where they and their babies can be cared for.
5.   A place where young women suffering from V.D. but requiring only treatment that does not prevent their working can live and secure their treatment.

The United Associations and others are moving to raise £25,000 for these purposes. Would you like to help?

A. E. Bennett, Honorary General Secretary, Australian Child Welfare Association, talk broadcast on 2CH (Sydney), 1 October 1944.

70. Seeing Clearly

During her life, Bee Miles became legendary in Sydney for stridently transgressing bourgeois mores and manners. She was most celebrated — and by many, feared — for her practice of forcing entry into cars and taxis. Her habit of reciting Shakespeare for money was regarded more indulgently. Bee Miles spent large periods of her life in mental asylums and prisons, but she differed from other homeless women who did not enjoy a private income. These excerpts from an unpublished account of her first experience in a mental hospital when she was twenty-one show she had a capacity to distance herself from her immediate situation and analyse it, that she was not bewildered by and submissive to authority, and that these qualities helped her to escape successfully. She had had the advantages of a middle-class education, and although she abandoned all the external signs of her bourgeois identity, she became an identity among the nameless band of Sydney derelicts because she could articulate the rebellion that others only experienced.

This is the afternoon for the Board ladies to make their sacred and silent appearance. They tiptoe — metaphorically speaking — through the refractory wards with fear on their faces. Sister and a couple of nurses form their bodyguard. I have not yet found out the actual use of these women but I wish Mrs Larkins would go for one of them. They're so respectable that a good savaging might make them a bit more human. I think they are here to see that no person is wrongfully incarcerated but, as they are in the hands of Super who just falls short of telling them what they must think, where are we!

. . . Am just in time to see Mrs Dawson give Walker a kick in the tummy despite the fact that Mrs Dawson is in a straight jacket and is strapped to a seat. Walker calls for aid and three of the attendants belt into the patient and leave her very subdued. Feeling nauseated I stroll back to our landing and open a onesided discussion (my side) with Gertrude on the evils of Mental Hospitals. These are many from the stupidity and ignorance of the Doctors and their unholy conceit to the ignorance and stupidity of the nurses and their disgusting cruelty. I state loudly that there is no cure. "We read", I say, "that insane people used to be thrashed. They're not treated any less cruelly now. I saw Watkins strangling the other day with her fingers, and what price the grazes on Mattie's throat from the stocking that Taylor twisted round it? We could tell Super but what on earth is the use? When the nurse denied it he'd put us down as delusioned. . . Besides when we do tell him Charge locks us up and tells him we have been violent to justify herself." To which Gertie answers with a hearty "it's true what you say".

. . . It is very sad when a devoted and good mother becomes insane. Kate, in one of her periods of insanity, was weeping for her babies. She had apparently been told by her husband that she would find peace and rest in hospital (the usual foul lie told by those who want their relatives to go quietly). But the ward she is in is the noisiest here and poor Kate is irritated and upset all day.

. . . Here's Bessie, the sweetest woman of all. She remembers the time when she was paraded before the psychiatry students. They had discussed her aloud for sometimes when we say to her "Bessie what sort of ear have you got", she will reply "a typically insane ear".

. . . Today there's some bad news for me. I am to be transferred to another hospital. The reason for this is, I think, that the doctors here do not feel they are making any headway with me and they wish to give another lot of medicos the opportunity to try and make an impression. The poor half wits. They say I'm insane but won't admit there's no cure for it. If a person returns to sanity in these hospitals he does so not because of any treatment he has received but as a rule in spite of the doctors and attendants. Any treatment he may be given is almost invariably irrational. . . . I feel very depressed and weep loudly. I have come to love many of the patients. Still I'd better be philosophic about it because I cannot alter Super's decision. I have been here long enough to realize that the wishes and happiness of a patient are rarely considered. At the least the short trip in a car to my new home will be a break in the general monotony. I have been a mental patient for about a year and a month and there doesn't seem any chance of leaving these prisons alive.

. . . after a year's observation of myself I have come to the conclusion that I am not mad and am begining to long very heartily for my liberty.

. . . I am off again. This time, with the very sensible help of some friends. I am successful in remaining away for twenty eight days after which, according to the laws of this state, one automatically becomes free.

Bee Miles, "Advance Australia Fair", unpublished ms. (n.d.).

PART 2

Private Lives

Introduction

The documents in this section have been selected to open the "private sphere" to discussion and analysis. The private sphere becomes less elusive if the family and sexuality are regarded from a social as well as a personal perspective. Therefore, we have included documents which express the intersection of personal experiences with public concern and with legislation. In this way, the personal experience of motherhood is illuminated by considering the State's concern with population and the restrictions on individual control over reproduction in the form of legislation on birth control and abortion. Prostitution is explored not as an outlawed form of sexual activity but as a social institution structurally linked to marriage. And the sexual exploitation of Aboriginal women is seen not as the aberrant consequence of single and lonely men on cattle- and sealing-stations, but as an extreme and unbridled expression of the sexist attitudes that determined women's personal experiences.

There are, of course, documents that describe personal experiences, but if these are to have a relevance beyond the particular, they should be interpreted within a framework that recognizes social as well as individual determinants. Thus aspects of life such as sexuality and childbirth, often thought of as "private" and inaccessible to the historian, can be seen to form part of a broader social experience.

The issues of birth control and abortion may be approached by examining the antagonism of interests between the individual woman and the State. In the 1880s, the birthrate in all colonies started to decline[1] and this decline accelerated in the inter-war period.[2]

Anxiety about the fall in the birthrate was well developed at the onset of the twentieth century. Royal Commissioners inquiring into the decline in the birthrate in New South Wales blamed the selfishnes of women, who tried to evade the physical and economic burdens of motherhood.[3]

As the lecture given by Mrs B. Smyth [133] in 1890 indicates, discussion of birth control in colonial Australia was relatively free and there was no restriction on the advertising of contraceptives. Earlier, at attempt in New South Wales to have Annie Besant's pamphlet about birth control, *Law of Population*, declared obscene had failed.[4] But after the First World War, the Commonwealth and the states legislated to restrict access to contraceptive information and devices. Regulations within the Customs Act of 1923 prohibited the importation of contraceptives. In the 1930s, Victoria, Tasmania and Western Australia passed legislation forbidding the advertisement and display of contraceptives and the National Security Regulations (Contraceptives and Venereal Disease) of 1942 covered those states that had not yet legislated against advertisement, as well as banning the dispatch of contraceptive devices by mail. State concern with population ensured that decisions about reproduction were not a personal matter.

Contraception was not illegal, nor was the local manufacture of contraceptives. In Sydney, the Racial Hygiene Association [140] and the Institute of Family

Relations [139] and in Melbourne, a clinic under the auspices of the District Nursing Association supplied contraceptives to married women. These organizations were careful to emphasize that they were not aggravating Australia's population problems. For them, the health of future generations was the paramount concern and they argued that the judicious practice of birth control would eradicate inherited disease, diminish maternal mortality, and ultimately result in an increased and healthier population. Abortion was universally condemned and the debate on birth control was carried on in the context of prevailing moral and social concerns. Women's right to determine control over their own bodies did not surface as an issue.

Some individual members of feminist organizations were active in the Australian birth-control movement, but feminist organizations considered birth control too contentious an issue and one likely to be too divisive. Jessie Street attended the 1930 Birth Control Conference in Zurich and became Australian corres-pondent for the London-based Birth Control Information Centre, but she would not publicly endorse birth control. [137]

One women's group, the Central Women's Committee of the Australian Com-munist Party, resolved that birth-control information should be available, but it emphasized that birth control should not be seen as a panacea for social problems. [141] This ambivalence expressed a fear that the employing classes might use contraception to manipulate the working-class population for political and industrial ends.

Eugenics (a theory that advocated the selective breeding of future generations so that hereditary disease and defects would be eliminated from the race) gained many adherents in Australia before it was discredited by the population policies of Nazi Germany. The logic of eugenics understandably appealed to those who believed that poverty and misfortune were the result of immutable weakness of character. Less obvious was its appeal for feminists committed to winning social and economic equality for women. It is likely that feminists, like liberals, were attracted to a philo-sophy that appeared to be both "scientific" and to offer solutions to problems liberalism was proving incapable of encompassing. In some ways, the thinking of the Women's Christian Temperance Union prepared the way for this alliance between "science" and social control.[5]

Rose Scott criticized the New South Wales Royal Commissioners who, in 1904, blamed the selfishness of women for the declining birthrate. She said there should be less emphasis on quantity and more on the production of "A population . . . of worth, physically, mentally and morally." [118] The same attitude is evident in feminist endorsement of sterilization and segregation of the "unfit", in the trade-off that one feminist politician suggested between child endowment for the healthy and segregation for the unfit and, less coercively, in the advocacy of premarital blood tests. [128]

While feminist groups were reluctant to advocate artificial contraception as an option for individuals, they had no such hesitation in lending support to programmes designed to control the "quality" of the population. In the areas of birth control and sexuality, before the Second World War, feminism did not challenge dominant opinion and prejudices. But this did not mean feminists thought women should submit to unlimited and unplanned pregnancies. Rose Scott and Dr Roberta Jull both voiced the opinion that reproduction should, for the welfare of society as well as women and children, be brought into the sphere of choice and rationality and Jull suggested a method, male self-control. [118, 120]

Sex education emerged in the inter-war period as a means of instilling sexual restraint. Fear of venereal disease was invoked to fortify morality. It was stressed that sexual activity had social consequences and that a responsible citizen postponed sexual gratification until it was socially acceptable and beneficial within marriage. [131]

Women's sexual needs were occasionally recognized, [140] but, more often, motherhood was assumed to be the main object of female sexual activity. Hence in their consideration of the declining birthrate, feminists were able to reconcile the needs of women and the welfare of the State. [123, 124]

Among the consequences of the First World War were the depletion by 59 000 of the male population, sickness and injury in the surviving male population and the widespread incidence of venereal disease known as the "red plague". In this context, a campaign for "celibate" or "eugenic" motherhood was begun by Marion Piddington. She proposed that through this method (artificial insemination was not referred to by name) women could fulfil their social and biological function and be secure in the knowledge that their children would by healthy. The campaign was taken up by the women's pages of the *Queensland Figaro*, but when Marion Piddington attempted to enlist the support of Sigmund Freud, he denounced its sexually repressive overtones. [127] Mary Fullerton of the (Victorian) Women's Political Association referred to it as a "conscription of virgins" and said "bastardy under the hedges was preferable".[6] Although "celibate motherhood" was a fringe issue, with its emphasis on women's procreative and social functions and the exclusion of sexual enjoyment, it encapsulates in exaggerated form the repression of female sexuality in the inter-war period.

The documents on prostitution record the sexual lives of an ostracized group of women and they also raise the question of the relationship between marriage and prostitution. Prostitution was anathametized by the clergy, politicans and philanthropic organizations. In the nineteenth century, two colonies — Queensland and Tasmania — introduced legislation to regulate prostitution, but it was never abolished. It was often stated to be an inevitable misfortune that society must cope with. If we look behind this bland and reluctant acceptance of inevitability, we see that while prostitution was publicly stated to be the antithesis of marriage, legislators recognized that prostitution also bore a positive relation to marriage. Prostitution was regarded as upholding the married state because it ensured the virginity of girls until marriage, protected the wife from the sexual onslaughts on her husband and left her free to bear and rear children, and channelled the extra-marital sexual pursuits of the husband into casual encounters that would not threaten the stability of the family. The institution of prostitution defined not only a moral division between women but also a division between sexual and procreative labour.

The problem was venereal disease, and it was for reasons of health, not morals, that the State attempted to regulate prostitution. Common sense argues that women could not be the only transmitters of venereal disease, but well into the twentieth century, attempts to eradicate syphilis and gonorrhoea were confined to the compulsory examination and detention of women, usually women deemed to be "common prostitutes". Contagious diseases legislation in Queensland and Tasmania was implemented to protect the health of men who had sexual contact with prostitutes. When the Superintendent of the Contagious Diseases Hospital at Cascades was asked by a Select Committee inquiring into the working of the Act, if men should also be subject to examination and detention, he replied that the disease was communicated by prostitutes and that prostitution was exclusively a female profession.[7] One reason why men were not included in the provisions of contagious diseases legislation was that marriage would indeed be under threat if married men were subject to the same scrutiny and detention as prostitutes. When the Venereal Diseases Bill was being debated in the New South Wales parliament in 1915, one member asked for a clause to be introduced making it obligatory for a doctor to tell a wife if her husband had venereal disease. He was told that this was undesirable because it would undermine the wife's trust in her husband and threaten the stability of the family. [8]

Venereal disease legislation did not disappear in Australia when the Tasmanian Act ceased to operate in 1899 and the Queensland Act was rescinded in 1911. Until the 1918 Venereal Diseases Act was introduced in New South Wales, the Vagrancy Act of 1907 and the Prisoners' Detention Act of 1908 combined to effect the detention of women suspected of having venereal disease. In the second decade of the twentieth century, all states (except South Australia) incorporated into their health legislation provisions for the arrest and detention of persons with or suspected of having venereal disease who did not present for examination and treatment. These provisions theoretically applied to both sexes, but were in fact used to ensure that prostitutes were free from disease. Women were vulnerable to hearsay and all states had a clause that protected informants, but which insisted that the person informed on, almost always a woman, be examined. During the Second World War, the Commonwealth entered the field of venereal disease legislation in the form of the National Security Regulations of 1942. The Queensland and Tasmanian legislation of the nineteenth century was strongly associated with an endeavour to protect the health of the armed forces and during the Second World War, the civil liberties of women were considered a necessary casualty to the paramount issue of protecting Australia's fighting men from infection.

The women's movement in Australia was essentially a post-suffrage phenomenon and it was not conspicuous in opposing the first wave of contagious diseases legislation in Australia. But during the Second World War, feminist organizations waged a relentless battle against the National Security Regulations and the double standard of morality that they embodied. At a time when the Director of Social Hygiene in New South Wales advocated shaving the heads of women who contracted venereal diseases more than once, Elizabeth Griffiths of the United Associations of Women attempted to change the nature and terminology of the debate on prostitution. In her evidence to the Parliamentary Standing Committee on Broadcasting in 1946, she argued that prostitution was a consequence of women's economic dependence. [103]

The situation of Aboriginal women is central to this discussion not only because as women they shared some experiences with white women but because the sexual exploitation of a whole race of women by white men dramatically illustrates the double standard that punished women and protected men. The situation was worse for black women, because their own society was in the process of dislocation, their poverty absolutely inescapable and because they did not have even the meagre protection that the ideology of chivalry and respect gave white women.

Black women in frontier regions such as the islands of Bass Strait and the north-west of Western Australia were almost inevitably drafted into prostitution, either because they were sold by black men in exchange for tobacco or flour or because they were abducted by white men. Mary Montgomery Bennett summed up the black women's passage into white society: "Originally 'property' they have now become 'merchandise'." [80]

It was not only the haphazard brutalities of individual settlers that black women faced. Legislation circumscribed their movements, employment, right to marry and their rights over their children. Much of this legislation was intended to control and diminish the part-Aboriginal population. Documents here suggest that the Western Australian Aboriginal legislation embodied a system of race control. The 1905 Aborigines Act made it a criminal offence for a white man to have sexual relations with Aboriginal woman, but no white man was ever convicted under the Act for co-habitation, while countless women, the sources of "temptation", were forcibly removed away from families and friends to distant settlements.

The ideology that promoted motherhood as the highest form of womanhood was modified where Aboriginal women were concerned. Attempts were made to exclude Aboriginal women from maternity wards in Western Australia and Queensland. [80, 82] One of the clauses of the Western Australian Act of 1905 provided for the "exclusion of the rights of the mother". Police were empowered to remove half-caste children from their mothers and a report here by Daisy Bates describes her execution of this policy while she was employed by the Western Australian government. [74] In 1936, Mary Montgomery Bennett disclosed the eugenic premises of this policy: "the design is to separate the half-caste men from the girls and send the girls out amongst the whites and so breed out colour by adultery and prostitution." [80]

Notes

1. W. D. Borrie, *Population Trends and Policies* (Sydney: Australasian Publishing Company, 1948), chs 4, 5.
2. Ibid.
3. *Royal Commission on the Decline of the Birth Rate and on the Mortality of Infants in New South Wales. Report* (Sydney: N.S.W. Government Printer, 1904).
4. W. C. Windeyer, *Ex Parte Collins: A Judgement* (Sydney, 1889).
5. See Kay Daniels "Introduction" in *Women in Australia: An Annotated Guide to Records* (eds) Kay Daniels, Mary Murnane and Anne Picot (Canberra: A.G.P.S., 1977), p. xviii.
6. *Queensland Figaro*, 18 October 1919.
7. "Report from the Select Committee on the Contagious Diseases Act", *Tasmania. House of Assembly Papers*, 1882, vol. xliii, Paper 112.
8. New South Wales, *Parliamentary Debates*, 1918, p. 3379.

Aboriginal Women

71. Barter in Women

One of the key features of contact between white sealers in Bass Strait and the Tasmanian Aborigines was the exchange of food and tobacco for Aboriginal women. Here George Augustus Robinson, Conciliator of the Aborigines, reports what some Aboriginal women told him of their contact with the sealers.

In answer to questions put to the TYE.REE.LORE. or the aborigines from the islands, they said that the sealers flog the women, that all the women have been flogged and that they tie them up to trees and flog them on the buttock. BULL.RUB said Black Jack flogged her because she had not caught some kangaroo, gave her two dozen, and at another time Jack Brown flogged her; and TAN.LE.BONE.YER had been flogged several times... "What do they flog them for?" "If they take biscuit or sugar they flog them; plenty women steal biscuit". "What do they steal biscuit for? Don't the white men give them plenty?" "No, little bit, sometimes very little bit". "How do the women live?" "On what they can catch; on limpets, mussels, crawfish and mutton birds. The white men flog the black women for nothing and flog the women belonging to other white men. Thomson beat the women on the head with a stick or tomahawk, plenty of blood. Plenty children killed". "How do they kill them?" "The black women kill them in their belly, beat their belly with their fist. Kill big boys; take them in the bush to kill them, men no see it; men angry". At one time... five black women and two black men took a boat which belonged to Harrington and run away to go to the main; the boat was lost on a reef and they were all drowned. Parish said a few years since five women attempted to swim from Swan Island and three was drowned.

G. A. Robinson, Journal, 25 October 1830.

72. All the Women have been Flogged

Robinson relentlessly denounced the trade in black women and collected evidence to refute the complacent popular belief in Hobart and Launceston that Aboriginal women were happy with the sealers and did not want to leave them. This account also reveals that black women were procured for economic as well as sexual purposes.

The aboriginal female Mary informed me that the sealers at the Straits carry on a complete system of slavery; that they barter in exchange for women flour and potatoes; that she herself was bought off the black men for a bag of flour and potatoes; that they took her away by force, tied her hands and feet, and put her in the boat; that white men beat black women with a rope. Fanny, who speaks English well and knows not a word of the Aboriginal tongue, said there were fifty women at the Straits and plenty of children; that the three women from Brune Island who were coercively taken away by Baker, a man of colour, were at Kangaroo Island. The aboriginal Fanny states that this slave traffic is very common in the straits, and that women so bartered or sold are subjected to every hardship which their merciless tyrants can think of and that from the time their slavery commences they are habituated to all the fatiging drudgery which their profitable trade imposes. Surely this is the African slave trade in miniature, and the voice of reason as well as humanity loudly calls for its abolition. This information is further confirmed by the man Baker, who was himself a sealer in Bass's Straits and had for a considerable length of time cohabited with the female Fanny. He was transported from Launceston to Hobart Town on a charge of having forcibly taken away three native women from Brune Island; but the charges not having been proved he was dismissed, although there was little doubt as to his guilt.

G.A. Robinson, Journal, 10 October 1829.

73. Capture

Robinson succeeded in removing many of the black women captured by sealers to his settlement on Flinders Island. On her arrival, one Aboriginal women gave this account of her experiences.

Sarah an Aboriginal Female Native of New Holland about twenty years of age has been living with the Sealers for some time past arrived at this Settlement on the night of the 1st June at 10 p.m. accompanied by the Corporal and two women belonging to the Settlement and who had been despatched the day previous to Wooddy Island in the Settlement Boat upon this particular duty.

Question	Where is your Country
Answer	Close to Kangaroo Island
Q	Who took you away
A	James Allen a Sealer and Bill Johnson was in company with him
Q	What age was you
A	Was a big Girl when they took me away
Q	How did they take you away
A	They tied me round the neck and led me like a dog
Q	Where did you go then
A	We stopt in the bush one night when they tied my hands and tied my feet
Q	What did you do in the morning
A	They took me in the Boat and took me to Kangaroo Island
Q	Was there anymore women
A	Plenty — All run away — James Allen and two blackfellows took me the other man looked after the boat.
Q	What did you do then
A	I stopt at Kangaroo Island a long time along with James Allen

After she had been living at Kangaroo Island for some time the Schooner "Henry"

John Griffith Master and bursar came to the Island and by and by Johnson stole her from Allen he tied her up and put her on board the Schooner with Harry Wally. They took her sealing and came to the Straits Johnson then gave her to Bill Dutton with whom she cohabited — Dutton about 12 months since/i.e. Plenty of moons (The Commandant counted with his fingers 12 the number of moons she said it was since Dutton left her) took away her little girl and left her, in the Straits on Wooddy Island and married a white woman and she understands he had gone whaling — She does not like to stop at Wooddy Island — likes to stop here best — does not like the Sealers — would like to go to her own country.

Q	Does the sealers beat the women
A	Yes Plenty — the Sealers cut off a boys ear and the boy died and they cut a piece off a womans buttock
Q	Did Dutton ever beat you
A	Dutton beat me with a rope
Q	Who made you
A	I never heard him
Q	Who is Jesus Christ
A	I never heard him
Q	Would you like to hear about God
A	Yes would like to hear it
Q	Who made the trees the grass and the sea
A	Dont know.

Would like to learn book and hear about God. She did not get plenty to eat with the sealers only got a little one. The Sealers get drunk plenty and women get drunk too. The statement she says is true.

Robert Clark, Catechist, account of an interview with an Aboriginal woman brought to Flinders Island from the sealers' camp at Wooddy Island, 3 June 1837.

74. Betrayal

The Western Australian Aborigines Act of 1905, in a clause designed to inhibit the growth of the part-Aboriginal population, provided for the "exclusion of the rights of the mother" and the removal of part-Aboriginal children to a settlement. A report from Daisy Bates demonstrates the implementation of this part of the Act. It is significant that Daisy Bates, who has acquired legendary status as a friend and defender of the rights of Aborigines, here implicates herself in the removal of part-Aboriginal children from their mothers, which was one of the tasks she was set by the Department of Aborigines while she accompanied the Cambridge Expedition led by the English anthropologist A. Radcliffe Brown.

A half caste girl called Mingenoogoo (Fanny) had two children with her one a baby in arms. She was camped with a young man named Marra about a mile and a half from Crowther Station. The young child a girl of 3 is called Lottie. She should be taken away from these surroundings I think . . . One half caste girl named Rita was with the Sandstone people and ought to be taken away from them, but it will I think be difficult to catch her her friends being exceptionally wary. The day before the half caste Polly and the two half caste children went away in the train. I took the Sisters of the Convent to jail to see the poor creatures and as Polly had worked for them when I told her they would all be taken to another Sisters' place she appeared to become somewhat more reconciled, and after the train had gone when I saw the mother of one of the children who had been taken away, but she seemed to believe my statement that the little children would be happy. They do not associate me as yet with the raids and visits of inspection, but they appear to think that Brown and Watson are connected with the visits of the police in some way, as if they accompany me to a camp the members hide whereas when I go by myself they do not fly from me. I do not want to destroy that confidence if I can possibly help it.

Daisy Bates to the Chief Protector of Aborigines, W.A., written from Sandstone, 31 October 1910.

75. "A Good Neighbour and a Generous Man"

In Western Australia, the Aborigines Act of 1905 made it a criminal offence for a white man to have sexual relations with an Aboriginal woman. It was often noted by opponents of the Act that the enforcement of the "cohabitation clause" punished the Aboriginal woman, while the conduct of the white man was excused or ignored. The following set of documents demonstrates such an inversion of the law. Further hardship and suffering was inflicted on Aboriginal women in these circumstances by the section of the 1905 Act that provided for the forcible removal of their part-Aboriginal children. In this case, both the Aboriginal women named as participating in sexual liasons with the station-owner at Dalgety Downs were transported, with their children, to the distant Moore River Native Settlement. The first, Ivy, died there; the second, Kitty, was allowed to return to the station. The last report in her file notes that she is again pregnant and claims that the overseer was responsible. Her claim was characteristically disregarded by the police constable making the report: "Kitty seems to take on anyone who comes along."

I recommend that the women referred to as Kitty and Ivy and their children be removed right out of the District and kept under Section 12 in the Moore River Native Settlement. My reasons are as follows: It will be a very difficult matter, almost impossible to secure a Conviction under the present Act, against [F——] for cohabitation. I understand he is a Justice of the Peace, his late father was a pioneer, who left a grown up family, all of whom are highly esteemed by all who know them. The position of [M—— F——] is known by everybody, and apart from the disgusting position he has dropped into or gradually slid into he is liked as a good neighbour and a generous man. I am personally satisfied that [F——] is more weak than vicious.

Inspector of Aborigines, to the Chief Protector of Aborigines, W.A., 12 August 1925.

Since writing my report I have listened to further representations of the male natives on the subject of Ivy. This is their point of view with which I agree. Give Ivy a chance to live her own life in her own country with her own man, an aborigine. If she will not live with him then remove her to a mission as she is a danger and a disgrace to the natives. Since I was here the natives have arranged that Kitty should go to Willie of Dairy Creek as reported. I am going to state that Kitty's return to decency has only being brought about by the fear of being removed.

I heard from the natives on Mooloo Downs that Ivy ([F——'s] woman) had been given to Young Noble of Bidgiemia. I did not ask any questions about this, but waited up to yesterday. The natives said nothing. This morning I was approached by responsible natives, including Young Noble, who assured me that Ivy had been given to Young Noble according to tribal rights and she should be taken away from [F——] and handed over to Young Noble.

The conditions at Dalgety Downs are a disgrace to the State. There is a simple way out; it will clean it up, save the Aborigine Department's face and is in accordance with the natives' idea of justice; that is, instruct the police to remove Ivy and her youngest child and hand both those over to Young Noble. The other children should be removed to an institution. Action is what is required now. The law abiding white people look to us, the male aborigines who desire to restrain their own wives look to us, and the fair name of the State demands action. If Ivy won't live her life with her natural protector, then she must be removed to a Mission or Settlement. Once this woman gives up the white man or is made to give him up she will, of her own will, remain with her native man in preference to exile, will be quite happy and contented once she hardens up to the new conditions. Ivy is merely a self willed naughty child and will get over it, taking her away from [F——] and giving her to a young and handsome fullblood is merely smacking her hands and telling her "not to be silly". Taking her other children away is hard but the Department in its wisdom has done that in innumerable cases, and it is the only thing to be done now.

Ibid., 14 December 1925.

76. Transportation

This warrant legitimated the removal of the Aboriginal woman Ivy and her children to the Moore River Native Settlement. There Ivy gave birth to her seventh child and later died at the age of twenty-one.

THE ABORIGINES ACT, 1905.

SECTION 12.

Regulation 12A (Form 10).

To _____THE COMMISSIONER OF POLICE_____*and all Police Officers*

within the State of Western Australia.

WHEREAS it is deemed expedient by me, the undersigned, the Minister

charged with the administration of "The Aborigines Act, 1905," that

~~Aboriginal woman "IVY", and her children Iris, Bob, Bessie, Johnny and Ralph~~

~~an Aboriginal~~, be removed ~~to and kept within the boundaries of the~~

~~————————————————————— Reserve (or be removed~~ from the

...............Dalgety Downs Station...........................~~Reserve (or District)~~ to

the......Moore River Native Settlement.................~~Reserve (or District)~~ and

kept therein):

These are therefore to require you forthwith to arrest and apprehend

the said...."IVY" and children Iris, Bob, Bessie, Johnny and Ralph..............,

and ~~him~~ them to remove from the.......Dalgety Downs Station...................~~Reserve~~

~~(or District)~~, and safely convey within the boundaries of the..........................

.......Moore River Native Settlement..................~~Reserve (or District)~~ and

~~him~~ them safely to keep within such Reserve (or District) during the Minister's

pleasure.

Dated this ....20⁴..........day of ....Dec............192⁶

Jas Hick

Colonial Secretary.

n 13657/21

Warrant issued under W.A. Aborigines Act, 20 December 1926.

77. Permission to Marry

Another inroad into the freedom of Aborigines in Western Australia was the law that made the permission of the Chief Protector necessary for marriages other than between full-bloods, and which was designed to increase the government's power to control the part-Aboriginal population. The Aboriginal woman Kitty, who had been removed by warrant to the Moore River Native Settlement in 1926, two years later wrote to the Protector, asking his permission to marry.

Dear Sir,
Would you be so kind to answer this question for me well Sir my mother is willing to let me get married to a boy name Caption Jones and I thought I would ask you first now as I am under you and he stop with my Mother in [illegible] and if they are not in there well they might be in Delgety Down because they told me they was going there in letter they wrote to me and Sir would you send for Caption Jones and my mother and father to come down to get married please sir have no more to say sir

Kitty D., an inmate of the Moore River Native Settlement, to the Chief Protector of Aborigines, W.A., 7 December 1928.

78. The Limits of Protection

It was a brutal irony that the Aborigines Act of 1905, which so successfully eroded the liberties of Aboriginal women in the guise of "protection", was powerless to protect them from physical assault. This letter suggests that sexual abuse was compounded by savage forms of punishment, a picture that reduces the Aboriginal women on the stations to the status of slaves.

On or about the 27th of March the Manager of the Cherubim Pastoral Company chained a gin to a tree, the mode of chaining was with a pair of steel handcuffs on one wrist, then attached with a chain to a tree and padlocked. The gin was on the chain for five or six days, on about the 4th day that the gin was on the chain the Manager (Jno. J. [S——]) went away early in the day and did not return until the following evening. On the afternoon of the day of Jn. [S——'s] departure the gin beckoned me over and told me she wanted to evacuate. I told her that I had not the key of the lock but that as soon as the gin who is attached to Jno. [S——] returned that I would ask her if she had the key of the lock. When the gin returned I asked her if Jack [S——] had left the key with her. That same night the unfortunate gin was left by herself the other gins who were supposed to sleep near her had gone to the other camp about ¼ mile away. I went over to where she was, she told me the gins had left her by herself and that she was frightened.

The sequence to the above occurrence is so disgusting that I consider myself justified in reporting the whole matter to you and risk being called an informer. A few days after the chaining episode I was in the garden while the garden was being watered and the gin who had been on the chain (her native name is Yebellee) goes by the name of Kitty said to me that Jno. J. [S——] had sent her to Jack [S——'s] bedside on two consecutive nights, that also on another occasion Jack [S——] had sent her to a man named Jack [C——] who when she came to his bedside and touched him, had lashed out with either his hand or foot and that she fled.

I may tell you that the gin previously referred to as being attached to [S——]
is named Kalpsy, she has two halfcaste children and prctically lives with [S——]
when she is at the homestead.

Letter from the cook at Cherubim Station to the Chief Protector of Aborigines, W.A., 4 June 1925.

There is unfortunately nothing in the Aborigines Act which enables me to take
proceedings against a man who chains up a native as in this case.

Memo from the Chief Protector of Aborigines, W.A., regarding allegations of cruelty concerning an
Aboriginal woman at Cherubim Station, 5 October 1925.

79. Apportioning the Blame

**The following comments by Mary Montgomery Bennett and Ada Bromham reveal a
thorough knowledge of the sexual exploitation of Aboriginal women by white men
and the failure of the law to protect the human rights of Aboriginal women. Mary
Montgomery Bennett was an outstanding crusader for justice for the Aborigines of
Western Australia. Her cause was taken up by the Women's Service Guilds and the
Women's Christian Temperance Union. Ernestine Hill, a novelist, comments from
an imperial perspective and pronounces white women responsible for the sexual
behaviour of white men.**

If a native woman complains to the police about a white man she is charged with
cohabitation, and is deported — perhaps 500 miles from family, friends and tribe.
The police visit the white man who denies the charge and is left to continue his policy
unchecked. We are apt to think that only a bad white man could molest a native
woman but this is not so. Where ever there is a white man's camp there is need for
protection for these girls. It is the average ordinary white man who is to blame for this
trouble.

Mary Montgomery Bennett, address to the Women's Service Guilds of Western Australia, Perth, 11
December 1933.

That exploitation by white people of both men and women natives does exist can be
proved, but it is the lot of the woman which must claim the attention of every intelligent white woman. They have neither human rights or protection against the irresponsible white man. The Chief Protector of Aborigines recently reported "that out of
33 coloured girls sent out to employment during the past three years, no less than 30
have returned pregnant. The law does not sufficiently protect these girls, they are
mostly unsophisticated and innocent of any intention to do wrong."

Ada Bromham, Secretary of the W.C.T.U., *West Australian*, 6 June 1932.

It is a social crime that should be charged, not to the men of the North, but — shall I
say it — to the women of the South, who leave them to live and die alone, uncared for
and unthought of, shouldering the white man's burden for Australians of the future.

Ernestine Hill, *West Australian*, 26 May 1932.

80. "The Terrible Plight of the Civilized Aborigines"

Mary Montgomery Bennett subjected the Aborigines Department of Western Australia to strenuous criticism during the 1930s. By delivering papers at conferences and addressing women's organizations, she publicized the violation of human rights suffered by Aboriginal women. This paper, given to the British Commonwealth League Conference in 1933, argues that consequent to their exposure to civilization, Aboriginal women were almost inevitably drafted into prostitution, and as mothers of part-Aboriginal children, then were punished further by the removal of their children.

An examination of the circumstances of aboriginal mothers in touch with civilization discloses that their condition has become much worse, and it concerns us much more nearly than the condition of wild aborigines, because the terrible plight of the civilized aborigines is the logical conclusion of our own dealings with them.

With aboriginal mothers are included half-caste mothers, who in Australia are deemed to be aborigines.

Two outstanding facts confront us: (1) slow starvation of natives through our depriving them of all land to live on and arising from dispossession and starvation; (2) wholesale prostitution of women. Originally "property" they have now become "merchandise".

Prostitution, wrote Mr Love, is the greatest evil that civilization has brought to the aborigines. The aboriginal has quickly learned to appreciate flour and tobacco. Too often the only way, in which he can procure these luxuries (perhaps they have become necessities) is by the prostitution of his woman. Having travelled across Australia from south to north and from north to north-east, I came to the matured opinion that nearly every black woman in the bush or on cattle station camps is at the disposal of any passer-by for the price of a stick of tobacco.

A letter from an educated half-caste man from the North-West division last year stated: "Our poor women folk don't get any protection up this way. We went through twelve stations. On every place you see half caste kiddies running with dark mothers. It is a disgrace to the station and half-caste women are living with white men on the outcamps." Dr Basedow protests against "ubiquitous concubinage" which is forced upon aboriginal girls by all classes of white men in the back blocks —that is the greater part of Australia.

The chief protector in Western Australia admits that he has no power to protect native women and that the means at his disposal are inadequate. There is only too much evidence that starvation and years of dispossession are taking their toll.

The report of the Aboriginal Department of Western Australia for 1930 says, "Loss of child life was greater than ever" and the report of 1932 says "Eking out an existence on government rations alone, they are undoubtedly deteriorating, particularly the children."

I would add, also that their mothers endure the first pinch. The Rev Mr Boxall of Narrogin, described to the newly formed Aborigines' Amelioration Association the hardships endured by expectant mothers for whom admission into hospitals was extremely difficult to secure, and for whom some provision ought to be made. Many hospitals refuse admission to natives and half-castes, for no reason, except that they are natives and half-castes and that white people would resent their presence.

Aborigines are deeply attached to their land and should not be transported. It would be as reasonable to attempt to solve the problem of the English slums by snatching children from their mothers and transporting them to a settlement in Teneriffe or Turkey, so vast are the distances of Western Australia.

The remedy for starvation and prostitution of Australian natives is to set apart in every division, adequate territories, where natives can live in communities of their own, unmolested by whites and can learn to grow their own food.

Further it is a particular responsibility of the women to require that the present ubiquitous practice of placing native women and half-caste girls at the disposal of police officers, should be made to cease at once.

Some police officers are upright men, but many are corrupt. I know a missionary who reports every white man who keeps a native woman in his camp. The police always provide an alibi for white offenders — but there are native women with half-caste babies.

The police provide an alibi because they so often need one themselves. A Queensland paper describes the use of an alibi: "A recent line-up of members of the police force at the Darwin police station, for the purpose of a young half-caste woman of the compound identifying a certain member in substantiation of certain sworn statements of hers. The lady in question picked out as the offender a member of the force, who, at the time alleged for the offence, was 2000 miles from Darwin." Some of my half-caste pupils are children of a police officer, who had several children by different aboriginal women.

There is another aspect of the position of the aboriginal mother of half-caste children, which demands the attention of women's societies — the effect of the mother's circumstances on the children. I know of aboriginal mothers who were hunted by the police to take their children from them to a remote Government settlement. Three women suffered an agony of fear, and the effects may still be seen in their children; I would refer particularly to one of my pupils, a nervy boy with a look of shock.

Aboriginal mothers are inarticulate and so endure untold sufferings of serfdom because we have deprived them of land to live on and refuse them education, with all other rights that are founded on education-medical services, wages when they earn them, and political standing, by which they might obtain other rights due to them.

I ask women of good will to press for definite reforms: (1) Adequate native territories in each division and (2) schools for thousands of our fellow subjects, intelligent native and half-caste children, who as a Government report admits, are growing up without training. Schools are fundamental to all other rights.

Mary Montgomery Bennett, paper given to the British Commonwealth League Conference, London, 1933.

81. Feminine Hysteria

The Department of Native Affairs attempted to divert attention from Mrs Bennett's allegations by discrediting her.

Mrs Montgomery Bennett is a cultivated woman and an excellent teacher, but suffers from ill health, at times severely. It is because of this fact that one is loath to take exception to any remarks she may make publicly . . . The wrongs of the Natives is an obsession with her.

Memo from the Commissioner of Native Affairs, W.A., to the Minister for Native Affairs, 21 February 1938.

82. Aboriginal Mothers

In the 1920s, a systematic effort was made throughout Australia to reduce the country's high rate of maternal and infant mortality by increasing the number of maternity hospitals and wards. The following letter reveals that the powerful racist attitudes of a local hospital committee in Queensland resulted in a campaign to exclude Aboriginal women from the new maternity ward. All the irrational components of racism are present: physical repulsion, fear of contamination and the belief that Aborigines do not need or deserve the same consideration (in this case, medical care) that white people do.

At a Special Meeting of my Committee held on the 4th Inst to consider your letter No 235994 of the 20th July 23 I was authorised to submit for your perusal a statement of its attitudes towards the question of the treatment of aboriginal women in the proposed New Maternity Ward at the Springsure Hospital.

In the first place I beg to assure you that my Committee is strongly in favour of the erection by the Government of such Wards, and is anxious to support to the fullest possible extent so humane and progressive an enactment.

We feel however that in this particular district, the admission of aborigines will inevitably defeat the beneficent object of the Maternity Scheme, since we are convinced that, should native women be admitted to the free use of it, the white community here for the most part will refuse to use the Ward at all.

Whilst we are fully aware that, in other centres where the native population is numerically negligible the same result may not ensue. We beg to submit that circumstances here are not the same as in most other centres. Springsure has a comparatively small white community, but at the same time it is the natural centre of a large area which contains a great number of natives and there is and always has been a very decided feeling hereabout against unnecessary contact between the two races.

This feeling is so pronounced that my Committee has no hesitation in saying that scarcely a white man in the whole district would countenance the possibility of his wife being compelled to lie up during or after confinement in the same ward as a native woman.

For reasons which will be advanced later we believe that when this ward is opened there will be no other Maternity facilities in this district.

The result will be that, instead of the community being benefitted by the Ward, its womenfolk will leave the district to be confined elsewhere and consequently will be put to greater expense and lose all opportunity for supervision and advice during the ante-natal period.

The dissatisfaction engendered by this will, we fear, result in a growing animus against the ward which will finally express itself in lessened support for the Hospital itself. Since the Ambulance Service has been established in this district giving increased facilities for travelling the aboriginals have shown a marked fondness for hospital treatment, and we have no doubt but that the Maternity Ward will become similarly increasingly popular amongst them. Already the increased number of natives requiring Hospital treatment has caused dissatisfaction in the district as we have not so far been able to provide separate accommodation for them in the General Ward.

Your letter states "inter alia" that ours is the first Committee to raise the question. We can only reply that probably in the majority of cases conditions as regards the number of natives in the district are not similar, and that when conditions do parallel ours we feel that the people supporting similar Institutions have not realized that their wives may be confined cheek by jowl with aboriginal native women.

Incidentally I beg to point out that to the best of my knowledge in no other civilised country in the world would such a state of affairs be entertained for a moment. Even supposing that only the poorest white woman were to use the ward which I take it is not the intention of the act the position would remain intolerable. We feel that sufficient consideration has not been given to the feelings of white women compelled at such a time to herd in with natives and we are convinced that were the position carefully considered from this point of view our position in the matter would need no further elaboration.

Futhermore we beg to suggest that the opinion of Maternity nurses on the question of attending to aboriginal patients needs careful thought. Our Hospital is small and the salaries we can offer are not large and we doubt whether we can make sufficient inducement for an entirely capable nurse to undertake such duties.

On the other hand we are not desirous of being forced to accept any less desirable nurse on that account.

In a district so isolated we already have considerable difficulty in securing and retaining the service of competent nurses. As regards the question of private Nursing homes and the Maternity Ward:— The conditions here are possibly peculiarly our own. All maternity work here is at present done at one such Home only, furthermore private patients requiring other than Maternity nursing are treated in the private ward of the Springsure Hospital.

Now the deflection of only a moderate number of patients from the private home would cause it do become an unprofitable venture and it is the declared intention of the proprietress to close down when the Maternity Ward opens.

Should public opinion thereafter turn against the ward to the extent which we anticipate we know that it is much easier to close down one such institution than to reopen another after its predecessor had declared it unprofitable.

There is in this district no visiting Maternity nurse to attend to patients in their private homes nor is such a practice desirable.

The position will then become that women wishing to remain in Springsure for confinement or unable to go away for financial or other reasons will be forced to use the Maternity Ward and then risk the possibility of aboriginal ward companions.

If the objectionableness of this is not obvious we can only regret our inability to make it clearer. As for the natives themselves — from time immemorial they have attended to their own confinements — receiving of latter years assistance when it was needed — and such assistance would never under any circumstances be withheld — but our experience of Natives leaves us under no delusion as to whether they will fail to use hospital facilities should such be provided freely and without some local control and we know that opening the Ward under the conditions apparently proposed by you will inevitably bring us a long train of their women for confinement and lead to the conflict with public opinion which we have already indicated.

Our opinion summarized then is, that in this district the admission of Aboriginal women will prevent the use of the ward of the white women, thus defeating the reason of establishing the Maternity Ward.

Secondly and still speaking of this particular district it will cause the closure of our only private Nursing Home, thus dislocating the existing Maternity arrangements.

Finally it will engender such dissention and bitterness in the district that the hospital itself will lose a great part of its public support.

For these reasons my Committee feel that they must request to be allowed to use their own discretion regarding the admission of Aboriginal patients to the Maternity Ward.

This does not mean their rigid exclusion as before stated, no native woman has or ever will be refused assistance by the Hospital when it was needed.

Simply my Committee feel that in this district such discretionary power would enable it to do its share to aid in the success of the Maternity Scheme by preventing its failure in Springsure in the purpose for which it is to be established. I have to request that you will ask the Works Department to suspend activities in connection with the building of the Maternity Ward here until my Committee has an opportunity of considering your reply to this letter.

President, Springsure Hospital Committee, to the Assistant Under-Secretary, Queensland Home Secretary's Office, 7 August 1923.

83. "He Had Only Married a Nigger"

While liaisons with black women were tolerated and regarded as the inevitable outcome of masculine sexual needs, interracial marriage was regarded as an abomination. Hence this police inspector's report on a marriage between a fifty-year-old boundary-rider and fourteen-year-old part-Aboriginal girl.

All those to whom I spoke said it was a mistake to allow this marriage . . . said he'd wake up to the fact that he had only married a nigger and would one day be discovered hanging behind a door in hopeless and futile disgust.

Police Inspector, Department of the North West, to the Chief Protector of Aborigines, W.A., 5 September 1924.

84. Race Control

The wide-ranging powers of the Western Australian Native Affairs Act of 1936 enabled the Commissioner of Native Affairs to embark on a policy of race control by vetoing marriages that he considered would propagate an "undesirable" racial strain. These powers were usually invoked to prevent Aboriginal women marrying white men and Asian divers. The following letter demonstrates that this policy was diligently pursued and that when the powers of the state Act were exhausted, successful appeals for support were made to the Commonwealth Government.

You spoke to me yesterday about the proposed marriage of an Asiatic named [S——b——S——] and Mary Bridget [S——]. . . . [S——b——S——] is a Mohammedan by religion and was born in Malaya. He is classed as an indentured Asiatic to the pearling industry, and is a seaman by occupation, but he enlisted on 20th May, 1943 and is now a member of the 51st Water Transport Coy. Fremantle. Mary Bridget [S——] is also known as Biddy [S——]. Although she is dark in appearance she only possesses one quarter Australian native blood; therefore she is not a native in law. Consequently, the proposed marriage of the parties is of no interest to me legally under the Native Administration act.

However, there was a similar application from the parties in 1940/41 and the matter was referred to the Rt. Hon. the Prime Minister, and it resulted in an intimation to [S——— b——— S———] that consideration would be given to the question of his deportation at the end of the pearling season if the proposed marriage took place. For your information I attach a copy of the Prime Minister's letter. Racially, it is not desirable that Asiatics, especially indentured Asiatics, should be permitted to marry women of Australian native ancestry. There has been quite a lot of correspondence with the National Government about indentured Asiatics associating with women of native ancestry at Broome, and since there is a considerable polyglot population at Broome as a result of these undesirable associations at Broome, I am personally of the opinion that the National Government has reached the right conclusion in its intimation that consideration would be given to the deportation of the Asiatic concerned in this case if the marriage took place. I would add that [S——— b——— S———] was convicted at Broome on 20th August, 1942 of (1) cohabiting with a native woman, and (2) with supplying liquor. He received six months' imprisonment on each of these charges. However, as previously stated, since Mary Bridget [S———] is now over 21 years of age, I have no legal jurisdiction in the matter of their proposed marriage.

Commissioner of Native Affairs, W.A., to the District Registrar, W.A., 18 January 1944.

Prostitution

85. "Vice has been Hitherto the Sole Dreadful Alternative of the Miserable Female"

This appeal to Governor Sir George Grey, to establish a refuge for women in South Australia, draws poverty, unemployment and prostitution into the one field of discussion.

The Memorial of Your Petitioner Richard Penney humbly sheweth—That your Petitioner has long been convinced that unless Man leads a life of usefulness he might as well not live at all and that those who occupy exalted stations do not fulfil the design of Providence in placing them therein unless they devote the influence and advantages they possess to ameliorate the condition of other classes of their fellow creatures and to diffuse happiness around them. *That* these considerations have induced your Petitioner — respectfully to call the attention of Your Excellency to the circumstance of the large number of females who are living by a life of prostitution in the city of Adelaide, out of all proportion to the respectable population, — a life productive of incalculable misery to themselves and producing important and injurious effects on general society; — to enquire into the causes that have produced so extensive and fatal a demoralisation and to point out, at any rate, a partial remedy which it is in the power of your Excellency to apply to the case.

That your Petitioner is assured that it is unnecessary for him to attempt to show the causes of prostitution; they are manifest and, as will, doubtless suggest itself to your Excellency's mind, are dependent on the imperfection of our common nature, and under the peculiar circumstances of our Society have been materially assisted in their operation by the influence of climate, by the demoralising example both in conduct and language, with which a long voyage familiarises the mind of the emigrant, examples eminently subversive of virtue in the mind; — early in the history of the colony, by the laxity of morals introduced by the importation of the lower classes of society from the neighbouring colonies; and then and at the present time by the obstacles almost insuperable, that stand in the way of our country population, who are mostly single men, forming matrimonial connections.

That — the consequences attendant on the introduction of labourers from the other Colonies, in the first settlement of the Province, a period in which great excitement and extravagant hopes prevailed, and also when the mechanics and labourers, mostly young men, earned wages far beyond what was necessary for the necessaries and comforts of life, — ... by the influence of their example the destruction of all moral distinctions; and both sexes, in that season of intoxication and delusion, readily imbibed the seduction and fatal principles of sensuality. The class of single female emigrants, thus lost their character for respectability, as a class — and settlers were unwilling to engage in their families any female servants with connections of doubtful character. This circumstance would, almost alone, account for the extremities to which so large a number of females have been exposed, for if having been once in service, an irritable master or mistress might give a discharge for a trivial fault, — it was very difficult to dissipate the idea that in the minds of others, that there was no other reason, of a graver nature than the one assigned. The worst construction was sure to be placed on the delinquency and many an innocent individual has thus fallen into the hands of those characters who are continually on the watch to pick them up — from the inability to counteract the prejudices of public opinion. *That* country settlers complain greatly of the difficulty of obtaining female servants of good characters, and, although, there is a very extensive and urgent demand for the services of that class of persons, that they are obliged to submit to great inconvenience for the want of them, rather than bring those whom they do not know into their families. *That* this same cause, has operated on the minds of single men desirous of marrying and prevented them from connecting themselves in that tie with that class, against whom, so much prejudice has existed; the frequency of prostitution amongst them having generated a mistrust with regard to all.

That it is impossible, but that, amongst so large a number, apparently devoted to hopeless misery and crime, — there must be many who would gladly embrace an opportunity of redeeming themselves, if it were offered; and it amounts almost to a certainty, that such would be the case, when we consider that their vicious courses are pursued for the sake of gaining their daily bread. — A hard necessity and circumstances against which they have not had strength of mind sufficient to bear up has reduced them to their present degraded position and bitter experience of every day must have produced a salutory influence on their minds. Your Petitioner would, therefore, humbly and respectfully suggest, Whether the Government would not be pursuing a legitimate and beneficial course by originating through the Colonial Chaplain, and assisting a society and institution having for its object — to afford refuge and employment to such single females, as may be without other means of livelihood — and, without making the previous character an obstacle to the admission of the applicant — to give females of this unfortunate class a chance of reformation. *That* this Institution should supply settlers in the country with servants, who might require them and that the simple recommendation of the Society should be rendered a sufficient testimonial of character by the guarantee, that the individual had been under their care a sufficient length of time to enable them to do so with confidence. The expense of this institution might be met by the labour of females admitted, either in needlework, straw work, washing or other employments as the Society might consider best adapted to their capacities.

Your Excellency will perceive that three important points would be effected by this institution, — objects involving a great change and improvement amongst the population of the Province —

Firstly — Country settlers would be provided with a valuable and indispensable class of servants —

Secondly — It would encourage matrimonial alliances by bringing the single men, who are almost all employed in the country into the society of single females, from whom they are now separated for months, under circumstances calculated to produce permanent and reputable attachments.

Thirdly — it would go a great way towards preventing future prostitution and would rescue a few at least from a course of life, the consequences of which cannot be contemplated without horror — Vice has hitherto been the sole dreadful alternative of the miserable female, placed in the untoward circumstances that have been stated to your Excellency, and this Institution would, at least, open a door to the path of virtue, so that she *could* have the opportunity of choosing between good and evil, or of finding a place of refuge, if, repentant, she would retrace her steps. But as far as the encouragement of marriage may be considered desirable, even the consequences to be anticipated from creating a more mixed society in the country, would be lost, under the present system, in which parties in the country are obliged to come from a distance into Adelaide to be united. Persons in the condition of servants cannot afford the loss of time and money that necessarily takes place in coming to Town, and the necessity that strangers would have of returning to a Public House after such a ceremony would be exceedingly to be regretted. There have been many instances, when marriage has been put off for months or even a year from this cause, and many in which the match has been broken off or the parties have ultimately dispensed with the ceremony altogether, believing themselves to be justified by the necessity in which they were placed. Your Petitioner does not know what obstacles may stand in the way of allowing proper individuals to celebrate the ceremony, under certain regulations, in the distant parts of the Province — but he is convinced, that if it were practicable, it would conduce materially to the comfort, prosperity, and morality of all classes of the people. Your Petitioner has now been more than two years in this Province and has been an attentive, if not a correct observer of the relations of the several grades and classes of our Colonial society, with the view, eventually, to operate on it in advocacy of the claims of the Aboriginal tribes.

Richard Penney, Memorial to Sir George Grey "respecting the establishment of an Asylum for abandoned Females", Adelaide, 2 August 1842.

86. Protecting the Domestic Hearth from Invasion

This tract shows that prostitution and marriage were often held to be in a symbiotic and not an antagonistic relationship. The writer appeals to the middle-class women of Hobart to denounce this rationalization of prostitution and make efforts to reclaim prostitutes.

These women exist in numbers almost beyond belief.* The profligacy which creates and supports them, insists upon the perpetuation of their sin as an institution inseparable from a condition of high civilization. Sisters ignore it. Wives and mothers "die, and make no sign." Statesmen justify the deterioration of the race and other consequences of this gigantic sin with economical reasons. The singular depravation of these women's lives, the long train of moral and physical evils inseparable from

*It has been estimated that in Hobart Town alone there are not less than three hundred and fifty of these unfortunate girls. The value of this sum total must however be ascertained by reference to statistics. The last census (1857) shewed that there were five thousand nine hundred and sixteen women in Hobart Town between the ages of fourteen and sixty; so that, of this number, one in every sixteen must belong to the class of which I write. The third Annual Report of the Hobart Town City Mission (1856) drew attention to "the existence of excessive social immorality among the lower orders of the population. The Agents report the existence of social vices and irregularities to an extent hithertoo unsuspected. It is found that the marriage tie is habitually disregarded by whole classes of our female community, and that habits the most opposed to those connected with piety, or even with social morality, are adopted without hesitation, and almost indeed without the sense of shame."

their mischievous behaviour, — this perennial transformation of the young and beautiful to the callous and sensual, this holocaust of virgin life, — is said to be essential to the prevention of yet greater social ills. It is said to protect the domestic hearth from invasion: it were better perhaps to speak without any ambiguity, though the thought should shock you somewhat: it is said to secure your virtue from assault . . . And so, on every hand, society stiffens up in a rigid conventionality, and the whole subject is avoided. It is left to the "moral sense" of the community, as though there was such a thing as a public conscience independent of the unit individual consciences; and all these consciences were sufficiently well instructed. Or, if enquiry be made, it is staved off by the theory that these women are all hopelessly irreclaimable; as though it became us to assign such doom to any . . . This cold-blooded philosophy deserves rebuke. There is no social ill which the Gospel cannot remedy.

"One of Four", *Words to Women: A Plea for Certain Sufferers* (1858).

87. "The Woman is Stoned While the Man May Go"

One of the most persistent battles waged by women's organizations in Australia was against the double standard of morality. This double standard formed the basis of legislation designed to regulate prostitution.

There are many phases of the Double Standard of Morals for men and women, but in nothing does it appear more unjust than in its application to the cases of young girls of the middle and poorer classes whose lives have been blackened by vice before they have yet reached the age of womanhood. Girls of tender ages found wandering in our streets, and who are known to be leading a life of prostitution, associating with bad characters, or living in houses of ill-fame, are picked up and brought before the court. In many cases they are sent to an Industrial Home, where such youthful offenders are trained for a noble, useful womanhood; and sadly do they need this training. This is all very well; but why stop here, for such provisions can only remedy in a very small measure the legitimate effect of existing causes. The modern physician knows that to cure the disease he must first remove the cause. Are our legislators less wise? As well try to bail out a sinking ship with a spoon as to attempt to stop the march of Vice by such weak efforts to remove its logical results.

Yes, the girl is sent to the industrial school; but what of the man? What sentence does he get who led her, in her childish ignorance, to take the first irrevocable step towards her own destruction? Is he searched out and sentenced to a like number of years of confinement? Oh, no! You see, he only started her on her slippery downward path; but she went on following it, so, of course, she must suffer and be punished — not he. So his part of the affair is left undiscovered, or, if known, is speedily forgotten, and he goes on his way unchecked, ready to seduce the next girl who places her trust in him, and, after robbing her of all that is beautiful in her childhood, sends her to join her unfortunate sister in the home. Does this seem overdrawn? No, not at all. It is only too true that often more than one girl is there through the treachery of the same man. Such men are Social and Moral Lepers, and should be dealt with as such; but they are not. Everybody knows that as long as they can keep up decent appearances even their social standing does not seem in the least affected by such "mistakes" as these. The door of every respectable house should be closed against such men.

But what of the victims — the girls who must spend the years of their young womanhood deprived of their freedom and cut off from the joys that should make this period of their lives so bright? They are safe and well cared for, for the present. But how do they regard the future? In the hearts of many of them — yea, most of them — there is an earnest, sincere desire to live pure, useful, womanly lives; but the past hangs like a millstone around their necks, holding them back and dragging them down from the high ideal to which they long to attain. One of these bright young girls told a lady connected with rescue work what she longed to be, and it was a noble ambition, "but," she cried in a tone that was pitiful in its hopeless despair, "I know I never can be that, for people will find out what I have been, and then nobody will want anything to do with me — at least nobody decent."

Another, in speaking of her fall, said, "I didn't know what the first step meant, and, when that was taken, I didn't care." That is the sad story of many, many wrecked young lives. They discover when it is too late that one false step has made them outcasts from society, and from all that is good and pure in life; and the despair of their hearts find expression in that bitter cry, "Nobody cares what I am; it is no use trying; I can't be good."

Much is said at the present time about equal pay for equal work. What we need vastly more is a like justice in the punishment of crime. If the stream of sin-cursed, wrecked young lives which is constantly pouring its ever-increasing volumes into our industrial homes and houses of refuge is ever to be checked, its sources must be searched out, wherever they may be, and fearlessly and faithfully cleansed.

> There was a maiden who went astray,
> In the golden dawn of her life's young day.
> She had more passion and heart than head,
> And she followed blindly where fond love led.
> And love unchecked is a dangerous guide
> To wander at will by a fair girl's side.
>
> The woman repented and turned from sin,
> But no door opened to let her in;
> The preacher prayed that she might be forgiven,
> But told her to look for Mercy — in Heaven;
> For this is the law of the Earth, we know,
> That the woman is stoned, while the man may go.
>
> A brave man wedded her after all.
> But the World said, frowning. "We will not call."

"The Double Standard", *Woman's Voice*, May 1905.

88. The Health of the Royal Navy

Queensland (in 1868) and Tasmania (in 1879) introduced Contagious Diseases Acts, in an attempt to arrest the spread of venereal disease. Such legislation was designed to safeguard the health of men who had sexual intercourse with prostitutes, specially members of the armed forces. The restrictive clauses of the Acts were applied exclusively to women who, despite evidence and logic, were regarded as the carriers of venereal disease. This letter from the surgeon on a British warship shows the important role the Royal Navy played in the introduction of contagious diseases legislation in Tasmania.

Sir,

I have the honor to address you on the subject of "The Contagious Diseases Act" in this Colony, in order to show what the effect of it has been so far as the crews of this Squadron are concerned, and to make one or two suggestions for its increased efficiency.

I feel it my duty to do so as the Senior Medical Officer in this Squadron, and because my action on former occasions has made me to some extent responsible for the introduction of "The Contagious Diseases Act" now in force in the Colony of Tasmania.

In my first letter, dated 15th May 1877, I reported that we had a short time before passed 14 days at Hobart Town, and had contracted 7 cases of venereal disease. This, I afterwards found, was below the mark, for 3 other cases of constitutional syphilis came subsequently under my notice, the men having been infected at Hobart Town. Of the 10 cases 4 were of gonorrohoea, 5 of syphilis, and 1 of both diseases combined.

In the course of our second visit, which took place in the last quarter of 1878, we spent 7 days and contracted 6 cases of gonorrohoea.

The present Contagious Diseases Act come into force on the 21st October last, since which date 63 women have been examined, and 40 of these have been found diseased and placed in the Lock Hospital. This ship arrived here on the 5th December, having thus spent 93 days in port. During this period we have only had 6 cases of gonorrhoea and 1 of syphilis. The "Emerald" has not been so fortunate: she carries 90 men less than we do, and has only been 38 days in port, but during this period she has contracted 9 cases of gonorrhoea and 5 of syphilis. One case of syphilis has also occurred in the "Renard".

The improvement, as contrasted with our former experiences, has been considerable; and I have no hesitation in saying, that if nothing had been done by the Government of Tasmania to remedy the state of matters to which I originally drew attention, you might not have felt justified in keeping the ships at this place for more than a very limited period.

Legislation, so far as it has gone, for the prevention of venereal diseases in the Colony of Tasmania must be regarded as tentative. In dealing with the evils which it is designed to meet prejudices have to be overcome, and it is often prudent to begin with measures which are not too decided in their action. The working of the Act hitherto has been encouraging. But I have shown that disease still exists in considerable amount. This, together with experience which has been derived from the operation of the Contagious Diseases Acts at home, shows that there is something further requiring to be done in order to make the present Act in this Colony more effective.

What is needed is, that all women certified as common prostitutes in Tasmania should be registered and medically inspected once a fortnight. As the law now stands it is very difficult for the officer appointed for duty to fix suspicions upon any woman, however notorious she may be, as a prostitute. He is expected to be informed by some one: but a man who has been infected by a diseased woman does not, as a rule, care to communicate the fact to a police officer; or he may have met the woman in the dark, or have been the worse of drink, and is unable to recognize her a week or ten days afterwards when he finds himself diseased.

Women sometimes, I find, inform on each other; but this is a dangerous privilege to place in the hands of prostitutes, from the spite or jealousy which these women often bear towards each other, or even towards those who may be leading virtuous and respectable lives. A grievous and terrible wrong may thus be inflicted on a good woman.

The present Act is too limited in its operation. A woman, though known to be diseased and to have spread disease in Hobart Town, cannot be arrested if she goes and lives six miles outside the city boundary. I know that women sometimes do this in order that they may avoid being placed in the Lock Hospital. To give an instance: On the 10th instant a seaman of the "Renard" came under my notice with true syphilis. He knew the woman who infected him, and where she lived. I accordingly sent him to Mr. Quodling, the Inspector of Police, and steps were immediately taken to have the woman medically examined. The result may be expressed by a quotation from a letter which I received from Mr. Quodling next day — "The woman by whom the seaman of the Renard has been infected has left town for a time, and thereby placed herself beyond the limits of the C.D. Acts, which are confined to a radius of six miles from the city boundary". I know that this woman must now be suffering from a loathsome disease, and it is too probable that she is engaged in disseminating it amongst the inhabitants of some country district.

On the 13th instant a seaman of this ship came before me, having been infected with syphilis on the 4th; but I find that the woman who infected him left for New Zealand on the 12th, having plied her trade until the day of her departure. She had already been in the Lock Hospital and did not wish to go again.

The Legislature of Tasmania might therefore follow out with advantage what has been done in England, and provide for the periodical inspection of common prostitutes. Unfortunately the beneficial influence of the Contagious Diseases Acts at Home is to a large extent rendered nugatory on account of their operation being limited to certain districts, so that disease is being constantly imported from the un-protected to the protected places by men as well as women. In order to prevent this as much as possible, and also to put a stop to diseased women going into the country districts to escape being confined in the Lock Hospital, I would advise that every common prostitute in the colony, no matter where she resides, should be registered and obliged to submit, if called upon by the authorities to medical inspection and if diseased, to detention to a Lock Hospital.

I feel satisfied that an Act including the provisions which have been roughly sketched in this letter would be productive of the greatest benefit to this Colony. I am assured by Mr. Quodling that there cannot be less than 120 women now earning a livelihood by prostitution in Hobart Town alone.

Of those examined 63 per cent have been found to be diseased. This is about the same per-centage which was found at Home when the Contagious Diseases Acts first came into operation. The number of prostitutes for a town of 20,000 inhabitants is certainly very large. In the course of a year or two through the operation of a good Contagious Diseases Act, this number might be reduced to at least one-half, and the per-centage of disease from 63 to something like 6 . . .

So far as I know, nothing has been done by the public in Hobart Town by means of voluntary organizations to aid these women in the Lock Hospital, some of whom are by no means confirmed in a vicious course of life. I admit there is often little hope of reclaiming an old prostitute. She is too often physically and morally diseased and vile in the very grain and fibre of her being. We can try however to minimize her evil influence. With a young girl it is different; and it is a pity that she should have to leave the Lock Hospital, as she must do at present, clad in the dirty drabs or decked with the tawdry finery of a common harlot. She is ashamed or afraid to go back to her respectable friends should she have any. She cannot get good employment because she has no character, while the very graces of her girlish nature make her more eagerly sought after by thoughtless men, and led on to hopeless ruin. Society cannot afford to neglect her, for in time she will have her revenge in the moral and physical contagion which she will spread through every rank.

The reclamation of fallen women cannot, for obvious reasons, be wholly undertaken by a Government which can only act through paid officials. But it is the duty of the Government of Tasmania to make the conditions of things, which I have pointed out known and I feel certain it will meet with a ready response from the public. It will be its duty to facilitate, as far as possible, the operations of any organisation having for its object the good of these unfortunate women. Indeed, work of this kind must be regarded as a proper and necessary complement to a good Contagious Diseases Act.

Walter Reid, Staff Surgeon of H.M.S. *Wolverene*, comments on the working of the Contagious Diseases Act in Hobart to Commodore Wilson, 26 February 1880.

89. "Better 'to Go on the Town' "

This prisoner, in her evidence to a board inquirying into the management of Queensland gaols, plots her social and economic decline, which dated from her husband's desertion. She suggests that little medical attention was given to women in gaols who were suffering from venereal disease.

I was married in Warwick, and my husband kept a restaurant in Brisbane. He left me. I went out to service. I came here for getting drunk. I was a good woman when I came here first, but I heard all sorts of bad things here. I was told it would be better to go "on the town" than keep on being sent to gaol, and they told me where to go. When I left here some of them met me in Brisbane at the Railway Station. I had 5s. which Mr Blaney gave me. Two women met me, one was about eighteen years old and the other about twenty years. I was twenty-four years old. They took me to a house in Albert Street. I had never been in such a house before that night. I got drunk. I lived there afterwards. I intended to go to Bundaberg, and that night I got drunk and was ashamed. A man was with me the next night. One of the girls brought a man to me. It was about five months after I first slept with a man that I was run in again. I was in the Lock hospital about four months after I went down. Sergeant Doyle came down to the house and asked me if I had a ticket. He knew me when I was married in Brisbane. He told me to get a ticket or I would get six months. After about four months I got ill, and after being examined by Dr Hobbs I was sent to the Lock hospital. Dr. Jackson told me I could go out on a pass, and I went out and got drunk and was sent up here. I never spoke to any bad women until I came into this gaol first. It was in this gaol that I was first asked to go on the town. I was by myself in the hospital for five months. I am in the general dormitory now. I expect the old hands tell other girls to go on the town. I would not tell them. I know I go out worse every time I come here. You do not care for anything when you go out. You have no friends. Ladies come here and talk to the girls. They have influence upon some of them, and the young girls try and keep away from the old hands after they have seen the ladies. I always go to see them. The Catholic priest never comes to the gaol; I have never seen him. The Sisters of Mercy come sometimes, I have seen them seven or eight times altogether. They never speak to us, they only read books of devotion to us. They only speak to the matron. Some prisoners are employed in the gaoler's house as servants. They come back about seven o'clock in the evening. Kate Mullins stopped at the house for two nights. I never saw Nellie Phillips or Emily Hansen the worse for drink but I heard of it; I was not here at the time. They were over at the house — one was cooking and the other was sewing. I have been sleeping with the other girls this time. Last time I was in the hospital. I am still ill. I did not ask to see the doctor; I knew it was no good. I have to keep clean the best way I can, but when I go down to the bathroom the others come down. I got some medicine from the chemist when I came. I asked him for a lotion which I have been using. There are utensils purposely for us. About six other girls are ill. The doctor does not seem to care, and they have to do the best they can.

Testimony given by an inmate of Toowoomba Gaol to the Board of Inquiry into the General Management of the Gaols, Penal Establishments and Lock-ups of the Colony of Queensland, 1887.

90. Lock Hospital or Lock-up

These Regulations suggest that the women admitted to Lock Hospitals were more prisoners than patients. The regime of the hospital was consistent with the virtual arrest of the women, also provided for in the Regulations: "That women found to be suffering from contagious disease shall be sent from the examining room in town to the Hospital in the Police Van: and it shall be the duty of the Police to see that this is done without delay — no woman being allowed to return home prior to her removal in the van."

The Patients:
1. All patients not confined to bed to rise at 6 a m. summer
                                            6.30 a m. winter
2. Beds to be made before breakfast.
3. Breakfast at 8 a m. Dinner 1 p m. Tea at 6 p m.
4. Wards and rooms to be cleaned and swept throughout before 10 a m.
5. All patients to occupy themselves with needlework or any other work for which they are considered fit by the Dr.
6. Each patient to take her turn as Cook for the day.
7. Bathroom & closets to be scrubbed every day.
8. No patient shall behave with disrespect to the Matron or Dr. or any authorised visitor, nor use bad language of any kind.
9. Any patient breaking any of the Regulations to be visited with one of the following penalties
    1. Solitary Confinement.
    2. Low diet. Bread & Water.
    3. Removal to lockup.

Regulations of the Lock Hospital, Brisbane, 1885.

91. Discriminatory and Ineffective Legislation

In her deposition, this young girl named the man whom she alleged infected her with syphilis. Similar testimony by a man about a woman would result in her compulsory examination and, if infected, detention in a Lock Hospital, but the Contagious Diseases Act did not recognize that men also transmitted the disease.

My name is Minnie [C——], and I am aged 14 years; I am at present at inmate of the Contagious Diseases Hospital at the Cascades; in December last I was at service with Mr. Priest New Town; during the time I was here I became acquainted with Maurice [B——], and on or about Boxing Day I had connection with him, and also on the night before the New Year. I never had connection with any other man before Maurice [B——]; I remained in the service of Mr. Priest until March of this year, when I left and became a servant at Glock's Derwent Hotel, Hobart. While at service here I became acquainted with James [W——], and had connection with him on the Queen's Domain on more than one occasion — on my first connection with him I got the disease, but was not aware until a fortnight or so afterwards when I happened to meet Hugh [O'R——] who said, he knew [W——] had the disease and that I must have it, he knowing I had been with him — I had also connection with Dick [J———], James [G——], and George [B——] but not until I had received the disease from [W——] — I informed my sister Fanny [C——] who is a domestic servant with Mr. Lovett, Sandy Bay, and was advised by her to apply for admission to the C.D. Hospital — I followed her advice and she accompanied me to the Hospital, and I was admitted by the Lady Superintendent. About the end of April I met [W——] at New Town who asked me if it was true I had informed Dick [J——] that he [W——] had given me the disease: this I denied having mentioned it to no one, as even then I was not aware I had the disease: he said he had had the disease but he was "all right now". I had connection with him on this occasion: about a week after this I knew for certain I had the disease — I am quite positive [W——] gave me the disease.

Minnie C., deposition to the Hobart Police, 1893.

92. Foreshortened Childhood

The Lock Hospital at Cascades, Hobart, was intended to treat women defined as "common prostitutes" by the Contagious Diseases Act. This correspondence indicates that venereal disease was not confined to prostitutes or to grown women.

Sir,
  I have the honour to bring under your notice that on the 10th inst., at Police Office Devonport, a child named Barbara [W——] or [R——], aged 10 years, was committed to this Department as a Neglected Child. Upon committal she was found to be suffering from Gonorrhoea and it has been necessary to send her to the C.D. Hospital, Cascades, where she is now located.

Secretary, Department of Neglected Children, New Town (Tas.), to the Commissioner of Police, Hobart, 18 January 1900.

Sir,
  Re attached correspondence the girl Barbara [W——] or [R——], arrived here on the 22nd December 1899 in company with Thomas Harper and Angelina Battle (tramps) on the morning of the 26th of December, the girl reported that a rape had been committed on her the previous night. On being examined by Doctor Smith it was then discovered she was suffering from "Gonorrhoea". I at once asked her

where and from whom she contracted the disease, she either did not know or would
not tell me. After some hesitation she said it was a boy who had intercourse with her
near Deloraine some time ago — on being questioned as to who the boy was, she said
she did not know his name, and could give no description of him. I asked her several
times while she was here waiting to go to Hobart, but could get nothing further from
her. She could not have contracted the disease here, as they were only 4 days in the
District before she was examined by the Doctor, and he stated the girl must have had
the disease on her over a fortnight.

Superintendent of Police, Devonport (Tas.), to the Commissioner of Police, Hobart, 23 January 1900.

93. Triumph of the Moralists

In this address to the National Council of Women, Rose Scott applauds the venereal
disease provisions of the Western Australian Health Act of 1915, particularly
because they applied equally to both sexes and thereby, she argued, repudiated the
double moral standard behind earlier contagious diseases legislation. However, the
informant's clause within the Act was later to be severely criticized by the Women's
Service Guilds of Western Australia. The clause, they maintained, was invoked to
the disadvantage of women.

... the conclusion arrived at by the majority of medical men is that as usual
Prevention is even better than cure and that women and men must be treated alike —
not only in the matter of *cure* but in that of Prevention also. The evil and lax belief
that sins *against women* were necessary for the Health of Men — has been contra-
dicted ever since the Brussells Conference — but there is more light, more discussion, more earnest desire to face the truth. And the truth really is as Josephine
Butler [leader of the movement against the English Contagious Diseases Acts] said
so long ago — that morality and science must always eventually agree — and so in this
terrible disease. That is the triumph of the moralists. Science has taken up the
teaching of morality — and insists that this evil is not necessary, on the contrary it is a
menace to any Nation and the loathsome C.D. Acts are a great deal worse than useless — The disease has taken such hold upon Humanity at large that nothing but
drastic measures can avail so far as cure is concerned. Western Australia has set us an
example and has an Act in force which though drastic is wise and humane. It insists
on *secrecy* and does not regard the diseases as a crime, since so many innocent people
are victims. The working of this Act is under the Board of Health not the Police —
and People who have the disease are compelled to undergo treatment till they are
cured and no one but a medical practitioner is allowed to heal such sufferers. A letter
from Mrs Cowan, the President of the NC of W in Perth tells me that the Act is
working well. There is strong protection for innocent people against blackmail and
she considers that what is going to be the most valuable help in stamping out these
diseases, is the way men and women, young and old, are now discussing them openly
and in the spirit that the subject is a high one in as much as it relates to *Life* at its
sources. The need for self control is being pressed on men by medical men on all
sides, and they actually had a lecture by Dr Blatchall to a mixed audience at the University. Any one can get a copy of this Act by writing to the Government Printing
depot Perth — they cost about 1/- each.

I feel that if we as a N.C. of W. are to ask for such an Act that we should also study the question from all sides (this question which has a very great interest to us seeing that its evils so seriously affect women and little children). Hence I wrote to Professor Anderson Stuart [Professor of Medicine, University of Sydney] both on our account and also for Mrs Cowan's information as to the effect of the Free treatment at Prince Alfred Hospital. Sir Thomas says a report will be ready in a months time, it is now being prepared, and then he will communicate with me — meantime the Medical Superintendent Dr Clayton has kindly written to say that he is of the opinion that the West Australian Act is a wise one.

Then I have received through the courtesy of Dr Cumpston [later Commonwealth Director-General of Public Health] in Melbourne a Report from Melbourne which is most enlightening — the result of the Federal enquiry into this matter. He shows that 1000s of lives are lost in Australia every year by this disease, that an immense amount of sickness and inefficiency is caused by it and that the *misery entailed* is terrible. The Federal commission considers the W.A. Act "a well considered endeavour to enforce the provisions they recommended" and they commend it to the careful study of all interested. This commission urges all legislation and regulations re the sale of alcohol should be carefully reconsidered as alcohol not only diminishes self restraints but it is believed that *resistance to infection* is diminished by alcohol — a checked disease is lit up afresh by alcohol — and many of the most awful cases of the nerve centres are partly conditioned by alcoholic excess.

Rose Scott, handwritten and undated address.

94. "They Blame the Woman for It"

When questioned on his attitude to the exchange of health certificates before marriage, the medical officer in charge of the venereal clinic at Sydney's Royal Prince Alfred Hospital responded:

It would be a good thing in the case of a man, more so than in the case of the girl. I think the man is more the cause of the spread of the disease than the girl. Most men look upon it as a woman's disease; they think it is effeminate to get it. They blame the woman for it. They really think it is her fault if they get it; that is they think it is inherent in the woman and they get it from her. The husband is more readily cured than the wife, and he blames the wife for not getting cured, although he has given it to her in the first place.

Testimony given by Gordon Wolsely Bray to the N.S.W. Select Committee on Prevention of Venereal Disease, 1915.

95. The Control of Prostitutes

The New South Wales Venereal Diseases Act of 1918 did not succeed in eradicating venereal disease, and here the Director of the Venereal Diseases Division of the N.S.W. Department of Public Health considers other measures. It is noteworthy that he does not take account of the role of men in spreading venereal disease.

The control of prostitutes is a problem which has engaged the attention of all nations and all times. They certainly exist in large numbers both professional and amateur. I have no scheme for their extinction. There is a demand for their services and supply will fluctuate according to that demand. I believe that as long as the human race lasts, there will be prostitutes who will ply for hire either openly or in secret, according to the conditions of the age in which they live. We can only hope to attempt to control their activities and to offer prophylactic facilities to those who have been their clients. A "red light" district is a menace to a city, although in a way that city benefits to a certain degree by having the women removed from the streets. A "red light" district is frankly a part of a city or town in which the use of a woman's body is for hire with the consent of the citizens. We could certainly establish prophylactic facilities in each brothel and so possibly minimise the risks of infection, but the idea is not a pleasant one. The examination of prostitutes at regular intervals is not a satisfactory procedure and is open to many objections. The control of prostitution by legal provision has never been satisfactory and nations which have sanctioned licensed prostitution for centuries, are still searching for effective measures of control. Unfortunately disease is only too frequently spread by the amateur and the professional prostitute is frequently blamed for more than she is responsible for.

I am in favour of keeping prostitutes moving. Those who are infected, might be sent to homes especially established in the country and there detained until cured or non-infective. Those prostitutes who are free from disease and who desire to become normal women, should be given an opportunity of learning a trade, again in a home in the country.

The young girl who through no fault of her own finds herself out of employment and penniless should become the concern of the State and provision should be made for her. I do not see how we can hope to reach the amateur except by education. Usually she is a girl in employment or who lives at home in comfortable circumstances.

J. Cooper Booth, "Venereal Disease Control in New South Wales and Some Suggestions for Its Improvement", *Transactions of the Australasian Medical Congress* (1929).

96. National Security Regulations: Evenhanded or Discriminatory?

Through the National Security (Venereal Diseases and Contraceptives) Regulations of September 1942, the Commonwealth entered the fight against venereal disease. These Regulations gave increased powers to the Chief Health Officers of the states, to compel those suspected of having venereal disease to present themselves for treatment and to issue a warrant for their arrest if they disobeyed the order. An informant's clause protected the privacy of the informant and ensured that all notifications of venereal disease received in this way would be followed up. It was claimed that these Regulations applied equally to men and women. The following account of the operation of the Regulations in Victoria undermines this claim.

Dear Madam,

Following our conversation today regarding the treatment in this state of women found to be suffering from Venereal Disease, allow me to summarise the points mentioned in our discussion.

Men or women infected with V.D. who place themselves under medical care are reported to this Department by number only. If they carry out the actions of the Doctor no Departmental action is taken. If they default from medical treatment they receive a registered letter or personal call in which they are ordered to resume treatment. If they disobey that they are liable to be detained for treatment in what is known in Victoria as "an appointed place". Appointed places in this State include gaol hospitals and an institution known as Fairhaven Venereal Diseases Hospital (accommodation 60 beds) for Women which is conducted by the Mission of St James and St John (Church of England). This institution has been built and equipped by the State and the whole cost of maintenance is met by the State.

Women who are known to the police as professional prostitutes or those women who, while under treatment, are seen constantly frequenting hotel lounges or consorting with Australian or Allied Servicemen, are by order compulsorily detained at Fairhaven.

Women whose names have been reported as infecting Australian or allied servicemen are in most cases warned or, if well known to the Vice Squad, are also detained until a certificate of cure is given.

Many women who have been reported as infecting servicemen are persuaded to submit themselves for examination, and if found infected are recommended to sign a form for voluntary admission to Fairhaven, promising to remain there until officially released. The only women sent to the gaol hospital are those who have a record of being violent or who have escaped from Fairhaven.

The treatment at Fairhaven is carried out by trained nurses and the State Director of Venereal Diseases visits the institution twice a week to carry out treatment.

All women who are ordered to submit to a compulsory examination are given the option of being examined by a woman specialist in her private consulting rooms, or at the Queen Victoria Hospital for women. A fee of one guinea is paid to either the private consultant or the public hospital for this service.

Director(?), Victorian Public Health Department, Melbourne, to Secretary, United Associations of Women, 22 May 1944.

97. "The Health of the Troops is the Paramount Consideration"

This document, pleading for more police control over women suspected of having venereal disease, shows the continuing link between the health of the armed services and venereal diseases legislation.

The question of the notification and reporting of cases where persons, either male or female, suffering from V.D. has been giving this Department and its Officers very grave concern, particularly in the present condition of affairs, owing to the number of Armed Forces in our midst — both local troops, and those overseas.

In making these comments it is to be borne in mind that the health of the troops is the paramount consideration, and anything that can be done to preserve that health must be given priority over any considerations of the feelings of the individual concerned, or of any organizations, such as Women's Service Guilds, Social Purity Leagues or kindred bodies.

In cases that have come under the notice of the Police it is found that the Police encounter difficulty in bringing the matter under the notice of those concerned in administering the provisions of the Health Act dealing with the treatment of V.D., and in a number of cases have been taken to task for their actions which have been solely prompted with a desire for the welfare of the community, and the infected individual.

It is recognised that, when the Bill was before Parliament, it was the desire, as shewn in the clauses of the Bill, that the Police should not in any way have anything to do with such cases, but it could not be foreseen the condition of affairs as they exist today.

Some young women, as must be apparent to anybody with a knowledge of affairs, have apparently lost control of themselves to such an extent that they are attracted by a uniform, and parade the streets of an evening until they link up with a man wearing the uniform of the A.I.F. or the U.S. The condition of the air raid trenches in the parks around the city and suburbs, when an inspection is made of them each morning, is such as to cause concern regarding the morality, or lack of same, of those frequenting same.

The attitude of the Health Department is that a person infected should complain to the Commissioner of Public Health that he has contracted V.D. from a certain person, and the Commissioner would then arrange for the examination of the latter. This procedure may be alright in normal times, but these are not normal times. Troops are on the move, and infection would not show until possibly some time after a body of troops have left, whereas I am desirous of steps being taken to prevent or minimise the risk of infecting.

I am forwarding herewith this Department's file which contains reference to several cases which have come under notice, and also the files regarding individual cases. Reference to these will show the difficulty that is experienced.

In the circumstances, and with a good knowledge of the position, I would recommend that the provisions of the Health Act be so administered during the present abnormal times to permit of members of the Police Force making reference to the possibility of individuals charged in Court of being infected with V.D., and to permit of the Magistrate ordering an examination. If such could be made legal by an order under the National Security Act, and possibly the Hon. Premier has such deputed power, there is not doubt it would be beneficial.

Commissioner of Police, W.A., to the Minister for Police, W.A., 23 March 1942.

98. "We should Direct Our Attention to the Seducers"

In one of the many letters the United Associations of Women wrote in protest against the operation of the National Security Regulations, which they said legitimated the apprehension of girls for the protection of men, Jessie Street argued for the inversion of the procedure.

It is time that we paused and took stock of our national health and of our moral standards. What are we doing to protect our young girls? Hundreds of them have been seduced and infected with disease. Many have had abortions performed, many are about to become mothers, many have been arrested and committed to houses and homes of detention; and horror upon horrors, as soon as one lot of girls are removed from the streets another lot are sucked into the cesspool of vice.

Why is this evil allowed to flourish in our midst? Why are the flower of our young womanhood, the future mothers of Australia, allowed to be debauched and diseased? One reason is that instead of trying to stamp out immorality and disease, those in control have tried to make sex indulgence safe. Never in history has there been any safe way of indulging promiscuously in sex. Immorality and disease go hand in hand. There is only one way of avoiding disease and it is an infallible preventive, and that is chastity.

Instead of persecuting and humiliating and terrorising the silly children who are lured by the blandishments and the uniforms and the cash of those who seduce and infect them, we should direct our attention to the seducers. We have a law in Australia that provides severe penalties for the carnal knowledge of a girl under 16, with or without her consent. Instead of raiding residentials and only detaining the girls, let the men found with the girls be detained and charged and brought before the courts.

I have been to a number of meetings lately where men have spoken of the spread of Venereal Disease and immorality, and almost without exception they have blamed the girls for spreading the disease and spoken of the need to protect the men.

Where is the man's sense of justice, of chivalry, where is his common sense? Can a man of 20-40 years of age require protection against girls of 13-20? Can he be overpowered and assaulted by these girls? The blame for the seduction of girls and the spread of disease must be placed where it belongs and that is on the shoulders of the men concerned. Any man found in bed or in compromising circumstances with a young girl should be detained and prosecuted.

It is time that the facts were faced. It must be recognised that a certain number of men are debauchers and perverts. While these men are at large they will continue to seduce and debauch our girls and to poison and destroy the springs of Australia's life. They are a greater enemy in our midst than a small-pox contact or a forger, or a thief, or a murderer. They must be removed from society. It is the only way.

The laws of supply and demand require this approach and our recent experience in Australia has shown that this law applies to the traffic in sex indulgence as surely as it does to trade in general. Remove those who create the demand and the supply will not be called into being. Our girls only want to have a little fun and excitement. No doubt they are often silly and ignorant — but they are not bad and they are not diseased until they have been seduced and infected by some man.

Jessie M. G. Street, Letter to the Editor, *Daily Telegraph*, 18 May 1943.

99. "Their Most Piercing Sin is Their Lack of Self-respect"

Elizabeth Griffiths of the United Associations of Women responds to suggestions by the Director of Social Hygiene that the penalties against recidivist female venereal disease sufferers should be harsher:

Dr Cooper Booth's suggestion that the heads of persistently vicious girls should be shaved is not new. Public contempt has always been the portion of the female purveyor of sexual vice. But ridicule will not reform these girls. Their fault is not in thinking too much of themselves, but of thinking too little. Their most piercing sin is their lack of self-respect. Any action calculated to further impair their human dignity would diminish their faith in themselves, without which they cannot be redeemed.

Elizabeth Griffiths, Letter to the Editor, *Sydney Morning Herald*, 21 July 1944.

100. The American Invasion and Venereal Disease

An extract from Kylie Tennant's novel *Tell Morning This* discloses a little-discussed consequence of the protection and presence of "our great and powerful ally" during the Second World War.

What had really attracted attention to Nonnie's Conference was the great Syphilis Scare. After the first hysterical outburst, the Department's [Moral Rehabilitation i.e. Social Welfare] policy was to tighten up by having any girls seen with Americans arrested, unless they could prove they were working, and to haul them off for a venereal disease test. Naturally it would have meant complications to arrest the men, but the authorities made things hard for the girls; and public opinion was vicious in its gloating over the wholesale corruption supposedly existent in the war-soiled city.

In the better brothels, the conversation ran with virtuous disapproval on the need for "cleaning up" these crazy kids who "didn't know how to take care of themselves". The homebred soldiery, who had been snubbed because they couldn't jitterbug, got their own back by sneering that the only thing a man could do was to find a well-seasoned whore of about forty-five, wait four years after the war, and then marry a girl of seventeen, thereby avoiding the venereal vintage. When a high-ranking American provost complained to the chief of the Australian vice-squad that he didn't know what the hell everyone was shooting off their mouths about, the vice-squad chief responded coldly, "Every night my men are pulling kids out of bed with your men — kids that aren't a day over thirteen. We don't like it. At least Australians don't sleep with babies."

There had been in the first days of the American invasion such tremendous jubilance, such admiration, such an exultant rushing forward to take the hand of the deliverers. But in that outstretched hand was a sheaf of dollar bills, and the deliverer merely drawled: "Well, at that price we'll take all you've got." A certain revulsion was noticeable.

Kylie Tennant, *Tell Morning This* (1967).

101. Venereal Disease: A Survey of Legislation

Feminist organizations in Australia had a long tradition of vigilant opposition to veneral disease legislation that discriminated against women. In this pamphlet, Ada Bromham of the Women's Service Guilds of Western Australia and the National W.C.T.U. demonstrates that state legislation and the National Security Regulations denied women equality before the law.

AUSTRALIA

What of the Australian Position?

Previous to the enactment of the National Security Regulations by the Federal Government in 1942, laws relating to V.D. were a State responsibility and will become so again in 1947 when the Regulations lapse.

SOUTH AUSTRALIA. — South Australia is the only State that has never enacted legislation for the control of V.D., yet the incidence has been lower than in any of the states under review and is decreasing. A sharp drop was reported in 1945-6. Some of the reasons given by an officer of the Central Board of Health, S.A., are improved methods of treatment which have induced more confidence in patients, opportunity extended to women for free, private and confidential examinations by appointment, greater co-operation from patients.

QUEENSLAND. — In Queensland the laws are similar to the old Contagious Diseases Acts which were repealed in the other parts of the Empire many years ago. They include notification by anonymous informers, compulsory examination of suspects and detention of patients in lock hospitals or prison wards. Another serious feature is the admission of the existence of tolerated brothels and the recognition of prostitution, by regulations requiring the periodic examination of women known to be leading irregular lives, on the assumption that it lessened the risk of promiscuous men contracting V.D. That this is misleading and dangerous is shown by the evidence given at the Royal Commission on Health in 1925. The then Commissioner of Public Health, Sir John Irwin said, "There is no guarantee that a woman examined at 9 o'clock in the morning will be free from V.D. at 9 o'clock that night." Yet the Queensland Government continues to sanction this infamous system, and 2,471 such examinations for V.D. were made by the Health Department during 1944-45. Whatever form of State Regulation is in operation, the incidence of the disease rises and it is not surprising that the present Director of General Health now states: "The menace for Queensland is not the professional prostitute, it is the amateur woman." Fear of gaol conditions had driven the problem underground. The failure of compulsory measures is further confirmed in the Queensland Health Report, 1944, under the heading "Sources of infection," we read: "Unfortunately too few of the notifications state the sources of infection so that the respective parts played by the professional and the amateur cannot be accurately estimated . . . the following table is given for what it is worth." The table mentioned shows that of 858 persons examined, in 681 cases the source of contact was unknown or unstated. This exposes the fallacy of "effective control" of V.D. in Queensland under out-moded laws.

VICTORIA. — Victoria has had compulsory notification since 1921. As is usually the case, the authorities considered it necessary to secure more power and in 1940 the police laws were amended to allow them to deal more drastically with women known as "common postitutes"; later these powers were again widened to cover the detention of girls arrested on vagrancy charges. The legality of forcing persons suspected of suffering from V.D. into the Crimes category is open to question, and is a gross infringement of democratic rights. From a social point of view it is tragic and defeats its own ends.

WESTERN AUSTRALIA. — In Western Australia control of V.D. has operated in much the same way as in Victoria. Girls may be reported on suspicion by anonymous informers, forced to be examined and if infected may be detained indefinitely. If free from disease they have no redress. The law makes brothels illegal but a red light district in the centre of Perth openly caters for promiscuous patrons. The latest figures available show an increase in new cases of V.D. Since 1939, statistics have not been made public, so we can assume the position has not improved.

NEW SOUTH WALES. — The Director of Health in New South Wales has had the right under the State laws to examine, forcibly, if necessary, a person if he has *"evidence"* that he or she is a known source of infection, but for some years the Department has been working under the more drastic powers conferred by the National Security Regulations, 1942, which gave the Director of Health the right to order any person for examination if he was satisfied that there were *"reasonable grounds"* for suspecting that such person was affected with V.D. Police Vice Squads have been widely used in N.S.W. and other states to enforce this legislation. In country centres the Medical Officer may report a suspect to the nearest police officer or magistrate, who may exercise all the powers and functions of the Chief Health Officer, excepting that the suspected person may not be detained for any period longer that six weeks. Responsible police officers agree that it would be difficult to define "reasonable suspicion", and that over-zealous officers might embarrass innocent women. Clause 10 of Regulations carefully protects all who administer them when wrong action is taken.

This legislation is unjust and undemocratic. It creates and protects the informer. The accused person has no right of redress. The name of the accuser is guarded with secrecy by the authorities. The National Health Council has recognized its dangers and made the following recommendation at a meeting in May, 1943, "That the Commonwealth Government should be asked to consider amendments to the 'V.D. and Contraceptive Regulations' to protect persons against false declarations." Nothing has been done about this recommendation.

The position of women. — During the war years these compulsory measures have been used mainly against girls and women. Adolescent girls have been drawn into the police dragnet of a gaol environment and emerge with a social stigma attached, and an experience that does not help them to a better way of life. Many lose their employment, have family difficulties and go down-hill to swell the underworld. Thousands of women have been reported, forced to be examined and found to be free of V.D. Official figures from the N.S.W. Health Department support this statement. In one year 2,000 women and girls were notified on suspicion, three hundred names had to be discarded on account of inaccurate information, and of the remaining 1,700 one in every three was free from the disease; 886 were wrongly accused.

Since then the position has deteriorated and it is officially stated that in 1945-46 there was a large increase in V.D.; the position as far as women is concerned is serious; 6,208 women were reported on suspicion and 38.6 per cent were not infected.

Ada Bromham, *V.D. Legislation: How It Works* (n.d., c. 1946).

102. For Women Only

Until the mid-1950s, prostitutes in Queensland were registered and compelled to present themselves for periodical examination.

When we were living in Cairns N.Q. some years ago I had a great friend who visited her sick Father in the Public Hospital regularly — one day she was sitting waiting there when in trouped a lot of handsomely dressed women, who queued up before one of the Dr's private doors. She saw they were not "Patients" and wondered what they were there for lined up each waiting her turn to go in. Later she enquired from someone and was told they were the cities "Prostitutes" who were *forced* by law each week to present themselves for examination to see if they were free from "V.D." . . . what a humiliating experience — for *women* only!

Letter from Mabel Critchley to Mrs Scrimgeour of the United Associations of Women, who were conducting an inquiry into prostitution, 7 October 1952.

103. "Very Few Women Can Get a Home for Themselves"

Elizabeth Griffiths, representing the United Associations of Women, gave this testimony to the 1946 Parliamentary Standing Committee on Broadcasting. Her principal task was to convince the Committee that the broadcasting of talks on venereal disease could play an important part in combating the spread of the disease, but she widened the field of discussion by tracing the causes of venereal disease to women's social and economic inequality.

This Committee's invitation to us to give evidence mentioned the subject of sex relationships. I gather that the Committee is concerned really with broadcast talks on sexual relationships. However, on the wider subject of sex relationships involving economic and social relationships as distinct from the biological aspect, we should like to stress certain points. As a society we believe in sex equality, and we believe that when we attain that objective we shall effectively combat these social diseases. We regard venereal disease as a disease of sexual promiscuity, but we regard venereal disease not as a cause but a symptom, and we are emphatic that the causes of sexual promiscuity should first be tackled. We believe in the Christian ethic of the essential worth of the individual. We believe in liberty as interpreted by a speaker at the Religion and Life Conference the other day, namely: "Freedom from external tyranny and oppression, and a capacity for self-discipline." We do not think that the quality of self-respect, which leads to self-discipline is developed by the prevailing attitude towards women. In regard to women, the emphasis is on the biological and recreational function, and the fact that women are creatures of brain, mind and spirit, is largely ignored. That is not conducive to self-respect among women. Although we live in a democracy, very few women have the freedom to obtain the things they need for themselves; they are always dependent upon somebody else. All women are told right from the beginning that they must have a "home of their own". They will have no security or status unless they have a home; but very few women can get a home for themselves. They can't earn sufficient. They can get it only through a man. A single woman with independent means can get a home, and therefore she acquires a good status. But there are very few such women, particularly among working women. On the other hand, a working man can get a home. He does not need to be very successful. A male shop assistant, if he gets tired of living in a boarding house can afford to obtain a flat or a little cottage. He doesn't have to wait until he is married; but a female shop assistant can't obtain a home because she cannot afford it. She must always live in someone else's house. Indeed, she is lucky if she does not have to share a room. But there is no little house or garden for her. All her training and tradition has told her that she must have a home; but in herself she has not the economic value to obtain a home. Her only chance is to induce some man to marry her and give her a home. She must make herself attractive enough to get that offer. Therefore she has to be pretty and smart and charming. That is of primary import- ance. If the development of her mind or spirit detracts from what is the feminine standard of the day — and the theory is that it does — then her mental and spiritual qualities must be dropped, or at least disguised. That is the external tyranny which denies to women liberty and self-respect. Even after she marries, and after she has done all that she is expected to do, and our society is arranged to urge her to do, she must still live through someone else. Her husband earns the money and she is dependent upon him. The law insists on his keeping and clothing her; but there is no legal provision for a wage for her. Now, would any man be satisfied with those terms? A man walks the earth with dignity when he does his work and takes his wages. Most married couples make happy arrangements, but that does not alter the fact that the wife is dependent upon the goodwill of the husband. Sometimes the association is very painful; and the state of being dependent, as every man knows, is not conducive to self-respect. Let us now consider the position in relation to young girls, particularly those of the classes which are causing much trouble at present in the sphere of social diseases. We find the same limitations. The girls cannot get the things they want themselves. Every girl, be she a princess or a factory girl, likes pretty clothes, scents, flowers and personal adornment. However they don't earn enough, but every book they read, every picture they see, and every advertisement assures them that the girl who has these things gets all the joy, romance and adventure. The ideal of woman- hood that is held before them is the glamorous creature with an elaborate hair-do, with a cigarette in one hand, a glass of something alcoholic in the other, gorgeous clothes, and a crowd of adoring men around her. Actually, nothing else is worthwhile; no counter attraction is offered. Thus these girls feel that they must have these fripperies. They can't buy them themselves, so they must get them from men, who always have more money than they have. Very often they get them for nothing. Sometimes they have to pay for them in their own currency. Of course, their self- respect should forbid them to do so, but self-respect and faith in themselves have not been cultivated in the feminine sex. We believe that in order to put the relations between the sexes on a healthier and more civilised basis, men should be taught to look for something more than a biological or recreational interest in women; and women should be given the confidence to develop and reveal true qualities of heart and mind instead of the miserable travesty of themselves which they have been taught to believe men expect. Radio is a medium for education along these lines. Talks should be given, necessarily by sympathetic and gifted speakers, to young people, who are naturally thirsting for romance and adventure, art, and music, to describe the adventure of science, and the excitement of making, and doing, and of overcoming obstacles, always with the idea of combating that sense of boredom and futility which so far has only found an outlet in sex excitement. In view of the unusual activities of many women during the war, the present is a most favourable opportunity for putting forward claims for the abilities of women. We believe that a great service can be done by improving the relations between the sexes, if talks are given now to show that the exploits of women during the war are normal. Such talks should show what should be expected of women, and what should continue to be expected of women, in order to build up a public opinion that women are fully com- petent human beings. I repeat that the surest deterrent to the social diseases of our time is the encouragement of greater understanding and respect between the sexes. We believe that the term sex relationships involves more than merely sexual relation- ships . . .

We agree that talks on venereal disease should be broadcast. . . .

We say that one of the means of eliminating the causes of venereal disease would be to give to women a higher status and greater dignity. If that were done women would not be so amenable to suggestions which are primarily the cause of social diseases. . . .

We believe that talks on venereal disease should be given over the air, and we are content to leave the handling of such talks to competent people. . . .

We say that by raising the status of women the conditions primarily responsible for social diseases would be greatly eliminated.

Evidence of Mrs Elizabeth Griffiths to the Parliamentary Standing Committee on Broadcasting, 1945.

Family and Motherhood

104. "The Women Have to Do the Work"

Australian historians have devoted a lot of attention to the male communities that were one of the features of a frontier society. Here Caroline Emily Clark describes the essentially female community of Adelaide during the gold-rushes of the early 1850s.

Sunday Dec. 14 ... We hear nothing but gold, gold, gold. People are leaving by hundreds and houses and land are being sold for half their value. Trade is very bad, shop keepers are in despair and people stand talking in the streets instead of going about their business. Fifty men went from Kensington alone last week and there are no less than twelve vessels advertised for Melbourne. The Government has offered £1000 for the discovery of gold here and today the children went out on a gold hunting expedition with a tin can and a spade. When they returned I asked Mary (aged 5) if they had found any gold "no" she said, "but we have found some yellow ochre". She is quite sure she will find gold and has already decided how she will lay out the thousand pounds.

Our grocer came here today to ask advice of Papa. He told us that in Norwood where he lives, and where there are three streets, there are but five men left, he being one of the five. He wishes to go to the diggings himself leaving his business for his wife to manage for it is so small now that he is in despair. Norwood is quite a village, there are rows of houses and a few weeks ago it was quite a busy place ...

Friday. It has been a hot day the thermometer at 90° in the shade. In the afternoon I walked to town to make some purchases, not a pleasant walk in such weather ... I found the town less deserted than I had imagined. There are a great many houses to let and the side streets have a forlorn look. Everyone talked about gold and I saw many shops where people were selling off, "Going to the Diggings" and other notices. "Gold purchased to any amount" etc. but altogether I found the place more cheerful than I expected. There was beautiful fruit in the shops, strawberries, cherries, goosberries, plums, and apricots ...

Dec. 30th. ... I heard of a certain Mrs Brown who keeps a bookseller's shop. The gold mania has destroyed her business, her husband went to the diggings in the hope of earning enough to meet a bill which will become due in a few days. He has sent the gold, Mrs Brown showed Howard two ounces in a lucifer match box as a sample but she cannot sell it, the banks having refused to advance money upon Melbourne gold as there is more in the market than individuals can purchase. Papa wants to buy some but he cannot get paid for his goods, the utter loss of business here is woeful and the scarcity of ready money. In the shops we are offered a reel of cotton or a packet of pins instead of small change and at the Post office Sidney laid down sixpence to pay for a fourpenny letter and after waiting for a few minutes asked for his twopence "we've no change" said the clerk, "you can take a pipe if you like", pointing to a heap of white clays upon the counter ...

Jan. 7th. 1852. Mr Greenway called to tell Papa that he had made up his mind to go to Melbourne, he cannot get enough to live upon now his customers are gone. He lives in Norwood and is one of the four men left . . .

March 18th. Sidney, Howard and I dined at Benwell, Mr Catcheside's, we brought Rosa back with us, she has had a very happy visit and I hope she is stronger but she still looks pale and thin. We have had a very pleasant day wandering about the garden and sitting under the verandah talking to our kind hostesses. The Miss Catchesides have been drying raisins and some excellent currants, they tried figs but without success. They are fearless independent girls, they have killed many snakes, they entirely manage the garden, horses, cows, and poultry. The other day they wanted wood, Rosa says they harnessed the horse to the cart and collected fallen branches in the paddock. They mow lucerne for the animals and when their brother was gathering his corn they each reaped for five hours every day. When most of the men have left the country the women have to do the work.

Caroline Emily Clark, "Memoirs" (1851).

105. Wanted — a Wife

The *Matrimonial Chronicle* published articles on various aspects of marriage, and as well, ran a column for those seeking marriage partners. A notable feature of many of the advertisements was the importance placed on the wife's contribution to the operation of the farm or business.

— Wanted a wife by a young man in the country, with a house and £500 a year.

— Wanted a Catholic husband by a servant girl 16 years old, and has saved £200. She is not very good looking, but I defy anybody to be a better cook or housekeeper.

— If I can get a suitable partner I would like to get married, but if I cannot I would sooner stop single. I am 18 years of age, good looking, fair hair, light blue eyes, tall, thin, am a good scholar, can talk French, draw, play the piano and sing well. If I get a husband he must be good looking, with a long dark beard, he must be fond of amusements, and take me to all the parties and balls that we can go to, and he must live in Sydney or Newcastle, and always dress well, I believe in enjoying this world while I am in it; I don't care what anybody says.

— Wanted a wife who can work; by a selector in the Manora district. He has a large amount of land and sheep.

— A lady 43 years of age would like to correspond with a healthy middle aged man, he must be a member of the Church of England.

— Wanted a Wife. A stipendiary of middle age, and unsullied reputation, wants a woman healthy and of mature years, say 50 or upwards.

— A young gentleman has decided to marry the first respectable young lady that offers, if any applies to this advertisement.

— Wanted a wife by a young man in Queensland. He has a comfortable business of his own, he is six feet high and light complexion, his age is 36, he will be in

Sydney shortly on a visit. The lady must be well able to read and write, so that she can assist him in his business.

Matrimonial Chronicle, July-October, 1879.

106. A Common Case

The bush wife, as Miles Franklin illustrates here, was expected to do general farm work, as well as her conventional tasks of housekeeping and child-raising.

Jim Ryan came all the way to Brogan's Gap from Duck Flat to court Polly Sweeney. Polly had many admirers for her eyes were bright and dark and the fame of her cookery and industry had gone abroad. More than all her admirers Polly favoured Jim, but her father liked him least and spoke of him thus — "He's a sneakin' lazy divil and its the pretty husband the gu-r-r-l that gits him 'll hev."

Polly differed from her father in opinion — girls and fathers mostly do in the matter of sweethearts.

Old Sweeney was over forty and not to be caught with chaff, but Polly's seventeen summers were not proof against the glory of Jim's tight check trousers and gaudy, heavily scented silk handkerchiefs, to say nothing of his green and scarlet neck ties and wonderful pipes.

Old Sweeney would have liked to see Polly the wife of Dan Bennett and continually sang his praises in her ears, but the length of Jim's spurs eclipsed all this wooer's chances in the first act.

Things went on till Jim proposed and Polly accepted and assured her father that if she could not have Jim she would die. Old Sweeney humphed rather cynically on receipt of this information but resolved "to let 'em rip" on condition that Jim started in life on his own account. Consequently he "selected" out at Duck Flat on the Jinnenah Run, and took his cheery little bride home to a two-roomed, bark-roofed residence, with a ground floor, possessing one door in the front one big chimney at the end and two little windows at the back. Duck Flat was a lonely hole, the nearest neighbour being a chinaman digger ten miles away. But bless you, Polly was never lonely. She was as busy as a bee and chirpy as a sparrow all day, making wonderful blinds for the crookedly erected little windows, and covers for the rough stools and boxes which with the equally rough table were her principal furniture. Jim was a host in himself to her in the way of company and his wonderful yarns about the horses he had ridden and the great strokes he had done never failed to find an interested audience.

When she had erected hen-houses, made a garden and put all her work behind her, she went out with Jim and helped him split posts, up a lonely gully, for the "improvements" which had to be on their holding within a stipulated time.

Jim had the best-end of the stick as Polly had to do all her own work after returning at nightfall and before setting off in the morning.

When the babies began to arrive in triplets or twins every year until she had five girls and six boys, she had not time to assist Jim, and in mending, poultry rearing, gardening, dairying, cooking and otherwise attending to her family was so much occupied that she felt she must really have a servant, especially as the old two roomed hut with stringy bark and gum trees growing close along side, had been succeeded by a fine large stone house which made a deal of work.

But she never had the nerve to propose such a thing. Jim grumbled so and was ever forcibly impressing upon her that a man had to be very long headed to get on these days when women were good for nothing but pottering around the house whereas his mother and the women of her day, used to be such a fine help to their lords . . .

"A Common Case", unpublished short story by Miles Franklin.

107. Wages for Housewives

In this pamphlet, the Sydney feminist group the United Asociations of Women argues that a wife should be legally entitled to a portion of her husband's income, in payment for her work in the home. The question of payment for housework is still debated by the contemporary women's movement.

Just as working men appreciate the right to their own money, so would wives appreciate a similar right. How can we make it possible for a wife who is working in her own home to have the right to her own money?

Let us here remember the requirements provided for in calculating the basic wage for men. Since 1912 throughout the Commonwealth the male basic wage has been calculated to provide for a man, a wife and a child or children, and so we can say that each man's earnings represent: (a) his wage; (b) the amount paid to him to keep a wife, i.e. marriage endowment; (c) the amount paid to him to keep a child, i.e. child endowment. So since 1912 we have actually had marriage and child endowment in operation in Australia.

It would be quite a simple matter from the point of view of legislation to make wives legally entitled to that portion of the basic wage which is alloted for their keep.

FAMILY WAGE

A fair and reasonable method of giving all married women economic independence would be to recognise marriage as a true and legal partnership. The husband's part as it is at present would be to earn the family income for which the wife makes a home for him and rears a family. The wife's part as it is at present would be to look after the home and bear and rear the family in return for which she would become legally entitled to a share of the family income. At present the wife does her part but is not legally entitled to any share of the family income while she and her husband live together. The wife's share of the family income could be estimated at the amount that the court would order to be paid to her as maintenance should the home be broken up.

THE WIFE AND MOTHER

In the majority of cases this arrangement would make no actual difference. Most husbands treat their wives with both fairness and generosity. An arrangement along the lines suggested would make no difference to these husbands, as they willingly give all they can to their wives — but in a small percentage of cases (which percentage added up makes a large number in the total population) we must all admit that wives do not always get a fair deal.

The fact that the wife was legally entitled to some money would make all the difference to herself and her family and would remove one of the commonest causes of family disagreements.

It is well known that should a wife leave an unsatisfactory husband, then he must pay her maintenance. It does not seem unfair to suggest that she should be legally entitled to the money for her maintenance while she remains with him.

MARRIAGE RELATIONSHIP

Marriage has passed from an act of capture through successive stages to proprietorship, when a wife was classified among a man's possessions along with his house and his ox and his ass. We have now reached the stage when it should be recognised as a true partnership between a man and a woman for their mutual benefit, comfort and service. It is only thus that marriage can reach its highest development which should be a physical, mental and spiritual companionship.

United Associations of Women, *Incomes for Wives: How Can It Be Managed?* (n.d., *c.* 1937).

108. Unmarried Mothers

Frequently, pregnant single women had to rely on the state welfare system for care during their pregnancy and confinement. The lying-in homes had a disciplinary as well as a welfare function, and inmates had to perform washing, sewing and other domestic tasks; and although they were encouraged to place their child for adoption, they were compelled to care for it for six months, for the child was considered a "humanizing influence" on the mother.

FORM OF AGREEMENT OR UNDERTAKING WITH THE DESTITUTE BOARD BY AN INMATE OF THE LYING-IN HOME.

ADELAIDE,_____19 .

I, the undersigned, having applied to the Destitute Board for admission as an inmate of the Lying-in Home, do hereby agree with the said Destitute Board as follows:—

I.   That I will during the period of my residence in the Home fulfil such duties as may be allotted to me by the Matron in the same manner as if engaged for household service under the "Masters and Servants Act of 1878," and will conform to all the regulations laid down for the inmates.

II.   That, on my admission, I will furnish the Board with all particulars requisite for my proper registration on the records, at the same time making declaration as to the paternity of the child of which I am *enceinte*.

III. That, within one month after the birth of my child, I will do all that is necessary to have such child duly registered in the public records, giving it a name, such child always taking my surname.

IV.   That I will remain in the Institution and under the control of the Board until such time as my child shall attain the age of at least six months, or until it is fit to be weaned, and will during the whole of this period suckle my child, unless at any time I or my friends can satisfy the Board that proper provision will be made elsewhere for my well-being and for the careful tending and rearing of my child.

109. Baby Farming

The single mother who kept her child and had to work to support herself often relied on other disadvantaged women for childminding. The childminders were frequently widows or deserted wives with children of their own to support. Time and money were scarce and a high rate of infant morality characterized this form of childminding, which became stigmatized as "baby farming".

Inspector Woodcraft, of the Q.S.P.C. [Queensland Society for the Protection of Children], said he knew Mrs Slater for about seven years, and for the last five years she had been occasionally taking care of infants. He had sent children to her. He had inspected the children, and found them kept very clean. Three had died within the last three months, and in his opinion death was due to want of suitable food. He was not sending her any children now. Mrs Slater was in very poor circumstances. After she took over the child, Ada Hardwick, she showed it to a witness. It was a delicate child. Subsequently he saw the child when it was covered with a dengue rash, which attacked all the children in her house.

Mr Neilson [Magistrate]: When did you come to the conclusion these children were being starved?

Inspector Woodcraft: I didn't say that.

Mr Neilson: You said lack of proper food. We have it here that the child died from malnutrition. Is it in consequence of the woman's poverty that she is unable to get proper food?

Inspector Woodcraft: Yes.

Mr Neilson: I understand that the woman in consequence of her means is unable to procure the food she may desire to give to the children. She may have the desire and not the means.

Inspector Woodcraft said he understood she had not been paid for two of the children for some months.

Mr Neilson: They go away and leave her without means? These people want some remuneration for their trouble. They must be protected, and the sooner the authorities take up the question the better, unless all these children's lives are to be sacrificed.

Margaret Fish, a boarding-house keeper, deposed that the mother of the child had now obtained employment. The child had been refused by the Salvation Army, and by two other parties as it was so delicate . . .

Selina Ann Slater stated she was a married woman, living apart from her husband, in Regent-street, Thompson Estate. She had her three children with her, their ages being 16, 14 and 11 years. Her husband was an engineer, and left witness eleven years ago, in consequence of his ill-health, and went to England. It was seven years since she had heard from him. She had since he left her, been in receipt of Government relief, and had also been taking charge of children to nurse. They had all been illegitimate but two. She had had about sixteen children through her hands; six of them had died, three during the past three months. The last child (who died) was Ada Hardwick, the subject of the present inquiry. Witness received her on 18th November last, and was paid regularly 7s. per week for caring for it. She gave it cow's milk and water. Dr Wield had seen it twice a week, and Dr Webb had also seen it. They had both approved of the feeding. Dr Wield prescribed medicine, which witness had made up at the Children's Hospital, and she gave it as directed. Witness also gave the child tablets, which had been prescribed by Dr Eleanor Bourne. Dr Wield was the last to see the child. She died on the 18th February last. Witness gave the child every attention, and carried out the doctor's instructions to the letter. It would have been to witness's interest to keep the child alive. She had two children at present, the payment for one being in arrears to the extent of about £5. The last payment was made on the 27th February, when she received £1 on account. The mother was anxious to pay. Witness should receive 5s. per week for the child. The father did not contribute, although he was able to do so to a small extent. Her house was clean. Witness had just handed a boy over to Mr Woodcraft, and the mother owed her £8 or £9 for its keep. He was 8 years of age. Altogether, about £20 was owing for children's care. Witness had never tasted any intoxicating liquors in her life.

The inquiry was then closed.

Brisbane Courier, 6 and 8 March 1905.

110. Foster Mothers

South Australia curbed the practice of baby farming by instituting the licensed foster mother system.

Licensed foster-mother system. — As far as I am aware, South Australia is the home of this system. It has been introduced for the purpose of protecting infant life, which too often comes into this world unwanted.

Occasionally it happens that our daily newspapers contain accounts of infants being found in the homes of so-called baby-farmers, either dead or dying, where it is conclusively shown that cruelties have been practised in the shape of starvation and neglect.

In an article recently contributed to the *Contemporary Review* by the Rev. Benjamin Waugh, of the London Society for Preventing Cruelty to Children, a most harrowing account of the cruelties perpetrated on little children is given. Humanity demands that childlife in either legitimate or illegitimate form should be nurtured and cared for, and not destroyed.

The law provides a severe penalty when human life is proved to have been taken in a direct manner, and the knowledge of this produces deterring influences. When children, however, are born into this world to bring nothing but a burthen, shame, and regret to those responsible for their existence, the frailty of early life, coupled with neglect, often proves the means of their destruction.

It would be claiming too much for our system to say that it completely prevents the possibility of cruelties to children being practised, but it is not too much to say that its adoption is the means of lessening and mitigating the evils so often attending baby-farming.

By our Act a penalty not exceeding £20 is provided in the case of any woman who takes a child to nurse without first obtaining a licence to do so from our Board, or for the father or mother of any such child who shall knowingly leave or place it with any person not being a licensed foster-mother or wetnurse.

Where a child has to be placed out at wetnurse, a certificate from a duly-qualified medical man exempts the case from the provisions of the law.

In order to obtain information concerning cases where the law is wilfully being broken, it is provided that half the stipulated fine shall be paid to the informer. Public attention is occasionally called to the existence of the law by advertising its requirements in the daily newspapers.

Persons who might be disposed to disregard its provisions hesitate to do so when they know that some near neighbour is likely to be pecuniarly benefited by supplying evidence which will secure their conviction.

Those who desire to be licensed to enable them to take children to nurse are asked to fill in a printed form of application, and a certificate of good character at the foot thereof is required from a clergyman or magistrate. As an additional safeguard, the home of the applicant is always visited by a lady in the employ of the department, and the granting of the licence depends upon the nature of her report. The licence when issued always specifies the number of children which the licensee is considered to be capable of properly nursing, and the home and children are regularly inspected by our lady visitor at about fortnightly intervals. Neglect when noticed is pointed out, and should no improvement follow the licence would be cancelled. A register of licences issued is kept in the office, and we are frequently applied to by persons wishing to place children with licensed foster-mothers. Our system guarantees the respectability of the women to those who wish to take advantage of their services.

As an additional means of protecting early child-life, a suggestion has been made that all private lying-in homes should be under a licensed system, and subject to inspection.

Measures could be adopted to secure all confinements of single women to these homes, and in cases where the mother could not retain the care of her child it should only be placed with a licensed foster-mother.

In conclusion, I would say that in South Australia we have had no baby-farming cases of notoriety for many years past, and it rarely happens that instances occur when a prosecution is considered to be necessary. The police are always ready to render every assistance to the Board in connexion with this branch of its work, and our immunity from cases of a sensational nature can fairly claim to be due to the legislative measures provided and the method adopted to make their existence known. A recent advertisement of the requirements of the law resulted in the number of licensed foster-mothers being increased by 22.

T. H. Atkinson, "The Destitute Poor Department of South Australia", in *Proceedings of the First Australasian Conference on Charity* (1890).

111. Abortion

This young woman, who describes an abortion performed on her, was fortunate in that the operation was performed by a qualified practitioner and that an anaesthetic was administered. These advantages notwithstanding, the curettage was not complete and she was admitted to hospital. Abortion was illegal and the doctor was charged.

Clara [L———] sworn states:
I am a single woman at present an inmate of the Gympie Hospital.
By Acting Sergt. Old. Do you know this man — pointing to Dr [N———]?
Ans. Yes — that is Dr [N———].
Q. Did you go to his surgery on the morning of the 19th inst?
Ans. Yes.

Q. Were you sick when you went to his surgery?
Ans. Not very.
Q. Were you in the family way?
Ans. I was about two months and a fortnight, but Dr [N——] said I was more, but did not know it.
Q. Did you ask Dr [N——] to fix you up?
Ans. Yes.
Q. What were your exact words?
Ans. I went up there about a fortnight before and he said you come up another time with the money and I will fix you up.
Q. You went up again with the money?
Ans. Yes.
Q. When did you go up with the money?
Ans. This Thursday the 13th day of July 1911.
Q. How much did you take?
Ans. Five guineas.
Q. Did you take that to Dr [N——]?
Ans. Yes.
Q. What did the money consist of?
Ans. Five single notes, two shilling pieces and one single shilling.
Q. Did Dr [N——] give you a receipt for the money?
Ans. No.
Q. Where were you when you gave Dr [N——] the money?
Ans. In the surgery.
Q. Was there any person present besides you and Dr [N——]?
Ans. No, nobody.
Q. What did Dr [N——] say to you when you gave him the money?
Ans. He said — "Sit down while I get some hot water".
Q. Did Dr [N——] go out of the room?
Ans. Yes he went out of the room.
Q. Did he return with anything?
Ans. He returned with some hot water.
Q. What did he do?
Ans. I was not in the operating room but he put those instruments in hot water.
Q. Did you see those instruments?
Ans. Yes.
Q. What were they like — Can you describe them?
Ans. I saw them but I cannot describe them.
Q. Can't you describe them?
Ans. I would know them if I saw them.
Q. Did Dr [N——] use those instruments on you on the evening of the 13th July?
Ans. Yes.
Q. Just describe how Dr [N——] used those instruments on you. Did he lay you on the operating table?
Ans. He laid me on the operating table and then began to use those instruments.
Q. In what way?
Ans. He put something round my neck and fastened it on to my legs. He pulled my legs up. He started to use the instruments.
Q. How did he use those instruments?
Ans. He put them in my privates.

Q. What then?

Ans. It was too painful. I could not stand it.

Q. What was done then?

Ans. He gave me Chloroform.

Q. Did you go off under that?

Ans. Yes.

Q. What do you remember next?

Ans. When I came out of the Chloroform he told me to have a rest.

Q. Anything else?

Ans. Yes. Mrs [N——] came in and gave me a dose of Chloroform.

Q. What next do you remember?

Ans. I remember coming round again.

Q. After you came round what happened?

Ans. Mrs [N——] gave me Chloroform a third time.

Q. What next?

Ans. I remember coming round again.

Q. After you came out of the Chloroform the third time what occurred?

Ans. The Dr washed me.

Q. After washing you what happened?

Ans. He took the straps off me. I mean the things he put round my neck and legs. I then laid on the table for a while. I them got up and Mrs [N——] helped me to get dressed.

Q. After you got dressed where did you go?

Ans. I went to the Exchange Hotel, meaning the Mining Exchange Hotel.

Q. How long were you at Dr [N——] on the 13th?

Ans. I went up a little after 8 p.m. and left about 11 p.m.

Q. Before you left did the Dr or Mrs [N——] give you any instructions?

Ans. Not that I can remember.

Q. When you returned to the hotel, what did you do?

Ans. I went to bed.

Q. On the morning of the 14th what did you do?

Ans. I got up and worked until about 12 o'clock. I then got sick and went down and told my sister I was going to bed.

Q. Did you go to bed?

Ans. Yes, I went to bed in my sister's room.

Q. Did anyone ring up for any person?

Ans. Yes, my sister rang up for Dr [N——]. Shortly after Dr [N——] arrived. He said "You had better come up to my hospital."

Q. Did you go to Dr [N——]'s hospital?

Ans. No.

Q. Where did you go?

Ans. I went to the Gympie General Hospital.

Q. What age are you?

Ans. I am twenty one years of age last birthday.

By Doctor [N——]

Q. Were you a servant at my place at one time?

Ans. Yes.

Q. Were you always well treated?

Ans. While I was there I was always well treated.

Q. Did you do some lifting in the hospital before you came up to me?
Ans. Yes I did.
Q. Did you tell me that you had strained yourself a bit?
Ans. Yes. I told you I thought I had strained myself.
Q. You had a bit of pain when you came up to see me?
Ans. Yes, a little.
Q. You had some bearing down pains?
Ans. No I had not.
Q. Did you notice you were bleeding?
Ans. No, I was not bleeding.
Q. Were you very sick at my place?
Ans. I was not sick when I first went up. I was sick when I took the chloroform.
Q. Did I say you would not be alright until the womb was empty?
Ans. Yes.
Q. I did not hurt you much did I?
Ans. I could not stand it.
Q. Did I ask you to stay in my place all night?
Ans. Yes, you asked me but I said I could not.
Q. Did I arrange for you to come in the morning if you were not better?
Ans. I don't remember.
Q. When I came down next day to see you were you in a good deal of pain?
Ans. Yes.
Q. Something had come away from you?
Ans. Yes I think so.
Q. I asked you to come up to my place, in a cab?
Ans. I forget what I said.
Q. Had you much pain walking home?
Ans. Yes, I had pain.

C. L., statement taken by and sworn before two Justices of the Peace at the Gympie Hospital, 15 July 1911.

112. A Cordon of Kindergartens

> The aims of the Brisbane Creche and Kindergarten Association extended far beyond the relatively straightforward tasks of childminding and elementary education. The kindergarten was seen as the site of the war between heredity and environment. For the welfare of the child and the community, the ascendancy of the moral environment provided by the kindergarten was considered crucial.

In May of this year the Creche was moved from its temporary quarters to more commodious premises in Ann Street, and the increasing number of children brought to us testify to the great need which exists for this branch of the work. At the moment of writing this report 46 little ones are being cared for at the Creche.

The object of the Creche, or day-nursery, is first and foremost TO CARE FOR THE CHILDREN, to give them wholesome food and tender love, to combat the evil which heredity has wrought, and that which in many cases a bad home environment is doing to give them healthy minds, and strong constitutions. Secondly, we find work for the mothers to enable them to keep the home together, and to strengthen the ties which should exist between mother and child.

Children are brought to us from as far as Paddington, East Brisbane, and Annerley Road, and it has been a matter of grave concern to us that owing to lack of funds, we have been able to reach so comparatively few of the children in other parts of the city, who so greatly need our care.

In May, a deputation waited upon the Minister for Lands for the purpose of obtaining a site at Paddington for a branch Creche and Kindergarten. Mr. Denham received us most kindly, and promised any available land provided the Association could find funds to finance the Branches. It is hoped we may soon be able to accept that offer, and that the people of Brisbane will help us to build at least one model Creche and Kindergarten in our midst. But in the meantime (with the proceeds of the Fete organized by the Mayoress of Brisbane in June, and with the subscriptions raised by the " 'Courier' Branch Extension Fund.") We propose without delay to rent and equip premises in two at least of these districts which need us most. . .

The Association has always sacrificed much to maintain a high standard of kindergarten teaching. We do not set a road mender to adjust a delicate scientific instrument, and we cannot expect to achieve results in character-building if we set the untrained teacher to deal with the most delicate and easily spoiled of all mechanisms — THE MIND OF A LITTLE CHILD. The hope of a country is bound up in its children, in those tiny mites lies our nation's treasure — with the character of the growing generation rests its prosperity or its downfall.

At a conference recently held in Connecticut the genealogy of a stock of notorious criminals, paupers and degenerates was traced back to one woman who began life as a neglected child. And what can we expect — "as the twig is bent the tree inclines," and the large number of neglected children who in the centres of population are a "satire upon our civilisation" will some day help to fill our prisons. I do not refer to the children whom the State deals with, but to those who have so-called homes — who would be often far better off if they had none, who (long before they reach school age) by the street and gutter influence have been robbed of that which is their childhood's right, and which all the years of life will never give back to them. We would see (as in Rotterdam) a cordon of Kindergartens to keep our children safe and clean, and in Brisbane we have such exceptional possibilities of success. As yet our city is not too densely populated, and the tide of hereditary pauperism and criminality has not grown too strong for us to breast.

Report of the Third Annual Meeting of the Brisbane Creche and Kindergarten Association (1910).

113. The Baby Bonus

The Maternity Allowance Act of 1912 legislated to give £5 to the mother on the birth of each child. This decision was criticized by the medical profession.

Maternity Allowance Act. 1912.
Maternal Mortality and Morbidity and Infantile Mortality.
I am directed to inform you that at the last meeting of the Federal Committee of Branches of the British Medical Association the following Resolution was passed, and the Branches have been requested to bring it under the notice of their respective State Governments, with a view to the Government taking such action in the matter, as it may deem appropriate:—

"That, in view of the national importance of securing a reduction in maternal mortality and morbidity and in infantile mortality, the *Federal Committee urges* on the *Commonwealth Government that* the *money now devoted to* the *Maternity Bonus* could *be more effectively expended along* the *following lines*, viz:—
  (i) the extension of maternity hospitals, ante-natal clinics and infant welfare centres;
  (ii) the provision of more efficient midwifery training for nurses and medical students;
  (iii) the provision of help for mothers and expectant mothers in necessitous circumstances;
  (iv) such other measures as are advised from time to time by medical experience."

Secretary, Queensland branch of the British Medical Association, to Under-Secretary, Queensland Home Secretary's Department, 14 November 1922.

114. Who Should Get the Money?

A variety of women's groups debated whether the money provided by the 1912 Act should be paid directly to mothers or spent on more and better maternity hospitals. Most feminist organizations opposed moves to take the cash grant away from mothers. During the Great Depression, the maternity allowance was reduced and income tested, but cash payments to mothers on the birth of a child continued until the Fraser Government abolished them in 1978.

On March 20 and 21 a conference of women from all parts of the Commonwealth is to be held in Melbourne to discuss the best method of helping poor mothers. The general idea is that if the money now spent in baby bonus payments (about £700,000) were devoted to the upkeep of maternity hospitals it would be better expended, but many of the country women are saying if that is done it is the city mothers alone who will get the benefit. They declared that if the bonus is withdrawn the money will be spent on erecting hospitals in the city, with the result that if a country woman — who usually has more children than her city sister — wants to get any help from the Government she will be put to heavy expense in coming to the city, whereas, under the present system, she gets the £5 without preliminary expenditure, and it helps to pay the bills of the doctor or nurse. On the other hand, it is claimed that the money can be spent to much advantage by the adoption of a scheme which was prepared some months ago by the Federal Health Department. The conference will be an open one, the sole question to be discussed being this — "Is the womanhood of Australia getting the best value from the maternity bonus?"

'The Baby Bonus", *Brisbane Courier*, 23 February 1923.

115. Better Babies

Eugenicists were critical of any method of child endowment that made payments to all mothers, believing that this practice would encourage even larger families in the poorer sections of the society.

The question of the "endowment of motherhood" is exercising the minds of many humanitarians. Sentimentally it is a beautiful and entirely desirable thing but is it practical and is it wise? If we could by such endowment ensure that the world would only get "better babies" then it would indeed be an ideal to work for, but alas, it would only mean a large increase in the number of feeble, unfit, and physically undesirable children being born. What the world wants is the sound teaching of Eugenics; healthy parenthood . . . and not the reckless propagating of a diseased and undesirable race.

"Plain Jane" column, *Queensland Figaro*, 22 July 1922.

116. Endowment for Mothers, Segregation for the Unfit

Millicent Preston Stanley was the first woman elected to the New South Wales parliament. Her contribution to the child endowment debate in 1927 reveals her sensitive awareness of the privations many mothers faced. It is also a striking example of the influence of eugenic thought on some feminists.

If it should happen that there are any members of the Nationalist party who do not find themselves able to support the bill which the Minister is bringing forward, it will be because of the question as to how the money is to be raised by which these families are to be endowed. If there are some members on this side of the House unable to support the bill I believe it will be because of the method of finding the money and the way in which the endowment is to be paid. For years past in the Federal sphere we have been paying the basic wage to a man, his wife and three children and in the State sphere to a man, his wife and two children. It is obvious that if we provide for a man with two or three children, then in the case of a man who has five, six or more children we are not providing in the basic wage for those additional members of his family. The result of that is very clear indeed. It means a lowering of the standard of living in the home, and can mean nothing else. I am prepared to say that although there is a general all-round decline in the standard of living in the family which has more children than those provided for in the basic wage, it is the unfortunate mother who is the greatest sufferer. The first thing that happens is a limitation of her pleasures. The next thing is a limitation of her clothing. The next is a general reduction in the food supply of the home — and it is the mother who suffers most as a result of that. The inevitable result of the lowering of the standard of living in the home is that every child in it is affected. May I point out that the feeding and clothing of the nation's children is a supremely important duty, and one which the State must be prepared to undertake, if they are not adequately provided for in other ways.

The three most important national functions are, the question of how a nation gets its living — the economic side — the question of preserving the existence of the nation through military service, and the question of the begetting and rearing of healthy children. The most important function performed by any person for or on behalf of the State is that performed by the working mothers of the community in bringing into the world and rearing children. It does seem to me the obvious duty of the Government of any democratic country to see that those children do not suffer simply because the father cannot earn an adequate wage, or has deserted or left them, or is suffering from ill-health or bad luck. It seems to me that these children are indeed the nation's greatest asset, and upon the years of childhood depends the physical and mental, and to some extent even the spiritual, structure of the child when it has grown a man or a woman. . . .

In my opinion there is another piece of legislation which ought to run parallel with this, and that is a measure for the segregation of mentally defective persons, for the purpose of effecting an improvement in the race-stock. This is not a laughing matter. It seems to me that if we had the kind of legislation I have in mind, which is perfectly practicable and which has been brought into existence in many countries, we should have improved progeny, and those whose maintenance we would be assisting by virtue of some such provision as this would be at least not mentally defective persons, and not feeble-minded stocks.

Millicent Preston Stanley, speech in the N.S.W. Legislative Assembly, 8 February 1927.

117. Wages and Child Endowment

Welfare payments are often manipulated to disguise drops in real wages. This article, from the *Working Woman*, the organ of the militant Central Women's Committee of the Communist Party of Australia, shows how child endowment in New South Wales concealed the fall in real wages in the early 1930s.

WORKERS ROBBED OF MILLIONS
HOW CHILD ENDOWMENT SCHEME WAS WORKED
PAYMENTS AGAIN THREATENED
BUILD SOLIDARITY COMMITTEES

How many workers know that during the time that the basic wage was reduced and Child Endowment instituted, a loss in wages of £6,000,000 took place? And during the first two years of its operation a further £24,000,000 was lost in wages, while only £2,634,664 was paid in Endowment?

How many workers calculated, that with the accompanying reduction in the basic wage, the institution of Child Endowment resulted in this enormous saving — *to the boss?*

How it Happened

This was brought about by reducing the family unit upon which the basic wage was calculated from one of four members to one of two members. Prior to Endowment, the family unit was a man, his wife, with two children. With Endowment operating, the unit was reduced to a man and wife alone.

In actual figures, the basic wage was declared at £4/5/- with Endowment, instead of £4/17/- for a man, wife and 2 children, the rise in the cost of living having increased to that extent.

This reduced standard was further reduced in 1929. The basic wage was then reduced to £4/2/6, and the first child was struck off from the payment of Endowment.

Another Attack Threatened

Today Endowment is in danger of being abolished altogether. Another reduction which the workers cannot stand! Premier Stevens promised and intends to carry out the Premiers' Plan. Along with that goes the abolition of Endowment. His reply to Mr Cahill (Arncliffe) is proof:—

"You would repeal the Family Endowment Act," asked Mr Cahill, and Mr Stevens replied, "*I would.*" The deepening crisis and the huge unemployed army has altered the capitalists' viewpoint towards Endowment.

This army has increased from 7 per cent. to 33 per cent. of the workers.

Endowment in 1927 was the method by which the workers' wages were reduced by £11,000,000 even after they themselves paid for the Endowment.

The new offensive of the capitalist class aims at further attacks on Endowment payments.

FORM SOLIDARITY COMMITTEES

Against this offensive the "Working Woman" comes forward to give the lead to working women to organise for the maintenance of Endowment.

Today, our only hope of maintaining Endowment lies in our own organised and mass strength determined to fight for Endowment for every child.

The Nationalist Endowment of 1929 could not reduce wages to £3/12/6 against your determined and massed opposition.

You can fight today against this further threatened attack!

Built up in your own district Solidarity Committees, and hold local demonstrations against an attack on Endowment. This will let Stevens and Co. know that they will not have it all their own way.

Watch for the day that the Child Endowment Act will be dealt with by the Government.

Hold mass meetings and protest demonstrations and be ready for a big central demonstration when Stevens and Co. launch their attack!

Working Woman, 1 July 1932.

118. The Declining Birthrate

In 1904, the New South Wales government appointed a Royal Commission to inquire into the decline of the birthrate. Rose Scott criticized the Commission because women were not included among the commissioners, but she also questioned the point of investigating the decline in the birthrate when the double standard of morality was not denounced. She saw the double moral standard as being the fount of prostitution, venereal disease, a high percentage of maternal and infant mortality cases, and inherited disease, and hence occupying a crucial and causal relationship to the declining birthrate.

There is also another subject it behoves me to speak of, and which has raised a whirlwind of talk and superficial comment, and that is "The declining birthrate," and its report. A Commission composed of men only, a report in which the only evidence printed was such as these men approved of, a commission which, like Adam of old, wound up very contentedly with assuring the public that everything was the fault "Of the woman thou gavest to be with me." My friends, so long as men keep up the demand for a supply of thousands and thousands of women in every city, who are to lead degraded lives, apart from the sphere of wife and mother, so long can they take the blame to themselves of a terrible evil which influences the birthrate not only directly but indirectly in three different ways — disease, selfishness, and immorality. Women, whether as wives or outcasts, are being sacrificed physically and morally. An instinct has been given to secure and protect the race. Quality should be placed before quantity, for population as population can be of no benefit to a country. A population should be one of worth, physically, mentally, and morally. What do we see? — thousands of little children handicapped as illegitimates, sick weaklings — a population of drunkards, idiots, criminals, lunatics! Slums where neglected children swarm, half-castes, the vast and ever-increasing army of unemployed, and worse still the women and girls who walk the streets at night! What does it mean? It means that licensed or unlicensed vice can only mean evil, and that a really great nation can only be built by inculcating the virtues of self-control and purity. It is not a question of many people or few people, but a question of what sort of people, and what sort of environment? Let us not add to the wrongs of children by adding insult to injury and publicly declaring that the one question is that they should be born — never mind how. We think more of our plants, our flowers, our animals, than we do of our children.

Rose Scott, *Presidential Address to the Woman's Political Education League* (August 1904).

119. Nine Months of Misery

> The *Woman's Sphere* ran a column entitled "The Population Question" and invited contributions from readers. The following contribution regards the question from the point of view of the mother.

As a teacher for more than thirty years, I have received the confidence of many women, and what I consider the saddest thing about the children question is the calm way in which married women talk of their wrongs and sufferings as though it was all part of the day's work. I remember one woman who had been married young, saying, "Though my husband has been good to me, we ought not to have had so many children." She went on to say that, though she was a young woman, only forty, her life was valueless, as her health was ruined and she could take no pleasure in anything.

Every child that a woman bears entails on the majority of them nine months of misery, more or less acute, with a culminating period of agony at the end. When this is repeated from ten to sixteen, or even twenty times, with intervals of only a year or more between, is it to be wondered at that many mothers die quite young of sheer exhaustion?

As a rule, the children who are produced at the rate of about one a year are delicate, and more than half of them are never reared.

I know of one woman who had twenty-two children, and less than one-third grew up. How is it possible for a mother to give her children proper attention when she has three and four babies to care for at the same time?

If she has means and can afford help it is difficult enough, but when she is the wife of a working man with a small daily wage it is impossible. As the small children grow up they are, while too young to do such work without injury to their own health, told [to go] off to mind the babies, and so practically have no childhood at all.

I think the greatest sufferers are the struggling farmers' wives. These women not only have their homes and families to attend to, but outside farm work as well, and one poor woman I have in my mind died of sheer exhaustion at the age of thirty, leaving eight young children behind her.

It is no uncommon occurrence to see a comparatively young husband and wife who have worked together, the wife having done her full share towards securing the competence which she hopes to enjoy with her husband and children, but while her husband is strong and healthy her health has been destroyed by the demands made upon her physical frame, and she dies, leaving her children motherless at the most critical period of their lives, and most probably knowing that another woman will reap the benefit, in comfort, of what she has toiled for.

The conclusion I have come to is that the man who has a large family at the expense of his wife's health and well-being ought to be reprobated by all right-thinking men and women, and, further, no man should have more children than he can support in comfort, nor expect children of tender years to go out into the world to help support younger brothers and sisters.

Clara Weekes, *Woman's Sphere*, 10 June 1903.

120. Populate or Perish

Dr Roberta Jull, a prominent West Australian medical practitioner and feminist, believed that Australia was imperilled by its low birthrate. She suggested that marriage and motherhood would be a more attractive option for young women if domestic help were available, and that this could be ensured by a system of domestic conscription. According to her, another advantage would be that the principles of efficiency would be brought into the home.

The question of the falling birth rate (for which as you know there are many factors) was actually discussed by a Committee in Sydney some years ago — It was then and still is to me a matter for amazement and mirth that the Committee consisted of men only — I believe a few women were examined as witnesses. How could a committee of men ever expect to really get to the bottom of this matter. A real understanding of child bearing and child rearing is only attained by experience — though before my marriage I knew a good deal about both, experience shewd me how short a way even the most sympathetic imagination can carry one. The result of the Committee's findings were chiefly so far as I can recall, fulmination against pleasure seeking, selfish women but no constructive policy was suggested. Some of the causes so far as I can judge for the acknowledged decrease in the birth rate are:— *1* The higher standard of living which obtains among us. *2* The desire to give the children greater comfort and care. Men and women who have worked and suffered much themselves desire to save their children. A mother whose life has been one long and grinding struggle, not infrequently advises her daughters either not to marry at all, to marry late in life or to limit her family. *3* The difficulty of obtaining help in the home. This reason is even more potent than either or both of the others and it increases instead of diminishes. It is well recognised among women that the households which need most help get least. Maids simply will not go to a house when there are children, they know by experience or observation how much harder the work is in such. *4* The want of control which is shewn by many men in the exercise of the procreative function — upon this it is not necessary for me to enlarge, but I can assure you it is a potent factor. I feel it is more than time that men of education and knowledge spoke out [on] the subject; that boys and youths were taught properly about marriage, its responsibilities and duties as regards the health of their wives and prospective children . . . a woman who has a child only once in three years is far more likely to be an efficient wife and mother, and to have healthy intelligent children than one who has a child once in eighteen months or oftener. I could give chapter and verse for all these statements but my letter would be much lengthened thereby — one case only will I quote — a woman, now middle aged, of brilliant intellectual abilities and also an excellent cook and housekeeper has had 4 daughters and 1 son. She is most able and prominent in all good works in her own city and is much sought after as a member of committees. Yet her usefulness is constantly curtailed by the fact that for weeks at a time she cannot procure domestic help, and is therefore obliged to do her own house-work with the assistance of one daughter. Her two elder daughters are in business — neither intend to marry. It isn't good enough they say. They cite case after case when their friends have married and say look at them: A. has been married 5 years and has 3 children, and is nothing but a wreck — B. has 1 child and has lost 3 (miscarriages) because she could never get help when she needed it. C. has had to give up her house and go into a flat because she couldn't get a maid and the children are all at boarding schools. The third daughter has married recently when nearly thirty years of age and openly says she doesn't mean to have many children. We must, men and women, go carefully and deliberately into this matter if we are to arrive at a solution of it.

1.   Life on the land must be made less lonely, less monotonous, less "all hard work" — The only way to do this is by some communal or co-operative system.

2.   If this were done and opportunities for good education and recreation afforded them parents would not desire as do many now to send their children away to better themselves in the towns.

3.   The status of domestic service must be raised. Employers must demand and maids must give a minimum standard of efficiency. Reasonable hours of work must be granted, and reasonable wages paid. My husband and I have often talked this over and he suggested that some form of service for girls equivalent to the military training of cadets might be enforced — there are distinct difficulties in the way but they could be overcome — a system of "apprenticeship" might be required, either to the girl's own mother or to some other housewife. Practical examinations could be set, and graded certificates of efficiency granted. Such a system would to some extent help the housewives, since "apprentices" could be obtained at low wages, but with strict con-ditions as to working hours and so on which would safeguard *them* from imposition. The gain to the race as a whole in a few years would be marvellous since no girl could escape the compulsion unless so extraordinarily "unfit" as to make marriage im-possible. Training in the functions and duties of motherhood would be included in this system . . .

     In Australia particularly with its very democratic governments and institutions it is urgently necessary that the gravity of this problem should be realised and some solution found for in no other way will it be possible to adequately people the vast spaces with a stable and thriving population: if that is not done by the white man it will be by the black or the yellow.

Roberta Jull, in a letter to an unidentified friend, 1916.

121. "A Race of the Best Whites"

This resolution of the Mothers' Clubs of Victoria suggests that, in the inter-war period, the conception that women's groups had of their civic responsibility was influenced by eugenic logic.

By 144 votes to 23 the quarterly meeting of the Victorian Federation of Mother's Clubs at the Central Hall yesterday passed a resolution in favour of voluntary sterilization of the physically and mentally unfit.

Mrs. G. Mann (Abbotsford) referred to danger of hereditary diseases: "Many people say that the world would never have had many of its geniuses had sterilization of the unfit always been enforced . . . but can one beautiful picture make up for the poverty of millions of people, or one rhapsody make up for the murders which have been committed from time immemorial by people with hereditary tendencies to murder? Research has shown that if two mentally deficient people marry at least two-thirds of their children will be mentally deficient."

Mrs. Priestly (Sale): "It had been estimated that in one generation mental deficiency would be reduced by half if sterilization was legalized. In Australia there was power to make the race we wished. It should not only be a white race, but a race of the best whites."

Argus, 10 September 1935.

122. Population Debate

Australia's population continued to provoke concern and debate. In the following excerpts from an A.B.C. radio programme, Dr Norman Haire, an Australian who ran a birth-control clinic in London, argued that the number of surviving children was likely to be higher if mothers were not burdened with too many and too frequent pregnancies. Dame Enid Lyons, federal politican and mother of eleven, suggested that greater interest in motherhood would be aroused if the matronly figure were promoted as the desideratum of female beauty.

Norman Haire: It is not the number of children born that really increases the population, but the number of children which survive. It is not the number of children born that is important but the number which survive to become healthy, happy and useful adults and to produce children in their turn. Even when a mother is healthy too frequent child bearing undermines her health, and her children are adversely affected by unfavourable conditions even before they are born. If too many children are born at too frequent intervals, all of them suffer from a competition for food and other necessaries of life, as well as from having to share the mother's care with too many rivals for it. I have had personal experience of this. Dame Enid is the mother of eleven children. I am the youngest of eleven — and I know the disadvantages of being one of a too large family. I know, too, what my poor mother had to endure for eighteen years. She was always either pregnant or suckling, usually both at the same time. For eighteen years she had scarcely a night's unbroken sleep. At the age of forty she, who had been an exceptionally strong and healthy young woman, had through her excessive and uncontrolled fertility become a devitalized, irritable, cantankerous, prematurely old woman. Only then, too late, did she attempt to prevent conception. . .

Dame Enid Lyons: . . . There is one other point of fashion which I think women find to be a great deterrent to having many children. That is our standard today of feminine beauty. Who are the people who decorate the magazine covers? The ladies of three husbands and no children — or at best two husbands and one child. It is not good enough. Who are those whose beauty today is extolled? Those who have kept the extreme slimness and suppleness of early youth. And really there is no beauty greater than that soft roundness of a young matron, and yet we cast it aside and regard it as nothing. I want to see the magazines showing happy mothers and happy babies. Not one baby, but many babies. I want to see the magazines refusing articles that exalt sex as an end in itself.

"Population Unlimited?", discussion broadcast on the Nation's Forum of the Air, A.B.C., 23 August 1944.

123. Saving the Mothers

Maternal mortality, the decline in the birthrate and the incidence of venereal disease were regarded by the United Associations of Women as aspects of the same problem. It is noteworthy that in the same year that the Birth Control Clinic of the Racial Hygiene Society was fighting for survival, Sydney's most articulate and prominent feminist organization recommended further restriction on the sale of contraceptives.

Having regard to the fact that Mother life is the *Real Basis* of Australia's well being and that the downward trend of Australian population must be checked, and serious efforts made to conserve human life if we wish to hold and effectively develop our heritage, the Standing Committee [Working for the Reduction of Maternal and Infantile Mortality] appeals to all Women's Organisations to put in the forefront of their activities for 1937 the best means of:—
1. Saving the Mothers.
2. Stemming the decline of population.
3. Commanding our most effective weapon — the VOTE.

RESOLVED: That Parliamentary Candidates to be asked whether they will support the programme of the Standing Committee for Reduction of Maternal and Infant Mortality summarized as follows:—
1. Enquiry:— expert, impartial, and privileged; into every Maternal death as it occurs for a series of say 500 cases — (2 years).
2. Improve and extend the training in obstetrics of all Medical Students *who intend to practise obstetrics*, and of all Maternity attendants.
3. Establish a new service of salaried midwives on an extended training (the British Parliament has just passed a Midwives Act on these lines for England and Wales and a similar movement is in progress for Scotland).
4. Standardize records; Statistics relating to Maternity; and compel notification of still births within 24 hours instead of within 3 weeks as per present Act.

RESOLVED FURTHER: That Parliamentary Candidates be asked: —

To consider the advisability of seeking legislation to make compulsory the exchange of a medical certificate showing the state of health of persons about to marry.

To enforce more restrictive measures to control the sale of contraceptives.

To condemn the erection of maternity annexes (or units) in close proximity to general hospitals. To make public the reasons governing the action of the New South Wales Public Health Authorities in sanctioning the erection of the "33 maternity annexes" referred to by the Minister for Health, in his address to the recent U.A.P. Conference.

To support the Contention of the Standing Committee that Economic insecurity creates an atmosphere of anxiety detrimental to the mental and physical well being of mothers and potential mothers and that therefore, the Federal Government should ascertain the financial capacity of the basic wage earner, or relief worker, or those immediately above this standard to provide himself and say, 2 or 3 children with such essential items of diet as milk, butter, eggs, green vegetables, and fruit.

To condemn the destruction of food stuffs suitable for human consumption (whilst competent authority tells us that we are building a C3 people).

To ask that the Governments order their paid experts, administrators and officials to put in motion, measures that will ensure to all mothers adequate incomes, to provide food, shelter, clothing, education, and all other social services that exist in abundance, and that security of tenure be assured to all parents in Australia.

Resolutions of the United Associations of Women's Committee on Maternal and Infant Mortality, 14 April 1937.

124. Women's Most Important Job

A conference on Australia's falling birthrate, convened by the United Associations of Women in 1944, reasserted the primacy of motherhood and child-raising, but recognized that economic considerations, increased leisure and concern for health and appearance made the prospect of motherhood unattractive to many women.

At a meeting of the United Associations of Women, held to consider the reasons for the falling birthrate in Australia, the following conclusions were arrived at:

(1)   Large families mean poverty, hardship, overcrowded homes, no holidays, no rest, work for the mother from dawn till dark till dawn;

(2)   Parents want to give their families a better education, better home, better food and clothing than they themselves had;

(3)   Women with large families are tied to their homes with few opportunities for rest or recreation, which could easily be provided by the establishment of kindergartens and creches;

(4)   Most houses available to working people are too small and ill equipped for large families. Large families are unpopular with landlords;

(5)   The strain of making ends meet and the continual household drudgery is likely to cause a breakdown in health and the mother grows old before her time;

(6)   The high cost of having a baby. It means medical and nursing expenses, new clothes for mother and baby, extra household linen and equipment and payment for household help during confinement;

(7)   The importance attached to figure and appearance generally, to the exclusion of all other attributes or responsibilities;

(8)   The growing realisation on the part of women that the raising of families and management of the home is regarded as of only secondary importance to the development of business and the pursuit of wealth.

(9)   The delay in making available to all child-bearing women the scientific discoveries of painless childbirth;

(10)   The increasing number of interests and amenities for men and women, and the fact that large families make it impossible, under present conditions, for mothers to enjoy these amenities.

Bearing and rearing the new generation is still the most important job a woman can do for herself and her country.

In this country the birthrate has been steadily declining until it has now reached a dangerous low level. Today, instead of the importance of family raising, all the emphasis is placed on youthful beauty, and sylphlike forms. The glamour girl has become the ideal rather than the mother. This is emphasised by all our advertising, our films, theatres, art and drama and literature.

Women are refusing to have children, even sufficient for replacement rate. Why?

Although great advances have been made by scientific measures in every field of men's work, this advantage has not extended to home making and family raising to any great extent. Actually with the general rise in the standard of living the burdens and difficulties have increased, particularly for parents who endeavour to give their families the advantages of modern standards of homes, education and so on.

A new approach is needed — it should be recognized that the work of bearing and rearing children is still the most important job a woman can do for herself and her country. She should be given every possible assistance to carry out her work. There should be a greater appreciation of the mother's job by the community. Preference should be given to mothers and children wherever possible, in trains, trams and buses, in shops and restaurants. Mothers with prams and babies are often regarded as a nuisance in public.

Resolutions of the United Associations of Women's Conference on the Birth Rate, 13 June 1944.

125. "I Was All Knocked About Inside"

This woman's account of the birth of her first child in Brisbane in the early 1920s shows the long-term effects that lack of money and medical attention had on her health.

My husband was out of work. Anyway he couldn't get work and I had a brother with me — out of work — and then I had these two children. I used to go to what they called the state hand-out, down Elizabeth Street I think it was, and you'd get a docket — you'd have to go to the police station first — get a docket for so much and you'd get something for the butcher and something for this and that and so on. My son, I think, was born around about that time at home. I'd had no doctor only a midwife and I said to her, I said, I rather fancy that I've had some funny feelings that this child is not being born right. She said, well, I'll get a doctor if necessary and so when I showed her some proof that I thought he was not being born right she said, well, let's get some help from somewhere. The poor woman didn't know what to do. She said it's too late now to try and get the doctor and she went and got a woman over the road who was three weeks off having her own child. She'd never seen a child born. The pains had left me by then and she got this woman to sit on my stomach to help to push the pains, to push it. And the midwife got one leg at a time (it's a wonder she didn't —). Of course he walked funny for a long time. Yes, and I had no attention and I was all knocked about inside.

He was about five or six months old and when the doctor examined me, Dr Connolly it was, he said, how old is your baby? I said, well that's him crying. He said, if you hadn't told me I would have thought you'd just given birth to a baby. You've got an awful lot to do inside, he said, we'll have to send you in the hospital. I said, I can't go to hospital. There's no-one to look after my children. I've got two little children and two brothers out of work and my husband's out of work. The men can look after themselves best they can. One was out selling pine-apples and another one was cutting up the meat off rabbit bones and other jobs like that for a mighty pittance. However, he said, well I'll give you a bottle of medicine; it might stop the hemorrhaging. But I've never had anything done. I've always been knocked about inside.

She [the woman over the road] had her baby three weeks later but the milk had left her. So I had plenty of milk for what it was worth — it was like water, because I wasn't getting the proper food — so I had her baby on one side and my own baby on the other. So that's how I repaid her for sitting on my stomach.

Interview with Nell McLeod, Brisbane, 1975.

126. Childbirth

Marion Piddington, a director of the Institute of Family Relations, emphasized the importance of specialist obstetric care at the moment of delivery, if the high rate of maternal and infant mortality were to decline. She believed that the survival of the mother was a national responsibility and denounced the graded hospital system, which enabled richer women to buy better treatment than that offered in standard wards.

In every State, in every home and in the minds of foremost members of the Medical profession and of the citizens who think throughout the Commonwealth, the grave fact has come to be realised that Australia is definitely failing in its duty to the parents and potential parents of the nation . . .

We hope to present an aspect of the problem, not yet examined, upon which governments, the Medical profession and the public, could speak with one voice and act upon without delay.

The published statistics of Maternal and infant mortality are known and there is no need to recount them here. Dr Watson Munro pointed out to the writer six years ago, that if deaths from abortion were included in the maternal mortality figures "They would swell the melancholy total by from 10 to 14 per cent". The figures of morbidity can never be known, so various and far reaching are their baneful consequences. But a strange result has, for some time, followed the prolonged campaign of enlightening the public as to our dangers. The official attitude is now thus expressed:

"There is no doubt that maternal mortality is far too high. Still it is no use stressing it — that only alarms expectant mothers. . . ."

At the present time, women, pregnant with hope and fears and anxious as to the outcome of the ordeal before them, visit a specialist in the hope that this ante-natal precaution may ensure a safe delivery when they resign themselves into the hands of a local practitioner.

The point overlooked in this policy is the most vital point of all. It is that the supreme moment of the mother's danger is the moment of supreme need for the highest order of human skill. In other words, all mothers should have available first class specialist advice, not only before, but at the time of delivery. . .

The Australian nation is tired of waiting for promises to be kept while the toll of suffering and death continues. It desires to see a settled plan of action and that plan carried out speedily.

Our proposal to Mr Hughes is, that at the coming Conference of Federal and State Premiers, a special grant from Federal and State Governments be made (whose promises at election time have always been to safeguard the mothers of the nation in childbirth) to permit specialists to control what ought to be specialist work.

The responsibility should be thrown on to the governments to provide such service throughout the Commonwealth. These Specialists would not interfere with the Doctors at the Base Hospitals, but they should be attached to and located near them and be made responsible for maternity cases in the area under their supervision . . . It is a national disgrace that there should be intermediate wards, in which some women, by paying a little more may have the advantage of a higher order of skill over those unable to pay. Each of the former has the attention of one qualified doctor, but the latter are too often delivered, without expert supervision, by those whose course of training is not yet completed. This training is necessary and it is at the Hospitals that it is obtained — But should not all mothers have skilled treatment in childbirth?

Marion Piddington, ''Another Aspect of Maternal Mortality'', duplicated information sheet distributed by the Institute of Family Relations, Sydney (c. 1933).

127. Celibate Motherhood

After the First World War, there was an attempt to promote the scheme of "celebate motherhood" in Australia, so that women likely to remain single because of the depleted male population could experience motherhood through artificial insemination. There was a strong eugenic element in the scheme — it was sometimes referred to as "eugenic motherhood" — and its supporters argued that the scientific procedures and tests associated with artificial insemination would eventually eliminate the transmission of defects and diseases. Marion Piddington, who later became well known in Sydney for her pioneer work in birth control, was one of the most enthusiastic proponents of the scheme. She attempted to enlist the support of Sigmund Freud for the celibate motherhood campaign in Australia. His reply was devastatingly critical of the scheme and the sex-denying assumptions intrinsic to it.

I am not indifferent to the honour that you should have asked my opinion on a subject of so big importance. But let me express the suspicion that you were somehow mistaken about my personality. I am simply an inquirer, not a bit of a reformer and the more I have learned the more difficult I found it to give advise about definite lines in the complex matter of sexual behaviour.

I pray you will consider whatever I say as the private opinion of an individual who can claim no authority for it.

This settled I confess to my doubt whether Eugenics be advanced enough to be used as the basis of practical measures. I further feel unsympathetic towards your proposition that childless women should procure children by artificial anonymous fecundation. I see lurking behind this device that tendency to sex-repression which will do more for the extinction of the race than war and pestilence combined. Lastly I think the children begotten in this way, doomed to be fatherless and only children and to bear the undiminished weight of motherly tenderness through life are likely to work under heavy psychological odds, compared to the other ones.

I pray you will neither by annoyed by my ''reactionary'' opinions nor by my bad English, as it is not my language.

Sigmund Freud to Marion Piddington, 19 June 1921.

128. Finding a Healthy Spouse

In 1916, when Jessie Street was treasurer of the Sydney University Society for Combating Venereal Disease, she urged the Society to campaign for the compulsory exchange of health certificates between persons about to marry. In the following decades, mounting concern was directed to the incidence of venereal disease, which many people believed was a major cause of Australia's other great worry: the falling birthrate. It was in this context that Jessie Street again advocated the exchange of health certificates before marriage. No legislation to enforce this measure was enacted, but the Racial Hygiene Association of New South Wales offered pre-marital examinations as a serivce.

One way of coping with the problem of providing adequate hospital accommodation for the public would be to reduce the number of the public requiring treatment. That is, instead of making progressively larger arrangements to treat those who are sick, that we should endeavour to prevent people from becoming sick. We already do this to a very great extent by means of health regulations and sanitary laws, whose sole purpose is the preservation of the health of the community . . . What further steps can we take to prevent diseases and ill health generally? We can do one very easy and very definite thing. We can make quite sure that everyone, at that critical time of their life when they are contemplating marriage, is informed as to the state of their own health and the health of their prospective partner in marriage. Enquiries are now made about the financial and social position of those about to marry — but although good health is of greater personal and national importance than any other factor, we entirely ignore any reference to it until ill health has come into the picture. Many people have complaints and diseases about which they are quite ignorant, but which they can hand on to their children and partners in marriage. Very many of these diseases and complaints can be cured and the consequent ill health to the sufferer, the partner in marriage and children could all be prevented.

If this is so, are we justified in not taking steps to prevent all this unnecessary ill health? Are we justified in allowing people to remain in ignorance about their health when the consequences of doing so are so serious to other persons, and also to the next generation, and so expensive to the State?

The answer to all these questions is, No! And the more you think about it, the more emphatically do you answer, No!

Well, what can we do about it? How can we warn people? It is quite easy. We can make it compulsory for persons about to marry to obtain a certificate showing the state of their health and indicating any complaint they may be suffering from, which can be handed on to others, and which can be cured. If this were done, untold misery, ill health, invalidism and in many cases death itself, would be prevented.

If persons about to marry were to exchange certificates showing the state of their health, we could reasonably anticipate that should either party be suffering from a curable complaint, that that party would undergo the necessary treatment to ensure that the trouble was not passed on, for surely no-one would knowingly infect a person of whom they were sufficiently fond to marry, or their unborn children, with complaints from which they could either be cured, or at least, rendered not infectious.

In addition to the talk about the shortage of hospital accommodation, we are hearing increasingly often about the low birthrate in Australia. How much of this low birthrate is also the result of preventable causes. Admittedly there are persons who for economic and other reasons do not want children, or at any rate, do not want more than one or two children. But there are a very large number of persons to whom it is a great sorrow that they are childless or have only one child. Much of the inability of these persons to produce children could have been prevented if they had been informed of the state of their health before marriage, and the necessary treatment given them . . . The great National question of the falling birthrate would in part be solved by the expedient of the exchange of certificates of health before marriage.

Jessie M. G. Street, "The Advantages of the Exchange of Certificates Indicating the Health of Persons About to Marry", unpublished paper, 5 November 1936.

Racial Hygiene Association of New South Wales, *Annual Report* (1939).

129. Preparation for Marriage

The Racial Hygiene Association of New South Wales was, as its name suggests, concerned with the health standards of the race and operated a pre-marital clinic, in the belief that if people were aware that they could possibly transmit serious diseases or weaknesses to their children, they themselves would refrain from reproduction.

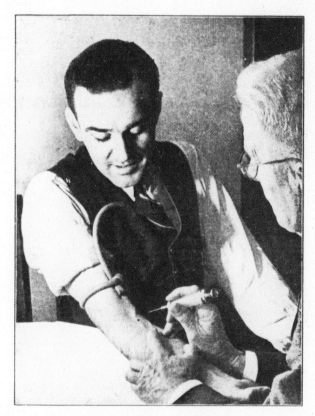

Pre - Marital Clinic

PHYSICAL TESTS

Support the Racial Hygiene Association of N.S.W. in its crusade for happy marriages and healthy children, by means of the exchange of health certificates. Avail yourselves of this opportunity to gain knowledge of yourselves, mentally and physically.

General Physical Examinations include :

Blood Tests.
Chest X-Ray.
Blood Pressure.
Diabetes.
Bodily Defects.
    Etc.
Inherited Diseases and Tendencies.

Pre - Marital Clinic

MENTAL TESTS

Support the Racial Hygiene Association of N.S.W. in its crusade for happy marriages and healthy children, by means of the exchange of health certificates. Avail yourselves of this opportunity to gain knowledge of yourselves, mentally and physically.

General Mental Examination includes :

Perversions.

Alcoholism.

Epilepsy.

Speech Defects.

Intelligence Test, etc.

Inherited Diseases and Tendencies.

Racial Hygiene Association of New South Wales, *Annual Report* (1939).

130. A Perfect Race

Herself, a woman's paper founded in 1928, attempted to popularize eugenics. Articles such as "The Race versus Ignorance" and "Women's Objective — A Perfect Race" emphasized the importance of blood tests before marriage, to alert parents to diseases they could transmit to their children. Women were reminded that motherhood was "not an instinct but a science".

'Herself.'

her present, past & future

AND AUSTRALIAN AFFAIRS

Vol. 1. No. 7. SYDNEY, APRIL 1929

NEXT GENERATION

CALLS

THE

EUGENICS

NUMBER

3D.

Photo kindly lent by "Glaxo."

131. Sex Education

In the inter-war period, sex education was increasingly seen as a way of instilling the necessity of chastity before marriage and thus a way of curbing the increase in venereal disease. In this pamphlet, the schools worked through parents, who were seen as having the major responsibility for sex education.

At the age of puberty, certain physical changes come upon boys and girls, and ignorance concerning their meaning and their dangers often leads to much physical and moral mischief in the children's lives. It is universally agreed that the proper person to impart to the child the knowledge which may avert this mischief is the parent, the father to the boy and the mother to the girl; and since past experience has proved that parents have avoided the performance of this duty, partly from a natural modesty, and partly from a feeling of inability to handle the subject satisfactorily, it has been considered the duty of the Government to furnish to parents the information that should be given to their children and to suggest at the same time a way of approaching the subject which may be helpful to overcome their not unnatural reticence in the matter.

Suggested Method of using this pamphlet.

The parent should first read the attached pamphlet by himself. Then it may be given to the child to read carefully alone, after a few words of sympathetic warning that it has reached a critical stage in its physical life, when it ought to know accurately about certain physical changes that are sure to come upon it shortly. After half an hour or so, the parent should talk with the child, briefly or at length as may be felt necessary, on the subjects in the pamphlet, urging him (or her) to set his (or her) face steadfastly against the evils indicated, and to adopt habitually the simple healthy safeguards which have been suggested for his (or her) protection. The pamphlet should then be taken away from the child, who should be made to understand that the information is confidential and not to be discussed with other boys or girls.

PAMPHLET FOR GIRLS

(1) *Menstruation or monthly sickness*

From the age of puberty onwards girls are subject to periodic discharges of blood. Those discharges (variously called menstrual period, monthly sickness, etc) as is well known usually last from two to five days and they recur with great regularity about every four weeks.

Owing to the mistaken ideas prevalent concerning menstruation, it is advisable to call attention to the fact *that this flow of blood is a natural process.* Therefore *anything that lessens or stops the flow such as wet feet or a cold bath, or anything which increases the flow such as violent exercise, dancing, or continuous standing must be avoided during the monthly sickness.* On the other hand, the effects of menstruation on the ordinary life of girls and women must not be exaggerated. Menstruation does not incapacitate normal girls or women from ordinary work. The troubles frequently met with are due to removable causes such as lack of physical exercises, constricting dress, lack of healthy living, and the idea so prevalent among women and girls that they should be incapacitated at that time.

Constipation especially affects menstruation, as well as the general health, by poisoning the system. Constipation also more directly affects menstruation by increasing the congestion and pressure around the already congested sexual organs, and may lead to chronic inflamation.

Girls should be encouraged *to take plenty of physical exercise in the open air between the menstural periods.*

(2)   *Self-Abuse (masturbation)*

It is necessary to call attention to the fact that girls indulge in the practice of self-abuse as well as boys. Many medical authorities are now satisfied that the practice is as common amongst girls as amongst boys, and that girls who masturbate are likely to indulge to a greater excess than boys. Mothers therefore must warn their daughters against this improper practice. Girls must be made to realize the disgusting and immoral nature of the habit and its possible dangers to Health.

The habit of self-abuse may be acquired accidentally from ignorance, or as the result of the example of other, usually older, girls, or from weakness of the girl's own character.

Remedies.

(i)   *Tight clothing should be avoided* as inducing irritation.

(ii)   *Cleanliness.* Want of cleanliness allows the natural secretions to collect between the folds of the skin and to irritate the genitals. Therefore girls should wash and carefully dry once a day the crevices between the folds of the skin.

(iii)   *Avoidance of constipation.* Unfortunately very few people realize how constipation undermines health. Poisons are liable to be formed in the bowels and then pass into the system, so that health suffers. Constipation is especially harmful to girls and women because it leads, as has already been said, to increased pressure and congestion to the already congested sex organs during menstruation. This interferes with menstruation and is liable to lead to pain and discomfort. Constipation often results from inattention to the calls of nature. False modesty often prevents girls from obeying the calls at once, the stimulation of the bowel is lost, and constipation results. A tendency to constipation may be often overcome by cultivating the habit of visiting the w.c. at a certain fixed time every day. Children should be impressed at an early age with the necessity of cultivating regular habits in this matter, and daughters when married should remember the dangers of constipation during pregnancy. In such cases, mothers are supplying their developing babies with poisoned blood, and the babies when born may in consequence be sickly or wanting in stamina.

(3)   *Illicit sexual intercourse*

Girls should be taught that their virginity until marriage is their most precious possession, and that it is a possession which once lost can never be recovered. They should be warned that men frequently ruin girls under a promise of marriage and then so despise them when ruined that they refuse to marry them. They should remember that a single connection may cause a girl to become pregnant and thus ruin her for life, also that a single connection may result in her becoming infected with a loathsome venereal disease.

These venereal diseases are loathsome in their nature, disastrous alike to the health of the woman and of her offspring if she have any offspring; they are extremely contagious and a girl may become infected as the result of a single connection with a man or youth, who may be suffering from the disease though appearing at the time to be healthy.

Safeguards.

(a)   Girls should avoid going to dances, evening entertainments, or walks at night time with young men without their parents' consent, and they should not allow young men in any way to take liberties with them. They should not accept invitations of any sort from strangers, either male or female.

(b)   They should avoid all unwholesome books and sensational plays and picture shows, and keep their minds and bodies busy with wholesome activities and out-door recreation.

Conclusion

A girl therefore who wishes to retain the respect of herself and her fellows and to grow into an honoured woman, healthy alike in body and mind, and strong and true in character, will steadfastly refrain from these evil practices.

She must not expect the task to be easy, for our sexual passions are strong and temptations are frequent; but there is no other victory in life that is so important for a woman to win.

Victorian Education Department, "Circular Addressed to Parents by the Education Departments throughout Australia with regard to Sex Hygiene" (*c.* 1925).

132. Marriage under Capitalism

Adela Pankhurst Walsh, youngest daughter of Emmeline Pankhurst, first gained notoriety in Australia as a feminist and socialist. After her marriage, she moved steadily to the right and founded the Australian Women's Guild of Empire. In her public addresses and in the columns of the *Guild of Empire Gazette*, she promoted marriage and family as women's proper and most rewarding sphere. She was interned during the Second World War because of her admiration for fascism, and particularly for the Japanese. The following extract from the *Working Woman* is typical of the attacks communist feminists made on Adela Pankhurst Walsh, for her celebration of marriage and motherhood and her neglect of the material difficulties that faced working-class wives and mothers.

Comrade Editor,

Mrs Adela Pankhurst Walsh, who used to pose as a revolutionary, has been recently telling the people what she thinks about marriage and children.

She starts out by saying that human beings are possessed of a selective power which works through a warm and passionate love for a mate and affection for their offspring. She continues in this strain, and paints marriage under capitalism in the most idealistic way. Not a mention does she make of the basis of marriage under capitalism, of the restricted circle in which the workers are forced to live, and of the slave conditions which force the women of our class to seek marriage, merely as a way out. She forgets all about her former beliefs that women under capitalism are the slaves of slaves, and of course, she fails to urge the women in her audience to organise to fight for better conditions, for themselves and their class.

In answer to the question as to whether women should produce children, whether they desired them or not, she stated, "It is the will of God". As one who has three, I say it is a pity what when God was "willing" the children, the means of feeding and clothing them was not "willed" at the same time.

"Sob-stuff Artist; Mrs Walsh on Children", by "A.E.A. of Rozelle", *Working Woman,* January 1932.

133. The French Pessaire Preventif

Mrs B. Smyth had a shop in Melbourne that sold women's lingerie and a variety of contraceptives. She wrote pamphlets of birth control, marriage and motherhood. The *following extract is from a survey on available contraceptive devices she gave to a group of women in the South Melbourne Town Hall in 1890. Mrs Smyth favoured the diaphragm, a method that she emphasized was in the control of the woman and could be used without the husband's knowledge or consent.*

12th Check — The Preventif Pessaire or Contraceptive Check. — *The best, safest, and most sure Check.* It has never been known to fail where instructions have been carried out.

The French Pessaire Preventif.

In offering this instrument to the public, a few remarks in explanation may be appropriate. There seems to be a lack of confidence in the Pessaires heretofore used, owing to the fact that they have been constructed without bearing any relation whatever to the parts with which they were to be brought into contact, consequently more injury then benefit has been caused by their use.

The French Pessaire Preventif is constructed on a common sense principle, and strictly in accordance with the anatomy of the female organisation. It is light in weight, being made of pure soft rubber, prepared expressly for the purpose; it is without stem, straps, or other cumbersome appliances; does not interfere with micturition or coition, can be easily adjusted, is not injurious in any way, and with proper care will last for years.

It affords a convenient and prompt means of cure to those afflicted with prolapsus (falling of the womb), leuchorrhoea (whites), and in the ready cure of the ulceration of the mouth and neck of the womb, so commonly the living torment of delicate women. In treatment of the cancer of the womb, it is a most admirable instrument. The ordinary treatment of female diseases by injections is uncertain, slow, tedious, disgusting and expensive.

In the use of local medication by means of the Pessaire Preventif, the cure is directly applied to the seat of the disease, and can be retained any length of time with ease, comfort, and success. By this valuable agent, old chronic female afflictions, seldom curable by former kinds of treatment, now yield readily. Many a poor woman who was completely broken down in the prime of life, a burden to herself, and worse than an utter blight to the marriage bed, is now restored to the enjoyment of domestic and social life.

The French Pessaire Preventif is of inestimable value to delicate females, to those in poor health, and to those who, by disease or distortion of the pelvis, cannot with safety bear children, as it is a perfect, convenient, and safe protection against conception and pregnancy, and the only article of the kind that can be used without the knowledge of the husband.

Injudicious and rapid child-bearing is the saddest affliction of the young women of America. It is destructive to the health of both the parent and the child. How often is the familiar spectacle witnessed of a young and beautiful girl, single today, married tomorrow, and next year a mother and an invalid. This instrument prevents the crime of abortion.

This being the fact, we can best serve humanity and Christianity by preventing the bearing of children, in such case as named above, which every woman may do, and should under circumstances that make it a crime to bear them.

The necessity of so doing reason teaches and conscience approves, since it would prevent much evil, crime, and suffering, in that it would prevent murder, annually, of tens of thousands of infants, save health and often life. This, together with the fact that it can be done without injury to the health, or violation of moral or physical law, makes it not only right but a religious duty.

DIRECTIONS FOR USE.

Smear the instrument with glycerine, double so that the concave or hollow surface is folded together, then introduce it with the concave surface upwards until it meets with an obstruction, when it will open out, then with a little pressure with the fingers around the rim, the instrument will be evenly placed in its proper position.

The instrument retains itself by air pressure, and it so accurately fits the parts that it adapts itself perfectly, and no apprehension of its going too far, or doing the slightest harm need be felt.

Mrs B. Smyth, *Limitation of Offspring* (1893).

134. Lack of Suitable Contraceptives

This letter from a young Hobart doctor to Marie Stopes, the founder of the first English birth-control clinic, illustrates the difficulty that even doctors had in obtaining effective contraceptives in Australia. Customs Regulations introduced in 1923 prohibited the importation of contraceptives.

As a general practitioner I have been extremely interested in your work on birth control, the more so as the colonial universities do not include it in the medical curriculum. I must confess that all I have been able to suggest to my patients, who I considered should not become pregnant, was that they should make their husbands employ a condom or douche immediately post coitum.

At present I have as a patient a young married woman with t.b. About two weeks ago I read your book and at once advised her to get a copy of it. She did so and then asked me to procure a suitable pessary for her. She objects to douching and her husband to the condom. From the Hobart chemists I could only obtain a "velvo" pessary which was too large, had no spring in the ring, and was of the shape condemned in your second diagram. I then wrote to Elliot Bros. in Sydney, perhaps the largest firm of chemists in the Commonwealth, and described carefully what I required. I received from them this morning a pessary which is quite unsuitable, being too large and with a cap of the wrong shape etc.

In desperation I have brought myself to trouble you. Would you be so kind as to have one of your clinic assistants leave the enclosed letter with a chemist who will be sure to send me the right article? I hope my helpless position at the other end of the world will appeal to you as I know no English chemists I can rely on.

Dr Eric Jeffrey to Dr Marie Stopes, 30 November 1922.

135. Bust the Customs

I am very grateful for your attempt to help one so far isolated as I am, but I regret to say the goods have been seized for which I will pay willingly. "Bust the Customs". It is no use me trying to argue with them as we are two hundred miles from the Post Office which sent the notice. I have again become pregnant when my baby was only six months though I was nursing her. I would to God you could write me on the subject. It sounds drastic but unless I can get relief somehow I will leave my husband, as I am just sick and weary of being a breeder. Just fancy travelling as we have to do long distances two or three days by coach to the nearest railway with a family of little ones then back again with another year in and out with never a friend near you, only looking forward week to week for the coach, sweltering just now at 98 in the shade. Mothers at home don't know what it is to have such a trying climate. My children Thank God are healthy and strong but what of me an anaemic wreck, struggling on baking our own bread and a hundred things a town woman never guesses. I have heard of an operation cutting the tubes. Would a woman then tend to stoutness as this would be a great burden in a hot climate like this. Advise me if you can as I am in touch with no doctor here and would not like to consult a man on the subject. I am enclosing 10/- to goods. If I still owe you anything let me know and if there is a balance in my favour then devote it to your cause.

Mrs M. W. of Queensland to Dr Marie Stopes, 19 November 1923.

136. The Ban on Advertising

When introducing the Police Offences (Contraceptives) Bill in the Victorian Legislative Council, Minister H. Pye justified legislation banning the advertisement of contraceptives on the grounds that this sort of publicity might arouse sexual curiosity in children. The legislation did not prohibit the local manufacture or sale of contraceptives, but by removing them from display, it discouraged embarrassed people from requesting them and it closed one avenue of information about birth control.

The purpose of the Bill is to prohibit the advertising, public exhibition, and hawking of contraceptives, and this I am sure will have the support of every decent-minded person in the community. Whatever may be our views on the merits or demerits of birth control, the indiscriminate distribution of advertisements throughout the State, giving particulars and price-lists of these articles, cannot commend itself to any citizen. One result of the present method is that this advertising matter, thrown over the fences of private houses, dropped in letter-boxes, or given away outside picture theatres, football grounds, and so on, gets into the hands of children and youths. Their curiosity is thus awakened and they gain a knowledge which can only be seriously harmful to themselves and distressing to their parents. There is ample evidence within the Chief Secretary's Department that widespread advertising is being carried out to an increasing extent. The police by moral suasion have endeavoured to restrict it, but the practice has grown beyond that stage, and the Government is convinced the evil is one that should be stopped. I hope that the passing of this Bill will give assistance to the many institutions such as mothers' unions and like bodies that are endeavouring at the present time to combat this evil. Protests have been received from every part of the State, and practically every woman's organization, including the Mothers' Union, the Girls' Friendly Society, and the Country Women's Association. The Australian Natives Association, schoolteachers, and many others have also urged the necessity for legislation; while a similar request has been made by many members of the legislature and by the press.

The Bill will not in any way interfere with the right of a person to purchase the articles if he so desires, nor will it prohibit or restrict the publication or sale of medical or scientific books dealing with the subject of birth control. It will, however, prohibit the printing, publication, or distribution of any advertisements for contraceptives, their public display, whether in shop windows or elsewhere, or their hawking from door to door. The result expected is that a knowledge of their existence will be kept from children of tender years, and men and women will not have these things flaunted before them. If a person wants to purchase them, he can do so, but he must ask for them and they must not be thrust upon him.

H. Pye, speech to the Victorian Legislative Council, 23 October 1935.

137. Feminist Reticence

Feminist groups in Australia were reluctant to publicly support birth control. Jessie Street gives some reasons for this and passes the responsbility for contraception over to the medical profession.

I feel I have not been a very effective correspondent but as I told you in a Report I sent you some years ago, more harm than good might come of publicity on this subject. At present there are no regulations against the sale or manufacture of contraceptive devices. There are some Customs regulations concerning importation of such things but these are merely with the object of encouraging their local manufacture. If any publicity does take place various Social Organizations raise their voices in protest and endeavour to have restrictions introduced against the giving of birth control information. I feel that the most effective way is to prevail upon Medical Bodies to pass recommendations that contraceptive instruction should be given in Medical Schools.

Jessie Street to Edith How Martyn, Director of the Birth Control Information Centre, London, 9 July 1934.

138. Medical Ethics

Norman Haire, a graduate of the University of Sydney, was, in the early 1920s, among the medical practitioners in England who advocated birth control. He was medical officer at two birth-control clinics in London and by his writings and lectures made information about contraception available to a lay audience. When he returned to Sydney at the beginning of the Second World War, he was appalled by the ignorance he found there regarding birth control and sexuality and his efforts to rectify this situation were frustrated by the reticence imposed by the ethics of the medical profession.

It is difficult to say just to what extent Australia's low birth-rate is due to the use of contraceptive methods. Indeed, the knowledge of reliable and harmless contraceptive methods seems to be limited, in this country, to a very few people. In Europe and particularly in Great Britain, books and pamphlets which give the best scientific knowledge available, in language understandable by the ordinary man or woman, are circulated freely. Doctors are free to write for lay readers and lecture for lay audiences, and many of them, including some leaders of the profession, do so frequently all over the country. The various birth-control groups have established scores of clinics where women may be examined by qualified doctors specially trained for this purpose and instructed by them in contraceptive methods. About twelve years ago the British Minister of Health issued a circular authorizing doctors at the Health Centres throughout the country, which are paid out of the government funds, to give contraceptive advice to married women, whose health is such, permanently or temporarily, that it would be damaged by pregnancy or childbirth. A few medical schools and many birth-control clinics train medical students and doctors in the technique of contraception. Contraceptive appliances are sold cheaply . . .

In Australia the position is quite different. Medical ethics here do not permit the doctor to write on medical matters, under his own name, in other than purely medical journals.

If he publishes books on medical matters for the ordinary reader, there are severe restrictions on their advertisements and sale. He may not lecture on medical matters to lay audiences.

Norman Haire, *Sex Problems of Today* (1942).

139. Education in Birth Control

Marion Piddington advocated greater use of birth control among married people, to ensure that the quality of life would not be undermined by more children than parents could afford, and so that those with inherited disease would not reproduce their racial weakness.

The following methods and instructions have been approved by the Gynaecologists supporting the work of the Institute of Family Relations.

The I.F.R. supplies the latest and most reliable methods of contraception for the wife's use. One method direct from Dr. Marie Stopes has been successful in 2,000 cases.

To determine size, state whether a child has been born or not.

Three advantages of the new contraceptive:—

(1) They are hygienic and harmless.

(2) Easy to make and place.

(3) No drug is used in making them.

The necessary contraceptives ready for use, together with instructions for using and making them at a small cost, will be sent upon receipt of postal note for 21/-. With the first outfit 1 doz. sheaths and contraceptive jelly (I.F.R.) are sent for use with the double method, or for the husband to use alone. The wife can learn to place her contraceptive soon after marriage.

After the initial expense of 21/- to the I.F.R. the wife can make her own contraceptives and the I.F.R. can post the best quality sheaths at 4/- per half doz. or 7/9 per doz. with contraceptive jelly (I.F.R.) 2/6 per tube for application with sheath.

When posting the outfit, information is also given which will ensure with certainty that conception can be prevented.

This special information is given in case of unforseen accidents (which should never occur) and it is thus hoped that the frequent anxiety experienced in marriage will be saved to both husband and wife.

Keeping baby on the breast will not prevent pregnancy. There is no "safe period" for thousands of women.

The method of birth control practised by some husbands of withdrawal before the climax (coitus interruptus) is harmful to both husband and wife, and is by no means sure, since numerous cases of pregnancy have been reported where this method has been constantly employed.

Quinine is valueless as a spermicide.

No caps are supplied by the Institute.

Marion Piddington, duplicated information sheet distributed by the Institute of Family Relations, Sydney (c. 1934).

140. "The Hard Road of Undesired Motherhood"

Dr Katie Ardill Brice, the author of this lecture on birth control, opened the first birth-control clinic in Sydney in 1933. The clinic was sponsored by the Racial Hygiene Association.

By speaking on the subject today I wish to make it perfectly clear that by BIRTH CONTROL I mean the use of measures which are calculated to prevent conception taking place and not to any attempt at the destroying of life once that has occurred. The spread of knowledge of Birth Control would do much to prevent abortion. Unfortunately abortion is more frequent than you in the security of your home realise.

We who work among the poorer classes can tell of the awful harvest of maimed bodies resulting from this practice. And are we wholly free from responsibility? Let us in the name of decency rise and make an attempt to deal honestly with the problem.

In consenting to address you today on the subject of Birth Control I realised that I was introducing a subject which was far from being unanimously approved but much of the sentiment and well bred humbug of the Victorian Era has vanished and a new freedom of thought and speech and action has arisen giving to men and women greater freedom to develop and grow to their full stature and bring out their best possibilities. We grow more civilised in the best sense as our lives become greater and freer, fuller of creative work and fuller of vital help, so that sooner or later we shall move on to that stage when men and women will conduct the great concern of pro-creation with as much foresight and planning as all other important factors that call for intelligent handling. They will have the children they desire and are in a position to bring up in comfort not chance comers into this world, not unwanted additions, straining their resources to an intolerable extent.

First decent living conditions of life then the living thing.

That this will make for the increased happiness of individual parents and individual families is obvious, that it will likewise make for a happier wealthier nation follows with an irresistible logic.

Where ever we meet with married happiness be sure it rests on a harmonious sex life. Sex and its urgencies play so large a part in our lives that where there is anything wrong on the central department, life as a whole is thrown out of gear, physically, mentally and morally. The needs of sex are next to food the most imperious of all the instincts implanted in us. Now marriage was instituted for the regulation and allaying of this need and where full mutual response and mutual satisfaction of this elemental need are lacking we may look for troublous times. For untold numbers of women every conjugal embrace is poisoned by the ever present fear of consequences — the fear of yet another unwanted baby, of yet another weary trudge along the hard road of undesired motherhood.

Our aim should be to make a happier world peopled by men and women who find in marriage the greatest mutual help and inspiration and whose children will have come to them by choice — not by chance. And this can be accomplished by Birth Control, but unfortunately this subject so often arouses controversy, antagonism, protests and lamentations from many quarters.

Briefly let us answer some of these main objections.

What an indictment of religious morality. Are we to believe that the whole edifice of Christian morality will fall to the ground if we remove the buttress of fear? Is the fear of the Lord as naught to the fear of the risk? The ignoble safeguard of fear must make way for a morality founded on our duty towards our neighbour and a nobler conception of sex love. Let us abandon a morality that has made goodness synonymous with dullness and seek a sane morality more worthy of the enthusiasm of youth.

The shrouding of the whole business of Birth Control in mystery and ignorance leaves the matter — a matter of crucial importance — largely in the hands of quacks and charlatans and here let me state emphatically that I advocate that this knowledge of Birth Control should not be left to commercial enterprise or voluntary effort but that we should have established mothers' welfare centres where such information could be given.

The poorer women plead for the knowledge which they know many of their richer sisters possess and are forced to obtain what help they can from the only sources open to them and these so often are only cheap advertisements. For every woman who rejoices because a man is born into the world there is another who weeps at the advent of the little one who will rob the living of their bread.

In an age when Science has harnessed natural forces shall woman still be their play thing? Is it not a crime against humanity that diseased and Syphilitic children should be thrust into life? Let us take Lord Dawson of Penn's famous saying "Choice not chance in the production of children" as our watchword to usher in the happier era when woman shall be free from the slavery of enforced maternity.

1. That a high birthrate is desirable and that a fall is "Race Suicide".

In spite of much that is said the population steadily increases, and as the infantile rate of death has fallen in most countries this argument fails. In countries with a high death rate it is almost invariably found that the infantile death rate is also high. More children's cradles often mean more children's coffins. We do not want an overcrowded mass of slum dwellers physically below par forming centres of wretchedness, let us have smaller numbers of orderly healthy useful citizens.

2. That Birth Control is artificial and unnatural.

All civilisation, as Lord Dawson of Penn, the King's Physician reminds us, involves the chaining of natural forces and their conversion to man's will and uses. There is nothing regular or invariable about conception and contra-ception does not violate any law as it does not interfere with any regular sequence but merely eliminates as it were (the 100th. chance).

3. That Birth Control leads to sterility.

No evidence has ever been produced that the use of contraceptives has proven injurious to women has been stated by Sir James Barr in evidence given before the Medical Commission.

4. That chastity will be no more and immorality rampant if birth control becomes general.

Before proceeding with the subject of Birth Control I have collected several cases at random from among the hundreds of women I see yearly at the Clinics and Out Patients Dept. cases which have made me become an ardent advocate of Birth Control.

Mrs G. Aged 35, mother of 3 children, eldest in Newcastle Mental Home for some years, next child at home mentally deficient also having spent some time in Newcastle, third and youngest child 5 already a confirmed Masturbator and far from normal mentally. The mother came and wept as she told me that owing to 3 mental children inquiries had been instituted by the Repatriation and she and her husband submitted to a test for Syphilis. Both proved negative but then she learnt for the first time that her own father was [in fact] her grandfather and she had married in ignorance.

Mrs X. Pulmonary Tuberculosis, had already had two Haemorrhages on the lung and been in Waterfall Sanatorium, 4 children 2 already diagnosed Tubercular.

Mrs. K. Patient had Nephritis (Kidney trouble). Has had three pregnancies. First baby was born while mother was having a "fit", child died at birth. Second pregnancy the mother although still subject from Kidney trouble was allowed to go almost to full time and then to save her life induction was resorted to. Baby lived a few hours. Third time the mother was induced again but the baby was born dead.

Mrs J. Seven children all suffering from some disability while the mother herself has pelvic trouble. The husband is a semi-invalid suffering from Aneurism and does know that he will die quite suddenly.

Mrs T. 6 children 3 suffering from kidney trouble, 1 from Infantile Paralysis. At 3 of her confinements the mother nearly died with Haemorrhage, while throughout the course of the pregnancies she suffered from marked kidney and heart trouble. On each occasion of her confinement she had been emphatically told to have no more children but no definite information as to how to prevent conception was given her.

K. Ardill Brice, address to one-day conference convened by the Racial Hygiene Association, Sydney, during Health Week, 1932.

141. Birth Control not a Panacea

The following views on birth control were formulated by the militant Central Women's Committee of the Australian Communist Party. Influenced by the Soviet Union's progressive legislation on sexual matters they, unlike bourgeois birth controllers, recognized abortion as a method of birth control.

In view of the fact that never before has any section of the Australian working class movement made a statement on this question, we print below the resolution, unanimously endorsed at the Sydney Women's Conferences last month:—

One of the most harmful ideas held by a section of the working class is that a knowledge of birth control will solve the problems of our class. This idea is nothing but an illusion which sections of the ruling class openly foster at this period, when the supply of labour power far exceeds the demand.

That family limitation will improve the lot of the workers, is an illusion leading to the opportunist conclusion that there is no need to struggle for increasing living standards.

Only a degenerate class commits suicide. Our class is the society of the future; therefore, we must fight for our right and the right of our children to enjoy a decent existence. We must fight for our right to bear and rear large or small families, according to our desires.

Thus we must repudiate the idea — "Working men and women, restrict your families. Demand the facts of birth control, so that you will be more easily able to exist decently on the pittance which is yours under capitalism."

At the same time, however, since we stand for the right of every man and woman to determine the size of their families, to make child-bearing a voluntary function, we must demand that birth control knowledge, which is today monopolised by the rich, be made available to the millions of mothers of our class, many of whom lose their lives or endanger and sometimes ruin their health, through ignorance and the dread of giving birth to another child.

This conference, therefore, believing that this knowledge should be accessible to the working women, demands of the Government that the necessary information and advice be obtainable at the health and baby clinics in the various localities.

In regard to abortion, which is illegal in capitalist countries, but freely available for women of the capitalist class, we demand that abortion be carried out under skilled medical attention in public hospitals, in all cases where requested by pregnant women, providing that the circumstances are considered justifiable by a committee of women workers attached to the local clinic, to which, in the first instance, the appeal is to be made.

In putting forward this demand, we take as our example the situation, so far as abortion is concerned, in Russia today, where such an operation is carried out free of charge at a public hospital, should a committee of working women, elected from the factory or locality endorse the request for such an operation.

"Women's Conference Resolution on Birth Control", *Working Woman*, January 1932.

PART 3

Working Women

Introduction

Each section of this book is concerned with "women's work", and the different and sometimes subtle ways in which women contribute to the economy. Women's unpaid work includes not only their domestic labour within the home but also the unpaid work of women in institutions and the voluntary philanthropic work of women's organizations. In the section on "Outcasts of Society", information about women's work emerged from institutional and welfare records: details are given of the employ-ment of women on the peripheries of poverty — women in the "precarious trades" of washing, sewing and cleaning — as well as about the work done inside the insti-tutions that provided competition in these already overcrowded areas of female employment. Documents concerned with the family add to these trades: there is, for instance, the "baby farmer" who looked after the young children of women who themselves had few opportunities of regular and well-paid employment and were not able to care for their children. Both the work of paid employees and the unpaid work of the ladies' committees are also described in the records of institutions. Both roles could be seen as merging in the figure of the welfare worker, a position of higher status and training, which owed much to the insistence of women's organizations that the care of women in the community should be placed in the hands of other women. Just as it is impossible to get a clear picture of some of the poorly paid female trades without looking at charity and welfare records, it is difficult to see domestic service clearly without taking into account that institutions trained girls and women for this work and continually provided a source of this kind of labour. A second source of supply is illustrated in this section — immigration. A further area of employment documented elsewhere is prostitution. While some of the documents dealing with women's unemployment link this with increased prostitution, few of the documents specifically concerned with prostitution view it primarily as a job, and while there is some awareness of economic determinants, there is an absence of any mention of the features commonly associated with discussions of work: conditions, pay, control.

In this section, then, we look at some specific kinds of employment in which women have been engaged. A broader picture of women's work also can be derived by referring to other sections of the book.

The peculiar nature of "women's work" that differentiates it from "men's work" is not revealed by looking at the nature and range of women's paid employ-ment. The idea that women have concentrated in jobs that are said to relate to their "traditional" roles in society — caring for others, providing food and domestic labour, as well as clothing and educating others — adds little to our understanding of the nature of women's work, especially when it is clear that men have also taken over traditional female jobs once they became industrialized and have dominated the upper reaches of all the "caring" occupations. Describing the exceptional women who have succeeded in work usually dominated by men, or who do jobs usually reserved for men, does little more than offer role models for other women or show the possibilities of variety within a generally more simple workforce pattern. What does seem to differentiate "women's work" from "men's work" in the community is the relationship between that work and the family. Employment outside the home has usually been seen as only one of a woman's alternatives. Because women have been seen as possessing an alternative unavailable to men, their "right to (paid) work" has therefore been tempered or undermined by the existence of that other, often only theoretical, possibility. Only in the most obscuring mythologies has the family represented a refuge from work rather than an alternative workplace.

This section is largely concerned with women in paid employment outside the home, although it also looks at those women poised halfway in the industrial process who worked in their own homes on the labour-intensive jobs that factory-owners found more profitable to leave to cheap outside labour. It is indicative of the problems presented by women's work that the first female factory inspectors were immediately diverted to the out-worker, whose own conditions were often appalling, but whose actual existence seemed to threaten the living standards of women in workshops, whose work could be more easily regulated and observed. Similarly, the domestic nature of the work of servants seemed to defy both industrial organization and regulation, and the domestic female employer/female employee relationship, if looked at too closely, threatened to undermine the fragile feminist belief in the common experience of women. These difficulties, however, are the result of the nature of the job and apply equally to the male out-worker and the male servant, who existed too, although in fewer numbers than their female counterparts. In these forms of non-industrialized work, the family producing unit persisted, just as it did among the self-employed on farms and in small shops. What is interesting, is why so many women were among the exploited and sweated out-workers who shocked the investigators and the charitable public at the end of the nineteenth century. The factory inspectors themselves were sure that the explanation lay in the double responsibility that many of these women faced, which kept them from factory work and in the home minding children, caring for relatives, at the same time that it made their paid work an economic necessity. The retreat of married women to unpaid work in the home might have been seen by many as a way of protecting the jobs of single women, female breadwinners and men, but the unregulated paid work of women whose home situation either enabled them or forced them to work for below subsistence wages threatened everyone's standard of living. Charity workers were among the first to see the results if not the implications of women's employment at these rates of pay.

Clearly, the position of the woman in the family is relevant to an understanding of her industrial position. Whether or not it ought to be relevant to her work situation was a dilemma resolved in different ways at different times by women's organizations, who asked for both equal rights and special considerations. The creation of professional jobs for women to care for and protect other women was a sign of the growing influence of women's organizations in the community, but it frequently led to restrictions on women's work under the guise of protection (factory inspectors) and restrictions on freedom (women police and welfare workers). This partly arose because of the emphasis placed on the family role of women by other women who had found for themselves a larger sphere of opportunity. The failure to take into account the implications of the "special relationship" between women and the family was dramatized in the failure of unionism, which narrowly defined the woman worker and was not successful in combating the characterization of the woman in the home as the "consumer" whose interests were antithetical to those of the productive worker. The extent to which these problems were recognized is demonstrated in the section "Women and Politics".

Women were usually thought of as having "somewhere else to go" : home to parents, home to have or look after children, home to care for husbands, or in the last resort, to someone else's home, to work for a token wage or none at all. Documents relating to the Depression of the 1930s suggest the belief that as long as a "servant problem" existed, there was no such thing as unemployment among women — the problem was merely to attract or coerce women into this area. The relief policies of depression governments illustrate the practical implications of this idea.

While women were thought to have two alternatives, one of which is encompassed in the phrase often used by respondents to government inquiries — "not employed, a housewife" — these documents show that for many women, paid employment was necessary either to provide their own economic independence or to establish the economic viability of that unit that was supposed to render their paid employment unnecessary. Margaret Catchpole's letter [142] reveals the variety of work one woman did in the earliest colonial period to preserve her independence, having as she did "no inklanashun" to marry, and Lucy Hart's letter [146] shows how similar work provided the basis for her family's upward mobility. Together, the letters suggest a source of conflict, as supported and unsupported women competed for irregular work. The same conflict appears in the documents concerned with schoolteachers a hundred years later.

While many of the documents in this section explore the working conditions and the economic circumstances of working-class women, two other major themes are touched upon. The use of migrant labour to fill shortages in poorly paid and unregulated occupations, and the consequences for the women involved, is shown in detail in the situation of domestic servants throughout the period. The increasing use of female immigrant labour from European countries from 1950 lies outside the period under discussion, but fits the same pattern. While today many of these women work in factories rather than in private service, they are frequently employed in the industrialized sectors of domestic work, in laundries, in cleaning, in the food industry; and in textiles, the modern counterpart of the "sweated worker" of the 1890s is usually an immigrant woman. Secondly, the documents reveal aspects of professional work often neglected by historians. Those concerned with teachers and nurses show the ways in which these occupations demanded of women a conformity to an idea of appropriate feminine behaviour, which reflected middle-class values and a double standard of morality. The extent to which the demand for higher professional standards could close an occupation to working-class women is illustrated in the case of midwives.

Most of the documents in this section relate the experiences of white women. As the excerpts from George Augustus Robinson's Journal show, the exploitation of Aboriginal women as workers was frequently enmeshed in a sexual exploitation as well [143, 144], and many of the documents in the section "Private Lives" describe this dual process. The documents included here show how some Aboriginal women (and children) were regarded not as cheap or unpaid labour, but as slaves, and how the "protection" of white authorities could alter this situation in so far as wages were paid, but not negate it, since the right of Aboriginal women to these wages and their freedom of movement were both restricted.

Earning a Living

142. An Independent Woman

Margaret Catchpole was sentenced to transportation for stealing a horse. In this letter, written in 1806. she describes the work she did to support herself in the country districts outside Sydney.

Binn for this 2 yeares past up in the Countrey at Richmond hill i went thear to nurs one Mrs Rouse a very respectfull person they Com from englent free they respect me as one of ther owen famely for Mrs Rouse with this larst child she had tould her husband that she must died Becurs i was not thear, Mr Rouse did live up at Richmond at his farm But the Govner giv him a places to be super and tender and marster Bilder at the Lumber yeard Parramitta then then i was Left over seear at his farm But it was so Lonsum for me so i left But i hav got fouer yowes and nine Breeding goates 3 wethers and sevenn Yong ones that is all my stock at present Mr Rouse keep them and Charg me nothing for them . . . i do not know any want Bliss God for i hav Binn nursen Lining in women and i will tak that keear i will not want it is a great word to say But i am well Beloved a monkst my Betters i niver hav knowen anething of punshment sinces i have Binn hear . . . i myself will not hav no husband But hear is no woman But must hav some sort of a man sum women do very well indeed uncle i tould you i was a going to a farm But id did not i Lived a Littell wille in a Littell houes of my owen i did not Lik that so i went to nurs one Mrs Skinnr they are the Channey makeres then i went to nurs Mrs Rouse and stopped with her one year and then went to Mrs Dightes thear is wear i arnt a year when i wast left at Mr Rouse farm and from thar i went to Mrs Dightes to nurs har and from thear i went to Mrs Wood and from thear to nurs Mrs Rouse a Gain now i am going to nurs Mrs fathfull Mrs Wood sister thar names wear Pitt wen they Cam into the Countrey they wear sum relashun to Lord nelson a very good famley i Liv very well and much respeted old Mrs Pitt is very fond of me But i sharll i Beliv soon goo to Live By myself Mrs Palmer hav often time wished me to goo to Liv with har again But the work was to hard for me in this hot Countrey But i all ways goo to see Mrs Palmer because Mrs Rouse and Mrs Dight was weat nurs to Mrs Palmer i might a gon to Lived with maney of the saillrs that is to a Binn thear wife and might a Lived very well But i hav no inklanashun i have a pieces of ground and i am thinken to Bild a houes or Buing a Cow But the prices of a Cow is from 30 to fiftey pound a pieces that is a grat sum of money

Margaret Catchpole to Uncle and Aunt Howes, from Sydney, 8 October 1806.

143. Mutton-birding

Aboriginal women were abducted and compelled to work for white men in a variety of manual tasks. On the islands off Tasmania, one of these tasks was mutton-birding.

Mutton birds — The women have a stick about three feet long called a spit and they put this into the hole. If there is a bird they tear up the ground with the stick and lay hold of him. They have gloves to lay hold of the birds. The birds come in the twenty-second of November and lay eggs. The eggs are very good and about the size of a duck egg.

G. A. Robinson, Journal, 12 November 1830.

144. Slavery

Here George Augustus Robinson describes the work Aboriginal women did for the Bass Strait sealers, showing the part that women played in occupations sometimes described as "exclusively male".

I had instructed Parish to proceed to Gun Carriage and to bring away the black women, and also a supply of potatoes. He said he would rush their houses for the women. I desired him to do no such thing, for there was fifty dogs on the island and before he could get to their houses the dogs would give the alarm; and that he would take TE.KAR.TEE with him, and that on reaching the island at night he would send her forward to inform the women that they would be well taken care of. There was no doubt of her getting to the women: the dogs would not bark at her as they knew her, and on the women being informed that their relations and friends was on the island, they would assuredly come and all that the men could say would not keep them away. These abandoned men had done and said all they possibly could to alarm and terrify these poor women in order to induce them to keep out of the way, and whenever they saw a boat coming they was ordered to conceal themselves. It had always been said that those women was quite contented with their situation, that they did not wish to leave the sealers, and that they would not run away if they was put upon the mainland, but this is false. There was not a woman kept in captivity but what earnestly desired and longed for their liberty, and many attempts have been made by them to get away and several of them had lost their lives in the attempt — many have been flogged by the sealers for attempting the same . . . The report that the black women long for captivity is contrary to human nature. Who feels pleasure in slavery, that galling appellation? And yet they are slaves. The men compel them to work hard, and they assist to work the boats in the place of men. They make them cook and do all kinds of drudgery, and they cohabit with them — the scene of debauchery is unfit to mention, and they have encouraged the most obscene dances, which is only peculiar to the islands, and is not known by the natives on the main [land]. They catch and clean mutton birds, their chief support, and they hunt for kangaroo and dress the skins. (Their only clothing is frocks made of wallaby skins.) They pluck the feathers of mutton birds and the sealers sell them to the merchants.

The black women from the islands are in considerable dread lest they should be sent back again. If they act contrary to my wish, it is enough if I tell them I shall send them back.

G. A. Robinson, Journal, 19 December 1830.

145. Emigrant Women

The ships' lists that give details of the disposal of female immigrants also give a picture of the pattern of female employment. While according to the lists, the greatest numbers were employed in domestic service, and less than 10 per cent in jobs such as glove-, dress-, and bonnet-making, and needlework, it is likely that some at least of the domestic workers had experience in these other trades, for which there was little demand.

The Committee, appointed for the distribution of the female Emigrants by the "James Pattison," have the honor briefly to report, for the information of His Excellency the Governor, that the several females amounting to 296, exclusive of 17 Children, being the whole number embarked, were safely landed on Thursday, the 11th February instant, and lodged in the temporary buildings prepared for their reception in the rear of Government House. The whole, with the exception of two who are of unsound mind, appeared to be in excellent health, and very cleanly and orderly in their dress and appearance, and bore strong testimony both in their demeanor and expressions to the kindness of the Superintendent, and to the order, regularity and harmony which he had maintained during the whole of the voyage.

The Committee have much pleasure in stating that they consider this to be the best importation of females, which has yet been received since the commencement of the present System, both as regards their usefulness and general moral conduct, so far as they have yet had an opportunity of judging. They deem it, however, proper to observe that there appear to be four, who ought never to have been admitted as Emigrants, two of whom are of unsound mind as above stated, and had been previously confined, and two are wives of Convicts.

There have already been engaged, 250; Leaving still unengaged at this date, 46; Total, 296.

Of the 250 engaged, 136 have obtained places in and near the town of Sydney, and 119 in the country districts.

The following statement shows the several capacities in which the females have been engaged, the number of each capacity and the average rate of wages per Annum they have obtained, vizt.:—

Capacity	No.		Average Wages.		
Governesses	2	..	30	0	0
Nursery Governesses	9	..	15	0	0
Housekeepers	4	..	14	5	0
Dress and bonnet makers	4	..	15	15	0
Glovemaker	1	..	8	0	0
Ladies' maids	2	..	14	0	0
Nurse	1	..	15	0	0
Cooks	8	..	12	5	0
Laundresses	20	..	11	13	0
Needlewomen	16	..	11	2	0
Housemaids	41	..	10	13	0
Nursery maids	32	..	9	16	0
General Servants of all work	100	..	9	18	6
Kitchen maids	3	..	9	6	0
Dairy women	3	..	9	0	0
Gone to their relations	4	::	—	—	—
Total engaged	250	..	10	14	6

The Committee think it right to state that they consider these wages to be higher than could have been generally anticipated, and than can safely be calculated upon in future. They are also of opinion that there was a larger number of females in this importation than Should be sent out in any one Ship, though they cannot but deem it fortunate that so many have obtained places on such favourable terms so soon after their arrival; more especially when it is considered that a Ship with 120 female Convicts arrived the same day, all of whom have been Assigned to private service.

The Committee have been very particular in allowing these females to engage only with families of respectability either known to themselves individually, or who produced satisfactory testimonials of character. It would be premature now to advance any opinion of the manner in which they may conduct themselves in this Colony; but the Committee are not aware than any have yet left their places for impropriety of conduct.

The Committee will have the honor of reporting more in detail for the information of His Excellency the Governor, when the whole of the females have been satisfactorily disposed of.

ALEX MCLEAY,   E. DEAS THOMSON.
W M. MACPHERSON.

Committee Room, Sydney, 29th February, 1836.

"Brief Report upon the female Emigrants by the "James Pattison," arrived at Port Jackson on Saturday, the 6th February, 1836, under the Superintendence of John Osborne, Esquire, Surgeon of the Royal Navy".

146. "I Do Nothing But My Own Work Now"

John Hart was a working man who worked hard so that he could become "his own master". Lucy Hart's letter to her mother in England describes not only the saga of a self-made man in mid-nineteenth-century Australia but also how she contributed to their earnings until they were "well off in the world" and she could stop working for others.

I think I told you when I was home that Hart was very saveing and very fond of money which made me very uncomfortable has I could not save anything out of his wages has we had so much sickness and of course I had many little things to buy for such a time I could not save much you might think but Mother I have never been without a *pound* in my pocket since I have been *John Harts wife* and I think that is a great thing to say.

Should I have been so well off in England NO work hard and be half starved Australia is the place to live I would not come back to England again unless I had enough to keep me without work on no account neither would my husband I am speaking now the very sentiments of our hearts but people must be *saving industrious* and *persevering* we have deprived ourselves of many things we might have had but what was it for all to try to do something for ourselves so that my husband should not allways work under a *Master* and happy am I to inform you that we have gained that point he is now his own Master, My Dear Mother after I had quite recovered from my confinement and quite strong I was determined to work to help get a living I began to take in washing and iorning at 3 shillings per Dozen so I used to earn about 15 shillings per week which was as much as I could do with a young *Baby* then we could save a pound per week for a house *garden* we was then getting on in the world very well for working people and just got things comfortable about us when my poor *husband* was taken ill with a violent *fever* fevers are very prevalent here and so they are in most hot climates when he was taken ill we had about 20 pounds in the house it was twelve weeks before he went to work again the very day he went to work we had but one shilling but thank God we did not owe any person a penny piece he went Back to his old place to work and you see My Dear Mother that through our own industry it kept us from the cold hand of *Charity* I still kept on my work all through his sickness so you might think my hands was full enough then/I never expected him to recover the Doctor gave me very slight hopes of him (after he got well and went to work again we was obliged to begin afresh and try to save a little more that is two years ago this month since then we neither of us has not had a days illness and everything have prospered) then in a month or two we bought a *cow* and she used to turn me in about 12 shillings per week and a lot of poultry of my own rearing we was then doing well I had by that time a great deal of washing as my little girl could run about/I did many weeks earn 30s. myself by my washing so I have not spent much idle time I was exactly like that when Mr. *White Brought* the letter to me that Stephen wrote and we had got 50 pounds in the Bank and all got by real hard work I must tell you Mother that Hart is a very steady sober man and would not spend a shilling in waste on no account neither would I myself my dear *Mother* now I will tell you how we got to *Melbourne.* I have no doubt you have heard of the gold diggins here at *Port Phillip* before this reaches you, the diggins Broke out soon after Mr White called on me well I beged my husband to com here and try his luck has so many *Adelaide* people have been here and done well at last he made up his mind to come and leave me in *Adelaide* has I could get my living with out touching the little money we had saved . . . in about 5 weeks after he left I received a letter from him containing the joyfull news that he had got his own share *200 pounds worth of gold* and also to tell me to sell my things and come to *Melbourne* as quick as possible so My Dear Mother gladly did I comply with that request I sold my things and took the first vessel Bound for Melbourne we had a very rough passage we was ten days coming we got to Melbourne the day after last Christmas day where I found my husband anxiously waiting my arrival he was then determined that I should not work so hard anymore of course I have no need to now for with the money that I Brought with me we could *raise 300 pounds* and now I consider myself well off in the world so I do nothing but my own work now we are living in a nice house called Devon Cottage . . . Hart bought 2 *Horses* and a *Dray* he gave 100 and 50 pounds for them he is now taking stores to the diggins for shop-keepers and he is making 30 pounds per week and making money fast but he will be off to the *diggins* again as soon as the rain comes . . .

. . . I only wish I could persuade you to come with all the children you *Mother* should have a good home and no work to do why not come *Mother* there was many older women than you came out in our vessel and are now doing well.

Lucy Hart to her mother, Mrs Lewis, and brothers and sister at Southampton, from Melbourne, 3 May 1851.

147. Apprenticeship

Indentured servants and apprentices suffered considerable restriction on their behaviour, including restrictions on their right to marry. Apprentice dressmakers, who paid to be taught, often became merely unpaid labour instead. In other trades, the absence of apprenticeships for women was more usual.

SOUTH WALES.

THIS INDENTURE WITNESSETH, THAT

doth put h   self Apprentice to
to learn his or their Art, and with him or them, after the Manner of an Apprentice, to serve from
unto the full End and Term of   Years from thence next following, to be complete
and ended; during which Term, the said Apprentice his said M   faithfully shall serve, h   Secrets keep;
h   lawful Commands every where gladly do; he shall do no Damage to h   said M   nor see it done by
others, but to h   Power shall let or forthwith give Notice to h   said M   of the same: The Goods of h
said M   he shall not waste, nor give or lend them unlawfully to any: he shall neither buy nor sell without
h   M   Leave: Taverns, Inns, or Alehouses he shall not haunt; at Cards, Dice, Tables, or any other
unlawful Games he shall not play; Matrimony he shall not contract; nor from the Service of h   said
Day or Night absent h   self; but in all Things, as a faithful Apprentice, he shall behave h   self towards h   said
M   and all h   Family, during the said Term.   And the said
for and in Consideration of the Sum of
to h   in Hand well and truly paid by the said   the Receipt whereof
is hereby acknowledged, the said Apprentice in the Art of   which he now useth,
shall and will teach and instruct, or cause to be taught and instructed, in the best Way and Manner that he can; and shall
find unto the said Apprentice sufficient Meat, Drink,   and Lodging, and all other Necessaries during
the said Term

AND for the true Performance of all and every the said Covenants and Agreements, each of the said Parties bindeth
h   self the one to the other, firmly by these Presents.   IN WITNESS whereof the Parties above-said to these Indentures
have interchangeably set their Hands and Seals, at   in this His Majesty's Territory of NEW
SOUTH WALES, the   Day of   in the
Year of the Reign of Our Sovereign Lord   of the United Kingdom of
Great Britain, King, Defender of the Faith, and so-forth, and in the Year of Our Lord One thousand eight hundred and

, Sealed, and delivered (no Stamps
g used in the Territory) in the
sence of

Eliza Ward Ewen, indentured to Hannah Jones, dressmaker, 25 September 1829.

148. Sweating and Charity

Many women attempted to support themselves through needlework and dressmaking throughout the nineteenth century, when other work was not available or when domestic duties prevented them from taking other employment. Overcrowding and poor pay frequently meant that women in these trades were forced to seek other assistance. The position of the needle-woman attracted attention late in the century when "sweating" became a topic for public debate. Here the link between sweating and charitable assistance is noted.

About the middle of the present year I was instructed by the Government to make a inquiry as to what extent the "Sweating System" existed in this colony, more especially in connexion with the clothing trade. Just at that time several articles had appeared in one of the Melbourne newspapers on this subject. I remember very well the first one. It was headed — "Sweaters in Melbourne. Horrors of the Clothing Trade," and sweating was referred to as mean, frowsy, depraved, and pitiful, and it was stated that it was carried on in Melbourne to a degree hardly less horrible than the incidents of its prevalence in London. The articles created a great amount of sensation at the time, and we all felt that the clothes we were wearing were very possibly made in some dirty loathsome den, reeking with filth and disease, and that we were spreading contagion wherever we went. I could not understand it. My official duties had taken me into all kinds of work-rooms, and although not wishing to say that all these rooms were, or are, everything that they should be, still I had not seen any rooms to which such terms could with truth be applied. Then, again, the articles referred to spoke of the long hours that sweaters employed their work-people. The Factories Act in this colony does not allow females to be employed more than 48 hours a week, but here we read of 78 and 80 hours as being an ordinary week's work. This, again, was astonishing. Employers of labour continually said that they could not obtain the female workers they required, and that when any extra pressure of work came they were compelled to make use of the privileges of the Act and obtain permission to work over-time. It therefore seemed unreasonable to say that women would work inordinately long hours in wretched rooms when they could get work in decent factories and work only 48 hours a week. As regards men, they have their unions, and it was felt that they were not likely to be imposed upon to any extent. With these feelings, I naturally commenced my labours in a very sceptical spirit, and what was found? That the whole question had been so muddled up and complicated by mixing together the various classes of work into which the clothing trade is divided that the articles were — to say the least — very misleading. The result of my inquiries was embodied in an official report, and laid before Parliament, and a copy can be obtained by any one who feels inclined to go into the subject more closely.

Before going further it will be well to state what is meant by sweaters and sweating. It is really necessary to do this, for the definitions are as numerous as they are contradictory. For instance, the members of the Tailors' Union look upon all men who do not work under their rules as sweaters. Some people urge that sweating is an abuse of the sub-contract system, and consequently there can be no sweating where there is no sub-contracting; others, on the contrary, maintain that sub-contracting is by no means a necessary element of sweating. Some people contend that a man who works a few hands, and does not work under what the trade looks upon as log prices, is a sweater; whilst, on the other hand, I have been told that the worst kind of sweating is carried on in some of the largest factories.

The committee of the House of Lords which inquired into "sweating" came to the conclusion that they could not assign an exact meaning to the term, but for all that they thought the evils known by that name to be a rate of wages inadequate to the necessities of the workers, or disproportionate to the work done, excessive hours of labour, and the insanitary state of the houses in which the work was carried on. I was compelled to give some meaning to the word, and after careful consideration defined it as taking advantage of the necessities of a worker to enforce a rate of wages which is below the current price, disproportionate to the work done, and which compels inordinate hours of labour. It was necessary in that report to mention every class of work in the clothing trade, but that need not be done here. It was soon found that the better class of tailors paid good wages, and whether they employed their work-people in their own factories, or allowed the work to be done away, it was done in clean and decent rooms.

Many cases which came under my definition of sweating were found, and they, without doubt, showed that the condition of this class of workers entitles them to assistance in some way. There are a great number of women who, through not having been brought up to any trade, and yet having from various circumstances to support themselves — and very often aged parents or young families — are compelled to work in their own homes and to accept as payment for the work they do almost any remuneration their employers will give them.

Perhaps a few facts connected with some of the cases inquired into will enable this to be better understood.

A women with a sick husband and six children, the youngest about three years old, was found making, or rather finishing, boys' coats. For this work she was paid 5s. a dozen, and she said that by working 70 hours a week she could manage to do 5½ dozen. That is earn about 27s. 6d. a week by working twelve hours a day. The husband was not in any lodge, and none of the children old enough to earn anything.

Another case visited was that of a vestmaker. The payment for this work was 12s. a dozen for men's waistcoats, 10s. for youths, and 8s. for boys. She told me that she often worked 84 hours in the week, and to earn 30s. was compelled to do so. She was a widow with three children to support, one a baby eight months old, and had to pay 7s. 6d. a week rent.

Another woman visited was a trouser finisher. This means sewing on buttons and making button-holes, turning up the bottoms of the trousers, putting in a band, and one or two other little things, and for this twopence halfpenny to threepence per pair was paid. She was a widow without children. Her house, a little wooden place in a right-of-way off a street in Carlton, was almost destitute of furniture. She paid 8s. a week rent, and told me that she could not earn more than 10s. a week, being too old to sit very long at a time. Two or three people lodged with her and paid her what they could. Judging from the appearance of the rooms and beds (indeed there was not a blanket in the whole house) the amount she would receive must have been very small.

Another case was a woman who is a slipper binder. There is a good deal of work about slipper binding. All the machine work has to be done and the slippers lined and got ready for putting on the soles, or for the putters-up, as they are called in the trade. For this work she got 1s. 3d. a dozen, a penny farthing each, and out of this had to pay for her own cotton and buy needles for the machine, the latter item being very heavy with certain classes of work. She was a widow with one daughter, a cripple, who was able to do very little to help her. Still, if work was plentiful, she could, by working long hours, earn £1 a week.

In another place a woman was found making canvas bags. The canvas was not new stuff that could be easily cut and fixed for working, but old canvas which is pulled off packing cases, and is often covered with tar or sewn up in such a way as to mean a lot of work getting it in order before the bag-making commenced. She did not buy the canvas, oh no, there was some one else, her employer who did this. The canvas was sent to her, and she made it into bags at the magnificent remuneration of 3½d. a dozen. She said it was a very hard day's work when she managed to make four dozen, that is earn 1s. 2d. Her husband was out of work, there were four children to be provided for, and 7s. 6d. a week rent to be paid. The bags were sold to the bone-dust mills. The poverty here was dreadful. As already stated, the husband was out of work. He was a hatter by trade, but there was no work to be done, so had got a bottle-boy's licence, and having hired a pony and cart, was going about collecting bottles to sell to the marine stores. These bottles had to be bought, but he could not afford to pay for them in the ordinary way, so invested 6d. or a 1s. in some toffee, which he broke up into very small pieces, and gave a piece to a child for a bottle. When it is remembered that 7½. or 8d. per dozen is a good price for bottles, and that the toffee and pony and cart had to be paid for before any profit was made, it will not be hard to see that the turnover would have to be considerable before very much could be brought home at the end of the day to increase the 1s. 2d. the wife had perhaps been able to earn.

A shirt finisher was visited. To finish a shirt you have to sew on eight buttons and make six button-holes, to fasten off four parts that have been left by the machinist, to cut off the ends of cotton, and put on a ticket. For this work she told me she was paid 9d. per dozen. This class of work is so wretchedly paid, that no one who is entirely dependent on it can attempt to do it, as it is impossible to make a living at it. It must be remembered, that the work this woman did, was of the roughest, and for the commonest kind of shirt made. Shirt makers as a rule receive from 3s. to 4s. 6d. per dozen for their work, and in my report, an average of sixteen shirt and under-clothing makers was taken, and it was found that by working 55½ hours, they were able to earn 11s. 3d. per week. It must, however, be remembered, that they have to pay for their cotton and needles, and very often the rent of a sewing machine as well out of this amount.

I could go on giving numberless cases, but they are all practically alike. The details are of course different, but the same hard work, long hours, and wretched pay exists. Even if all could go to work in factories, and there are many who cannot, whose domestic duties of one kind or another keep them at home, still the factories are not big enough to hold them, and it is feared that many employers are not anxious to have them, seeing that without doubt the work is done more cheaply in this way.

It may be wondered what has this to do with a conference on charity. It has this to do with it. All the cases mentioned, and, indeed, a very large percentage of outside workers, are to be found on the books of one or the other of the various charitable institutions about Melbourne. The pay these women receive is so wretched that they find it impossible to live entirely on what they earn. The work is intermittent, and in the instances given the amount of the earnings is always to be qualified by the remark "if the work is constant." It would, therefore, appear as if this subject could be discussed in connexion with Class D. in the appendix to our President's letter of 30th June last, viz.:—

Outdoor Relief. — In the official report already referred to various suggestions were made in the direction of legislation, but it was felt, and indeed said, that unless prices could in some way be increased they would assuredly fail to achieve the desired object, and that they after all were simply tentative. If the condition of these workers could be so improved as to enable them to support themselves, it would be a great point gained. And now, is there any way of doing this, and if there is, what is it? It is undoubtedly much more easy to find fault than to suggest remedies. It would appear as if the only way in which these people could help themselves would be by forming an union amongst themselves. If this were done, they could, backed up as they would be by public opinion, secure better pay and not have to work such long hours. It is feared, however, that this is impossible. There are so many dependant on this kind of work the necessities of whom are so great that they will work for anything rather than not work at all. There is also another class, who are not compelled to work — those who have husbands earning good wages, or in some way have a certain income coming in every week — who will also work at any price, simply because, as they say, it does not matter. They only work in their spare time, and at the end of the week have a few shillings which belong to themselves, and which they can do as they like with. These two classes (and the number of people who would come under them is very great) would, it is feared, effectually prevent any such a thing as an union of outside workers being formed. Then, if they cannot help themselves, who is it that should help them? Surely the employers and the public — the employers by paying a little more for the work done, and the public by paying a little more for the article purchased. It is only a little. Sixpence more paid for a pair of trousers, or threepence for a shirt, would, if this additional money were allowed to go to the workers, make all the difference to them. People in this colony earn good wages, and surely, if they realized what this cheap clothing means, they would not always try and buy it. It is the keen competition of the age, the desire to make business no matter who may suffer thereby, that is very much the cause of this sweating. If the owner of some large clothing factory would start and put up the prices paid to these outside workers, pay them the same as the inside workers get (for at present there is a difference in favour of the inside worker of at least 40 per cent.), and then in some way let it be known that the maker of the article in question has been fairly paid for her labour, surely the public could be induced to buy it, at a little higher price truly, but not at a higher price than is absolutely necessary to enable the maker of it to live.

The sweating system is, without doubt, gradually obtaining a footing in this colony, and, if it could be grappled with at once, it might possibly be eradicated before it has got too strong a hold amongst us. In what way this can be done is the problem to be solved.

J. A. Levey, "The Sweating System", in *Proceedings of the First Australasian Conference on Charity* (1890).

149. A Shirtmaker's Life

In this statement, a 32-year-old shirtmaker describes her working life. The attached memo was written by John Bannigan, South Australian factory inspector.

History of the Case of Mrs (A.) a shirt maker.
Bearing on the Sweating Evil.

This woman has supplied the following Statement —

In March 1896, my husband being unable to follow his usual employment through being afflicted with rheumatism, we decided to undertake shirt making as a means of livlihood. My husband being almost a cripple I could not leave him & our child, the latter being now 3½ years old.

I first applied to a firm named (B.) & asked them for shirt making — they gave me a line of men's working shirts to make at 3/- and 3/6 per doz. At first I could only manage to make about 1 doz per week, but gradually improved till I could, with the assistance of my husband who made the button holes sewed on buttons etc, make 1 doz per day. We did this work for about 18 months, but got it in such small quantities and at such irregular intervals that our average weekly earnings did not amount to more than 10/- between us.

Out of our earnings we had to pay house rent & 2/6 per week on sewing machine. About this time the work got so slack that I applied to a Syrian storekeeper named (C.). We did the undermentioned work for him at the prices stated opposite each article.

Tweed trousers (mens) 6d. per pair; Serge ditto 6d.; moles ditto 6d.; dungaree ditto 4d.; Women's aprons with shoulder straps 10d. per doz; Colored petticoats 10d. per doz; Women's night dresses 6/- per doz; Women's Chemise 3/6 per doz; Slip Bodice 4/- per doz; Children's pinafores 1/6 per doz; — men's working shirts 2/6 per doz; Boys Shirts 1/9 per doz; men's flannel shirts 1/6 per doz; men's Dungaree Coats 3½ each; men's summer coats 5/- per doz; men's beaver mole coats 5 d. each (takes 3 hours to make).

These articles were all received ready cut out & I had to make the garments & finish them at the above prices. We continued at this work for about 12 months, I doing the machining & my husband — who by this time was totally deprived of the use of his lower limbs — doing the finishing.

Our hours of work were from about 8 in the morning till 12 midnight & I have often worked till 4 in the morning. We could not afford to buy firewood & my husband's legs used to become so painful that he had to lie down about 10 o'clock.

Our united earnings amounted to about 15/- per week, but this was swallowed up by house rent & cost of machine, so that we had very little to buy food — We did not have any breakfast & about 12 noon we had a cup of tea & a little dry bread. At 6 pm we had a frugal meal & when we could afford it we got 2d. worth of meat but this was not often.

Early this year we were out of work for 6 weeks & had to pawn every little thing we could raise money on. We then got work from a Syrian named (D.) — We cut out and made up men's shirts at 3/- per doz. After a time we got work from a firm named (E.). For them we cut out and made up men's shirts at 3/6 & 4/- per doz; Pyjama Suits 10d. per suit; Butcher's aprons, hemmed top and bottom & 2 strings, 6d. per doz, do all cutting out ourselves. — It takes about one hour to make one of the shirts mentioned above. There are 9 buttons and button holes to make & this with the finishing takes from 40 to 45 minutes smart work.

Towards the end of April we got work from a Firm named (F.) — For them we made up men's shirts, double stitched, lined & 3 gussets at 5/- per doz. This work was very heavy & we could only make about 15/- per week both working hard. My husband often said it was killing him & I believe it did at last have that effect, for the poor fellow died on Sunday morning 20th inst, & I am now trying to finish the work we had in hand.

I am 32 years of age & have one child 3½ years of age. I have no money to pay for burial of my husband, but I am hopeful that I will be able to pay it off by instalments. A man named (G.) held a bill of sale over our furniture & he has this morning (9th May 1899) removed every stick. I am now going to live with my mother at Kent Town.

(Memo
The Firm (F) actually disputed the small a/c which this woman presented for her work after her husband was dead, & insisted that they pay 0/½d. less per shirt than that claimed. They also brought forward an old standing a/c said to be due from the deceased husband & put as a set-off against the pittance the poor woman had earned. Tho no part of my duty I intervened in this case & after an interview with the head of the firm they promptly paid the amount claimed & threw in half a sovereign to help the poor woman out of her difficulties. JB)

CONFIDENTIAL
(A.) Mrs F. N. [F——], 81 Franklin Street, Shirt Maker.
(B.) G. & R. Wills & Co, Wholesale Clothiers, Rundle Street
(C.) Habib — Storekeeper, 93 Waymouth Street
(D.) Antonie Mattei, Storekeeper, Elizabeth St
(E.) Bridgeland & Atterton, Tailors & Outfitters, Hindley St
(F.) G. & W. Shirelaws, Tailors & Outfitters, Hindley St
(G.) G. Dodd, Furniture dealer, Victoria Square

Report from John Bannigan, Inspector of Factories, 1899.

150. Working-Class Extravagance

In this letter, referring to the shirtmaker whose story was told in the previous document, Factory Inspector Bannigan reveals the gap in comprehension that could separate bureaucrat from "client".

Dear Madam,
In reply to your letter of yesterday's date I beg to say that I am unable to give the name of the woman referred to without first obtaining her consent.

Her most pressing want just at present is, I believe, the means to pay for the burial of her husband, in doing which she (in my opinion) somewhat foolishly incurred more expense than the circumstances warranted, & is now working hard endeavouring to earn the means to pay it off.

I will probably see her tomorrow & if she has no objection, will send her name & address to you later. In the meantime anything you may be disposed to do for her may be done through me. She has plenty of work at present and is a bit "high minded", so that it is difficult to assist her.

John Bannigan, Inspector of Factories, to Miss E. Raston, Kent Town (S.A.), 13 July 1899.

151. "Cases Worthy of Sympathy"

The interconnections between sweating and charity have already been suggested. In this letter from South Australia's female Inspector of Factories to the wife of the governor, philanthropy is shown operating in the changed circumstances of the 1890s, during which time women's unions and female factory inspectors made their appearance.

Your Ladyship,

You were pleased some few weeks ago, when I had the honor of waiting on you respecting the evil of "sweating"in the Clothing Trade, to express your desire to help any deserving case of distress that might come under the notice of the Factories Inspectors in the course of their investigations.

I now venture to bring under your notice in compliance with that expressed wish the undermentioned cases, which I believe worthy of sympathy and assistance.

Mrs. E. [B——], of Young Street, Adelaide, widow, who has for the last three years supported herself by making shirts, & whose case perhaps your Ladyship will remember I mentioned on the occasion above referred to. Recently through illness she became unable to pay for certain repairs to her sewing machine, which, in consequence, was detained by the Singer Sewing Machine Company for the amount due, & the poor woman is now deprived of the means of livelihood. One pound (£1) would enable her to recover the machine, and she says she could then earn sufficient to pay the firm the instalments due.

2nd. Mrs F. J. [F——], of Rundle Street, Kent Town, widow, a history of whose case appeared in the morning papers of 30th June last.

This woman with her husband & child recently endured all the terrible trials of a life of semi-starvation. She is now earning a precarious living by shirt-making, but is handicapped by a debt incurred for the burial of her husband. Any assistance that could be rendered towards paying this off would help to establish her in a position to live more comfortably.

With regard to the first case, I beg respectfully to suggest that in the event of your Ladyship being pleased to advance the sum required for the recovery of the sewing machine, that the amount be donated to the "Working Women's Union", which body could be empowered to receive repayment from Mrs [B——] in the event of her being able to re-fund the money, and this sum might then be made the nucleus of a fund to assist other similar deserving cases.

Thanking your Ladyship for the very kindly interest you have evinced in these matters,

I have the honor to be,
Your Ladyship's most obedient servant,

Agnes A. Milne, Inspector of Factories, to Lady Tennyson, 13 August 1899.

152. "A Better Day Dawning"

Agnes Milne, a shirtmaker who became South Australia's second female factory inspector, was involved in the Women's Christian Temperance Union and in the Working Women's Union. She recognized that the working conditions of women had to be changed for women's emancipation to be complete.

Not to generosity, man's first impulse to woman, nor to justice, his highest act, but to passionless science must be credited the vastly extended area of the field of female employment which, during the latter half of the expiring century has profoundly changed her character, and promises to further complicate social conditions. And yet not alone to passionless science can be ascribed the emancipation of woman, when I read that nearly nineteen hundred years ago, the first commission ever given in this new era was given to a woman. And although she has been crushed and trampled under foot of men, yet to-day, by the power of the All-Good and science going hand in hand (for science after all is only the handmaid of the Great Ruler of the universe), there will rise up a noble band of women who in their turn will be wise to counsel and command.

It may appear that the social conditions of women seem to be more complicated than ever; yet we are hopeful, that by wise and judicious legislation, out of the chaos and complication, order, peace, and plenty will come. But we are now to take up the practical parts of "Woman's Work and Wages."

An article from the *Advertiser*, 1898, states that, according to some interesting facts and figures recently published by Lloyds concerning exploits of women, nearly four millions of American women are earning incomes as lawyers, authors, journalists, Government clerks, physicians, farmers, ministers of the gospel, and public school teachers. Many of these are receiving large salaries — from £400 to £700 per annum.

But while facts and figures such as the above are very gratifying, we have to acknowledge the fact that to-day there are thousands of women workers who are still held in the iron grasp of commercialism. Hence to-day we find her narrowed and cramped, while many a poor creature has to work long hours for a very small remuneration.

Still we trust there is a better day dawning, when such things as the following shall be a thing of the past. . .

Inspector Kingsbury, in the *Age*, states that in one of the Victorian factories one girl machined forty pairs of uppers for a remuneration of 10s. 6d., while another turned out eighty pairs for 12s. 6d. He also states that apprentices were only receiving 2s. 6d. per week when they should have been receiving 5s; and we have to admit the same thing obtains to-day in many industrial pursuits in our own province.

The Hon. W.A. Robinson, in an article to the *Advertiser* some time ago, wrote:— "There is a point which cannot be passed by the workers, and which can never be insisted upon by the capitalists, that is the starvation point, and this point has been reached in many instances (we do not say in all). And," says the writer, "we can go further and say, without fear of contradiction, that this semi-starvation system of payment for female industrial labor has been in existence for many years, notwithstanding the powerful appeals of reformers."

We have still with us to-day the bargain-hunters, who never trouble to ask themselves the question how much the worker receives for her share of the work in the bargain that is so cheap.

Therefore woman's emancipation is not yet complete, when it is known as a fact that numbers of women are working hard and long hours, and the most they can earn is from 7s. to 10s. per week.

Girls in Adelaide factories to-day are making men's tweed suits (dark serge) for 4s. the suit. Another woman, to keep her workroom going during slackness of her own work, took a line of tweed trousers to make, not knowing what she was to receive for same, and when taken home received the handsome sum of 7d. a pair (well made). She, paying her employees a fair day's wage for a fair day's work, had nothing whatever for her own labor.

Henry George says:— "Where wages are highest there will be the largest producers and the most equitable distribution of wealth. There will invention be most active, and the brain guide best the hand. There will be the greatest comfort and the widest diffusion of knowledge, the purest morals, and the truest patriotism."

May this soon be so in South Australia.

> . . . . . Where, floating free
> From mountain top to girdling sea,
> A proud flag waves exultingly;
> And freedom's sons the banner bear;
> No *shacked slave* shall breathe the air —
> Fairest of Britain's daughters fair —
> > Australia.

"Woman's Work and Wages", Agnes A. Milne, *Journal of Agriculture*, February 1899.

153. "The Full Fruits of Their Labour"

Legislation on hours and conditions of work particularly designed to protect women and children was one way in which attempts were made to improve their working conditions. Another way was to set up special factories in which concerned and philanthropic people could invest.

In consequence of the cruel hardships which the sweating evil has inflicted on a large section of the working women of Adelaide, it is proposed that an effort should be made at this opportune time to start a small Shirt Factory on principles which will give to the workers the full fruits of their labour.

It is proposed to raise by the issue of debentures the sum of £200, bearing interest at the rate of 4% per annum, in shares of £1 each, the debentures to be redeemable at any time by giving reasonable notice to the holders.

The objects of the Association — which it is proposed shall be called "The Working Women's Shirt Making Association" — is to establish under competent management a Shirt Making Factory, consisting of about eight women, including the manager for a start, the number to be increased later on according to requirements. That the property of the Association shall be vested in trustees to be used for the furtherance of the object for which the Association was formed in perpetuity, subject however to the payment of principal and interest on all paid up shares.

An earnest appeal is hereby made to all lovers of fair dealing to help this worthy object by taking a few shares in the Association, through the efforts of which the promoters are hopeful that an initial blow will be struck at the pernicious evil of sweating.

Friends and well-wishers of this worthy object, who are willing to assist by taking shares are requested to attach their names hereto, stating the number of shares they are willing to take in the Association in order that sufficient promises of assistance may be forthcoming before any unnecessary expense if incurred.

It was intended to add a few extracts to this notice from reports by the Inspector of Factories respecting the starvation rates paid to workers under the sweating system; but it having been pointed out that the facts are already widely known, the extracts are omitted in order to economize space.

> We, the undersigned, hereby agree to take the number of Shares at £1 each set opposite our names herein, in the proposed W.W.S.A., & we promise to pay the whole of the amount due on the said shares within 14 days of the formation of the Association . . .

Working Women's Shirt Making Association, Prospectus (n.d., c.1899).

154. "Blood Money"

The investigations of the early female factory inspectors into the conditions and pay of working women took them out of the factories and into the homes of the out-workers. Some of the most graphic descriptions of this work were given by the first female factory inspector in New South Wales, Annie Duncan.

In the course of my rounds one day I was arrested by the sight of a pale harassed-looking woman, seated in front of a window, and evidently working against time. The case proved to be a very pitiful one; a deserted wife left to support three children between the ages of 3 and 11. She was struggling to make a living by making shirts for a factory at 4s. a dozen; each shirt was made with a turned-down double collar, finished with three buttons and button-holes, a well fitted front, a breast pocket, cuffs, and four gussets; buttons were provided by the factory, but she was obliged to find all cotton at the rate of 11d. per dozen reels, and button hole cotton at 2½d. per reel; the shirts were of a good class, well cut, and of good material, and demanded careful work. Questioned as to her probably weekly earnings, she replied that she had that week worked all Sunday, had risen early on Monday morning, and stayed up till midnight, and during that time had made five shirts, working continuously except for the necessary interruptions of meals and of dressing and undressing her children. She had occasionally made linen pillow-cases at 2s. per dozen, finding both buttons and cotton, and took in any chance work she could get. With the aid of Government relief of 7s. 6d. a week and 5s. rent received from a lodger, she was just able to pay for her cottage, make her weekly payment for the machine, and feed and clothe herself and her children scantily enough. "He is a poor little half-starved creature," she said, speaking of her bright-faced little boy; "but I can't help it. I am always just as you see me," she went on, with patient endurance, "working as hard as I can go; it's a cruel price; but the employer is very nice to me, and indeed he ought to be, for it is blood-money." The bed on which her work was laid out was covered with an old table-cloth; and she told me that for two years she had had no blankets. Happily this want has now been supplied.

Another sad case was that of an elderly woman, who for years had lived in comfort with her brother. On his death she was cast on her own resources, and in a spirit of true practical charity she sought to make a home for other helpless and homeless women, who might otherwise have drifted far enough on a cruel fate. By taking in work from factories and sharing work, expenses and profits — the latter, I fear, an unknown quantity — with other women, she hoped to make a living. She had many disappointments amongst those she wished to befriend; but had not lost heart, and when I visited her was at work with a respectable-looking Irish girl, who with an ignorance of the true condition of things that was pathetic, expressed her pleasure at the thought of learning "a profession which would make her independent." The elder woman told me that she had been making moleskin trousers (very heavy work) for two factories for 6d. a pair; but that since Christmas, 1897, there had been a fall of a halfpenny, with additional pressing and taping to be done. For ordinary "colonials", in 1897, she got 6d. a pair; for "raised seams", 7d.; but in each class there was a fall of a penny since the new year. She said that she rose early and worked late; that she had not, from Christmas to May, averaged 10s. a week; but that with much effort she had contrived to keep her rent paid up, and spent from 2s. to 2s. 6d. a week on food. Curious to know how life was kept up on such conditions, I asked her what she lived upon. "Bread and black tea," was the reply. "I have bought sixpenny worth of damaged potatoes since Christmas, half a pound of butter in four or five weeks; and when I feel very weak, I get two or three pennyworth of the cheapest meat." Such are the conditions under which lonely women drag out a sorrowful existence at our very doors.

Annie Duncan, "Report on the Working of the Factories and Shops Act for 1898".

155. Co-operation

The necessity for women's co-operative industrial ventures to compete with other commercially run factories led to this experiment in South Australia. Catherine Spence was one of the women involved in the scheme, investing in it herself and launching it on its way.

SOUTH AUSTRALIA

The first factory in this State to be run by electricity is just about to be opened. It is being started by a small company, of which the shareholders are all women, and the manager and secretary are women. It is beginning in a small way with eight or ten women operatives who must be shareholders. A number of very practical level-headed women are the promoters of the scheme, which promises to be very successful. It will have the good wishes of many, and its progress will be watched with lively interest. Any scheme which helps women to help themselves is worthy of enthusiastic support. There are still people who speak with contemptuous dislike of women who work for their living, but as many have no male relatives able or willing to provide for their needs, it is absolutely necessary that they shall enter the ranks of wage-earners, if existence and self-respect are to be maintained.

Woman's Sphere, 10 March 1902.

156. "Living Death"

As in the eastern states, exposés revealed the conditions experienced by dressmakers and needle-workers. In this Western Australian case, the women were not out-workers but were employed in city workrooms. Heading the campaign against sweating were members of the labour movement, including Mamie Swanton, leader of the tailoresses' (and, later, the tailors') union. The First World War had resulted in considerable expansion in the clothing and textile industry.

THE WAIL OF THE WHITEWORKER

"Suicide or Shame?"
Arbitration Court Evidence
An Appeal

In the course of his magnificent "Vision of the Future," Ingersoll says: — "I see a world . . . where the poor girl, trying to win bread with the needle — the needle that has been called the 'asp for the breast of the poor' — is not driven to the desperate choice of crime or death, of suicide or shame."

Unfortunately, the realisation of Ingersoll's "Vision" appears to be a very long way off, judging by evidence recently submitted in the Perth Arbitration Court in the Whiteworkers' case.

1. Miss ——, a dressmaker employed at Goode Durrant's, said she had been seven years at the trade, and was now earning £1 4/- a week. She lived at home, had no father, and had to take in sewing at home to make ends meet.

2. Miss —— worked at the Broadway making shirts, flannels, blouses, and underclothes, at piecework rates. Her wages averaged 16/1½ a week.

3. Miss ——, a trouser finisher at Goode Durrant's, has been five years at the trade, and now earns £1 a week. Pays 18/- a week for board, and gets financial help from her parents who do not live in the city.

4. Miss ——, a milliner with six years' experience. Has worked for Murray's, Moore's, and Luckey's, and averaged 25/- a week. Has to do homework to enable her to meet expenses, and consequently has practically no time for recreation.

5. Miss ——, a milliner with six years' experience, is now employed with Boan Bros., and earns 17/6 a week.

6. Miss ——, a milliner with five years' experience, is now employed at Boan Bros., and earns 15/- a week. Has no father.

7. Miss ——, a dressmaker employed by Bradshaw's, Fremantle, has been seven years at the trade and is paid 17/6 a week.

8. Miss ——, a dressmaker employed by Fisher Beard, Fremantle, has been five and a half years at the trade, and earns 30/- a week. She and her sister "batch", and have to stay at home of nights and week ends doing private sewing in order to pay their way.

Imagine, from the above instances, the appalling conditions generally under which our W.A. Whiteworkers are existing? Thousands of beautiful young Australian girls daily placing their blood sacrifice on the alter of Commercialism! What chance has the bud of womanhood in these girls of ever growing into a sweet and fragrant blossom? None! Capitalist society has sentenced them to a sour and sordid living death. BUT IT MUST NOT BE!

These girls in their hundreds must be rescued, and the Labor Movement alone has undertaken the task. A Woman Organiser has been appointed, Unions are being formed, and the aid of the Arbitration Court is to be invoked! All this means heavy expense. WITHOUT YOUR FINANCIAL HELP THE WORK IS HANDICAPPED. Can't you spare something?

The poet, Thomas Hood, thus describes the wail of the Whiteworker: —

Work — Work — Work
  Till the brain begins to swim:
Work — Work — Work
  Till the eyes are heavy and dim!
Seam, and gusset, and band,
  Band, and gusset and seam,
Till over the buttons I fall asleep,
  And sew them on in a dream!

Oh, men with sisters dear!
  Oh, men with mothers and wives!
It is not linen you're wearing out,
  But human creatures' lives!
Stitch — stitch — stitch
  In poverty, hunger, and dirt,
Sewing at once with a double thread,
  A shroud as well as a shirt.

But why do I talk of Death?
　That phantom of grisly bone,
I hardly fear his terrible shape,
　It seems so like my own—
It seems so like my own
　Because of the fasts I keep;
Oh, God! that bread should be so dear
　And FLESH and BLOOD so CHEAP!

Work — work — work!
　From weary chime to chime,
Work — work — work
　As prisoners work for crime!
Band, and gusset, and seam,
　Seam, and gusset, and band,
Till the heart is sick and the brain benumbed,
　As well as the weary hand.

Contributions, large or small, should be sent to
ALEX. McCALLUM, Trades Hall, Perth
and will be acknowledged in the "W.A. Worker."

MISS E. HOOTEN (Treasurer for the Fund),

Trades Hall, Perth

Pamphlet issued by the *Western Australian Worker* (c. 1917).

157. Women's Organizer

Jean Beadle, pioneer worker in the labour women's movement, was employed during 1918 by the Australian Labor Party Metropolitan Council in Western Australia as women's organizer. In a series of letters, she described her progress as she attempted to get woman workers to join the unions. In December 1918, she considered that enough unions had been established to cover the industries employing women and her work in that capacity ceased.

Dear Comrade,

Since my last report I have been actively engaged in the shops and factories in the metropolitan area, I continue to add a few new members to the Shop Assistants and Clothing Trades Unions, but I regret to state that I cannot report any new work.

The members of the Laundry Workers Union still maintain their interest and pay their dues regular. I visit the various laundries as often as possible to collect dues and enroll new members.

I have not been successful in getting a meeting of the food Manufacturing Employees in the metropolitan area for the last three months; at first this union appeared most promising, but all efforts to get employees to attend a meeting seems now futile — I am keenly disappointed and can offer no reason other than the closing down of the A.F.L. Jam Factory and the fear of victimization.

The work in Fremantle is most encouraging. The Fremantle Branch of the Food Manufacturing Employees Union is over 60 in membership, each meeting is well attended and great interest displayed.

The Jute and Hemp Workers meet regular. This union is comprised principally of girls (only 6 male members on the roll!). A competition is being arranged for the best essay on "Economics", the sum of £1.0.0 goes to the winner, it is expected that every employee in the industry will shortly join up — since my last report I have visited all of the factories in the Fremantle area, on behalf of the Food Manufacturing Employees and the Jute Workers, only one factory has refused to be represented, the employees of Mews have stated that they are well satisfied with their wages and conditions and they have no intention of joining the Union.

Yours fraternally,

Jean Beadle, Report to the Metropolitan Council of the Australian Labour Federation, Perth (n.d., c.1918).

158. "A Powerful Influence"

This paper, given before the 1909 Australasian Catholic Congress, is notable not only for its survey of women's working conditions in Australia but also for the importance it attaches to the political organization of women in effecting changes in this area. Annie Golding was a schoolteacher and president of the Women's Progressive Association. Her sister, Belle Golding, was an inspector of shops and factories and her other sister, Mrs Kate Dwyer, founded the Women Workers' Union in New South Wales and was one of the commissioners on the Royal Commission that inquired into female and juvenile labour in New South Wales in 1912.

The industrial, social, and moral development of a nation may be judged by the position of its women. In all decadent nations women are in a state of bondage or intellectual atrophy; regarded as slave or puppet. Mahommedan nations furnish a striking example.

In British-speaking countries the progress of women in industrial and social avenues has been rapid during the past fifty years. The advancement is the logical corollary of the spread of education and its enlightening, humanising influence on legal and industrial reforms in regard to women.

The scope of this paper will not permit of entering minutely into every avenue open to women. They are so numerous and varied that a brief survey will only be possible, and in addition a comparison between New South Wales and Victoria in regard to the industrial and professional position of its women, as these States lead in industrialism and population.

The Commonwealth and New Zealand stand out prominently amongst the nations of the world even taking precedence of the United Kingdom and America in progressive legislation where women and children are specially concerned. Great Britain is swayed by her old and conservative traditions, America by her rings and trusts, into which the inhuman system of child labour so largely enters — the latter a rock on which the industrial ship of the Commonwealth may be wrecked if a vigilant watch is not kept. Fifty or sixty years ago there were few occupations open to women, other than domestic service, laundry work, and sewing. The low rate of pay and insanitary conditions were appalling in the older countries, even young Australia did not, by any means, present a clean record.

As regards accommodation, sanitation, and shorter hours, industrial legislation throughout New Zealand and Australia reformed abuses, removed glaring anomalies, shortened hours, and generally ameliorated the hardships of both male and female workers; but left the wages of women and girls at a disgracefully low standard, so low, indeed, that it is marvellous how they were able to live clean, respectable lives. To this low rate, with its attendant privations, may be attributed many of the unhappy marriages, and much of the street degradation that has so often called forth stringent remarks from our leading magistrates and judges.

As industrialism is daily claiming a larger percentage of our women, their position, health, and protection should be jealously safeguarded. The interests of the future motherhood of the race demand it, as the environment of this generation affects the virility of the next. To verify this assertion one need only contrast the undersized, weedy appearance of the youths grouped about the street corners, or even issuing from our industrial city hives, with that of our country youth, where healthier surroundings, better food, and freer lives combine to produce a more stalwart and vigorous physique.

That the claims of women to a living wage, sanitary conditions, and shorter hours were criminally overlooked in the past is an undeniable fact, and such were the causes that led the more fearless and advanced women to agitate for the vote. They realised that the claims of the unrepresented are too often slighted in consequence of the weightier and more insistent demands of the represented, who receive recognition because they have the means to remove abuses and the power to signally punish neglect. It can be stated with assurance the granting of votes to women has been an effective lever in improving the sweated and inequitable conditions attached to their employments. The machinery to still further improve matters is provided by the recently introduced Industrial Disputes Act and the Minimum Wage Bill. Both just and humane Acts, if properly administered. The administration of the Industrial Disputes Act to a great extent rests with those concerned, it being the first to give women the opportunity of representation on the Boards.

Thus, they have the right to appoint representatives of their own sex, women who thoroughly understand and can voice their requirements.

By these means men's wages have been materially improved. The scale of women's wages, though increased, has not done so in the same ratio, and they are still far below a decent living wage. This is wholly caused by the apathy they display, and their culpable ignorance of their industrial value, and the potential influence they can wield through uniting and registering under the Act, also by means of the vote. This apathy and ignorance have been evinced, and with disastrous results to themselves, by not securing representation on the Wages Boards. They had the power to insist on women representatives on Wages Boards for every industrial occupation in which women are engaged, and to thus protect their interests.

The relatively low scale of wage fixed must clearly emphasise the old adage, "God helps those who help themselves". There are women in every walk of life fully competent to advocate their claims, and where they have done so their status and remuneration have invariably improved.

The Wages Boards in Victoria have bettered the condition of women workers, though, as in New South Wales, the discrepancy between men and women's wages is unduly accentuated. From an economic standpoint, this is a grave error, and if not amended, will eventually undercut men in occupations where her work is as efficient as his, or even where slightly inferior, as two women can be employed for the wages, or even less, of one man.

An equitable and practicable remedy would be equal pay for equal merit, and there are so many avenues, professional and otherwise, in which the work is equal. This principle has worked well in the Commonwealth Public Service, where it prevails up to £110 per annum. Mr. Austin Chapman, when Postmaster-General, testified to its efficacy, and the suitability of girls in postal departments, for clerical work. The discrepancy mentioned is a fruitful source of low wages to men, increase in the number of unemployed, a decrease in the marriage rate, and a general lowering of the standard of living. Work should be paid for its economic value, not on a sex basis.

The unequal standard has steadily increased the ratio of female to male workers. According to latest Federal statistics, it has increased in Victoria at the rate of, in 1886, about 1 to 5, in 1907 1 to 2. In New South Wales in 1886 about 1 to 7, in 1907 about 1 to 3. According to the Annual Report of Labour and Industry, New South Wales, for 1908, the male employees were 66.8 per cent., that of females 33.2 per cent., or in round numbers, 1 to 2. The chief occupations in which women work are the clothing and textile industries (the former embracing tailoring, dress-making, and wholesale manufactories), tobacco, and preserving works, drugs, chemicals, foods, furniture, and various others; the number employed being 22,402. In the Commonwealth, 1907, the total number was:— Males, 184,897; females, 63,944; as against 149,246 and 46,564, showing a relatively larger increase in the number of female than in the number of male workers. . . .

. . . on the whole, Victorian women have fared better under the awards than in the Mother State. For example, under the Soap and Soda Board in Victoria, the scale ranges from 8s. 6d. per week under 15 years of age, to 22s. 6d. at 21 years and over. The award in New South Wales is based on years of service instead of age, but practically works out the same. The scale is under 16 years 8s. for the first three months, after that 10s. weekly until 16 years of age, and then ascends till the fifth year and over, culminating in the munificent sum of 18s. 6d; a leading hand, or super-intendent, receiving 20s. per week. The advantage is to the Victorian women. The award for the aerated waters fixes the minimum for men at 42s., and for women 21s. Before the award women's wages were from 12s. 6d. to 15s. per week. They have benefited to a certain extent, but nothing in comparison with men, yet many of them are the bread-winners for the family. The Victorian award for aerated waters says:— Persons over 20 and under 21 years of age, 25s. per week; sex is not mentioned, so again Victoria scores. For the confectionary awards both States are the same — for females over 21 years of age ranging for dippers, and chocolate dippers and coverers from 18 to 20 years of age, only 14s., under 18 years 10s. per week, over 21 years the rate is 17s. per week. Yet these girls have to work the regulation 48 hours per week, they have the same need for food, clothing and housing. How are these to be supplied on such a beggarly pittance?

In the jam trade the award in New South Wales grants 18s. 6d. per week to girls over 20 years, and in Victoria for 18, and over that age the rate is 14s. for the manu-facture of jams, etc., for their preparation for sale, 16s. per week. The minimum rates for adults in New South Wales are — males 40s., females 20s. Victoria, males 36s., and females 16s. per week; not even half — both are mean and paltry. I do not advocate lowering the man's, but increasing both, and bringing the women's more in line with that paid to man.

In the hairdressing and grocery trades equal pay for equal work has been adopted, and will be watched as an interesting experiment.

Many other cases might be cited; but those quoted will serve to illustrate industrial conditions in both States. As far as investigated the Victorian women are slightly better paid on the whole. Western Australia is coming to the front. The Premier is advocating a levelling up, and said the low rate of wage in Tasmania made her a serious competitor in trade.

New Zealand has enjoyed till recently industrial success, and may be regarded as a pioneer in the political, industrial, and educational progress of women.

THE DOMESTIC SPHERE

Domestic duties and marriage absorb the greater number of women in Australia, as in older nations; but it is regrettable that they are not more pronounced factors in preventing the overcrowding of women in the labour market, and the consequent lowering of wages. The causes may be sought in the avenues themselves.

Domestic duties have not been considered of sufficient importance to devise means to raise them to a more dignified status, and therefore are most sedulously avoided, preference being given to other occupations where hours are shorter and greater freedom is experienced, even though such occupations are more trying, and tend to stunt the physical and intellectual development of our womanhood, and as a natural sequence that of our race.

Domestic duties of every type are — as yet — ill regulated, inadequately appreciated, and, in general not sufficiently remunerated. Domestic service, in particular, is avoided, though better paid than many industrial occupations, and this will continue till it is raised to a more honorable position in the social scale. Nursing was once a despised calling, but training, education, and a due appreciation of its onerous and noble aims have placed it in the front rank of women's occupations. The same attitude towards domestic duties would lead to better training and sound instruction, skilled work, inspired by conscientious and intelligent effort would be rendered in return for due respect and adequate remuneration.

Much of the educational effort of the nation will be directed to the training of its womanhood in all the functions that make for the production of a physically, morally and intellectually well-developed citizenship, and this should be the chief ideal of our educational establishments, from the lowest grade of primary to the highest grade of university education. . .

Representations have been made by the various women's organizations of New South Wales, and deputations have waited on Premiers, asking for the establishment of a Domestic Science College; but so far without practical result. In the scheme of University reform so long and consistently urged by the Women's Progressive Association of New South Wales, a Chair of Domestic Science was one of the most important reforms advocated. The status of home-making and domestic instruction would be raised, and result in greater scientific research work or investigation in food constituents. Its influence would be distributed throughout the State. More capable and intelligent interest in the domestic sphere would be evinced. The cleanliness and ventilation of the home, its improved sanitary surroundings, suitable food combinations, and all that tends to the promotion of a vigorous population would rank first among the avocations open to women. The kitchen, instead of the Cinderella, would then become one of the chief domains in the domestic sphere.

It is very disappointing that in the University Reform Bill now before the Legislative Assembly of New South Wales, among other notable and far-reaching reforms, provision has not been made for a Chair of Domestic Science.

Though highly appreciating the need for a Chair of Veterinary Science, as a woman, I think there is even more need for a Chair of Domestic Science, as the care and production of cattle cannot be quite so momentous to the welfare of a nation as the improvement of its race, yet as Agriculture, Domestic Science, and Veterinary Science are interdependent, it would not have unduly strained the financial resources of the State to have estabished it in addition to the other two. The three should not be separated, all perform important duties in building up the State or nation.

The "one" not included has for its function the building up of the perfect human casket, capable of enshrining the perfect human soul, ready to respond to the promptings and aspirations implanted by the Divine Inspiration. I may be charged with unduly exalting the power of domestic science training to produce such results, but eminent economists and scientists recognise that physical degeneration is speedily followed by moral and intellectual decadence. Slum areas produce such degenerates.

The causes of so many unhappy marriages, divorces, and a not-sufficiently high marriage rate are partly attributable to the problems mentioned. Industrialism claims too great a percentage of girls and women, and so the marriage age goes by. On the other hand, a low rate of wage to the husband often forces the wife into the labour market to compete with and undersell her single sisters, widows, and deserted wives. This militates against domestic happiness, and the care and moral training of the children are neglected when the mother is called from the domestic hearth to contribute to the support of the family. This undesirable phase of industrial and married life is rampant in older countries, and with deplorable results. It was recently ascertained in the United Kingdom that upwards of 50 per cent. of married women were compelled by adverse conditions to return to the industrial market after forty years of age; after the child-bearing and child-rearing period, and thus swelled the ranks of unskilled workers. It should be the chief endeavour of legislators and economists in Australia to prevent similar conditions undermining its prosperity.

Of course there will always be the competition of unmarried women, widows, and deserted wives, but this may be kept in a fair condition by a proportionately just scale of wage, but even better by equal pay for work of equal merit. The objection put forward to the latter is that women will not have a fair chance of being employed. But if the work is of equal merit, it is hardly likely to displace the women. In some instances, it may displace her, but the man will be employed at a more equitable wage, and will, thus, be in a position to marry. In other occupations it eliminates woman from work for which she is physically unsuited, and conserves to her more suitable avenues.

The comparative economic independence of women has removed the incentive to marry merely for a home, and will eventually place marriage on a higher plane. The more thoughtful and intellectual women disapprove of the inequality of the married partnership.

When a man marries he removes his wife from the industrial or professional walks of life to look after the home and rear the children, thus performing the high, but onerous duties of wifehood and motherhood; but he is not legally bound to provide for her or her children's future. He may mortgage, speculate, or even gamble away the home, furniture, or other property without his wife's consent, or even knowledge.

The wives of notable citizens, though thinking themselves protected against want, have on the deaths of their husbands found themselves and their children destitute.

They have not a legal say in the guardianship of their children, nor in the distribution of the accumulations of the married partnership. In this respect the States of the Commonwealth are behind many older and more conservative countries.

Many good and humane acts for the care and protection of women have, nevertheless, been enacted, and in time legislation will remove the anomalies enumerated.

Among the Acts that have greatly benefited women and children in Australasia are: — The Shops and Factories Acts, Early Closing, The Industrial Disputes Act, the Minimum Wage, The Infants' Protection Acts, and in New South Wales a Girls'

Protection Act is now before the House. The Old Age and Invalid Pensions Acts have placed women on the same footing as men, and have lifted a burden from many women either invalid or too old to earn, yet who shrank from charity or entering an asylum.

In the professional occupations, which, according to Federal statistics, include all persons engaged in the government and defence of the country, and in satisfying the moral, intellectual, and social wants of its inhabitants there are 111,134 so engaged; of these 41,235 are women. . . .

. . . [in Victoria,] the salaries of women teachers is a standing disgrace to that State, many ranks of industrial, and even unskilled, labour being more highly paid than that of trained and most efficient teaching.

Efforts are now being made to raise salaries, but until women urge their own cause little material benefit will result.

Whatever the salary, women in private and public are doing excellent work in education. The universities are open to women and students are on an equality as far as instruction and degrees are concerned. It is when honourable or lucrative positions are to be filled that sex distinctions are made. There are no women on the Senate, or on the professional staff. In New South Wales, though according to published lists, women medical students hold their own, they are not appointed as medical residential officers in public hospitals. The conjoint Boards are chiefly filled by University men, and only once, in response to public opinion and a spirited public demand, was a medical woman appointed. They were careful to avoid making it a precedent. The other universities are more liberal in this respect, as women medical officers are eligible for such appointments. Medical women are appointed under the Department of Public Instruction in New South Wales, also to health departments and asylums. As yet women are not eligible for school inspectors, as in some of the States. Women are appointed as Factory, Early Closing and Sanitary Inspectors.

Australian women have eminently distinguished themselves in literary, musical, and artistic circles, both at home and abroad. Eminent vocalists have drawn the attention of the civilised world to the quality and purity of the Australian voice.

There is scarcely a cultured and intellectual avenue into which women have not entered, and with marked success. These advances have chiefly followed the introduction of woman's suffrage, showing what a powerful influence it has wielded in raising the status of women, and the greatest triumph of all is that this progress in the industrial, political and social position of women has been achieved without abating their womanly dignity, and without raising the sex antagonism and bitterness that have been displayed in the United Kingdom and parts of America. This, in itself, is a marked tribute to the womanliness of our Australian women, and the justice and chivalrous spirit of our Australian men.

Australasia has made precedents that may well be followed by older nations, and this remote Southern land will shine steadfastly as the beacon light of faith, justice and humanity.

Annie Golding, "The Industrial and Social Condition of Women in the Australian Commonwealth", in *Proceedings of the Third Australasian Catholic Congress . . .* (1910).

159. Protection for the Most Helpless

The increased concern shown regarding women's working conditions from the 1880s resulted in protective legislation, which was itself sometimes criticized because it made women less able to compete in an already difficult labour market. In the inter-war period, this criticism gained strength with the growth of feminist organizations, such as the Open Door International, whose charter demanded that legislation should be based on the nature of the job, not the sex of the worker, and that the same restrictions should apply to men and women in so far as hours, overtime, nightwork, lifting and danger were concerned. Feminist organizations in Australia tended to be more in accord with other Open Door demands (such as equal pay and the end of restrictions on employment for married women) than with their opposition to protective legislation. Factory inspectors, whose own work had largely contributed to the passing of this sort of legislation, were particularly opposed to what they saw as putting "equality" first.

The question of protective legislation for Women in Industry is of vital importance to a Pan-Pacific Conference. In the countries bordering on the Pacific are demonstrated the beneficial effects of such protection as shown in Australia and certain parts of America; also the urgent need of protective measures for the Women in Industry in Japan, China, India and Persia, and other countries.

In the Eastern Countries organisation among the women themselves is so slight that little can be achieved by such means to amend any bad conditions in industry. Women in Industry in all countries form the majority of women gainfully employed. The conditions of labor show urgent reasons for protection to be granted by legislative enactments.

The health of women and girls as mothers and potential mothers, should be safeguarded for the benefit of the race. It is claimed by certain sections of women — professional and others — that no legislation should exist to grant special protection to Women in Industry until men also are granted exactly the same conditions of employment. This claim is made on the score of "Equality First." It is not recognised by these opponents of protection that women are less able than men, by their own efforts, to bring about the better conditions so urgently needed. Men have been organised in their Trades Unions for nearly a hundred years. The organisation of women in Trades Unions is of recent date — and then in only a few countries.

The prohibition of night work and limitation of working hours is of more importance to women than to men. Whatever may happen in the future, it is true that at present, Women in Industry often carry a double burden — their work in the factory and their work in their homes. To ensure satisfactory conditions for both men and women, it is necessary first to improve conditions for the lowest branches of industry, where, unfortunately, women are employed. Only by a gradual levelling up of industrial conditions can improvement be gained for all.

At the present stage of industrial development, measures of protection must first be obtained for those who are the most helpless and downtrodden in the labor market, in order that the position may be safeguarded for those who have already obtained improved conditions. This applies between the different countries — as between the sexes — and also between the different grades of employment.

The opposition to protective legislation by certain groups of feminist organisations, on the plea that it prevents equality between the sexes, has aroused the Women Trade Unionists the world over to defend their own interests, and the welfare of their sister women in less industrially developed countries.

Resolutions passed at the International Conference of Women Workers at Paris in July, 1927, and previously at the National Women's Trade Union League of America in July, 1926, leave no doubt as to the attitude of industrial women in favour of special protection for women. A report issued by the Joint Standing Committee of Industrial Women's Organisations in Great Britain, states, inter alia:—

"In the present state of affairs it is often easier to secure protection for Women than for men, while conditions which men's stronger organizations can gain for them, can only be won for women by legislative enactment.

"The worker who cannot be exploited at the employers' will because the law does not permit it gains a stronger and not weaker position in the industrial world. Legislation has had to step in to give women a chance of achieving a more equal footing with men. Without protection it is not equality that the woman achieves but far greater inequality. . . .

"The greatest evil in the industrial employment of women is low wages — whether of men or women. The low wages of men often compel married women who are already fully occupied at home, and who are bearing children, to compete for employment in industry. The low wages of women are an important factor in dragging down the wages of men. In our efforts through Trade Boards to abolish sweating, regulation affects both sexes — but the worst sweated trades are those which mainly employ women. The fixing of minima, both wages and hours, which has, therefore, been of special benefit to women: Would the feminist organisations regard it as 'restrictive?' Would they prefer that the employer maintain his right to sweat his workers in the name of equality?

"These considerations apply to industrial workers in factories and workshops. They do not apply to the professional and clerical workers. We are also entirely against prohibition of the employment of married women on the ground of marriage. It is because we believe in the emancipation of women, economic, social and political, that we stand for the protection of industrial women workers against the ruthless exploitation which has marred their history in industry."

"Women in Industry", paper written for the *Pan Pacific Bulletin* by Elizabeth Clapham, Inspector of Factories, W.A.; reprinted in *The Dawn* (Perth), 20 February 1929.

160. The Front Room

In this interview, two women describe their experiences as dressmakers in South Australia in the 1920s and 1930s, during part of which time one was the employee of the other.

Madge:

We lived on a farm at the Hundred of Younghusband, fifteen miles above Mannum. There were seven girls in the family, no boys. I worked as a domestic a few times but I always got homesick so I went back home again. I'd last a few weeks and I'd get homesick. So then I started sewing with a girl friend. We went into Mannum and she'd started sewing and she taught me sewing. From there we went to Murray Bridge and I used to sew down there. I was about twenty-two then. I had my own business and people used to come along when they wanted a dress made — all different kinds of people from the working class to society people. I used to charge anything from 7/6 up to a guinea or something like that in those days. If you wanted a blouse or something it might be three or four shillings then.

When we came down to the city I worked in dress shops. First at the T. & G. I was the only one there. I used to do alterations and if they wanted a dress made, like an order, I'd do that. There were only two ladies in that shop serving. It was only a small shop but it was stocked with frocks and things like that. Then I worked at Waxman's in the work-room. That was about 1929, I think it would be. At Waxman's it was quite a big shop and there were thirteen girls there in the workroom. I got £3 a week for a start and then I went up to about £3/15/- and commission. That was good money in those days. We were kept fairly busy doing alterations most of the time and then we'd do stock work and perhaps an order now and again. I sewed there for three years. Then I sewed at Bowman's Arcade for eighteen months. And then I started on my own in Rundle Street. It was during the Depression, when I couldn't get work. You see, I was gradually getting less time at Bowman's Arcade, perhaps three days a week, sometimes two days, and it got that way that, well, there wasn't much to do and I thought I'd start on my own. Everyone said I was mad. But I tried it out. That's when Jean came to work with me. I was there nine years.

Jean:
   I left school at fourteen years and I didn't have much idea of what sort of work I wanted to do. At the end of the year, when I left school, I had a temporary job at a draper's on Unley Road, it was what we called Christmas trade, and I was there for about three weeks before Christmas. I didn't last any longer than the Christmas period. I did a commercial course at school but I didn't go very far. At fourteen — you can see that I only had two years at what we called Central School — I wasn't really a trained typist or at shorthand. I should have gone to business college but I didn't know really what I wanted to do. I was best at sewing. It was the only thing at school that I got a credit for. But I didn't think of taking it up as a job. Didn't enter my head. I more or less had to leave school because things were very, very bad at home. I had to get work. That was about 1931.
   At the beginning of the year after I had done the Christmas work I had to look for a job and I answered quite a few ads for housework. I did get a job doing house-work which I kept for about eight or nine months and then the opportunity came to work for my aunt Madge in dress-making. I wouldn't have been much more than fifteen, about fifteen and a half, then. And I stayed with aunty until I was twenty-one. Then I worked at home for two years.
   Aunty just had the one room. It was a room that was separated into a little kitchenette where we made our coffee and had our lunches, a little, tiny fitting room and the actual work-room. The whole thing wasn't very large. When I started there was just a senior, then there was me, and after a while aunty took on a junior. So at one particular time there would have been three apart from aunty. I was never under any contract. They called me an improver. I worked as long as aunty had work for me to do, which turned out to be nearly six years. I remember starting off at 4/8, but I think probably I got a little bit more fairly regularly as I stayed there, it might have been perhaps every two or three months. I could afford to buy practically nothing. It all went on tram fares and lunches. I couldn't pay any board. If I wanted a pair of shoes if took me months to save up for the cheapest pair of shoes. I know we used to pay about 14/11 for a pair of shoes and I'd be putting a shilling a week or something like that aside for shoes.
   In the work-room I started by being the messenger girl, going to the stores and getting the haberdashery, going to the dress material departments and getting a whole lot of patterns, because we used to have to get linings and trimmings and things like that, and I would get the samples and bring them back. I was the lunch girl, used to make the tea, and sweep, pick up pins, take out tackings. That was the very beginning — put in tackings and take out tackings. But aunty taught me to sew and she taught me all the basic things. Most of it was done in working hours.
   The girl that was senior to me, she had worked in a big store in the city doing sleeves, doing skirts (skirt seams). They would never do a whole garment. They'd just go on and on doing the one type of job. When I left aunty's, when I was twenty

one, I tried to get a job in what we termed factory work and the first job I applied for, I remember the fellow said to me, "How many dresses can you make in a day?" I nearly dropped dead because ours was all order work and we never completed a dress in a day. We could have done but we didn't because people came in for fittings. There was always a second fitting. He had a dress factory. And I just didn't have the faintest idea because I'd never worked on the power machine and this was all power machine work. I didn't get past the door. He just asked my experience, what experience I'd had in that type of work. And when I said none, well that was the end of that. I knew then that I wouldn't have a hope of getting factory work without a certain amount of training because I was too old. I was too old to get work in the same sort of work that I was doing, because they wanted girls under twenty-one. And that gave me the idea of starting up at home.

I felt my aunt had been very, very good to me. I think that the last few months that I was there in the work-room she was really keeping me on when she couldn't afford it. She'd taught me thoroughly. I was quite confident of starting up on my own. Quite confident that I could do the work because of the basic training that I'd had. I think I was very relieved when they told me I wasn't suitable at the dress factory. We had worked on complete garments and we weren't terribly rushed. It was rather leisurely — we worked on the whole garment right from the start until it was complete. I suppose we took a certain pride in the finished thing. I'd hate to have done seams, seams, and never seen the finished garment.

My mother said I could have the front room. I had to buy a large table for cutting out. That cost me 25/-. To get myself known in the district (I had lived in the district all my life but to let people know that I was dress-making) I had 500 pamphlets printed. To cut down the cost of those I went to one of the local drapers and he put an advertisement on the back of my pamphlet and that brought the cost down to half. The 500 pamphlets cost 15/6 and by having the advertisement on the back that brought it down to 7/9. I had to buy adaptors and flex for the cords. I used my mother's treadle machine and I bought a mirror that was put on a stand. And I had a board on the front gate, advertising. I was "Jeanne", "Dress-maker". My first year's income was £76/2/2½. I paid £41/12/0 board. The second year was probably much the same. I paid my mother 4/- a month for the electricity I used. Apart from that I had no other expenditure.

By the time I was to be married I had enough saved to buy a few things like crystal (we were all mad on crystal in those days) — a few nice things to put in my home and I had enough to buy the material for my wedding dress and the accessories for my wedding. And then I was flat broke.

Interviews with "Madge" and "Jean", Adelaide, 1976.

161. Unemployment

Although unemployment was a major cause of poverty among women, unemployed women and girls were not given the dole during the Depression. Charitable committees, partly government-funded, gave out rations, found work if it was available and attempted to train girls for employment. Some set up workrooms, thus threatening the employment of women still in work. This report shows how unemployment relief organizations offered an area of work for public-minded women and women's organizations, as well as facilities for unemployed working-class women. In the tradition of other philanthropic organizations, domestic service was emphasized. Soon after this report was written the work went into recess through lack of finance.

Fellow Members,

On behalf of the Citizens' Committee for the Training and Relief of Unemployed Single Girls and Women, I have much pleasure in presenting a Report of its activities since its inception.

No. of positions filled 3,758
No. of rents paid .... 8,166. (5/- to 10/-)

All rooms and bedding are inspected.
Maximum Wage £3.15.0
Minimum Wage   10/-

No. of girls and women registered .... 5,115.

Attached hereto is a full Report of all moneys raised including Government Subsidy, Overseas Settlement Fund, Stamp Campaign, McNess Fund, Golden Apple Appeal, Lord Mayor's Fund, Refunds from Girls, Sundry Donations, and Shop Assistant's Union.

There is always plenty of domestic work for reliable girls, but the untrained unemployable girl will always be a big problem unless some steps are taken to cope with the situation. Facilities are needed for training these girls if they are to become independent and useful members of the Community, which is the right of every individual.

Sick girls are catered for in several ways. If necessary, two or three weeks at the M.C.L. Cottesloe, or at the Y.W.C.A. to recuperate. If necessary, Milk orders are given from two to four weeks at a time. That is, a girl gets a pint of milk a day from her local milkman for a given period. Also orders are given at chemists for tonics etc. When necessary a girl is taken to a doctor at the expense of the Committee. When a girl is found a position, her clothes are overhauled and she is sent out equipped with overalls, underwear, and clothing etc. New shoes are bought or her old ones repaired. A girl is given a small sum of money for travelling expenses, necessities, and meals on the train etc.

In addition to domestic work we have filled several clerical positions, shop and nurses positions. If a girl is to stay in town all day, waiting for an interview, she is given a midday dinner.

I would like here to comment on the wonderful assistance the Y.W.C.A. has always given this work. The General Secretary, Miss Godlee and her staff have always given hearty co-operation and assistance. The Y.W.C.A. has given access to all its Clubs. Under Miss Godlee's direction, classes have been formed for Arts and Crafts, Shorthand Speed and Cookery. An opportunity has been offered to any girl to learn whatever she wishes. An unemployed girls Club called the Arana Club, under the direction of Miss Bailey, is going well, and some of the girls have been attending regularly for over two years. And I think I can safely say that every girl's need has been met, when at all possible to do so.

Girls are not encouraged to be idle. No assistance is given unless a girl is willing to offer for work.

All Government Departments, especially the Women's section of the

Unemployment Board (Miss Muirson), co-operate and help to make the work more satisfactory.

Ethel C. Orgill, "Citizens' Committee for the Training and Relief of Single Unemployed Girls and Women: Report, From June 1930 to 19th July, 1935", Perth, 19 July 1935.

162. The Extra Quid

This description of the strain of piecework appeared in the Communist women's paper the *Working Woman* during the Depression.

I am a packer at a sock factory. The other day as I was coming up the passage I heard the foreman of the packing room talking to the boss.

"There is no doubt about it," the foreman said, "piece work is the only satisfactory way to get them working all the time. If we put them on the task system, they put on a spurt and finish them and then spend the rest of the afternoon doing nothing. Supposing we gave them 400 to do, well they go for their lives and do 350 by about three o'clock and take till five to do the other 50."

I can see what we girls have done alright — we have worked too hard and too fast, and that is where we have cruelled ourselves. We have less girls in the packing room than we used to and we get through the same amount of work. We got on to piece work and went so fast that a great number of girls were put off.

When we had the task system, we did go at a terrific speed to get rid of the pile of work, but we'd be fagged out and would have to have a spell. The boss thinks we should keep up that speed every minute of the day. We are urged to compete with one another to see who can do the most work.

We've been cut down ha'penny a dozen twice in a year, and we have to work and work without stopping to make up that shortage. On the task system we could get £2/9/6, and on piece work we can earn a pound more, although to do it we get through three times as much work. We need that extra quid and that is where the boss has us licked, especially now when nearly all of us are helping to support those at home who are out of work.

We have to keep on at a terrible pace to earn every penny we can, although we get tired and sick. Unless you've done piece work like this you have no idea how it makes you giddy and your head swims round and round. At home every night they say I am bad tempered and irritable, but I am really sick — too sick to eat my tea. If your paper is going to show factory workers how to stop the boss from putting it over them, well, I'll be glad, and I will give you news about my job whenever I can.

"To Hell with Piece Work", *Working Woman*, August 1930.

163. Keeping a Hold Over Their Money

Among the women who received no payment for their work or were given a token amount were many Aboriginal women. Under the Western Australian Aborigines Act of 1905, Aborigines and half-castes could only be employed by persons granted a permit. The Aborigines thus employed received only a small portion of their wages and the remainder was sent to the Department of Aborigines.

Just lately I placed a girl through the Department of Aborigines. She was most efficient and satisfactory until the Department wrote to her mistress and said they must only give her 7/6 per week, and the balance to be sent to the Department. As her mistress said, this broke her heart and she just slacked off and slacked off until she was fit for nothing. Another girl that I sent away to one of my good friends places had her employer written to telling the same thing, that out of 30/- a certain amount had to be sent to the Department. When the employer, a mine manager, wrote and said he was banking the money the Department said either the payments must be sent down regularly or the girl must be sent back.

One girl whose aunt comes to see me was many years in a position and she can get absolutely no satisfaction as to how much money collected is in hand. Two others tell me they have been put in debt with the Home where their children are, though one was six years in one position and only three years in the Home, and the other had done something like ten years work with these deductions made.

All who come to me say they cannot get a statement of their financial position or a bank book or any satisfaction. Perhaps a £1 at holiday time may be doled out and told to be taken care of, as they have no more to be given.

It is a most extraordinary position. It cannot be imagination when all tell the same story: that they cannot get a Statement of Affairs. Another great cause of dissatisfaction is that they may only be employed by people with a "permit". They think this is being done to keep a hold over their money and over them, and I respectfully submit that this matter should be very carefully looked into and that a recommendation should be made that at the age of twenty one they should be allowed to handle their own money and handle their own affairs.

Evidence of Mrs Nesbitt-Landon, Royal Commission on Aborigines, Perth, 1934.

164. "Station Chattel"

An Aboriginal girl, Rosie, who was born on a station, lived there on a permit held by a Mrs Darcy, whose sister's husband managed the meat-works at Wyndham. When Mrs Darcy was to leave the station, Rosie was sent to work at the meat-works. The authorities intervened and this telegram sums up the government's view of the twelve-year-old child's status.

HALF CASTE GIRL BORN ORD RIVER STATION HELD UNDER PERNICIOUS GENERAL PERMIT AS SLAVE AND HANDED OVER AS STATION CHATTEL FROM ONE PERSON TO ANOTHER SHOULD BE LEGALLY ADOPTED OR PLACED IN INSTITUTION FORTHWITH

Resident Magistrate at Wyndam, W.A., to the Chief Protector of Aborigines, 23 July 1921.

165. Wage-Fixing

An authority on Australian wage-fixing practices, George Anderson was described by Muriel Heagney as someone who not only had high academic qualifications but was also a master printer with experience of the practical side of labour relations. His essay presents a particularly clear exposition of wage-fixing in Australia in relation to women.

Basic wages for adult females are declared by the State basic wage-fixing authorities of Queensland, South Australia, and Western Australia. Commonwealth and State female basic wages are either exactly or approximately 54 per cent. of the appropriate male basic wages, with the exception of the State female basic wage for Adelaide, which is approximately 50 per cent. of the State male basic wage. The female basic wage is based on the cost of living of a single woman living away from home with only herself to support, and provides her with a sum sufficient for her normal and reasonable needs.

In March, 1928, a Judge of the Commonwealth Arbitration Court determined a standard of living for women employed in the clothing industry after a lengthy inquiry, and fixed a basic wage of 49/6 per week, which worked out at 55.6 per cent. of the male basic wage of 89/-. That amount of 49/6 would, in the opinion of the Judge, afford a single woman in the clothing industry, without dependents, a minimum standard of decency and comfort. He allowed for board and lodging 25/- per week; for clothing, handbag, brushes, comb, soap, tooth-paste, and hair attention, 11/- per week; for fares, 3/-; notepaper, envelopes, stamps and telephone, 10d.; library, books and newspapers, 1/-; doctor's or lodge fees, 1/-; union dues, 4d.; social organizations, sports and recreation, 2/-; church and charity, 1/-; annual holiday, 2/-; a total of 47/2 per week. He brought the amount to 49/6 per week by adding 2/4 to provide for two and a half weeks' work which females in the clothing industry lost from different causes. It will be noted that a provision was made for an annual holiday. Such a provision is unusual in basic wages.

In Australia women generally are not paid the same rates of wages as men, even if the work done by men and women is of the same kind, *e.g.*, clerks' work. The man is the bread-winner of the family. The male basic wage is essentially a family wage. It is based on the needs of a man, his wife and children. The average woman has only herself to support, and as her needs are less than those of the average adult male worker, Industrial Courts prescribe for her a basic wage suited to her needs.

In a number of industries where a certain kind of work is recognized as men's work, women who are employed on that work must be paid the same wages as the men. The object of the equal pay is the protection of men in their employment.

George Anderson, "Industrial Tribunals and Standards of Living", in *Australian Standards of Living* (1939).

166. Lamingtons

Keeping a shop is a way in which women traditionally have contributed to the family income. In times of unemployment, the shop sometimes became the only source of income, as this story from the South Australian river town of Murray Bridge shows.

My fiance and I decided to get married. So we bought the cafe and worked for about twelve months and then we got married. Just the two of us for a start because Joe was out of work. He'd been put off. He was foreman at the Farmer's Union in the cheese department and just at this time the Depression started to set in and things were very bad. So we ran the cafe and we managed to get a living ourselves out of it. It

used to take us all our time, by the time we paid 25/- a week rent for the shop and 25/-
a week for just one room at the back which we were going to live in when we got
married. And then of course it took a while to work the cafe up. We had to work —
we used to get up early in the morning and work all day and all night until 12 o'clock
and 1 o'clock in the morning. We served meals. We used to cook ham and eggs,
grilled steaks, chips, and I used to cook 40 dozen pies and pasties a day and about 6
dozen small cakes, whip up sponges as they came in and ordered them, and sausage
rolls and cream puffs and lamingtons, make my own sauce and pickle my own onions.
My husband used to sit up at night and help me strain the sauce. And we used to do
the lamingtons — he used to say he'd never eat another lamington. We used to have a
big wood oven, a very big oven that I used to make all the pies and pasties in and it
used to be 117 degrees at 11 o'clock in the morning. It used to be a lean-to kitchen.
Well everything went alright and we had three girls working for us, and then in the
meantime we'd had a little baby. Two girls lived in at the back because we had taken
one room at the back and put a sleepout on the side, just an ordinary verandah that
was covered in, and they stayed with us and lived in with us and they used to work all
hours but they didn't mind. They were quite happy. They used to get 12/6 a week and
their keep. We'd have young chaps come in who would have walked, come all the
way from Melbourne or from Mt Gambier, on foot . . . They used to come in and
we'd give them a meal.

Just before the war started they came up and wanted Joe to take his job because
they wanted a cheese maker — and you know why that was. When the war was
coming on they had to have cheese. So of course he went back. I had 3 or 4 girls in the
shop by then. It's a terrible thing to say but business was booming. It started to boom
then when all our nice young lads all went off to the war.

Interview with "Valerie", Adelaide, 1976.

167. The War

Early in the Second World War, women's organizations such as the United
Associations of Women were concerned that women in wartime employment should
not be exploited.

Dear Madam,

We have been considering the subject of women being used in occupations
hitherto reserved for men. We have decided to make the following recommendation,
which we would like to bring under your notice:

"In order that the rate of wages and standard of living obtained by male employees may
not be undermined as a result of the war, the United Associations of Women
recommends that when women are taken on for any work hitherto performed by men,
either because of the enlistment of male employees or because of the shortage of men
resulting from war time needs, that women shall be engaged under the same conditions
and awards as govern such work at the time, and that the policy of equal pay and equal
opportunity for men and women shall be generally adopted throughout these
occupations. We request all women's organisations, patriotic, philanthropic and social,
to support this policy."

We ask you to give this recommendation your serious consideration, and to use
what influence you can to bring it before as many people as possible in order to
prevent the undercutting of male labour, by cheap female labour, in war time.

During the last war, women were employed in many occupations previously reserved for men. The women were employed at a lower wage, and when the men returned, the industries concerned, having been geared down to the lower wage, found it uneconomic to re-employ the men.

At the same time, we believe that women who undertake work in connection with the war industries should be protected. They should not be dismissed and left stranded when the men return. These women have to support themselves, and many of them have dependents. We believe that other employment should be found for these women, and until such time as this is done, they should receive unemployment pay of a sufficient sum to keep them, and any dependents they may have, decently housed and clothed and fed. Every care should be taken to see that women war workers should not be thrown on to the street in the general dislocation of industries which will occur when the war comes to an end. This is a matter that we will have to give particular attention to when the time arrives.

Meanwhile, we ask for your support of the foregoing recommendation.

Circular letter from Jessie Street, President of the United Associations of Women, 22 July 1940.

168. Work for Victory

Patriotism, better conditions for women and pro-Soviet sentiments are linked in this wartime leaflet.

The fascist aggressors in Europe and in the Pacific have let loose total war.

In the life-and-death struggle for freedom, women in the democratic countries are rallying to the sides of their husbands, sons and brothers.

The bestial ill-treatment of women by the fascist marauders has convinced women everywhere that the defeat of fascism if of vital concern to them.

Australian Minister for External Affairs, Dr. Evatt, recently visited some of England's war factories.

One great plant he visited was engaged in filling 65 types of munitions with explosives. At this highly dangerous job, 84% of the production staff were women. More than half the factory's women workers were married, and most of these had children.

Dr. Evatt said he was deeply touched by the magnificent work the women were doing.

In England to-day, 4 million women work in war factories, in America 3½ million, and our Soviet ally has over 30 million women engaged in war industry and agriculture.

Here in Australia our Government is calling for another 50,000 women for war industry.

You may be one of them!

Thousands of women are needed, not only to replace the men being called up, but to supply the labor for many new war industries.

Women are needed to build production to a level that will enable us to win the war in the shortest possible time.

How can we ensure that all this new
energy will be used and none of it wasted?

by Limiting Working Hours . . .

Long hours mean tired bodies and frayed nerves, accidents and absenteeism — all of which add up to reduced production.

by Equal Pay for Equal Work

Shorter shifts and higher wages mean increased production. Equal pay for equal work should be paid to women who are doing the same work as men.

by Improved Working Conditions

Long shifts without breaks cause strain and industrial fatigue. Bad ventilation and bad lighting mean headaches and eye-strain. Good rest rooms, lockers, showers and well-equipped canteens open to all shifts would make a great difference to health and efficiency.

by using Married Women . . .

under a system of short shifts which would allow them to attend to their home duties. Day nurseries and kindergartens would be needed where small children could be left while Mother is working, while factory canteens supplying well-cooked meals would solve other domestic problems.

All these things exist in Soviet Russia as a normal part of factory life. If our ally can do it, so can we — provided we organise.

Every woman working in a factory should be a member of a trade union.

Every woman who joins a trade union strengthens the campaign of the unions to have the improvements suggested here adopted by the Government and employers.

Women! Ensure by strengthening the National Front against fascism that the people of Australia play their full part in this war which is deciding the fate of mankind.

UNITE ALL FORCES — COMMUNISTS, TRADE UNIONISTS AND ALL ANTI-FASCISTS!

FIGHT AND WORK FOR VICTORY!

National Front pamphlet issued by the Legal Rights Committee, Sydney, n.d.

169. Women in the Metal Industry

During the war, Muriel Heagney was women's organizer for the Amalgamated Engineering Union. Her address to the first meeting of Sydney women shop stewards in November 1943 gives a history of women within the union and their dealings with the Women's Employment Board.

SISTERS: . . .

WOMEN'S WORK AND WAGES IN THE METAL INDUSTRY

For the benefit of Shop Stewards who are not familiar with the methods by which wages and conditions in the metal industries are fixed for women and juveniles a few explanatory notes may be helpful.

Since 1935 all sections of the metal industry are covered by a consolidated award of the Commonwealth Court of Conciliation and Arbitration Court entitled the Metal Trades Award. The Judge dealing with this industry at the present time is Judge O'Mara. The award is binding on metal trades employers and on all the metal trades unions having members in the industry covered. Since the war began several legal agreements have been made in respect to aircraft and other sections of members.

In March 1942, the Federal Government at the request of the A.C.T.U. removed from the jurisdiction of the Commonwealth Arbitration Court women who were coming into the industry to replace men or do work usually done by men or which had not been performed by men or women prior to 3rd September 1939 when this war began.

Male labour of all grades continues to be covered by the Commonwealth Arbitration Court awards or agreements. In so far as males are concerned the Metal Trades Award is a fairly comprehensive document with 241 well-defined classifications carrying various margins for skill over and above the needs base rate and loading as well as many clauses relating to conditions which have been established by collective bargaining over many years. The men in the industry understand the application of this award and in every workshop action is taken by the shop stewards to enforce the award in its entirety.

The position of the women in the industry is quite different. Prior to 3rd September 1939 when this war began there were relatively few women in the metal industry in Australia, and those so occupied were limited to certain sections in radio and electrical work and to mass production in the lowest types of sheet metal and general small metal manufacture.

They had no collective bargaining power and were given scant consideration by the Commonwealth Arbitration Court in regard to wages and conditions. Actually there are only two rates covering adult women in the M.T.A. namely, one which determines that women with three months experience in the trade shall be paid 75% of the male needs base rate plus a 3/- loading and no margin for skill or responsibility, and a lower rate for those deemed "inexperienced". This, in hard cold fact, boils down to the miserable current rate of £3:13:6 with which you are all so familiar as the rate beloved of the Metal Trades Federation which they want applied to all grades of work upon which women are engaged throughout the war industries.

WOMEN'S EMPLOYMENT BOARD

When women began to invade the industry at the behest of the Federal Labour Government early in 1942 the trade unions became alarmed because it was manifest that this pool of cheap labour ready and willing to serve the nation in its hour of need for patriotic purposes irrespective of the rates and conditions of work, constituted a menace to established standards in peacetime as well as during the war. The A.C.T.U. called a conference of all the unions likely to be affected by the use of female labour in war industries which demanded that women replacing men or doing the same or similar work as men should receive the full male rate.

Negotiations with the Government followed and the A.C.T.U. abandoned its claim for equal pay by compromising for the setting up of the Women's Employment Board to fix wages for women replacing men doing work usually done by men, or performing tasks that had not been done in Australia prior to the outbreak of this war. The Board was authorised to fix wages and conditions, with the proviso that the rate fixed must not be less than 60% nor more than 100% of the appropriate male rate.

The W.E.B. authorised the employment of women in 85 of the classifications in the Metal Trades Award already referred to which carry margins of from 8/- to 27/- and awarded all grades 90% of the appropriate male rate on the ground that women did not produce as much as men, were not as efficient as men, and showed greater absenteeism records than men.

Regarding conditions the W.E.B. adopted those of the Metal Trades Award described in these terms:—

"The Metal Trades Award of the Commonwealth Arbitration Court of Conciliation and Arbitration made wide provision — after adequate inquiry — for the working conditions for the employees male and female covered by it, and it is proposed to continue those as part of this decision."

I have already described the "adequate" consideration given to women in the metal industry by the Commonwealth Arbitration Court so you may judge for yourselves the value of this opinion.

You are all familiar with the outcome of the W.E.B. over the last year and a half. You know that 90% of the male rate where it is accepted by the employer usually means 90% of the process workers rate no matter what operation women do and that in actual cash this means £5 for a straight week of 44 hours without overtime or penalties for shift work.

Because of the tangible benefit in the difference between the £3:13:6 of the C.A.C. and the £5 of the W.E.B. we have a kindly feeling for the W.E.B., nevertheless, we deplore the fact that the Board has done very little towards the recognition of sex equality whilst in a formal document the W.E.B. unanimously declares with due solemnity — "The Sexes are not equal — heaven forbid." — in justification of the 90% standard which threatens to become as rigid as the C.A.C. standards.

ATTITUDE OF THE A.E.U. TOWARDS EQUAL PAY

Alone amongst the metal trades unions the Amalgamated Engineering Union in Great Britain as well as in Australia has always stood unreservedly for equal pay based on the rate for the job, and it was because of the failure of governments and industrial tribunals to recognise sex equality in the workshop that there has been opposition to women entering the skilled sections of the trade. The engineer is essentially a craftsman and he places high value on his craft but he also realises that by that craftsmanship he is contributing to the rationalisation of processes and he wants to preserve the rates of the process workers as well so that the worker may benefit directly from the inventions that aid production.

The Australian Section of the A.E.U. has therefore striven to maintain the male rate for the job. When the W.E.B. was established the Commonwealth Council of the A.E.U. protested and demanded that the Federal Government implement its own policy of equal pay for the sexes by a regulation eliminating sex differentials in the metal trades. If the Federal Government had taken the same line as that taken by the State Labor Government in providing by legislation that where no female rate exists the male rate shall prevail, the 241 classifications with rates and margins set down in the M.T.A. would have operated legally from the outset for skilled work and another regulation forbidding sex differentials in the metal industry would have obviated all the sittings of the W.E.B. and consequent litigation in so far as this industry is concerned.

The A.E.U. was mainly responsible for the 100% rate paid to women in a Western munitions factory which was so much advertised for many months.

The A.E.U. however, accepting the position as it is, applied to the W.E.B. for a variation of the 90% to 100% of the male rate and will present a comprehensive case in support of the contention that women do produce as much as men, that absenteeism is a failing of men as well as women and in any case it should not be considered as a reason for lowering rates to punish people whilst at work, and, thirdly, that sex differentials conduce to industrial unrest and militate against a maximum war effort.

Members of the A.E.U. have ceased work in demands for the 100% for women working on men's work, and a mass meeting of the Sydney District members supported their action. Recently at the Quarterly shop stewards meeting a resolution was carried promising renewed support for the demand for equal pay and directing the attention of the Sydney District Committee to the decision of the mass meeting to take drastic action in support of the full male rate for women in the engineering sections of the metal industry.

We are now striving to secure the implementation of the W.E.B. determinations for 90% of the male rate for large sections of workers entitled to it but not yet paid and at the same time we are vigorously endeavouring to secure the elimination of all sex differentials from metal trades wages.

VISITORS TO THE WORKSHOPS

I have visited nearly all the workshops in the Sydney District where women are employed in general engineering work or in government munition annexes.

In the Munition Factories under direct government control the W.E.B. rates are paid without question and the amenities and health services are good, consequently, I have not spent much time on this phase of our work but have devoted myself to the private establishments where the struggle to maintain decent standards is as difficult in wartime as in peacetime.

The large heavy industry sections that undertook the management of annexes or employed relatively few women recognised the W.E.B. rates and paid them continuously from the date of the award. As a rule they also provided amenities and health services comparable with the average, so that one might conclude that in this section the standards set by the W.E.B. for women in the metal industry have been generally observed.

A recent check-up on the firms paying the W.E.B. rate after the decision of the High Court confirming its validity revealed a very interesting situation. In the heavy industry section and in a number of decent firms where only a few women came under the W.E.B. the employers stated their approval of the W.E.B. standard and several frankly said that in the jobs upon which women have been placed they are doing as well or better than the men whom they succeeded, and that the employers would welcome the rate for the job. One old-established company which shall be nameless because they are breaking the law benevolently expressed belief in the rate for the job, pays all women including those entitled to pegged M.T.A. rates, the 90% and adds merit money in some cases bringing the recipients nearly up to the 100% rate.

The third section in this industry, namely the private firms who have in the past employed largely male juvenile labour or have employed women on a small scale, and, who having tasted the rich plums of small metal production under war conditions, are determined to continue large scale operations in mass production of domestic and other light metal commodities after the war.

This group has been strongly organised by the Metal Trades Manufacturers to resist every legal and administrative action of the Government to secure equal pay for women in light metal production and for the most part they were recently paying the Metal Trades Award rate of £3.13.6 even when they are only agents for the Government in the administration of government munition annexes. . .

Sometimes I feel distressed at the frustration in efforts to secure the implementation of the W.E.B. decisions. From time to time I have appealed to every Federal and State authority and always receive the same reply: the Federal authorities have no power because of constitutional limitations and the State authority is doubtful where Federal control exists.

The new regulations governing the Women's Employment Board and the recent provision for Committees of Reference are being tested by an application for hearing in four cases and if these fail and speedy action is not taken by the Federal Government to remove anomalies, there will be no option but to permit the workers to exercise their inherent right to withhold their labour-power rather than to submit to the intolerable and unjust conditions still affecting women in metal sections of war industries though the Women's Employment Board has been nominally functioning since March 1942.

Muriel Heagney, "Report of the Organiser of the Women's Section of the Amalgamated Engineering Union to the First Meeting of Women Shop Stewards of the Sydney District, 10 November 1943".

170. Back to Depression Days

The implications for working women of peace-time employment policies are clearly illustrated in this pamphlet.

REMEMBER THE WAR?

762,653 women were employed in industry (1943 figure).

They were paid   100%
90%
80%   of a man's wages.
75%

The Women's Employment Act and the Female (Minimum Rates) Regulations fixed these rates.

WHY?

Women would not work in important war industries — the rates were too low.

NOW ITS PEACE TIME

- Employers, through the High Court, have torpedoed the Women's Employment Act.
- The Female (Minimum Rates) Regulations have gone overboard as from 31/12/1949.
- The Commonwealth Arbitration Act has conveniently been amended to provide a separate female rate.
- The N.S.W. Act already says 54% of the male basic wage is the woman's rate.

All nice and legal, isn't it?

BUT

IN £. s. d.

If you are in the Public Service (clerk, mail sorter, tram conductress, railway porter, postwoman, etc.) and receive say £8 per week, as the law now stands *you can lose at least £2 per week.*

If you are a seventy-five per center and the rates are reduced to 54% of the male basic wage — *you will lose at least £ 1/8/5 per week.*

Isn't it wonderful to be a woman!

You'll have to cut your weekly budget.
Here's a few suggestions how to save £2 per week.

CHOP	The weekly hair set	2	0
CHOP	Cosmetics — be natural	2	0
CHOP	Fruit from your lunch	2	0
CHOP	Cigarettes — sweets — movies or other simple pleasures	6	0
CHOP	The landlady or mum by	10	0
CHOP	Sheer nylons — wear service weight mediums	4	0
CHOP	The glory box — rely on presents	4	0
CHOP	Dry cleaning, shoe repairs — don't be so fussy	2	0
CHOP	Clothing costs — go to the jumble sales	6	0
CHOP	Presents — its the thought that counts	2	0
		£2 0	**0**

IT'S BACK TO DEPRESSION DAYS

UNLESS YOU —
ACT NOW!

Everyone says they believe in equality, including
the Prime Minister
  Federal Government
  Federal Opposition
  Liberal Party
  Labor Party
  Make them live up to their words:—
The A.C.T.U.
  N.S.W. Labor Council
  Trade Union Equal Pay Committee.
  Believe in action to secure EQUAL PAY.

War and Peace, issued by Trade Union Equal Pay Committee, Sydney (n.d.).

Domestic Servants

171. At the Tub

In the early days of settlement, women who were used to having servants in the home were sometimes deprived of them and had to adapt to new tasks, not always willingly, as this letter from Western Australia shows. The situation in which washerwomen had too much work or other sources of income seems to have been more of a feature of the early days of settlement than later, when competition between washerwomen and the laundries, and between live-in general servants and trades-women, made these jobs a precarious way of earning a living. The Bussells were a pioneering family with a property outside Perth, and as the early labour shortage became less severe, the women of the family were relieved of these domestic tasks.

... there is not a single thing here that can possibly suit a person of luxurious habits, therefore if such come they must feel wretched and unhappy as long as they remain and which they [illegible] rail against a place because they have to wait upon themselves and perhaps wash their own clothes for money here will not procure you servants to do those things for you. They are not to be had for money; there are so few in the colony and those few so independent that they care little about those they serve. Mrs. Barsey turned out infamously. She worked for up 12 months and gave us nothing but trouble the whole time so that I was thankful when at the expiration of the year, she was allowed her fare home and Barsey permitted to work for John until their debt was liquidated. Since Mrs. Barsey left we have been obliged to wash our own clothes and this like every mountain Fanny has dwindled into a mole hill. I assure you I think nothing of it, we manage everything so comfortably that we do it with the greatest ease and I often have, when standing at the wash tub, one sleeve tucked up above one's elbow, wished you dearest with us, *enter into the pleasures* of our occupation, poor dear Charley; he was dreadfully distressed when first we commenced it and used every exertion to prevail on Mrs. Dawson, the only washer-woman in our neighbourhood, to do the whole for us at her house at the enormous price of four shillings a dozen; I believe mine and dear John's were the only light hearts in the house when Charles returned from Wonnerup and told me he had been unsuccessful in his application to Mrs. Dawson. She had so much to do already with her dairy, her children and the washing she already had that she could not receive any more — John and I were in secret excessively pleased at her refusal; we both thought it an immense expense to enter into for one large household though as all the ladies had such a dread of the wash tub we would not raise our voices against Charley making the application — the dear old Charley came up to me (when I was walking in the garden afterwards with my little Capel in my arms) looking so distressed and anxious that I could not help exclaiming "What is the matter Charley?" "Oh Charlotte this is a most disgraceful thing is it not?" "What Charley, having to wash our own clothes?" "Yes, it appears to me a break up of everything like domestic comfort". "Oh, Charley, not at all. Why should it? We shall only have to be very, very busy one day every fortnight, there is no reason whatever why things in the house should not go on just as comfortable as it does at present. You will see that all the difficulties will vanish the moment we commence. . . . but that same evening poor dear Fanny followed me into my room when I retired for the night and after seating herself by the side of my bed in an easy chair you so well remember, in which you too have often sat. She burst into tears — "Fanny what is the matter, are you ill?" for I was really frightened at seeing her so distressed. "Oh no Charlotte, you will say I am very foolish; nothing is the matter but I have such a dread of the washing. I cannot describe to you my horror of it. I hoped such days would never come again but I think they are come upon us now as a punishment for hating the occupation so much. I suppose now I shall never do anything else from Monday morning till Saturday night but stand at the wash tub" and with this speech there came such a torrent of tears that it positively astonished me — however, as well as I could I began to cheer her — told her it was impossible washing her own clothes could employ her a week and that I was quite sure she should be able to do it quite comfortably if she would only look on the bright side and enter into it cheerfully — the following week we commenced. John and I were the first to make the starch. I soaked in the white clothes the day before which made them more easy to get clean when we began to rub the next morning — being young beginners we did not get thro' our work that day so quickly as we do now, but we managed most comfortably considering it was the first time — now we begin in the morning and get it all finished and on the lines by dinner time, our dresses changed and seated at dinner as though nothing of the kind had been going on — the next day all our clothes are in our drawers again and looking much better washed than they ever were in Mrs. Barsey's time — so you see Fanny we are pretty well satisfied with our work. I should like you to see Mrs. Spicer, dearest Fanny and tell her with my most kindly most affectionate love that I often thank her in my heart for the invaluable lessons she gave me when a child; in a hundred different ways I have felt the benefit of them since I had been out here and often wish she was present to be rewarded with a sight of the child she brought up now busying about quite in her own style and rejoicing that it fell to her lot to have such a kind excellent teacher in her early days — in this respect there will be always a great difference in the girls her and myself; they think hardships of what I consider trifles and I suppose this arises from them never having been allowed to do anything of the kind when young. At that time they knew nothing of domestic occupations and though they have entered into them since they have been out here, *they have never liked them* — dear Fanny however has completely conquered her aversion to the washing and enters into it as cheerfully as possible and finds instead of being a whole week about it her clothes are often finished in the morning and in the drawers in the evening.

Charlotte Bussell to her "dearest Fanny", 1842.

172. Two Servants

If "the servant problem" was an issue that preoccupied middle-class women at least until the Second World War, there were times when the problem seemed to be more severe. This was so in Adelaide during the Victorian gold-rush, and in this letter to her aunt in England, a young Adelaide woman describes an encounter between mistress and servants. Less than four years later, the boot was on the other foot: female immigration had resulted in unemployment among domestic servants.

My dear Aunt,

We were very glad to hear from Croxley that you are so well and strong again. I suppose you hear all the news about us from Croxley and the curious state the Town is in owing to the gold diggings. The greater part of the female servants have gone off to Melbourne where they get 12/- a week for wages and those that remain are a very bad set. The other day we were dining at Judge Cooper's and a lady present related her own experience in a very amusing manner. It appeared that she had engaged a cook and housemaid the week before; and they called each other Miss Thomas and Miss Tomkinson all day long, and their Master they spoke of as the Captain. After a few days Miss Tomkinson came to her mistress when the following converstaion took place:

MISS T: We are going to the theatre tonight and as there is a Ball afterwards, we shall not be able to return till the day after tomorrow, and besides we should be too tired to do our work.

MISTRESS: . . . And who is to get the dinner and do your work if we are left without any one in the house?

MISS T: Oh, I'm sure I don't know, Mum, we couldn't possibly disappoint the party and Miss Thomas is such a particular friend of mine, she must go.

MISTRESS: I can only say that if you go you shall not return here again.

However, they did go, and the next day Miss Tomkinson came back elegantly dressed in a blue silk dress, magnificent shawl and white silk drawn bonnet. Her mistress desired her to take her bundle and leave the house, but she earnestly entreated to be allowed to send for it, saying: "Oh, Mum, I couldn't possibly carry a bundle in Adelaide in my present dress". However, she was made to take it.

Penelope Belt to her aunt, Miss Bentley, 19 June 1852.

173. An Excess of Irish Female Immigrants

The importation of single women, most usually from Ireland, to act as domestic servants in South Australia led to the setting up of country depots, in an attempt to disperse the women. In his memorandum, the governor reveals that the words "domestic servant" frequently meant in actuality "farm labourer", and many of the girls were neither strong enough nor sufficiently trained for this sort of work.

Memorandum by His Excellency the Governor of the Circular ordered by the Board to be sent to the Country Depots.

1. In reference to the circular of the Immigration Board of the 5th instant, on the subject of the re-admission to the several Immigration Depots of girls who have left those places for service, I must remark that I think the power given to the Matrons of the Depots to re-admit girls, hired specially for short periods, is opposed to what ought to be the primary object of the Board, viz., the permanent settlement and dispersing of the immigrants amongst the general mass of the population.

2. If a very great effort is not made now, in the height of the harvest, to get rid of the immigrants, there will be less hope of attaining that object when the harvest is over. The re-admission, however, of immigrants in the manner so publicly sanctioned by the Board must lead the farmers and other employers of labor to use the services of these girls for only just so many days or weeks as they may have profitable use for their labor, and then to return them to be fed and supported at the expense of the public for perhaps several months, till it may suit the employer of labor again to apply for the services of the girls for a brief period.

3. The Colony might thus be called on to support some hundreds of girls for ten months in the year, that their labor might be available for the remaining two months. This is a serious question when it is considered that there were yesterday upwards of 759 Irish adult female immigrants rationed by the Colony, either in the depots or on shipboard, exclusive of 157 supported as destitute poor.

4. I cannot, therefore, think that it is fair to the Colony, or that it would eventually prove advantageous to the immigrants themselves, that they should thus learn to look on the depots as asylums, to which they can retire after short periods of labor, whilst those *who would otherwise lay themselves out to find permanent employment for them* will make their arrangements with a view to consigning them back to the depots at those periods of the year when the employment of labor becomes least profitable.

5. The principle is essentially bad, and can only be recommended by the pecuniary saving temporarily effected in the rations of the girls so employed — a saving likely to be fearfully counterbalanced in the end by the indefinite adjournment thereby occasioned to the final absorption of the immigrant girls in the mass of the population.

6. A girl, leaving the depot, should feel that, on her exertions to give satisfaction to her employers, and on the character she may acquire for industry and integrity during a short period of service, must depend her chance of getting her term of service prolonged, or finding some other engagement. If she feels assured that, no matter how she behaves during a short engagement, she has a comfortable home and good diet secured to her in a depot, the Government will lose the best guarantee for the girls' making, in their own behalf, those exertions to secure permanent employment, which are, and must always be, worth ten times as much as the utmost help which the Government alone can give them.

7. I therefore think that, except when a girl receives actual ill-usuage from an employer, she ought not to look for further aid or protection from the Government. If, unfortunately, despite of her best exertions, she becomes destitute or falls ill, I think she should receive the same relief, and no other, as is afforded, either by public or private charity, to the destitute now, but on no account should such relief be administered in any immigration depot, it being important to preserve distinct the principles on which an immigrant is supported and a destitute person relieved.

8. For myself, I see no measure so effectual for grappling with the gigantic and costly evil now becoming rooted in the heart of the State, as enlisting the utmost exertions of the girls themselves in aid of their settlement and dispersion; whilst I do not believe this can be effected until they are made to feel and understand that, once they leave the depot, its door is shut to them for ever. If any special reasons are to be considered as justifying their re-admission, the Board alone should decide on the adequacy of those reasons; and any matron re-admitting an immigrant *ad interim* under such circumstances, should do so at the risk of having the cost of the rations of such person deducted from her salary.

9. It is probable that the majority of these girls can, and that, under these circumstances, they will find employment, if not in in-door work, yet in that species of labor to which alone the great majority of the immigrants in question have been accustomed, viz., out-door farm work. Such may possibly not be the employment to which one would give the preference, and numbers of the immigrants are qualified for a superior employment; but, on the other hand, there are many, if not *the majority of them*, who at present are fitted, by their previous habits, for little else, and, therefore, from the first, I have never wished to encourage amongst the immigrants an expectation of obtaining other work for which they are really unfitted. In the circular sent last June to the Magistrates and District Councils, I remarked "that the *majority* of the Irish female immigrants had not acquired the experience necessary to render them useful as in-door servants, but that they were willing to be employed as farm servants, having most of them already served in that capacity." The above observations were penned after personal examination and inquiry by myself concerning all the female Irish immigrants then in the Colony.

10. I confess that, as an Irishman, I infinitely prefer seeing my countrywomen employed in any honest work, whether reaping, stacking, or other out-door farm occupation, to seeing them leading, as at present, a life of forced idleness, demoralizing to themselves and injurious to some of the best interests of the Colony. I consider that those who are physically capable of such hardship would be more respectably engaged even whilst digging, than whilst eating the bread of charity; and I have no doubt, that by commencing thus, they would increase their chance of settling prosperously.

11. The above observations are intended to explain why I think it more judicious not to give the Board's direct sanction to the employment of immigrants for short periods, on the understanding that at the termination of such periods, they can *claim as a right* re-admission to one of the depots.

12. I take this opportunity of suggesting the urgent necessity, and the moral duty which devolves on the Government, of finding some industrial occupation for the inmates of the depot. It is not likely such occupation will at first prove very remunerative, but if, in the end, it repays only the cost of such additional supervision as it may entail, it will have accomplished a great object by keeping the girls employed, and enabling them to obtain some useful instruction in knitting, washing, baking, cooking, sewing, or any other occupation which the Board may judge suitable for them. I would, therefore, suggest that the Board should not be deterred from making the attempt, by the various difficulties of detail, or even by the increased expense consequent on their first efforts to afford industrial occupation to the immigrant inmates of the Town and Country depots.

13. In connection with this subject, I would also suggest that, where any country depot has been found to work satisfactorily, the Board would do well to pause before closing such an outlet for the superabundant immigrant labor now in the Colony.

R.G. MacDonnell, Governor-in-Chief of South Australia, to Female Immigrant Board, 9 January 1856.

174. "Impolitic, Unjust and Cruel"

This letter suggests the consequences of a policy that sought to deny female immigrants who remained unemployed the shelter of the immigrant depots. In it, the

Superintendent of the Female Immigrant Board shows an understanding not only of the difficulties these women faced but of the way that work inside an institution could "interfere" with the livelihood of other "industrious" women.

Sir—1st. The Female Immigrant Board, having maturely deliberated upon the Memorandum of His Excellency Sir R.G. MacDonnell, bearing date the 9th instant, have now the honor of forwarding a reply to that document.

2nd. The Board believe there are two reasons why female immigrants are maintained at the depot after their time on shipboard has expired. *First*, that there has lately been an amount of immigration of unprotected females altogether in excess of the present demand; *second*, that it is the duty of Government, for the sake of morality and ordinary humanity, to find shelter and sustenance for that excess.

3rd. With reference to the important question of denying re-admission to all females at the depot who have once obtained situations, the Board would respectfully observe—

4th. That, while it seems proper that no girl who can find employment of even a temporary nature, should be allowed to remain in the depot, and that it becomes the duty of this Board to re-admit no girl into the depot unless it can be clearly proved, that being thrown out of employment is not owing to any fault of the young woman applying for re-admission, the Board believe that no general rule can be framed adapted to meet the peculiarities of every case; each must be decided upon its own merits; and all that the public can expect the Board to do, is to use every means in their power to prevent any case of abuse arising. The Board having thus expressed the principles upon which they conceive they ought to act, regret that they cannot on all points agree with the views enunciated by His Excellency the Governor-in-Chief.

5th. The Board are impressed with a firm belief, founded on long Colonial experience of the constant fluctuations in the labor market, that should the present stream of immigrants of that class be arrested, this serious evil will, ere the lapse of many months, remedy itself, and that many girls now rejected will before long be readily engaged. This is the impression of the Board after a careful consideration of the subject in all its bearings. The present prosperous state of the agricultural community (the most numerous class of any in the Colony) for whose sevice a majority of the girls is more especially suited, justifies this opinion, which is further strengthened by a return, herewith forwarded, showing that, from the formation of the Board, in October, 1855, to the present date, a period of little more than three months, no less a number than 1,343 females (return enclosed) have been sent from the depot.

6th. To adopt the harsher line of policy, and refuse admission to all girls once engaged, even but for a week, the Board consider to be highly impolitic, unjust, and cruel, and that it would lead to many disastrous results.

7th. Many deserving and virtuous girls would thus inevitably, without money, home or friends, be sacrificed and driven to prostitution for their support; and by withholding such reasonable support and shelter from the deserving immigrant, if the girl [does] not got on the town, she becomes an inmate of the Destitute Asylum, and thus undeservedly loses caste as well as heart, and may probably become a permanent pauper — as few persons requiring servants will engage them from the poorhouse, where they must associate with prostitutes and diseased men, and have ample means, therefore, of forming bad acquaintances.

8th. The Board have practically found it necessary to provide by its rules as well against the caprice and oppression of employers, as against the misbehaviour or laziness of the servants.

9th. The Board have thus endeavored to show that the practice adopted by them of re-admission of the *deserving* to the town depot is politic, just, and merciful. They, therefore, urgently advocate its continuance under the present system, which excludes the unworthy; and they would further remark with reference to the engagement of servants, the arrangements made between employers and employed ought not to be interfered with by the Board.

10th. The Board fully concur in the sentiments expressed by His Excellency, that occupation and employment should, if possible, be found for the inmates of the depot. They will, therefore, with hearty zeal endeavor to grapple with the difficulties, perceptibly in the way of establishing so desirable a system; but it must be borne in mind that there is a danger of interfering with the labor of a numerous class of industrious females, who by washing, mangling, needlework, and other such occupations are endeavoring to support themselves and families in an honest and respectable manner.

11th. As regards the impolicy of closing country depots after being once established in any locality, the Board would remark that they never contemplated the necessity of forming such for any permanency; their great desire has been to remove every establishment to some other part of the country so soon as the demand for female servants at each station has been fairly met. The Board consider it highly impolitic to overstock the country depots, where girls are far less under control and supervision than at head quarters.

M. Moorhouse; Superintendent, Female Immigrant Board, to Colonial Secretary, 21 January 1856.

175. Expulsion

Not only the disposal of the women but their behaviour while awaiting disposal attracted the attention of the authorities. The unhappiness that many of these young girls felt at being sent into employment in far-distant areas like Robe and Penola is even more understandable in the light of the pay they received and the nature of the work they were expected to do.

Sir,

I have the honor to report for the information of His Excellency the Governor in Chief that since my last communication, five of the Irish Female Immigrants have been hired at Penola.

I have sent a party of twelve to Mt. Gambier and I hope to hear shortly that the whole or greater part of them have met with employment in that neighbourhood.

One of the girls Bridget [H———] has been so insubordinate that I have been under the necessity of expelling her from the Depot. She in the first instance, having been named one of the party for Penola, refused to go, which the matron passed over; she was afterwards selected for Mt. Gambier, but on the morning the party left, she hid herself away & did not make her appearance until night; besides these two cases of direct opposition to orders, I was informed by the matron that her general conduct was very bad, I therefore considered that I had no alternative but to expel her, as an example for the other girls, which I hope will have the effect of preventing the necessity of having again to resort to such a measure.

Charles Brewer, Government Resident, Robetown to the Colonial Secretary, 1 September 1855.

176. Fighting Back

Some of the women in the immigrant depots did not accept their situation passively. In this case it seems likely that the virulence of Smith Kell's attack had a sectarian basis, and that some of the local antagonism to the women was a response to their Irish-Catholic origins.

I am sorry to report, that this morning there was a great disturbance at the depot, so much that I was obliged to call in the police. The dispute arose in consequence of my having forbidden them to go to a distance in the country, returning at all hours of the night without leave. After peace was restored, there was still one girl, of the name of Catherine Leary, whose conduct it would be impossible to overlook. She not only attempted to assault me at the time, but threatened to murder me the next time I came to the depot. I must, therefore, insist on her being recalled to Adelaide by the next mail.

The boxes of the girl you sent out last have never arrived; she is in great want of them.

Since writing the above, it has been reported to me by the police, that the majority of the girls at the depot are fully bent on a row, threatening every person who contradicts them, and stating that they only want three more police and a few soldiers, and then they will have a fight. They appear to be instigated in this by the girls you last sent out. I must beg of you to take some steps to put an end to this affair, either by sending for the ringleaders to Adelaide, or breaking up the establishment.

Smith Kell, Chairman of the District Council, Willunga, to M. Moorhouse, Superintendent, Female Immigrant Depot, 10 October 1855.

177. "The Poor Girls"

Some of the hardships faced by the girls in looking for work can be glimpsed in this letter from the matron of one of the country depots, the inmates of which had been severely criticized by local authorities.

Respected Friend — I am very sorry that your mind should be so much disturbed with such barefaced falsehoods. What I stated before, I would declare on a *death-bed*; as to the other frivolous accounts, I firmly believe is envy and malice, for the Corporal made use of a profane expression, and said he would get them out of this place, or he would get himself out. Gentlemen — I hope you will not lay anything to the poor, innocent girls' charge, for they do not deserve what has been charged against them; for they are always in and the doors locked, and the keys in my pocket. The Police do not want them even to have their windows open at night; if they were closed, they would, at times, be suffocated with heat and smoke, for I am obliged to keep my door always open, when I am in the room, owing to the smoke.

Gentlemen — It is anything but pleasant for me to make such entry, my feelings yearn with gratitude for your kindness in forwarding the copy. Please pardon my burdening you, or my own mind, with such malicious accounts as have already, and, I believe, are now, being stated by the Police in reference to the poor girls; if you require any further particulars they shall be duly forwarded; in reference to the girls, they are all that I can require. I have not had the pleasure of seeing Mr Kell, since my last. I can assure you, Gentlemen, that what I state is nothing but the truth; three of the poor girls walked yesterday, barefooted, about sixteen miles, between the hours of ten and four, to get a situation. Mary Cain will leave today, at five shillings per week — and the other two expect to be sent for this week. Catherine Uninn was hired, yesterday, at two shillings and sixpence per week. My husband gave Mary Cain an old pair of boots to enable her to go to her situation.

Matilda Eliza Lewis, Matron, Willunga Depot, to M. Moorhouse, Female Immigrant Board, 16 October 1855.

178. The Immigrants

A Select Committee was appointed in South Australia in 1855 to look into the large number of female immigrants who were unemployed and supported by the colonial government. The matron of the Female Immigrant Depot, Adelaide, was asked about the backgrounds of the immigrant women and their employment at the depot.

343. Have you any means of knowing the general reasons for emigration on the part of these girls? — Because they were told of high wages being given, and their friends have doubtless advised them to come out, at the same time sending good accounts to them of the state of things in the Colony.

344. Are they chiefly from the poorhouses in Ireland? — I think a great many of those who have come recently, have come from their parents or friends direct to this Colony; and a great number have come from manufactories where needlework, a kind of embrodiery, was made — many certainly from the poorhouses.

345. Do you know of any means by which they could be instructed in domestic service, so as to fit them for taking situations? — No, I do not know with such numbers of them how it could be done.

346. Have you any suggestions to offer to the Committee as to any improvements in the present system, for the management or disposal of those in the Depot? — No, unless there was some establishment to which they could be sent. The returned servants used formerly to go to the Destitute Asylum, but they have great objection to that because of the hard work there.

347. Could you not give them work in the Depot? — There lies the difficulty.

348. Do you know how much the girls earn for themselves by sewing, and other work of that kind? — I do not.

349. (*By Mr. Forster*) — You stated that the Country Depots have been of considerable service in getting girls into employment, particularly the Mount Barker Depot. Do you think it likely that after harvest a great number will return to the Depot? — Yes, I am afraid they will, because such has been the case before.

350. Then you think a great many of them have been employed from the Country Depots chiefly for harvest work? — Yes, I think it most likely such was the case.

351. You stated that the girls in the Depot washed their own clothes, and scour their own rooms; those things must furnish a very small portion of work for them? — Certainly, especially among so many, and where they take it in turns to do it.

352. There is in existence, I believe, a Committee of Ladies, who, having taken an interest in the Depot, have furnished the inmates with cotton to manufacture articles of needlework and embroidery, and also to knit stockings with. What

becomes of the proceeds of the labour or material thus furnished by that Committee? — The girls have the proceeds themselves.

353. Then they get cotton for nothing, and they are allowed to sell what they make for their own benefit? — Yes, but the amount they can earn is very trifling. There were some girls who were lace-makers, who have left the Depot, and taken a room, where they pursue their employment of lace-working.

354. Are there a great many of the girls who come to the Depot, who have been brought up in better circumstances, and have not been accustomed to work? — Yes, there is one now in the Depot, and she has been a long time there, and yet is very anxious to get a situation, and yet her appearance is against her; she does not look like a servant.

355. Have you ever heard the girls say under what arrangements they came out to this Colony? — No, I have not.

356. Then you do not know what is the moving cause of their coming out in large numbers? — No, Sir.

357. Did you ever hear them say that any person visited Ireland for the purpose of getting emigrants, or have you heard them say anything of that kind? — No, Sir.

358. (*By the Chairman*) — Do any of them appear disappointed on their arrival here? — Many of them do. They seem to think there is very little, if any, chance for them, and I have found them in tears from this cause frequently.

359. (*By Mr. Forster*) — Then you fear that they will not all be employed very speedily? — I think not, there are nearly 400 of them there now.

360. What do you think would be the best plan to adopt to employ them? — Some persons have recommended washing, but I think if they were to be employed in that manner, it would have the effect of throwing out of employment many poor persons who now earn their subsistence by that means, and they would be compelled to go into the Destitute Asylum. I think a manufactory would be best.

361. Supposing a manufactory could be established, would the females themselves be willing to engage in it? — I should think they would not at first; but when they found they must employ themselves they would fall into it.

362. Do you think it would be well to put it to the girls as an alternative, either to engage in that, or give up all claim to support? — I think it is desirable, especially as regards girls who have returned from situations.

363. You find them generally worse than the new arrivals? — Those who have been in the Colony a long time are the most difficult to get rid of.

364. The Government have felt a difficulty, and so have the Committee, in finding employment for them? — I think the difficulty arises from the great numbers to deal with.

365. Do you not think it would be better to keep those girls as at present six or twelve months longer, if there was no prospect of their leaving the Depot and uniting and mixing with the bulk of the colonists, than to employ them in a manufactory? — I think there are some who will never be fit for service, and who have not strength enough. I should say there are forty who, from ill health, are unfit for service. One woman who is in the Depot I have known in fits for two days at a time.

366. Then they will become a permanent burthen on the Colony? — Yes; and I consider it very wrong that those persons should have been sent here to get rid of them.

367. Have you heard many of them say where it was they wished to have gone? — Yes, many of them wanted to go to Melbourne, and they thought Adelaide and Melbourne were one and the same; or that they were so near as that they could easily go from one to the other.

368. (*By Mr. Blyth*) — Can they wash well? — Yes, but they cannot do ironing; and that is the reason they are not employed.

369. Have you noticed whether there have been many respectable persons calling recently for the purpose of hiring servants? — There have not been so many lately. Persons are not aware that there is an office expressly for their accommodation when they wish to hire girls; and consequently they shrink from the task of going to the Depot, and the possibility of being mixed with two or three hundred girls.

370. Have you noticed a scarcity of cooks? — Yes, there has always existed a scarcity of that class of persons.

Minutes of Evidence, Select Committee on Excessive Female Immigration; evidence of Mrs Ross, Matron, Female Immigrant Depot, 11 February 1856.

179. Overworked

The evidence of Mr Ennis, Yard Overseer at the Female Immigrant Depot, revealed the harsh outdoor labour and the poor pay the immigrant women received in South Australia.

488. (*Mr. Forster*) — Are there many girls draughted to the country now? — No, not many.

489. What is the reason? — There is not such a demand now as there was for them.

490. Have you reason to apprehend that many of them will be thrown out of employment? — I think not, many parties who never had a servant before are able to keep them now.

491. Supposing that no more immigrants arrived, how long do you think the Colony will require to absorb the number of girls at present in the Depot? — They are absorbed at the rate of about twenty a-week, and there are three hundred in the Depot.

492. Do you mean twenty above the number that return? — Yes.

493. Then in six months the numbers will be absorbed? — Yes, but perhaps it would be safer to say eight months.

494. Do you know any person who is likely to be a permanent burden to the Colony among the inmates of the Depot? — No, I think they will be able to obtain employment. Some of the younger girls have been frightened by the state in which girls' hands have been on returning from service in the country.

495. Has that impression been produced by the representations of the girls returned from service? — Sometimes by those representations, and sometimes by the state in which they saw the girls' hands and also by the answers to their enquiries.

496. Do you think such impressions could have been created upon the mind of persons who had been accustomed to service? — In some cases it would where they could see how the girls had been knocked about.

497. (*By Mr. Angas*) — What do you mean by knocked about? — Overworked.

498. What evidence have you had of that? — I have seen their hands stripped.

499. Would not that be the case with your own hands if you went to work for a few days in a garden? — In the cases I refer to, the girls were accustomed to service.

500. (*By Mr. Forster*) — Would not the girls' hands get soft by being twelve months out of employment. Hands become hard by continuous employment? —

Yes, but one of those girls had gone from a place to that in which her hands became sore.

501. Then how do you account for the state of her hands? — The only way I can account for it is by the way she was overworked. She told me she had twenty cows to milk, to churn without assistance, and a great deal of work besides. From what I know of that girl, I believe she was quite willing to work. His Excellency the Governor was present upon one occasion, and saw that girl's hands. She has since gone to a situation.

502. Do you know any other case? — Yes, I know other cases.

503. Do you know anything of the nature of the representations made to the girls before they came out to this Colony? — Yes; that servants were so scare that they would be certain to get high wages.

504. By whom was this representation made? — By friends of their own, in letters written home.

505. The object of this Committee is to ascertain what has led to the excessive immigration of young females; and presuming that I might obtain some evidence on that point, I asked the question. Then you think it was owing to the representations of relatives and friends? — A great deal of it has been caused by that.

506. Do you know whether the Emigration Agents have made any representations of that sort? — No, I know nothing of the sort.

507. (*By Mr. Neales*) — Can you give any idea why girls should be in one case twelve months, in another case nine months, and in other cases seven months, in the Depot, without having ever been engaged? — Some of those you refer to have been engaged, but the time stated that which they have been in the Depot from first to last.

508. And not continuous residence there? — No.

509. What do you set down the long continuance of some girls in the Depot to? — Some cannot get employment; others are, perhaps, not inclined to accept offers of employment.

510. Do you not think that all those who have been so long in the Depot are disinclined to accept engagements? — I think, generally, they are. Some are not inclined to accept the current wages; others would take the wages if they could get situations to suit them.

511. (*By Mr. Blyth*) — What are the current wages? — Four or five shillings a week.

512. I see by the papers that some have hired at half-a-crown a week? — In the country parts some have been taken out at that rate.

513. Are there any regulations with respect to accepting or refusing situations? — Any girl refusing half-a-crown a week would be dismissed, as I think any would who were reported for refusing even less than that.

514. Have there been complaints of insolence on the part of the girls? — There have, but not generally. Those coming back to the Depot are required to produce written characters; and if the employer complains of insolence, the Board will notice the case.

515. (*By Mr. Forster*) — Several of these women are of a superior class? — Yes; many of them will make good servants.

516. Have you any suggestion to make as to the best mode of employing those girls? — The question has come unexpectedly upon me. I have not at present.

517. Will you be good enough to favour the Committee, in writing, with any suggestion that occurs to you? — I shall be most happy to do so. I may say that the making of bags for Mr. Dutton will supply many of the girls with boots.

518. How many women could you employ? — We could employ upwards of a hundred if we had work for them.

519. They all understand knitting and the like? — Yes; they understand some sort of knitting or crotchet-work.

Minutes of Evidence, Select Committee on Excessive Female Immigration; evidence of Mr P. Ennis, Yard Overseer, Female Immigrant Depot, 13 February 1856.

180. Boots

While the inquiry was concerned with establishing that the female immigrants were unsuited to many of the tasks expected of them, graphic details about their lives often emerged. The hardship caused by the shortage of boots, which meant that some women looked for work barefooted has been mentioned. The girls who made sacks for Mr Dutton received boots "for their labour".

529. Do those girls generally express disappointment at not being able to obtain employment? — Not so much as to the employment as to the rate of wages.

530. Do you learn from them why they came to South Australia? — Certainly, to better themselves.

531. Do they say that they had information as to the rate of wages? — Yes, they speak of the statements in letters and in the papers, and chiefly complain of the circulars sent through the country, professing to give information to the rate of wages here.

532. Then they seem to expect a higher rate of wages than they find current here? — Yes, much higher.

533. Did they, so far as you know or have heard, all apply for passages to South Australia? — A good many expected to be sent to Sydney or Melbourne, who were sent here.

534. Are the girls generally too young to go to service? — Generally speaking they are.

535. About what age are the youngest? — They are seldom under sixteen years of age.

536. Are not healthy girls fit for work at that age? — Very few at that age are fit for the work in country service. They would with teaching make house-servants, but they are not able for the work put upon them.

537. What work do you refer to? — Drawing water from wells, and attending to cattle and horses.

538. Do the girls who return from country service generally state that such is the employment given to them? — Yes, and others are deterred from taking places by those statements.

539. What do you consider those girls fit for? — A great many of them left their fathers' houses to come here, without having ever been at service. They came partly for companionship with others, and partly in the hope of getting high wages.

540. Then they expected high wages without possessing domestic qualifications? — Yes, very few.

541. Are they not able to wash and cook? — They are generally able to wash, but not to finish; as to cooking, they know nothing about it.

542. Do they generally behave well; — Generally they are well-disposed girls.

543. Are they inclined to be actively and usefully employed? — Generally they are anxious for employment . . .

580. Are there a number of girls employed in making sacks? — Yes.

581. Do they make any objection to that work? — They are very anxious for that work, but it is only given to those who are in want of boots. Some of the girls are sadly off for boots.

582. Then they are to receive boots for their labor? — Yes, they are to receive boots.

583. (*By Mr. Neales*) — Can you give any reason why some girls remain so long in the Depot — one, twelve months; four, nine months; fourteen, seven months; fifty-four, six months; and so on? — I think a person in the Depot twelve months should have had a situation before that time.

584. Or even six months? — Yes.

585. Then you believe that those are the worst of the girls who remain in the Depot so long? — So far as willingness to go to service.

586. (*By Mr. Blyth*) — Can you give the Committee any idea of the proportion who wish to go to Sydney? — About twenty or thirty have received money from their friends.

587. How many of the whole number of the girls originally intended to go to Melbourne? — From ten to twenty told me, that at home, when getting the form, that they expected to go to Sydney or Melbourne.

Minutes of Evidence, Select Committee on Excessive Female Immigration; evidence of Mrs Ennis Assistant Matron, Female Immigrant Depot, 13 February 1856.

181. "A Good Place for Any Girl Handy at Her Needle"

A number of female immigrants were interviewed during the inquiry into excessive female immigration. Here Sarah Keogh, a young woman from Dublin, describes her capabilities and expectations.

837. (*By the Chairman*) — How long have you been in the Colony? — Eight months.

838. What ship did you arrive by? — The *Grand Trianon*.

839. What part did you come from? — Dublin.

840. Had you been in service before you came here? — Never.

841. What did you do for a living, anything in the way of domestic work? — I am a dressmaker.

842. Have you been at dressmaking for many years? — For two years.

843. What did you do before? — I lived with my father and mother.

844. What were they? — They kept a shop.

845. What did you expect to do here? — I was told it was a good place for any girl handy at her needle.

846. Then you are handy at your needle? — Yes, I am.

847. But not accustomed to domestic work? — Just so.

848. Were you healthy when you came on board ship? — Yes, but I have not been healthy since my arrival here.

849. Did you fall ill on shipboard? — Yes, I had a great deal of illness on shipboard.

850. Did that reduce you to your present feeble state? — It might have done so.

851. Have you been at service in this Colony? — I have been a fortnight in one place at Gawler Town.

852. What were your duties there? — To do for nine in family; I found I was not capable of doing the whole of the work.

853. Of what description was the work? — I had to cook, wash, and milk one cow, that I was not competent to do; I had also to go and get wood and cut it up.

854. Did you have to use the axe? — Yes, and to go for the wood.

855. Far? — Not very far from the house.

856. Why did you leave? — I got sore eyes, and my master said I was not capable to do the work.

857. Have you been any where else from the Depot?— Yes, I have been at Encounter Bay.

858. Did you not get any offer of employment at all there? — No, they said they wanted country girls who could milk and do out-door work. Four of us girls were sent back as not fit for that part of the country.

859. How long is it since you returned from Encounter Bay? — Two months.

860. Have you endeavoured to obtain employment in the shops at needlework? — There is a shipmate of mine who promised to get me as much work as I could do. I was about to apply to the Board for a month's rations to keep me while I was doing work to begin with; but the Rev. Mr. Ryan told me that the girls outside were not doing very well.

861. Do you think you could get employ outside? — I have tried to get into a shop, but was unsuccessful, and I knew that it was no use for me to try to get a situation, for I could not keep it.

862. What then do you consider you can do? — Needlework is the thing I am capable of doing.

Minutes of Evidence, Select Committee on Excessive Female Immigration; evidence of Sarah Keogh, 18 February 1856.

182. "If the Ladies Desire Servants . . ."

General Booth of the Salvation Army addressed the Second Australasian Conference on Charity held in Melbourne in 1891. His "Darkest England" scheme and proposals on immigration attracted attention, particularly when immigration was linked with "the servant problem".

MRS. GLENN suggested that 50 of the first 100 should be domestic servants, as they were suffering in this colony from want of domestic labour.

GENERAL BOOTH said he could understand that, as he was suffering from the inconvenience caused by three servants at the house in which he was staying having announced their intention of leaving. Somebody had told him in Sydney that if he would bring out 5,000 domestic servants they could place them in that colony alone. He had no doubt he could supply domestic servants to any amount. There were thousands of girls in England who would be delighted to come out, but they would not come alone. Even the poor rescued girls would not come alone. If the ladies desire servants, let them subscribe for them. "How much would it cost?" might be asked. Supposing it cost £20 to prepare the girl and send her out here, and that the wages were to be £35 per year, would those wishing for servants advance the £20 in each case? During the first year the £20 might be deducted from the girl's wages. If the girl left them they could get another, so as to get services to the value of what they had subscribed. If they agreed to such a project it would, of course, be understood that the servants were to be at liberty to attend the meetings of the Salvation Army and wear the uniform. There were thousands of lasses who would be glad to go anywhere provided they were allowed to wear the uniform.

The statesmen, the Christians, and the philanthropists of Australia were with him in his scheme. The only real objection was raised by the workingman. The eight hours question would be discussed at the conference to be held at the Trades Hall later on in the day. He proposed to meet the difficulty by showing that when the working man became his own master he could work what hours he liked.

Proceedings of the Second Australasian Conference on Charity (1891).

183. The "Notorious" Gulf of Siam

While the idea that immigration should be used to solve the servant problem was a recurring and popular one, in actuality, the arrival of single female immigrants continued to pose problems: of employment, dispersal, protection, suitability, and as these documents show, of morality. The "notorious" *Princess Royal*, which arrived in Hobart in 1832, was thought by many to show that, in moral terms, there was little difference between government-sponsored free immigrants and convicts. In Western Australia, where there were no female convicts, the women from the *Gulf of Siam*, sixty years later, were greeted in the same way.

Dear Sir Malcolm,

I have waited to make some enquiries about the young women referred to in the Report sent to you by the Hon. S. H. Parker, Colonial Secretary, who went out with Free passages to Western Australia in the "Gulf of Siam".

It is a matter of very deep regret to me that some of them have turned out to be unsatisfactory.

There are however two points which I personally cannot pass over unnoticed in this letter, one, "looking at the characters which are attached to the papers of these girls, it is obvious that they are obtained far too easily, and that they afford no criterion even as to personal respectability of the recipients."

If this were true, then indeed all the great trouble which I take and the exhaustive inquiry made into character would be quite useless — The two Secretaries and my own private Secretary are persons who spare no trouble in their correspondence, in getting characters spreading back over several years history — and where-ever I consider it necessary, additional enquiries are made after the applications come into me. My system too of having the women interviewed in different parts of the kingdom, by persons who are in the habit of interviewing people of the working classes, is an additional security when a reference is taken up by writing to person referred to — and several persons are written to cover dates of a servant's service life — there does not remain more to be done unless a personal interview was required with the employer — which of course could only be carried out at enormous expense.

I think that the trouble and care which is taken deserves some recognition on the part of the authorities.

I am informed by Mrs Salter who as you know meets the various parties, that she considered there was a very large proportion of superior girls in this last party.

She also writes, that the young women from the previous party, are doing better than would have been expected from the report of them during the voyage, which shows that the conduct there was caused by the persons who gave so much trouble from amongst the other passengers.

I notice that Dr Nix writes in his report; "The girls in this ship were under the impression that whatever their behaviour might be on board the ship, the Government were bound to provide them with situations, and that the report of the Matron and Medical Superintendent was of no account, if the rules had been explained to them before starting I am afraid it had not been done in a clear and distinct manner".

I beg to hand you an extract from a little leaflet which is given to every young woman, pp 2 paragraph 3 which I shall be obliged by your sending with this letter to the Colonial Secretary.

I may add that as you are aware I or my son make a rule of coming up to the Depot before the young women embark, and I see each separately and then address them together, especially warning them that their conduct will be reported on by the Matron and that upon her Report as well as upon these written testimonials they will be accepted in the Colony.

I should like to suggest that rules to which absolute obedience should be required, should be posted in their compartments, and I enclose for your perusal a copy of Rules which I have made for my Canadian parties and which everyone of the Canadian girls signs before going on board, and unless you prefer to furnish me with a copy of Rules you may wish to issue, I shall require every one of the young women in future selected for Western Australia to sign — I shall add the words "and of the Medical Officer" after Rule 5.

I now proceed to send you some details of information about the young women, whose conduct is reported on.

I enclose one of three good characters belonging to Kate [H——], sent by a lady who employed her for 6 years and who knew her for 15. Kate [H——] was selected to be Sub-Matron on board, when one of these Sub-Matrons fell ill, and received her gratuity; the Matron reports exceedingly well of her and says she on one occasion declined to have any Brandy — I think she will re-establish her fifteen years good character.

With regard to the [L——] girls. Their conduct appears to have been most insubordinate and offensive. I think however it is due to myself to enclose you the letters written by each of them, which prove that I had required definite assurance of their having done domestic work and of their purpose of taking service. Miss Lefroy at my request wrote definite questions and you will see equally definite answers.

Miss Lefroy saw Miss [L——] at intervals during several months and never detected any sign of insubordination or want of discipline, but they were so extremely anxious to be employed that I suppose their want of discipline did not betray itself — their Father was a dissenting minister. I can only suppose they had been unused to self discipline.

About Mrs [MacC——] there is nothing to be said excepting a deep regret that she had deceived and imposed upon persons who had known her from the year 1890 to June 1894. I have written to Col. Rideout and informed him of the great disgrace and scandal of recommending such an infamous and abandoned woman, and I can only repeat my great regret and annoyance that such a vile person should have obtained any assistance or been introduced into your Colony.

The Hon. Mrs Ellen Joyce, United British Women's Emigration Association, to Sir Malcolm Fraser, Agent-General for Western Australia in London, 11 December 1894.

184. "An Infamous and Abandoned Woman"

References demanded of women immigrating as domestic servants show a variety of backgrounds and a common economic precariousness. Two women on the *Gulf of Siam* were the daughters of a clergyman, left without support on the marriage of their brother. Mrs. MacC.'s references show a search for employment that had already taken her from England to Port Said.

March 26 1891, Chatham

I believe Mary [McC——] to be a thoroughly respectable, honest, sober woman. She has recently lost her husband and is anxious to obtain some suitable employment in domestic service.

J. Bramley Rideout, Lt. Col.
Hon. Sec. Soldiers and Sailors Assoc.

24 September 1891, War Office, Pall Mall

Mrs [McC——] was here only a short time while one of our women was on leave. I liked her much, she was always in to her time, and kept her room nice, she seems a poor friendless little woman. I do hope she will meet with some nice kind lady to befriend her, as far as I know she is a deserving woman. I was sorry she had to leave. I am sure she would have been able to have kept her work all right during the summer, but she could never have done it in the winter, so it was impossible for me to keep her on.

I advised her to try and get with a lady, she does not look at all fit for cleaning work. I hope she will meet with a kind mistress, and I trust she will prove a faithful and good servant.

H. Knight, Assistant Housekeeper.

References for Mrs MacC., enclosed with Mrs Joyce's letter to Sir Malcolm Fraser.

185. "Emigrant Single Women are Expected..."

Women immigrating in parties were expected to sign contracts, to ensure that they reached Australia with their respectability intact. Mrs Joyce enclosed a copy of these "rules of conduct" in her letter to Sir Malcolm Fraser.

Rules for Emigrant Women Joining Protected Parties under S. P. C. K. Matrons.

1.—Emigrant Single Women are expected to rise in the morning at whatever hour ordered by the Matron.

2.—They are to go below deck when directed by the Matron. In the evening the hour for going below will vary with the season of the year. They are not to come on deck again after roll-call in the evening on any pretext whatever, without asking permission from the Matron. They are to go to their berths at 9 o'clock.

3.—They will have to keep the articles of their Ship Kit thoroughly clean and in order. They will have to do their own berths, and keep them clean and tidy.

4.—They are expected to attend the Services held during the voyage, and any classes for Religious Instruction given by the Chaplain. *and as to the classes of the*

5.—They are to consider themselves under the direction of the Chaplain. *and of the medical officer*

6.—Young Women are on no account to hold any communication with the crew or with the male passengers, excepting in the case of Fathers and Brothers, and then only with the sanction of the Matron. When on deck they are to keep together in such places as directed by the Matron, and to be under her charge.

———

Infringement of the Rules will render the Young Women liable to forfeit the recommendations with which they are introduced into the Colony.

CONTRACT.

I promise to obey the Matron, to keep the above Rules and Directions, and to support the authority of the Matron as long as I am travelling under her charge.

Signature ....

Witness ....

Date ....

WARREN, PRINTER, WINCHESTER.

"Rules for Emigrant Women", as used by the United British Women's Emigration Association.

186. Service in the Colonies

Ellen Joyce's booklet, *Letter to Girls on Leaving England* is largely concerned with telling the immigrant women how they ought to behave on board ship and what to expect in the colonies. This passage suggests that service in the colonies was different from service in England, and that greater "democracy" did not necessarily mean less work.

Expect to find things very different — God made the climates different, and the fruits and vegetables different, and so the hours and customs must be different. Say to yourself, "It is I who am strange to it all, and I shall get used to it as they have done." Their way is the best for their country. Whatever you do, don't write home and grumble in a discontented way before you have had time to settle down. If you want to grumble, in three months time it will be time enough, for you only make enemies instead of friends by finding fault with Colonial ways; I have so many friends in the Colonies, and know that after a little seasoning people get to like the freedom of life, and the prospect of doing well and settling comfortably, far better than the life in the old country. Service is different, because when a mistress works herself, as many ladies do, she expects a servant to work all round and not be particular, and you will be asked to do some things which we don't ask our servants to do here; but you have chosen to earn your bread on the other side of the water, and you must earn it as they do there. I am thankful to know you will always be sure of well paid employment if you keep your best friends. When you have to change your situation write before-hand to your patron-friend, and tell her; she will be sure to know of a good situation for you, and in most cases will arrange for you to come back to the House or Lodge where you were received. "What service do you wish for?" asked the lady who was waiting to receive some of our Girls' Friendly Society members at Sydney. "We wish to go into a nobleman's family," answered the travellers. "There are a great many noble men and women here, who think the noblest thing they can do is to show that all work thoroughly well done is noble work, but there are very few people with any titles in a new country," replied the lady very quietly. Now these girls had good reason for wishing to live with those they called "titled people," for their parents had lived in "the family's service" and they had been educated and brought up in the households of those who were doing their duty in that state of life to which it had pleased God to put them, and who had spent their lives and incomes amongst their Irish tenants, sharing with them the bad times, and trying to infuse their people with courage, energy, and thrift. Letters had been written by them about these emigrants with a tenderness and forethought which was quite maternal and which showed how strong was the link existing between them.

So it was no wonder that the girls wished for such friendly employers again, but in the Colonies these Old World relations of "*doing duty by the people who live on the property*" do not exist. Everyone stands on their own worth, and mistress and maid alike get on according to their self-reliance and capability.

One set of young women who had great ideas of their own value wrote back, "We could have got plenty of places with employers who had come out as emigrants like ourselves last year and who are now keeping servants, but we didn't want that sort of service." A strong testimony to the rapid progress of the working class, though showing an absolute want of appreciation of the true spirit of rendering service on the writers' parts.

Ellen Joyce, *Letter to Girls on Leaving England* (1894).

187. In the Matron's Opinion

Matrons escorting parties of girls immigrating to Australia to become domestic servants kept records of their opinions of these women, and frequently it was the matron's impression that determined the employment given on arrival. These comments come from two different record-books kept by matrons escorting immigrants for the South Australian government prior to the First World War.

Ethel [A——]
An inexperienced girl, very young. Very easily led. Obedient and very willing to help. If placed with a good lady will do well. She is very willing to learn all she can.
I think her far too young to have come out without her parents, not only in years but in ways.
She has gone with her sister to Lady Stirling who will thoroughly train her.

Emily [C——]
A very bright girl and I believe very good at her work. Rather frivolous in her ways. I think very easily influenced especially with men folk. Very determined in some things, but in others very lax. I do not think her principles are what I call very high, still I believe she will work well and I hope do well.

Ellen [E——]
A very capable girl, very good principles. I had no trouble at all in the boat with her, she kept all rules and was very willing and always ready to help the others. Very capable with her needle. She should do well in the new land.
I have heard her mistress is very satisfied with her.

Beatrice [G——]
I have reported on this girl in my diary. She is very self willed and objects very strongly to be told of anything. For the last 4 years she has had no one to check her in anything which has been bad for her. From what I can gather I believe her to be a capable girl, but will require a very firm mistress. She will I think be much better in the country. I had to watch her very closely.
She has gone to the country but at present have not heard how she is getting on.

Florrie [G——]
This girl at first was very quiet but got very friendly with Florence [M——] and was quite led away with her. I had several times to reprimand her, especially when I found her dressed up in man's clothes after I had seen them all in bed for the night. I think this very disgusting. I spoke to her very seriously and the Captain also spoke to her which made her very ashamed of herself. I shall suggest her going to the country I believe that will be much better for her, she will I am sure be a hard working girl, but not any refinement for a refined house.
She has gone to the country.

S.S. *Commonwealth*, Matron's notebook, reports on individual girls, 2 May 1912.

Annie [P——]
A good reliable type of woman, will make an excellent working housekeeper.

Elsie [L——]
Has a refined and ladylike manner. Been in good service in England, will do best in good family in town. She is very resourceful.

Sarah [G——]

A real, strong country girl, has a hasty temper and was too familiar with a man on board.

Gertrude [C——]

A bright, strong little woman — not afraid to speak her mind — selfwilled. Quick in her movements and would make a good waitress or general.

Hilda [B——]

Rather flighty, has seen a little of the world and not been used to hard work.

Edith [S——]

A good faithful woman. Will be splendid for a farm as she understands poultry and dairy work thoroughly.

S.S. *Geelong*, Matron's notebook, reports on individual girls (n.d., c. 1913).

188. True English Womanhood

Apart from a report on each individual immigrant girl, the matron kept a diary of the voyage, in which she confided the events of the trip and her general impressions of the girls.

May 14. My last entry. We arrived at the Home safely, after a most satisfactory voyage, and found a hearty welcome from Mrs Moore, who interviewed each girl after tea, and began her difficult work right away to choose the right girl for the right place. Today every girl is fixed and only waiting their time to go to their places. I am glad to think they have begun so well, and I am sure that everyone will do her very best to uphold the high standard of true English womanhood, even those of whom I have not approved.

S.S. *Irishman*, Matron's diary, 14 May 1914.

189. A Signed Undertaking

The organized immigration of women and girls for the purpose of engaging in domestic duties continued throughout the nineteenth century and into the 1930s. Some applicants who were accepted in the early 1920s had been in munitions or nursing during the war. As well as giving the information requested, applicants also supplied a medical certificate and at least two references giving evidence of character and suitability for household work.

Adelaide

THIS SPACE FOR OFFICIAL USE
ONLY.

P.M.
L.M.
R.W.
M.S.
Date

GOVERNMENT OF AUSTRALIA.

WOMEN'S APPLICATION FORM FOR MIGRATION

Under the Assisted Passage Scheme agreed between the Government of Australia and the British Government under the Empire Settlement Act, 1922.

(ALL QUESTIONS MUST BE FULLY ANSWERED.)

Name in full (IN BLOCK CAPITALS, SURNAME FIRST)   H   B

Full Postal Address (IN BLOCK CAPITALS)   Mountain Houses, Pontsticill,

Nr Merthyr, Breconshire.

Present Occupation   Nurse Attendant.

Age 24   Date of Birth 11. 4. 1877 Place of Birth and County   Tantyglo, Monmouthshire.

Married, Single or Widowed Single   Height 5 ft   Weight 7st. 8 lbs Religion C. of E.

If married, Husband's full name, age, occupation and address

Children (Names, ages and sex):—

_____ Age ____ Sex ____ _____ Age ____ Sex

_____

_____

Are you in good health?   Yes   Have you at any time been subject to fits?   No

Name and Address of next-of-kin. If under age, give name and address of parents or guardian :—

Mrs H , Mountain Houses, Pontsticill, Nr Merthyr.

Have you ever been engaged as a domestic?   Yes

If so, how long? 1915 to 1918   At what wages? £48 per annum

Upon what work (if any) other than domestic and war work have you been employed?

Nursing

Domestic Experience.—1. Can you do plain cooking?   Yes.

     2. Can you do general housework?   Yes.

Name and Address of Present Employer

Unemployed

Name and Address of Previous Employer   W. S. Jones, Surveyor, 12 Station Rd,

Cymmer, Port Talbot, Glam.

When did you leave your last situation?   September 1923.

What class of situation do you desire in Australia?   If possible Nurse Attendant.

Do you prefer a situation in the city or in the country?   City.

Can you pay the reduced passage fee of £22 and £2 landing money?   No

If not, how much can you pay?

Have you any friends or relatives in Australia? If so, give relationship, names and addresses :—

Are they prepared to nominate you?

Form B.

Have you at any time resided in Australia or New Zealand. If so, when and where? ...	*No.*
Have you any preference for a particular State of Australia?	South Australia.
If you cannot be accepted for the State you prefer, are you prepared to settle elsewhere in Australia?	*Yes.*
Have you interviewed or communicated with a passenger agent? If so, furnish name and address ... ...; ..	
Have you previously communicated with the Australian Migration and Settlement Office or any Employment Exchange? If so, when	
When do you desire to sail?	ith Church army party to Adelaide.

I declare all the above statements to be true.

Signature of Applicant *B. H.* Date *22. 9. 1923*

(Must be signed by applicant personally; a signature by another person on her behalf will not suffice).

If any statements made by the applicant are found to be incorrect, the passage may be cancelled, even after the applicant has joined the ship, in which case the passage money will be forfeited.

PARENT OR GUARDIAN'S CONSENT IN THE CASE OF APPLICANTS UNDER
21 YEARS OF AGE.

I (Insert full Name, Occupation and Address)

the (father) of
(mother)

who has applied for an assisted passage to Australia through the Migration and Settlement Office, Australia House, Strand, London, hereby consent to my daughter proceeding to Australia.

Dated this day of 192 .

Signature of Parent or Guardian

Witness*

Address

The Witness must be one of the following, viz.: a Member or Official of any Banking Firm established in the United Kingdom, any Mayor, Magistrate, Justice of the Peace, Minister of Religion, Barrister-at-Law, Registered Medical Practitioner, Solicitor or Notary Public, resident in the United Kingdom.

INFORMATION FOR APPLICANTS.

At least **two Original References** (copies not acceptable) from responsible persons as to character, domestic experience (if any) and suitability for household work, must be submitted in support of this application.

A Medical Certificate must also be furnished when asked for on the official form which will be supplied.

Applicants are warned against leaving their employment or disposing of their property until advice is received of the name of the steamer on which their passages have been booked.

On completion, this form, with references, should be forwarded to:—

DIRECTOR OF MIGRATION & SETTLEMENT,
Australian Government Offices,
Australia House.
STRAND, LONDON, W.C.2.

A

Signed undertaking issued by the Director of Migration and Settlement, Australian Government Offices, Australia House, Strand, London, W.C.2.

GOVERNMENT OF AUSTRALIA,

MIGRATION AND SETTLEMENT OFFICE,

AUSTRALIA HOUSE, STRAND, LONDON, W.C.2,

UNDERTAKING to engage in DOMESTIC DUTIES in Australia.

I, *B   H*

of *"Mountain Houses", Pontotcill, Nr Merthyr. S. Wales.*

having been accepted as a domestic/lady-help under the Empire Settlement Act do

hereby agree to engage in domestic duties only, for at least twelve months

after my arrival in *Adelaide, South* Australia. I do this on the

understanding that if I am placed in an unsuitable post, I shall be at liberty

to take up another situation in domestic duties either through the Government

Bureau or by advertising, after having given the necessary notice. Should I

during the first twelve months seek any employment other than domestic

duties, I agree to repay the sum of £11 granted to me as an assisted passage

under the Empire Settlement Act.

Signed *B   H.*

Date *12 Oct. 1923.*

Signed undertaking issued by the Director of Migration and Settlement, Australian Government Offices, Australia House, Strand, London, W.C.2.

Agreement.

Migration of   BLODWEN H____. 226/47/19

PASSAGE RATE £ 22
£ _ Cash, £ 22 on Loan.

IN CONSIDERATION of the Director of Migration and Settlement, of the Commonwealth of Australia, Australia House, London, advancing to me the sum of £ 22 to assist me in the payment of my passage money from Great Britain to South Aust. in the Commonwealth of Australia, I HEREBY UNDERTAKE AND AGREE with the Commonwealth of Australia (hereinafter called the Commonwealth) :—

(a) to repay to the Commonwealth the said sum of £ 22 by equal monthly instalments of £ 2 , and to pay the first instalment within one month after my arrival at South Aust. aforesaid, and each further instalment one calendar month after the previous instalment was paid, until the whole of the said sum of £ 22 has been repaid;

(b) that if any instalment is not paid on the due date for payment the whole of the said sum of £ 22 , or so much thereof as then remains unpaid, shall immediately become due and payable, and the Commonwealth may recover same in any Court of competent jurisdiction;

AND for the same consideration I hereby irrevocably appoint the Commonwealth my true and lawful agent for so long as any portion of the said sum of £ 22 shall be unpaid to receive from my employer for the time being in Australia any moneys then due or from time to time to become due to me from my employer and to apply same so far as it will suffice in repayment of the amount of the advance then due and unpaid;

AND I HEREBY AGREE AND DECLARE that a certified copy of this document shall be sufficient authority to my employer as aforesaid to pay to the Commonwealth the said moneys.

Dated this *twenty third* day of *October* 1923

Signature *B H*

Witness* *[illegible]*

Address *[illegible]*

* The Witness must be either a Clergyman, Magistrate, Police Officer, or an authorised Agent of the Migration and Settlement Office.

NOTE.—The attached duplicate undertaking must also be signed and witnessed. It must not be detached

Signed agreement issued by the Director of Migration and Settlement, Australian Government Offices, Australia House, Strand, London, W.C.2.

190. Success

This excerpt from a letter written by an assisted immigrant in South Australia was possibly used by the Department to encourage other women to emigrate as domestic servants.

Though only two years in the State I have many more friends than I had the means of making in England and am most happily married to an Australian. The State and its people have ever been kind and friendly to me and I have no regrets in leaving my homeland, though loving it dearly.

Life is more equal and free in this sunny land and I would heartily recommend it to all young men and women who are willing to work and win the way through for themselves as I did.

Letter from Mrs N. Hawthorn of Norwood, S.A. (n.d., *c.* 1923).

191. Repayments

Women immigrating under the Assisted Passage Scheme were expected to repay the sum lent in monthly repayments, usually of £2.

Dear Madam,

The Commonwealth Crown Solicitor has forwarded to me your letter to him, in reply to his demand for repayment of the loan of £10, which was granted to you by the Migration and Settlement Office, London, towards the cost of your passage to Australia. You mention in your letter that if you could get a regular situation you could pay your way. I would point our that you were granted an assisted passage to Australia on the understanding that you would engage as a domestic helper. I am informed that on your arrival in Australia, notwithstanding the fact that there were abundant openings for domestic helps in South Australia, you were unwilling to accept a position, but desired to join your brother who was living at Broken Hill. The State Immigration Officer, Adelaide, advises me that if you are willing to accept a position as a domestic helper in South Australia, and are prepared to apply yourself to work, he would have no difficulty whatever in securing you a suitable position at 25/- per week. There is absolutely no justification for any earnest young woman in this country capable of performing domestic duties being destitute through lack of employment. When you came to Australia it was open to you to write to the State Immigration Officer, Adelaide, at any time and seek his advice and assistance.

I shall now be glad to hear further from you on this matter before replying to a request for instructions received from the Crown Solicitor.

Letter to an immigrant woman from the Assistant Director, Commonwealth Immigration Office, 6 March 1923.

192. Advantages

Domestic service, while it involved long hours and hard work, offered the advantage of "living in" to young women who could not support themselves on wages given for other jobs. Sometimes, too, it offered work that women could take pride in doing well. The time described in this interview is the early 1920s.

I decided I'd like to try out working in a restaurant. So I stayed with my aunt and took on a job in a restaurant. You used to start at 8 o'clock in the morning and finish, get home by the last bus, at 12 o'clock. You had one uniform which you supplied yourself and you washed it out at night when you got home and pressed it and put it on the next morning. And that was seven days a week. That was a city restaurant. It was downstairs in Rundle Street. I stayed there only for about 6 or 8 months because it was pretty tough. You had six tables. You had to memorise everything that was given to you. You weren't allowed to write anything down. You had to take the whole six table order and go out and get it yourself, give it to the chef and get it ready and bring them back. But those days you did get quite a few tips from different ones. But it used to be really tough. And there used to be some tough girls there — that was why I left. I think we used to get about 15/- a week. We didn't save anything. It would take us a long time to save up for a pair of Prestige stockings (they were 14/6 a pair) which would last us for over twelve months or more because we'd look after them.

Then I left there. My cousin was working in a house job at Kensington Gardens and she was going to leave and she spoke very highly of these people and said, "Well, why don't you go there because you get your keep and half a day off a week and Sunday afternoon off, and most evenings". I think I got 25/- and my keep. Well, that was good money in those days. You really had nice food and they were lovely people to work for but they had three children and a very big house. You'd be up at 4 o'clock in the morning and you'd have the washing done before breakfast. You'd take grape-fruit in at 6 o'clock and they would have their breakfast at 8. You'd do all the cooking. You'd do all the cleaning and all the washing and all the ironing. The lady of the house didn't do anything. You'd do the whole lot yourself.

You'd have everything set out, special things for special days. You'd work all day and you'd cook a hot meal every day — a three course meal. In fact sometimes I'd start after lunch to prepare. They'd have soup and of course in those days they'd have everything laid out beautiful. They'd have a silver service, which you had to clean, and the meat and everything was put on these. They even had finger bowls for washing their fingers. You didn't really wait on the table, only take the meal up. Everything was put on the table and they'd serve themselves. You'd go and remove the dirty plates and you'd then take in the fruit plates. Oh, the silver and the crystal fruit plates and everything like that was beautiful. In fact you'd get a real thrill setting the table — everything used to look so beautiful and most of the people were really nice, the guests. I used to have lots of them say to me, "If you ever want to leave here come over with us, we'll have you". Because if you could cook — we used to have all these dishes, you know — jugged hare. I used to say you'd want a peg on your nose when you'd go to get it. I ate the same meals but I never ever had my meals with them. I preferred to have my meals in the kitchen. They used to treat me like one of themselves. But while I was having my meal I could be washing up, especially if I wanted to go out to a dance that night.

You'd have Wednesday afternoon off and Sunday afternoon — or I think it was Sunday afternoon the following week. Once they knew that you were reliable, that they could trust you, they didn't mind what time you came in, as long as you were up in the morning to do your work.

There was a lot of work. In the winter time we had winter curtains and when the summer came they were taken down and we put up summer curtains. Everything was taken down. Once a week you'd sweep all the walls with the cobweb broom. The windows could be cleaned once a week and of course you had to scrub kitchen floors, then polish them. And the verandahs, well, that would be done a couple of times a week, down on your hands and knees, polished. Brass and silver — everything. Pillowslips would be starched and of course they used serviettes and they'd only be used once and be folded in a special way with the serviette rings. And the table cloths would all be starched. Everything was done with the old scrubbing board. We had a flat iron for a start and then the one you put the coals in. But we never had any electric irons. Washing at one particular place I worked, we used to have two dogs. They were pedigree dogs and we used to bath them, then put them in the blue water and tie them up and let them dry themselves. It was funny.

I stayed at the Kensington Gardens place for about twelve months. I left because I wanted a change. I think that you got that way when you were at a place for that long, you felt as if you wanted a different environment, when you were doing housework. And you really had to do housework then, because you got your living. You could live in. They were all live-in jobs that I did. Otherwise when you went in a shop or anywhere like that you had to pay board and you wouldn't have enough money to pay board then. So you had to do house work. Most times it was looking after children too. But they were good to me.

Interview with "Valerie", Adelaide, 1976.

193. The House Service Company

> This document details Jessie Street's attempts to solve the servant problem to the satisfaction of both worker and employer. Her emphasis, however, on training (the absence of which was the employer's constant complaint) rather than on improving working conditions (which was what the servants themselves wanted) betrays the middle-class orientation of the feminist movement in this period. In 1937, she suggested to the Premier of New South Wales that part of a federal grant for training unemployed youth be allocated to training girls for domestic service, but was informed in reply that the money was to be spent on youths and young men.

In my opinion, the shortage of workers is mainly attributable to three causes.

The first is the lack of regulation or uniformity in the conditions of employment of domestic workers in private homes. In support of this, I would point out that there is no shortage of domestic workers for employment in hospitals, hotels, boarding-houses or clubs, in which institutions the conditions of domestic workers are regulated by an award. This would lead us to the conclusion that the statement frequently made that young women will no longer undertake domestic duties, is a misleading statement. The true state of affairs being that when domestic duties are performed under proper conditions that conform to the requirements of the more educated type of workers that we have today, young women have no hesitation in undertaking domestic duties.

The second cause is the low status of domestic workers. The reason that their status is low is largely because of the absence of any recognized standard of training. There is a tendency to regard domestic work as a job anyone can perform, whereas, it is a very highly skilled occupation. To become a good cook or parlour maid, requires a high degree of intelligence and skill. If domestic workers had to qualify in some organised course of instruction, their status would automatically improve. The extremely low status of hospital nurses before they were trained, is an example. With the introduction of an organised course of training, their status has now been raised to one of high esteem.

The third cause of the shortage is, I believe, the absence of any organised scheme to recruit, train, and place girls as domestic workers. By an organised scheme, I mean such arrangements as exist to recruit, train, and place girls in the businesses and professional occupations. Every girl sitting for the Intermediate or the Leaving Certificate examinations, receives letters and circulars from business colleges, setting out the possible courses of training, in order to enable them to enter the commercial or professional world. These circulars describe the possible achievements of girls entering these occupations in the most glowing terms. Moreover, any of these colleges undertake to find positions for the students upon the completion of their term of training.

If an organised scheme of a like nature was put into operation to encourage and assist girls to take up domestic work, under some more or less regulated conditions of employment, I am confident that a large number of girls would take up domestic work. There is no question that the domestic worker earns considerably more money than the average office, shop or factory workers. She has no expenses in fares, laundry or keep, which are really worth to her at least 25/- a week, in addition to her pay. Since any average girl with little training can earn 30/- a week, the earnings of a domestic worker may be put down as at least £2/15/- a week. This wage compares favourably with the wages of most of the positions that business colleges are able to offer girls.

Having suggested the causes which I believe are responsible for the shortage, I submit the following outline of a scheme for training and placing girls in domestic work. The scheme is one which I called by the name of the Home Training Institute, and was operated by me through the House Service Company from 1927 to 1935, when, owing to the depression and the losses suffered by the House Service Company through bad debts etc., I was compelled to abandon this experiment. The scheme was as follows:—

I appointed as Supervisor, a woman who was experienced in running a home, who had some business experience, and who was able to handle girls.

The House Service Company advertised for young girls wishing to train for domestic work and for mistresses prepared to take young girls. Each girl had to supply two references as to character and the mistresses also had to supply a reference.

When the girls were engaged they became members of the staff of the House Service Company.

The House Service Company supplied each girl with four uniforms, two caps, two aprons, and the necessary materials for the Technical College Course. They insured her under the Worker's Compensation Act, arranged and paid for classes at the Technical College, and the girl became a member of the recreation club.

The House Service Company placed her in a private home, under conditions drawn up in the form of an agreement between the mistress and the House Service Company.

The House Service Company paid the girl weekly, a wage agreed upon with the girl. The wages of each girl varied, according to her age, apparent intelligence, and previous experience, the minimum wage paid any girl was 7/6 a week.

The mistress paid the House Service Company weekly or monthly the amount of the girls' wage, plus 5/- a week. It was from this 5/- a week that I expected to finance the scheme when it expanded.

The aim of the House Service Company was to enable each girl to attend the three year course in Domestic Arts at the Technical College, and give a diploma to those girls who passed their tests successfully. One of the terms of the agreement with the mistress was that the girl should be allowed off once every week in time to reach the Technical College at 9.30.

Mr Nangle, the Principal of the Technical College, and Miss Wilson, in charge of the Domestic Arts Section, were most helpful. At Mr Nangle's request, Miss Wilson arranged special classes for these girls which laid emphasis on the practical side of domestic work, and Mr Nangle arranged the classes at times and places convenient to the girls. Classes were held at Darlinghurst, Ultimo, and Mosman Domestic Science School.

The House Service Company employed a recreation officer for every afternoon. She used to meet the girls after their class, and pay their wages. She also arranged tennis, swimming, hockey, or any sport decided upon by the girls; if requested, she assisted the girls with their shopping. In the late afternoons in winter, the girls did dressmaking and millinery.

The Technical College classes served more than one useful purpose. They primarily taught the girls the proper way to do domestic work; (incidentally, through the girls, the mistresses acquired a lot of useful information) they also enabled the girls to make friends, which eliminated one of the greatest drawbacks of the domestic work, that is, loneliness. By enabling the girls to get diplomas, I hoped that the status of domestic workers would be raised.

I submit the outline of this scheme with the hope that you will be able to do something along similar lines. If some such scheme were started, and all the girls that were leaving school were circularised with a copy of the enclosed handbook with a suitable letter, I am sure that there would be an immediate response, and as the scheme became known, the response would be greater. Before long, a regular stream of trained domestic workers would be entering the market. When this occurred, the fact that many of the these girls had diplomas, would raise the status of domestic workers, and if the agreement under which these girls were placed outlined model conditions that were practical, before very long, these conditions would become general.

I believe a scheme along these lines would cure the shortage of domestic workers, raise their status, and could be made to operate so that conditions of domestic work will become uniform and regulated more or less by consent. Any further information you may require I would be pleased to supply.

Jessie M.G. Street, ''Re the Shortage of Domestic Workers for Private Employment'', submission made to the Premier of New South Wales, 1937.

Professional Women

194. The Schoolmaster's Wife

Many jobs that later became professional occupations for women were, in the early colonial period, reserved for the wives of men employed by the government. This was often the case in charitable and punitive institutions until dissatisfaction with the standard of care in those institutions led to a greater insistance on training. The expectation that a schoolmaster's wife, particularly in a one-teacher country school, would help with the teaching for a stipulated period during the week, persisted, however, until after the Second World War. Unmarried male teachers were at a disadvantage in country areas and frequently were not given charge of mixed schools.

My Lord,
   The Establishment of a general system of gratuitous Education for the poorer classes of this Community has already engaged the attention of His Majesty's Governmt., and I have been favored with a communication of your Lordship's views on the subject. In order to proceed successfully in the manner proposed, I find it will be necessary to introduce into the Colony some well qualified and respectable School-masters and Mistresses. I therefore, beg to propose to Your Lordship to authorize the Colonial Agent to send out as early as possible two Men and their wives, who have been accustomed to teach according to the method of Lancaster or Bell. The men should also be competent to instruct in the higher branches of Mathematics and the latin language. A more particular instruction as to the required qualifications of both Masters and Mistresses is given by this opportunity to the Colonial Agent, who is desired to obtain your Lordship's commands on the subject of these appointments.
   It is presumed the services of a competent Master may be engaged for about £150, and of his wife for £100 a year. A small house will be allowed them. An outfit of from £100 to £150 will, I imagine, be required to be advanced, and the Parties might be made useful by being embarked on board Prison Ships.

Despatch from Sir Richard Bourke to Lord Glenelg, 17 June 1837.

195. The Governess

The difficulty of finding work for English women with genteel accomplishments led to the setting up of societies that helped such women to emigrate. But while there was often a demand for domestic servants in the colonies, governesses who emigrated found a different situation.

My dear Miss Rye,
   I am very sorry I was prevented writing to you by last Month's Mail but I have

no doubt you have already heard from Mrs A Beckett of the safe arrival of the 2 Miss Musketts, Miss Burrows and myself at the place of our destination. I am thankful to say we had a very pleasant passage and enjoyed tolerably good health all the way. Upon landing as I was disappointed in not finding anyone to meet me, I went with the Miss Musketts to Cooper's Railway Hotel, where we staid a fortnight. Before I had been in Melbourne a week I was fortunate enough to meet with a situation as Governess in the Family of Mr James the Registrar of the University. I have now been here 6 weeks and during that time have been very happy and comfortable. Mr & Mrs James are quiet Christian people and both extremely kind to me. I saw the Miss Musketts last week the younger has a situation as Saleswoman in a Drapers in Melbourne but has to board out. The older has not yet met with anything owing to her not being able to teach Music. They are for the present boarding together at 37 Victoria Street. Miss Barrow [*sic*] was met by her brother upon her arrival and from that time we did not hear anything of her till last Sunday when I met her in Melbourne on my way from Church. I believe she has some engagement but I do not know what. And now my dear Miss Rye I know you are anxious to hear what prospect there is for Governesses out here. From what little I know of Australia or least this part of it I do not think there is much encouragement for them I would not advise any young person to come out unless they have friends to go to upon arrival in the event of their not meeting with engagements. This in Melbourne is not very easy to do and to go up the Country is very expensive. The Salaries in the Bush are higher than in Town I believe from £80 to £100 (I have £60) Musical Governesses are the most required in fact unless they are able to teach Music which seems to be more thought of than anything else they are almost sure not to succeed. Female domestic Servants seem very much wanted. Good house servants get from £30 to £35 — Cooks more — I think Governesses would do better at Sydney. I called with the Miss Musketts upon Mrs Perry Mrs A Beckett and Mr Franklin the latter put an Advertisement in the Herald for Miss Muskett but it did not lead to anything. When I went to Geelong I called at Mr Willis but he was then up the Country so we have neither seen nor heard from him. Should you send out any more Governesses I shall be very happy to do anything in my power to assist them.

Accept my thanks dear Miss Rye for all your kindness and believe me with kind regards to yourself and Miss Lewin.

Caroline M. Heawood to Maria Rye, Women's Migration and Overseas Appointment Society, from Melbourne, 25 March 1862.

196. Pupil Teacher

The humble origins of professional teacher-training for women can be found in the pupil teacher system, the details of which are delineated here. The system opened up work opportunities for the more malleable daughers of the "respectable" working class.

Sir,

I have the honor to report for the consideration of the Commissioners, on the application of Emma Marshall to be admitted as a pupil teacher in the service of the Board.

Miss Marshall has spent two months on probation, in the Girls' School, and has given satisfaction to the Mistress, who speaks highly of her industry and docility. Her attainments are very limited, but her progress, since she commenced to attend the School and receive instruction, has been creditable, and such as enables me to recommend her application to the favourable consideration of the Board. Her parents are, I have reason to believe, persons of respectable character. I, therefore, suggest that she be received as an Apprentice, at a salary commencing with Twenty pounds per annum, and dating from the 1st of the present month.

R. Macdonnell, Inspector of Schools, to the Queensland Board of Education, 3 October 1860.

197. Free Education

Headmistress Margaret Berry, in her evidence before the Royal Commission inquiring into education in Queensland, gave a very clear picture of students and teaching at a state girls' school in Brisbane in the 1870s, revealing the way that these schools were the training-ground for female pupil teachers.

1768. Have you any pupil teachers under you? I have twelve; that is, including those in the infant school.

1769. Do the girls that you train as pupil teachers generally follow their profession? Several have married and have abandoned it.

1770. But as a rule? I think, as a rule, they will follow it; I do not think they will abandon it for any other occupation. We have had some very successful teachers trained in our school, and we have received excellent reports of them from the country inspectors. . .

1836. Would it be possible, supposing you had a stronger staff of teachers, to impart a higher education to the girls? Yes, I think so on scientific subjects, if there was a stronger teaching power.

1837. Do you keep up your acquaintance with the girls after they leave your school? I do not socially, as regards visiting their families, as I object to that; but I often meet the girls, a great many of whom go into shops; of course all those who are pupil teachers in town, I meet frequently.

1838. Do you think after they leave school that they devote much time to their education or endeavour to improve themselves in what they have been taught at school? I cannot say, but I am afraid they do not, I am afraid they forget a great deal of what they have learnt; I think they read a great many novels and books of that character; the "Young Ladies' Journal" is very popular with them, I understand; I do not think they study much after leaving school.

1839. Have your Inspectors ever said anything to you in reference to your older pupils studying for middle class examinations, such as are now conducted in Sydney and Melbourne? No, I think not; I do not remember that they have.

1840. Is the career of a pupil teacher now preferred to the prospects offered to young girls in shops? It is; parents frequently come to me and ask me to say candidly whether I think their girls will succeed as pupil teachers, as if I thought they would not they would place them in a shop; in some instances I have told them that I thought they would not, and they have taken them out of the school to place them in business.

1841. Then you really do get the most promising pupils? Yes, but some of the best girls do not offer themselves as candidates for pupil teachers.

1842. What is your opinion of the present system of having a training master? I think it has improved our girls, especially as to the method of teaching; they have derived great advantages from both Mr. Kerr and Mr. Platt.

1843. Is it part of your work to point out to pupil teachers the best method of teaching? It is, and to show them when they are wrong; they require constant supervision and instruction.

1844. Have many of your pupil teachers gone to country schools after their training has expired? About eight altogether; they all went as mistresses.

1845. Single women? Yes.

1846. *By Mr. Hockings:* In reply to the Chairman you mentioned that the girls in the highest class of your school did not receive instruction in geometry and the higher branches of education? Yes.

1847. Do the pupil teachers receive such instruction from the training master? I do not think they do.

1848. I think I understood you to state that you were of opinion that the girls in the highest classes would strive to pass a higher examination if such a system was established? Yes, I think they would.

1849. Do you think that the girls in your school would be capable of doing so? Most of them who have passed as pupil teachers, if it went by that standard.

1850. *By Mr. Mein:* Do you think there is any great good resulting from teaching young girls geometry? I cannot say, as I do not know geometry myself.

1851. You think education should take a more practical turn? Do you mean that we could make it more practical?

1852. I mean by teaching them domestic economy? I think that would be more useful.

1853. What do you think has been the result of free education, how has it affected the schools? I think it has increased the attendance, and has also perhaps produced some greater irregularity of attendance than would be the case if parents paid for education.

1854. Do you think it would be possible to go back to the system of paying? I am afraid it would be a very unpopular step to take; people seem to like free education very much indeed.

1855. Do you think it would be advisable to introduce a compulsory system of education? I should like to see one introduced.

1856. Do you not think it would cause inconvenience to parents in many instances? I think it would — to the parents of the poorer classes especially.

1857. But taking children up to twelve years of age being placed under such a law, could such children be of service to their parents at home? Yes, they are of service in the house in many ways.

1858. Are the teachers satisfied with the remuneration they receive at present? They often speak of that and say that they ought to get more; the salaries are no doubt low when compared with the cost of living at the present time.

1859. What is your own opinion on the subject? I think they require more — I am speaking of female teachers.

1860. I believe there is a considerable distinction between the amounts paid to mistresses and masters? Yes; that is a subject on which I should like to say a word or two, namely that before the schools were made free the mistresses received exactly the same scale of fees as the masters; it was reduced then, and now the mistresses receive only at the rate of two-thirds of that allowed to the masters.

1861. That reduction has been adhered to ever since? Yes, it has been adhered to ever since; I think that considering the subjects taught are the same in both schools, and the efficiency required by the Inspectors is the same, that the mistresses are entitled to the same compensation for fees as the masters are; even on that score they are, but on the score of having had it before I consider that they have an additional claim. . .

1869. Is sewing the only branch of domestic economy taught in your school? No: other branches are taught — just to the extent I mentioned to the Chairman — in object lessons.

1870. Not cutting out dresses? No; only sewing — I never encourage cutting out dresses, because mothers might say that the material was spoilt in cutting out — they used to do so in Sydney, and I have known teachers there obliged to replace the material at their own cost in consequence of such complaints.

1871. You said, just now, that a good deal was forgotten by the girls after they left school? Yes.

1872. Then it would be better, would it not, to teach them something that they would be likely to remember — practical domestic economy, for instance; — would it be practicable in your schools? That would depend upon the kind of instruction: supposing it was washing, then we should be obliged to have a laundry. In Dublin, where I was trained, they have all those appliances, and I think they might be introduced here with very great benefit in the form of industrial schools.

1873: *By the Chairman:* Do you not think it would be well if some of your girls could be induced to go into respectable families, to get lessons in domestic economy? Yes, I think it would; but many of our girls are very well trained by their mothers; they come to school beautifully clean and neat, and many of them can cook and make jams, &c.

Evidence of Margaret Berry, for fourteen years headmistress of the Girls' Normal School, Brisbane, before the Royal Commission to Inquire into the Working of the Educational Institutions of the Colony, Queensland (1874).

198. Ocular Proof

The close observation of the behaviour of female teachers is revealed in this letter written by the headmaster of a Victorian country school to the Education Department. When confronted with this report, the teacher alleged that the headmaster wrote it because she had refused his sexual advances. The investigating board rejected her explanation, and while not commenting on the truth or otherwise of the headmaster's charges against her, found her to be "quite an unfit person to be employed in any school or to be entrusted with the tuition of children".

. . . since the appointment of Miss [W——] to the above school I have often heard reports against her character but never paid any attention to them, until about 20 March it was reported to me that she was *pregnant*. I immediately made inquiries and found that her *Menses* had ceased for about four months and other symptoms such as loss of appetite, sick-headache and nausea were apparent.

Being aware of these circumstances I deemed it my duty to report the matter to the Department. Having often heard about her immorality I was convinced from the above symptoms that there must be some grounds for these reports. I have had no ocular proof of any immoral action on her part so I cannot prove anything, only I thought it proper to put the Department in possession of the facts for fear anything should happen to prove the truth of these reports. Having had the advice of a Chemist she now appears in perfect health and is about to be married in a few months.

I must here state that as a workmistress she has always done her duty well.

Headmaster, Winslow State School, to the Secretary, Education Department of Victoria, 19 April 1877.

199. An Act of Indiscretion

A woman teacher was said by her head teacher to have been "guilty of improper conduct with a married man". She denied the charge and asked that the allegation be investigated. The investigating board's report shows the standard of "womanly" behaviour expected of female teachers, expectations that applied also to out-of-classroom behaviour.

The Board appointed on the 26th July by His Excellency the Governor in Council to investigate certain charges preferred against Miss Rebecca [N——] a Teacher in State School No 755 Gordon, have the honour to report that they investigated the case on Saturday Aug 4th at Gordon and found that Mrs Jane [W——], the wife of Mr Thos [W——] of that place was the person who preferred the charges.

The statement of Mrs [W——] was that on the 10th June last she saw her husband and Miss [N——] come out of the Registrar's Office about 9.45 p.m. — that is [W——]'s own office, he being the Registrar for the district.

Several witnesses were called by Mrs [W——] who stated that on different occasions they had seen Miss [N——] going to and coming from [W——]'s office after office hours but they could give no dates as to when it took place.

The Board consider that the charge made by Mrs [W——] loses much of its force from the fact that the Registrar's office cannot be seen from the position that she occupied at the time. That she saw her husband coming from that direction is not doubted, but there is less certainty about Miss [N——] having been in his company.

In the opinion of the Board the charge against Miss [N——] is not sustained by the evidence. But we consider that she has not been sufficiently guarded in her conduct at all times it being shown that she has been in [W——]'s office assisting him to post up accounts without a lady friend to accompany her.

The Board recommend that for what they consider an act of indiscretion Miss [N——] be removed from the school.

Report of board appointed by Education Department of Victoria to investigate charges against Miss Rebecca N., a teacher at Gordon State School, 10 August 1877.

200. Character

While teaching as a career provided women with opportunities for possible economic independence and social mobility, they were expected to conform to particular standards of behaviour. In this case, the headmaster of a school at Sandhurst had spoken to the inspector of a female teacher's drinking habits. He later regretted this when his comments resulted in her dismissal, and put in a plea for leniency on her behalf.

... Miss [S——] has no father and has been brought up and still lives in a hotel kept by her mother, and I very much fear that the example set her has not been the very best — I thought when I spoke to Mr Craig, and even now believe that if Miss [S——] could be removed to some other school away from the temptations of home that it would prove a great blessing for her and that when among strangers she would have too much self respect to fall into disgrace again — Had I known that her first warning would be a public investigation I would have spoken to her on the subject, cautioned her and I feel that I may have been a little to blame in not doing so — Miss [S—] seems very anxious now to retrieve her character if possible, and thinks if she might be allowed to remain in her present position for a month or so and then removed to some other school, that she would be able to render a good account of herself in the future — I most respectfully beg to add that Miss [S——] is a good teacher, very much liked by her fellow teachers and scholars, and that it would be a matter of very great regret should she be ruined now without the chance of retrieving her character—

Headmaster, German School, Sandhurst, to the Secretary, Education Department of Victoria, 31 August 1875.

201. No Prospects

Advice to the prospective immigrant often drew attention to the need for domestic servants and the lack of opportunities for women in the professions. Florence Hill had only been in Australia for a short time when she wrote to friends at home about the dearth of employment for middle-class women. From the end of the nineteenth century, however, this situation began to change with the increasing professionalization of areas of women's employment, in welfare, nursing and teaching.

Although I am unable to speak positively, I much fear from what I have heard that women above the hard-working servant class are practically as "redundant" here as at home. I am amazed by the number of unmarried women of the middle class, many of whom have a hard struggle to maintain themselves. Cooks, house-maids, and laundresses are in great demand, their wages being 10s. a week and even more, besides board and lodging...

Though in many respects life here is so like that at home, that I often find it difficult to realise I am out of England, still, in most families the mistress has hard work to do, and when, as not unfrequently happens, she finds herself destitute of any servant, her work is very hard indeed, and in the case of a young woman with a large family tells sadly upon health, physical and mental, and even life itself. This would make me hestitate additionally in advising women above the servant class to come out. If they don't marry they will have a hard struggle to support themselves; and if they marry they may sink under their many toils, especially in the great heat of summer. Women born and bred here feel these evils less.

Letter from Florence Hill, reprinted in *Englishwoman's Review*, October 1873.

202. "The Class of Persons Most Desirable"

The turning-point in the professionalization of nursing in Australia came when a group of London-trained nurses were sent to take up positions at the Sydney Infirmary. In this letter, Florence Nightingale describes the differing qualities she expected in matrons and head nurses.

My dear Mrs Wardroper,

In reply to yours of December 12th, I concur entirely in your view as to the class of persons most desirable to send out as Matron and head nurses to Sydney.

It would be a grave mistake to send to New South Wales any but a *good working* head of the Nursing Establishment and *good working* (Head) nurses under her.

The head should be a well educated gentlewomen of very active habits, with firm but gentle manners — thoroughly trained up to her work, so as to be able to train others.

The "Sisters" (Head Nurses) should be of *the best kind* of what forms the class of London Hospital Head Nurses, highly trained capable of bearing *hard* work — of nursing as well as teaching others to nurse. We must look to the persons who will *offer* themselves, (and who, during training are found most suitable,) for this kind of work. I would not therefore specially exclude or specially recommend any class, but I would say that there must have been a habit of physical exertion and physical strength from childhood a habit not of being waited upon but of waiting upon others to fit people for this kind of life.

I am quite sure that the selection, as well as training, must be a most careful one, and, after the most careful selection, a year is not too much to ascertain whether the physical powers will bear the Hospital life, (to say nothing of the mental powers) before sending out. But I am also quite sure that you, for one, will select the *persons* most desirable for the purpose, so I will say no more about the *Class.*

With regards to Salaries — I think that £150 (with Lodging and Board) for Superintendent (Matron) and £50 (with Lodging and Board) for Head Nurses ("Sisters") is enough and not too much and I think the New South Wales Government would be consulting their own interest, if they were to give an increase yearly.

Of course as passages are paid out, they, Superintendent and Nurses, ought to come under certain obligations as to service. I am afraid that it was not perhaps intended, by Capt. Mayne, that to give Board and Lodging, or at least not Board (they must, of course, *lodge* in the Hospital). But I have stated what my opinion is. . .

I cannot but add what a grand opening I feel it to be for a gentlewoman who has capacity and energy to found this Training Institution at Sydney.

Florence Nightingale to Mrs Wardroper, Matron, Training School for Hospital Nurses, St Thomas Hospital, London, 13 December 1866.

203. "Not Ladies At All"

Professionalization within nursing did not always proceed smoothly. In 1886, the Lady Superintendent of the Hobart General Hospital was relieved of her position and not given a testimonial. Her efforts to claim a testimonial led to an official inquiry, during which a picture of nursing in Hobart emerged. Mrs Wilson's gentility and meagre professional training are contrasted with the training and social backgrounds of a group of Scottish nurses, the arrival of whom precipitated the events leading up to Mrs Wilson's dismissal. During the inquiry, Mrs Wilson was said to have "revolutionized the Institution" and "got together and trained a nursing staff which was a credit to the Hospital and the Colony". The nurses from Edinburgh, who were not only well trained but "rebellious", were from a different class background — one had been a domestic servant — and this was presumably thought by Mrs Wilson to threaten the newly acquired respectability of her profession.

I have been advised to ask Mr. Fysh for a proper testimonial, which my services certainly deserved, looking at the state the Nursing Staff and Home were in when I took office as Lady Superintendent, and as they were till the Scotch Nurses upset everything. I am sending Mr. Fysh a copy of the lovely testimonial the Board gave me, and which you may remember. I came to the Hobart Hospital with testimonials showing I was a gentlewoman and a trained nurse, and after working nearly five years for them they turn me adrift, though they can find no real fault, without a character, making it impossible for me to get any post in the Colonies without a testimonial. This may be Colonial justice, — it is certainly not English.

ESSIE WILSON.

EVIDENCE

TUESDAY, NOVEMBER 1, 1887.

DR SMART *called and examined.*

1. *By the Chairman.* — What position do you occupy? Chairman of the Hobart General Hospital, and occupied that position when Mrs. Wilson was appointed Lady Superintendent.

2. Were there several applications? Yes, a good many.

3. Was Mrs. Wilson chosen after reading testimonials from several applicants? Yes, there were about 30 applicants. . .

6. When was the Lady Superintendent first engaged? Mrs. Wilson was engaged as head nurse on January 1st, 1883, and continued in that capacity until about December 17th, 1883. She was never under my observation during that time; she was in Dr. Bright's ward. I had nothing officially reported against her during that time. She became Lady Superintendent of the nursing staff on December 17th, 1883, and her services terminated on February 28th, 1887. Her whole services at the Hospital extended over four years and two months.

7. *By Mr. Fitzgerald.* — Did you consider her testimonials not so good as some of the other applicants? I will not make a comparison, but some of the others had testimonials of examinations; Mrs. Wilson's testimonials were for 1 year and 10 months, and included no examination.

8. Do you consider she was the best, so far as training and testimonials went? I do not.

9. *By the Chairman.* — What was your first cause of complaint? It was not officially recorded, at my earnest request. I did so simply to prevent trouble and mischief arising out of it, and I thought by trouble and care it might be got over. I will explain the whole affair. — In 1883-4 the Hospital was very badly off for trained nurses and after consideration the Board recommended to the Government that I should communicate with my brother, Dr. Andrew Smart, of Edinburgh, with the

view of securing from the Training School of Edinburgh three trained nurses. The Government approved, and authorised me to communicate with my brother in order to carry out the wishes of the Board. Three nurses were selected from the very best Edinburgh school. They were certificated, and holders of testimonials as having served from five to eight years as head nurses in the Royal Infirmary of Edinburgh. The arrangements were made, and one of them, Miss Milne, now Lady Superintendent of the Launceston Hospital, arrived in Hobart on March 23rd, 1883. Some considerable time previous to her arrival I was in possession of the testimonials and qualifications of these nurses, and these Mrs. Wilson, then Lady Superintendent, was made fully acquainted with, and was made clearly and distinctly to understand that they were women who had served a long period of service, and who possessed the highest qualifications. On March 21st, 1885, Miss Milne arrived by steamer at Hobart, and came straight to my house. I received her as I thought she had a right to be received, and took her in a cab to the Hospital with the view of introducing her in proper form to the Lady Superintendent. On our arrival at the Nurses' Home (Mrs. Wilson's quarters), we were admitted to the hall by a servant, and I asked if the Lady Superintendent was in. The servant said "Yes," and I said "Tell her I have called with one of the nurses from Edinburgh, and I want to introduce her to Mrs. Wilson." I distinctly heard the servant deliver the message. We stood waiting in the hall for a considerable time, and I felt that some misunderstanding had arisen, or else I was being grossly insulted. Feeling that something was wrong, I pushed open the door, and stepped into Mrs. Wilson's room. There I found Dr. Graham and the Lady Superintendent having afternoon tea. I made known my mission, and without moving from her chair she waited quietly. I told her I had brought Miss Milne round, and she asked me what right Miss Milne had to go first to my house, and how dare she do so? I said I supposed it was because she had my address, and added that she was standing in the hall. Then, without moving from her chair, the Lady Superintendent said, "I will ring the bell, and the servant can show her to her room." This was done, and I, feeling that a distinct affront was being done, retired. We waited a long time again in the hall, and my face burned with shame and indignation to think that this lady had come such a long way to be so treated. The most abject menial could not have been worse treated. I at last said to Miss Milne, "You had better wait; the bell has been rung, and I suppose the servant will attend to you." I came away, being ashamed to stay longer. I acquainted the Committee with these facts, and am prepared to repeat them on oath. The Lady Superintendent never left her chair to see me out, and I came away feeling I had been grossly insulted. I was waiting in the hall several minutes in each instance. The Lady Superintendent knew all about Miss Milne, her testimonials, position, &c., and it seemed to me to be a very wrong proceeding on the part of the Lady Superintendent. The Committee urged me very strongly to take action and have her suspended, and I have been accused of being too soft-hearted in the matter, but I had a strong desire that no disturbance should take place at that time. I did not reprimand her at the time, but did so shortly afterwards with other matters.

10. Was that officially reported or recorded at the time? It was not officially recorded or brought before the Board until the Committee was sitting about Miss Turnbull's case, which was about a year later. About a month after Miss Milne's arrival the other two Edinburgh nurses arrived, and shortly after that the Lady Superintendent stopped me abruptly in the hall of the Hospital and demanded to know "what my brother could have meant by sending out such women; they were not ladies at all, they were only common women, and it was lowering the tone of the

nursing staff to have such women here." I then reprimanded her pretty severely — I do not say fiercely — for her remarks, and explained to her, what I had often explained before, that they were thoroughly trained and approved nurses, and that it was her duty to receive them and treat them as such. The result was that she burst into tears, and I left her.

Claim for a testimonial made by Mrs E. Wilson, Late Lady Superintendent, General Hospital, Hobart.

204. Retrenchment

The precariousness of teaching as an occupation for married women is clearly illustrated by the strictures introduced by the Victorian Education Department to cope with an "excess" of teachers in a period of unemployment.

MEMORANDUM—
Early in 1894, the then Minister of Public Instruction, the Honorable R. Baker, had under consideration the question of retrenchment in the Education Department, and, as the teaching staff was in excess of the requirements, he decided to recommend to the Governor in Council that the services of Female Married Teachers should be dispensed with, and he sent notice accordingly on 1st March to the teachers interested.

Before the expiration of the period of notice, certain of these teachers appealed to the Minister to be retained, on the plea that their circumstances were such that, if dispensed with, it would mean ruin, as their husbands were either incapable of supporting them or were out of employment and without any immediate prospect of obtaining it.

The Minister dealt with each case on its merits, and, in some cases, withdrew the notices unconditionally, while, in a few instances, the notices were withdrawn with the condition that the teachers must be prepared to go at the expiration of 12 months. These latter had their services dispensed with on the recommendation of the present Minister when the condition mentioned had been complied with.

All female Teachers — with the exception of a few cases of special hardship — who were either 50 years of age or of 30 years' service, were asked to tender their resignations, and did so; and as they were entitled to pensions, the Department had no option but to grant them.

Those teachers who were dispensed with are entitled to compensation only, and there is no legal authority to pay anything else. The judgment of the Full Court in the case of Mattingley V the Queen confirmed the action of the Department.

The Minister no doubt stated that he would endeavour to obtain pensions for the teachers dispensed with, but he added that, as this would be outside the law, he would have to consult his Colleagues. He did consult them, and it was decided that, as the teachers in question were not legally entitled to anything more than compensation, the Government would not place an amount on the Estimates to provide annual pensions for them. . .

The law, as it stood in 1894, and the policy of the late Government, which has been endorsed by the present Premier, are distinctly opposed to paying anything except compensation to married female teachers who were in excess of the requirements of the Department.

This statement as to the Singing and Drawing Masters, Truant Officers and several Clerks, whose services were dispensed with, and who were allowed pensions, where pension rights existed, is perfectly correct. The majority of those persons were Breadwinners, and consequently were not in the same position as the married female teachers. It might be mentioned that the Government which granted pensions to the Singing and Drawing Masters, Truant Officers and Clerks referred to above was the Government which dealt with the question of retirement of the Married Female Teachers.

Undated memorandum, Education Department of Victoria.

205. Shirley School

The last twenty years of the nineteenth century saw the development of kindergarten teaching in Australia, with the first free kindergartens established in the 1890s. While the expansion of primary education had brought increased work opportunities to girls from the less-affluent sections of society, kindergarten teaching was seen as a genteel occupation particularly suited to a young, single lady. In 1900, Miss Newcomb and Miss Hodge, two Englishwomen with wide educational experience, established the New School and Kindergarten in Sydney, where teachers could be trained and progressive teaching methods were demonstrated. Like many other women involved in teaching in this period, Newcomb and Hodge were advocates of women's rights and became involved in the suffrage movement in England on their return.

The New School (GIRLS) and Kindergarten.

SHIRLEY, EDGECLIFF ROAD,

SYDNEY, N.S.W.

Principal: Miss NEWCOMB.

Cambridge Higher Local Honours Certificate, 1885.
Cambridge Teachers' Certificate, 1886.
Form Mistress, Exeter High School, 1886-7.
Mistress of Lower Division, Maria Grey Training College, London, 1887-9.
Mistress of Upper Division, Maria Grey Training College, 1889-97.

THE NEW SCHOOL AND KINDERGARTEN.

The aim of this school is to give the pupils an education which shall develop individual power and widen the range of interest and sympathy in every direction. Book-study, though of the highest importance, is but a means to this end, and in the early years of life it is not as important as the training of the eye and ear, the hand and voice. The methods which will be employed are the result of many years of school experience, together with the study of educational principles to which so much attention is now given in England, Germany, Sweden and America. These principles have hitherto been most completely carried out in the system called the Kindergarten. In the Kindergarten the natural activities of little children find full scope in joyful play. The same principle of natural development by self-activity will be adhered to throughout the school, and consequently intellectual forcing will be wholly avoided. The physical well-being of the pupils will be secured by a thorough system of gymnastic exercise, as well as by games and gardening. Much of the school work, as well as the Kindergarten, will be carried on in the open air. The greatest importance is attached to the maintenance of a high moral tone in the social life of the school. There will be no dogmatic religious teaching, but Scripture lessons will be given in careful confirmity with the wishes of parents.

CURRICULUM

The entire School Course (ten years) will include English Language and Literature, History (ancient and modern), Foreign Languages (ancient and modern), Mathematics, Science, including Domestic Economy, Drawing, Needlework, Class Singing, Drilling (Ling's Swedish System) and Ball Exercises.
    There are no extras excepting Instrumental Music, Solo Singing, Advanced Drawing, Wood-carving, Dancing and Swimming.

TERMS (Payable in Advance).

KINDERGARTEN	per quarterly term	ONE-AND-A-HALF GUINEAS.
TRANSITION CLASS	per quarterly term	TWO-AND-A-HALF GUINEAS.
LOWER SCHOOL average age 9-13 years	per quarterly term	FOUR GUINEAS.
UPPER SCHOOL average age 14-18 years)	per quarterly term	FIVE GUINEAS.

A charge of five shillings per quarter for stationery is made throughout the Kindergarten and School.

SCHOOL HOURS.

KINDERGARTEN   *9.30 to 12 a.m.*   *SCHOOL*   *9 a.m. to 12.45 p.m.*
    Pupils can attend in the afternoon from 2.15 to 3.30 for the preparation of Home Lessons and for Lessons in Intrumental Music, Solo Singing and Dancing.

Prospectus, Shirley Girls' School and Kindergarten, Sydney (1901).

206. Pioneer

The life of the woman teacher who taught in a one-teacher school in the outback (as Dorothea Lock did in Western Australia in the 1930s) frequently illustrates the isolation and hardship more usually associated with the male "pioneer".

I beg to inform you that it is almost impossible for me to attend school on wet days, as it is necessary for me to walk, when such occur. Today being very wet with a violent gale, I was compelled to attempt the walk to school, a distance of six miles. However, I tried a shorter route, and after walking four miles through blinding rain, discovered I was on the wrong road. It was then too late to try to reach Miamoon, so I returned home. This is the second wet day on which the above school has been closed by me since assuming charge on 5th June.

As there will possibly be other wet days, and I possess no conveyance, it may be necessary for me to close the school again, as the walk to school affects my health, causing a pain in my side.

Undated letter from Dorothea Lock, teacher at the government school at Miamoon, near Wubin, W.A., to the W.A. Education Department.

. . . I have to inform you that the above school was closed on June 12th and on July 18th, owing to adverse weather conditions. On the first day mentioned, I did not know my bearings sufficiently well to walk, while on the second day mentioned, I became lost. I do not walk daily to my school, but am given a lift by some of my pupils in a cart. It is only necessary for me to walk on very wet days, as these children do not attend on such days. Accommodation may be available with Mrs Withell who resides 3½ miles from the above school, but since there is a possibility of the above school, being moved 5 miles west of its present site, I would then be forced to return to Sanders', with whom I now board. If the school were moved, Withell's home would be situated 8 miles from the school, while Sanders' place would be 1½ miles distant, that is, within walking distance.

Ibid., 28 July 1935.

207. No Job for a Woman

Although a high proportion of teachers were female, women tended to concentrate in the lower echelons of the profession. In Victoria in 1928, the Director of Education felt obliged to justify a decision to accept only male applicants for the position of Chief Inspector of Secondary Schools, in the light of a complaint from a potential applicant, Miss Julia Flynn.

For your information I will state the reasons why I regard this position as being essentially one that requires a man.

The field of post-primary education presents the most difficult problems in the whole educational field at the present time. For the first time in our history, education for all beyond the primary stage is being provided, and it is essential in the organization of this field that the education should be adapted to the future needs of adolescent boys and girls. So far as girls are concerned the problem is much simpler than that presented by the needs of the boys. Some girls enter into wage earning occupations but even of these the great majority will become housewives and drop out of these occupations in a few years. The boys, on the other hand, have to start on their life's work, and the educational system should be directed to fitting them for their future vocation in the best possible way. Their needs are not nearly covered by the relatively simple curriculum that is necessary for girls. Varying types of courses including an increasing amount of practical and pre-vocational work must be provided, and I hold strongly that only a man with the full knowledge of modern conditions and of the educational needs of boys can adequately fill such a position. On the administrative side the Chief Inspector has to interview parents and councils, discuss all manner of details, even those dealing with sanitary arrangements, holding inquiries into complaints often involving sex matters, and these duties, I am satisfied a woman should not be called upon to undertake.

In issuing the advertisement in its present form, I consider I was saving Miss Flynn from any disappointment she might possibly feel. I do not consider that Miss Flynn with all her outstanding merits, can possibly fill the position of the Chief Inspector of Secondary Schools. I might mention that on her appointment 14 years ago I urged her then, as the first woman inspector, to make a special study of the problems of girls' education. Miss Flynn is very much interested in education, but rather on the older academic lines and our schools of domestic arts for girls have been developed without her assistance in any way ... Recently Miss Flynn has shown greatly increased interest in these schools, but since she has not guided or inspired the development of these modern schools for girls, I think you will realise how hopeless it would be to expect her to lead and direct the development of modern schools for boys. I would regard it as unfortunate if so fine an officer as Miss Flynn has shown herself to be were to become soured and embittered through inevitable disappointment in the present instance.

Minute prepared by the Director of Education of Victoria, 2 August 1928.

208. Hostility

In Victoria in 1928, the position of Chief Inspector of Secondary Schools was opened, under pressure from the Minister, to women applicants and Miss Julia Flynn was appointed. The Director, however, announced that she was not to be confirmed in the appointment. In this letter to the Public Service Commissioner, she describes the difficulties of working with a superior who was hostile to her. In her battle to win promotion, Julia Flynn was actively supported by feminist organizations throughout Australia.

After my appointment had been made by the Governor in Council on your recommendation, the Director wrote to the Schools Board, asking the members to express their opinion as to whether my appointment was acceptable. This was a complete surprise to me and the indignity was imposed upon me of having to leave the room to permit of free discussion of my merits by professors of the University and headmasters of State and registered schools. The discussion was entirely favorable to me but I do not know what the Director had intended to precipitate by his action...

I sought no advantage from the Director on account of my sex through all the years I have worked with him, nor did I receive any. On the contrary, no man appointed to a corresponding position has ever been subjected to such unusual tests during his probationary period. For six months I have been placed in this position — if I consulted the Director before reaching decisions, he would at once conclude that I was unable to cope with my work. Now he states that I failed to approach him sufficiently often, though I repeat that I know of no suggested action of mine on any important matter which I have not first submitted for his approval.

Julia Flynn to the Public Service Commissioner, 25 March 1929.

209. Professionalization

One aspect of professionalization of nursing with wider social implications was the passing of legislation to restrict the practice of nursing and midwifery to people with formal educational training in those areas. Legislation in South Australia in 1920 prohibited the employment of unqualified women, regardless of the length of their experience, if they did not apply for registration within one year of the passing of the Act. Women in country areas and women with little education particularly fell foul of this requirement. Their enquiries brought the following typed circular in reply.

Replying to your letter of the 5th inst. I have to advise you that only persons who have trained in a recognized Training School and passed the Board's Examinations may be registered by this Board.

Unless therefore, you are the holder of such a certificate of training as a midwife, you are not eligible for registration as a midwife.

I would point out that the Nurses Registration Act provides that no person who is not registered as a midwife shall practise midwifery.

Letter sent by the Registrar, Nurses' Registration Board of South Australia, to women whose applications for registration were received too late, 1923.

210. Nursing the Poor

In this report, a woman police officer in Adelaide describes the case of one unregistered midwife. Ironically, the registration of midwives and the existence of female police officers to investigate them both owed much to the efforts of women's organizations, who exerted pressure resulting in the expansion of professional jobs for women in this period.

Enquiries were made by the W.P. Constable in Harriet St Adelaide re this woman... She is Mrs Mary [M——], widow, aged about 70 years, an old age pensioner. She has been doing midwifery for a number of years, principally among poor people, but also has nursed for various doctors... On August 21st Mrs Mary [M——] was interviewed by W.P. Constable and Miss Priest W.P.C. She then stated that she had nursed the cases mentioned above, but only did it to oblige either old patients or friends. Her reason for not registering under the Nurses Registration Board was because she was getting the pension, she did not think she would be allowed to do nursing except a very few cases, as she thought that pensioners "were not allowed to earn anything over a few shillings now and again", but people came to her and begged her to nurse them again, and she did so under persuasion. She did not know that she was offending against the Nurses Registration Act by taking these cases without being registered.

Report of Woman Police Constable M. M. Wilcher into unregistered persons practising midwifery, 18 August 1923.

211. "Capable of Nursing"

Insistence on professional qualifications in midwifery sometimes created problems in rural areas and among women dependent on attending maternity cases to support themselves, as this letter from Wallaroo in South Australia shows.

Dear Sir,

Having received notice from the Secretary of Children's Welfare . . . warning me against taking in maternity cases as I am not a Registered Nurse I am writing you to explain the state of affairs in Wallaroo at the present time. There is only one registered Nurse here, a woman 66 years of age and too old to attend cases, she has a small house and only takes in one or 2 cases per month, there is no one here that goes out nursing, so what are these women to do. I thought that as there was no convenience for them that I would open a place as I have had a lot of experience in nursing and my home is 3 doors from each of the Doctors and enables them to visit oftener and render more attention to patients and both of these Drs know that I am capable of looking after them. I have had more experience in nursing that even Mrs [B——], the registered nurse here, and Mrs [H——] also, who was the other woman to be warned of same, although her home is only a small skillion house and I pity the women that were laid up in Summer time there, so what are the women here to do, where are they to go, they must be attended to and I am not going out to nurse anyone. I have gone to a good deal of expense to make everything as it would be and I am relying on this to keep myself and little boy 12 yrs of age. All day today I have had women calling and asking me, whatever are we doing to do, whatever is wrong. I can assure you it is putting them to a lot of worry and it is unreasonable to think of them going to Moonta or Kadina as the Lady Inspector suggested they could do, it is 8 & 12 miles and would cost 10 & 14/- each way and double at night and mean risking their lives besides, if I were not capable of nursing maternity cases I would not undertake the work.

Will you please grant me a Licence and let me have a reply as soon as possible.

Mrs M.D., Wallaroo, to the Inspector-General of Hospitals, 5 June 1928.

212. An Attack on Marriage

In New South Wales in 1932, during the Depression, the Married Women Teachers' and Lecturers' Dismissal Act was passed. The threat to dismiss all married women teachers, excepting those who could prove economic necessity, was seen as a negation of the right of female teachers to marry, and as such as an attack on the family. This position was taken up by A. B. Piddington in a speech before the Bar of the Legislative Assembly.

. . . all this is done in a bill that contains the gravest attack upon marriage that can be found in any statute. All this undermining of the economic safety of marriage is without any saving of existing engagements, without any consideration at all for the incapacity of a woman to practice her profession anywhere but in Crown employment.

This attack upon the marriage life of the community and upon the marrying young woman is made in an age of the freest scepticism, so that if it is the desire of the Legislature to accept what the Countess Russell says, that the time has come "to translate into law and more common practice" the growing opinion with regard to free unions outside marriage, this bill provides a pioneer opportunity. And the attack is made at a time when the population of Australia was never in greater danger. I learn from the Government Statistician that last year the natural increase of Japan — now stirring, as every thoughtful observer must see, not in the Far East, but in what is for us the Near North — was 914,000. The natural increase of Australia in the same year was 73,000. The birthrate of Australia was never lower, and it has been steadily declining for many years past. It is at this moment that marriage, which is at present the keystone, not only of happiness, but of upright, wholesome and useful public life, is denied to a great army of faithful servants, suited for marriage, or likely to be married. Our case is grave. I do not say that this bill will do any more than break the hearts of a few hundred people. I do not say that it will do any more than dispeople many homes that would have been made, but its principles are what I have already described.

A B. Piddington, *The Matyrdom of Women* (1932).

213. The Imposition of Celibacy

Some opposition to the dismissal of married women teachers tended to suggest that because of the Act women would be prevented from marrying. While A. B. Piddington stressed the implications of this for the birthrate, this statement by a spokeswoman for the United Associations of Women emphasized the restriction placed on personal freedom.

This week we read in the cables from Italy that Mussolini has pronounced the edict that *unless* men in the Government services marry they must resign. Just about twelve months ago Mr Drummond issued the edict that *if* women in the Government Education Department are married they must resign.

Every man on reading about Mussolini's decree must have felt that it was an impertinent interference with the personal liberty of Italian men. Whether a man marries or not is surely his own concern and to force marriage upon a man will probably make for the unhappiness of two people, the man himself and the woman he is forced to marry.

We hope this pronouncement of Mussolini's will make the Government of New South Wales realise the injustice of Mr Drummond's decree that if women teachers are married they must resign. Whether they marry or not should be their own concern and only unhappiness is caused by imposing celibacy on women teachers.

The Married Women Teachers Dismissal Act was introduced as an economy measure. Conditions have improved so much during the last year that we feel justified in hoping that this reactionary piece of legislation will be repealed before long and that no further interference will take place with the personal life of women workers.

"Mussolini and Mr Drummond", statement by a "Spokeswoman" for the United Associations of Women, Sydney (n.d. *c.* 1933).

214. Feminist Broadcast

Feminist organizations such as the United Associations of Women interpreted the threatened dismissal of married women teachers as a threat to all women workers and attempted to organize opposition to the legislation, utilizing radio programmes and printed leaflets for this purpose.

The Married Women Teachers Committee of the United Associations, has taken legal action on the position of the Married Women Teachers, and wishes to inform them that they cannot be dismissed at present. It also wishes to warn them against accepting dismissal until they get legal advice that their dismissal is in order.

All Married Women Teachers should communicate with the Teachers Federation for help and advice.

It is urgent that every Married Woman Teacher should resist dismissal as this Bill endangers all women workers.

You are advised to get in touch with the Federation.

Statement by the United Associations of Women scheduled for broadcast by 2UW, Sydney, during 5-6 October 1932.

215. "Putting Back the Clock of Emancipation"

This article on the dismissal of married women teachers puts forward a feminist view of the entry of married women into the workforce.

. . . women teachers have been singled out of all our women workers for dismissal for the crime of completing and enriching their lives by marriage.

There seems no limit to the stupidity and injustice of this Married Women Teachers' Act, which seemed so popular at the time of its enactment, but whose limitations and effect have been so lamentably unknown by the public. Do the readers of "Woman" know, for instance, that the compensation cost of dismissing several hundreds of married women teachers has been so great as to make it farcical to suggest that this is a measure of economy, brought in to make employment for ex-students? Do they know that a valuable married woman teacher of 14 years' loving and faithful service has just been dismissed from the work which is her life . . . And do they know that many retrenched married women are now in dire need because their husbands' positions are now very poor, or lost altogether through the depression?

There is more to it than this, however. The case for the women teachers is the case for all womenkind. Legislation like the M.W.T. Act is the first step towards putting back the clock of emancipation and self-respect for every married woman who wants to enjoy economic independence, and that widening of mind and vision that comes with following a career outside the home.

Many women seek only the sheltered busy life of the home, and their work as home-makers and child-rearers is none the less valuable for their choice. But to many also, aided by the increasing labor-saving devices of modern science, by the growing tendency towards smaller and better spaced families, by the more equal education of the sexes and the modern acceptance of women's entry into industry and the professions, will bitterly resent any attempt to force back into economic dependence and into the more cramping walls of the home, those women who deliberately choose the sterner path of the pioneer — those who, for love of their career, choose to combine with the responsibilities of home and children the arduous tasks of teacher, doctor, nurse, business-woman, writer, architect, or whoever else. The great and noble army of fighters and writers for the cause of women's rights — the Olive Schreiners, the Charlotte Perkins Gilmans, the Pankhursts, the Rose Scotts — would weep in despair to behold the retrogression of such legislation as the N.S.W. Married Women Teachers' Act.

"Today, as never before," writes Vera Brittain, an English wife and mother, and author of the famous "Testament of Youth", "it is urgent for individual women to show that life is enriched, mentally and spiritually as well as physically and socially by marriage and children; that these experiences render the woman who accepts them the more and not the less able to take the world's pulse, to estimate its tendencies, to play some definite, hardheaded, hard-working part in furthering the constructive ends of a political civilisation."

"Kathleen Winn" (Clarice McNamara), "The 'New' Married Woman", article dated 12 January 1933, written for publication in *The Woman.*

216. Women Teachers' Guild

Attempts by the United Associations of Women to organize teacher groups against the dismissal of married women teachers (and, incidentally, elicit their support for equal pay) were not always successful. Teachers' organizations, staffed largely by single women, were concerned with defending their own interests and suggested that married women teachers had advantages not always enjoyed by single women.

Dear Mrs. Street,

I thank you for your pamphlets and information regarding the question of employment of married women in the Education Departments of the various States. This matter was placed before our Advisory Committee, fully and freely discussed, and the *arguments against it* were as follows: —

1. During the last war, married women were employed. Most of them had ties in the metropolitan area, and were therefore exempt from country service. The single teacher was therefore transferred into the country schools while the married woman was given an appointment in the city or suburbs. This, I believe, caused much bitterness among the single women.
2. Because of a second income the married woman was independent and could adopt that particular attitude towards her superiors and her work.
3. Divided interests are not conducive towards good teaching; the married woman's interests are chiefly in her home.
4. Students leaving the Training College may not receive an appointment, if there are not sufficient vacancies. By the introduction of married women security of appointment would be lessened.
5. There is provision in our regulations for the employment of married women as temporary teachers under special circumstances. Some have been retained after marriage. (I have one on my staff.)
6. As far as we can ascertain no schools here have been closed because of enlistments of men teachers.
7. There is also the question of Child Endowment.

8. Because of the different conditions and differences of administration in each State, I should say that while the matter was of paramount importance in some States (e.g., Tasmania) it was not an urgent one in others such as South Australia.
9. The meeting was, therefore, against employment of married women in this State.

Re the other matter, viz. the principle of equal pay, we are unanimously with you and would be glad to be notified of any further progress in the matter.

J. M. Cooper, President, Women's Teachers' Guild, Adelaide, to Jessie Street, President, United Associations of Women, Sydney, 29 July 1941.

217. Recognition

Work in nurseries and kindergartens, the junior branch of the teaching profession, was given recognition during the Second World War, when trained workers were forbidden to transfer to other work. In this way, the work of one group of women (those employed in war-work and in factories) created work for the professional woman who taught or cared for her children.

I have been informed by the Director General of Man Power that he feels that Day Nursery Workers and Assistants and Kindergartners should not be permitted to enlist in the Women's Auxiliary Forces.

It is felt that there is a growing importance in the work of these persons whose training should not be lost by acceptance into the Auxiliaries.

It has therefore been decided not only that these trained workers shall be forbidden to enlist but also that they are not to be permitted to transfer from these occupations to other forms of employment.

These prohibitions seem to carry with them an implication that reasonable terms of employment must be given to the employees.

If you think that publicity in the Press to this decision is desirable I will arrange this if you will inform me.

Deputy Director-General of Man Power to the Secretary of the Kindergarten Union, West Perth, 24 December 1942.

PART 4

Women and Politics

Introduction

At the most superficial level, discussion of women in Australian public life has been concerned with outstanding women. In politics, attention has been given to women who were "first" — first in the franchise movement, as political candidates, or in parliament, while among black women, Truganini achieved the more tragic prominence of being said to be "the last". Most of the documents in this section deal with white women, but the section begins with Aboriginal women, and these few early documents dramatize the need for any evaluation of women's political activity to move beyond simple feminist criteria and into an examination of the broader social and political implications of women's actions.

The debate about women's political activity in Australian history has largely revolved around the vote: whether women were the beneficiaries of a political campaign initiated and conducted by men, as MacKenzie, Encel, Biskup and Dixson claim, or whether, as Summers argues, women actively sought and struggled for the vote.[1] The documents selected show that "women in politics" can claim a significance beyond this debate, and that the impact of women cannot be measured and discounted by the small number of women elected in parliament.

The women's movement in Australia expanded in numbers and activity in the post-suffrage period, and the thrust of feminism in Australia was directed towards achieving reform through influence rather than to getting women into parliament, although women did stand as parliamentary candidates, frequently on a "vote for women" platform. The suffrage movement similarly did not limit itself to the campaign to get the vote. Women's franchise was always more than a symbol of the equal status of women as citizens. For the suffragists, it was an instrument by which women could reform and purify society, and their programmes embodied a vision of a society that would be more moral and more compassionate. Three themes dominated the women's movement after franchise and expressed this vision: protection for women and children in employment, their support and protection through welfare, and the concept of equality and justice before the law. In the euphoria of the Sydney celebrations that marked the granting of the vote in New South Wales, Rose Scott invoked this vision when she spoke of "the advent of the mother-woman's world — the wide, loving heart and sheltering arms". [226] This belief, that women had a special role to play in purifying and elevating society, became institutionalized in both a programme of social reform and in the concept of non-party feminism. The motivating force behind this was the same belief in women's moral superiority that had led Adelaide reformer Caroline Emily Clark to reject the idea of votes for women.[222]

With the disbanding of the Womanhood Suffrage League after the vote was granted, Rose Scott founded the Women's Political Educational League, to show women how the franchise could be used to further women's rather than party interests. A number of documents included here show how this essentially uniting

strategy both channelled women's political energies but produced a source of
divisiveness and contradiction. Rose Scott argued that the special interests of women
would not be given prominence in party platforms and it was necessary for women to
remain outside the constraining influence of party loyalty, a view later reformulated
by Vida Goldstein in the *Woman Voter*. But women's groups attached to political
parties increasingly provided an arena for women to express themselves politically
and even such a staunch advocate of non-party feminism as Catherine Spence was
sceptical of what came to be the two prongs of feminist strategy. In private, in letters
to Alice Henry reproduced here, Spence criticized both Rose Scott's belief that
Liberal women would be unable to retain a voice independent of their party and Vida
Goldstein's decision to appeal directly to the woman voter. [236, 238]

Documents included here suggest that the strength of non-party feminism lay
in isolating issues and in searching across party lines for parliamentary support. The
weakness of non-party feminism lay in the assumption that "women's issues" did
not vitally impinge on the core philosophies of conservatism and labour, an
assumption that paradoxically suggested that women's issues were at the same time
"greater" than and less significant than party issues.

From the early twentieth century, the debate about non-party feminism (or the
autonomy of the women's movement) divided women activists. Two early groups,
the Women's Liberal League in New South Wales and the Queensland Women's
Electoral League, combined an appeal to women with an attack on socialism, arguing
that women's interests would not be served by the election of a "socialist party".
From an opposing perspective, committed Labor women and later Communist
women maintained that non-party feminism camouflaged the right-wing bias of
prominent feminists and women's groups. With the advent in the inter-war period of
an extreme right-wing organization, Adela Pankhurst Walsh's Women's Guild of
Empire, which like the older groups stressed its non-party innocence, the dilemma
posed by the ambiguities of the concept became acute.

While conflicts between women's organizations illustrated the difficulty of
uniting all women in a common cause, many non-party women, too, found that the
single-minded pursuit of the feminist vision led them beyond the circumscribed area
of women's issues. Essential to non-party feminism was the middle-class, liberal
belief that Australia was progressing towards a more humane, more just and more
democratic society, and that women had an essential part to play in that process.
Without the women's vote, there could be no real democracy; without equality and
protection for women and children, society was not just; and only through women's
involvement in public life and politics could society be humanized. In this sense,
feminist goals were limited and the transformation of society that feminists sought
was partial. Consequently, non-party organization, concentration on women's issues,
women candidates to represent all women and across-party lobbying were all
appropriate tactics. However, in pursuing their humanitarian and often moral goals,
feminists were frequently thrust into confrontation with a society that revealed itself
to be more complex, unyielding and contradictory than this progressive philosophy
suggested. Rose Scott was led by her moral and protective endeavours on behalf of
women and girls in factories and shops to question an order of society that rewarded
the few and disadvantaged the many. Vida Goldstein, pleading for "love instead of
hatred, for arbitration instead of bloodshed", found herself and the *Woman Voter*,
during the First World War, in direct confrontation with police and government.[248]
The pursuit of women's issues led, uncomfortably, into broader questions about the
division of resources and the regulation of the economy. The pursuit of a moral and

humane society — the "soft" politics of the women's movement — was capable of abrupt transformation into the "hard" politics of foreign policy and welfare, politics that divided the parties.

Documents relating to the Depression reveal the difficulty with which women's groups were able to confine themselves to women's issues while continuing to present an adequate defence of the rights of all women in the community. In Perth, for instance, the main feminist organization, the Women's Service Guilds, showed little official concern with unemployment, although leading members (along with members of other women's organizations such as the W.C.T.U.) were active in the relief committee, which gave aid to unemployed women.[66, 67] W.S.G. president Bessie Rischbieth was also at one time president of the relief committee. Even so, their actions remained charitable rather than political, their "politics" being restricted to a feminist emphasis on unemployed women and girls rather than men and boys as the recipients of their efforts. The failure to relinquish the limited perspectives of non-party feminism reduced organizations such as these to the status of charitable auxiliaries to the State and opened them to the criticism that their efforts sometimes harmed rather than helped working-class women. The documents in this section that refer to unemployed women in Perth illustrate the activities of another group of women who moved from "charity" to "politics" by mounting a critique of government sustenance policy and who criticized the relief committee for sending women to positions at less than award rates.[267, 268] One of the women active in this group was Katharine Susannah Prichard and these and other documents in this section show how women in the Australian Communist Party moved beyond the non-party feminists in locating the problems of unemployed women within a broader analysis of the economic situation. Similarly, Jessie Street's response to female un-employment — to set up a training scheme for domestic servants while opposing domestic service being brought under an award — was firmly within the tradition of non-party feminism, but clearly reflected a middle-class response to the issue. The autonomous feminist movement remained wedged between a grave concern for the casualties of unemployment and a disinclination to look critically at the basis of a society that allowed this to happen.

On the other hand, the experience of the Depression had an important influence on the political attitudes of many feminists. Vida Goldstein's 1943 campaign platform, while using the older terminology of humanitarian feminism, asked for the "establishment of a Financial System which will make Money the Servant and not the Master of the People".[271] Jessie Street's experiences prompted her to repudiate some of the basic beliefs of non-party feminism when she joined the Labor Party. In an interview with Jean Devanny, Street said that prior to the Depression her commitment to a non-party stance was based on the belief in the willingness of all political parties to enact reforms, but she had joined the Labor Party because she had come to believe that "the opportunity to make profits and not to render service was the major concern of those who control our present social and economic system".[272]

Jessie Street's expanded range of interests included spearheading the "Sheep-skins for Russia" campaign during the Second World War and publicly defending Soviet society. [274] When Street began the Women's Charter Movement in 1943, Bessie Rischbieth, then President of the Australian Federation of Women Voters (the co-ordinating organization of the state non-party organizations) denounced it as communist. At this time, Rischbieth and Street, while both agreeing on major feminist issues, disagreed over the type of society most likely to usher in the best possible world for women.[2]

While lack of consensus over the broad political issues created divisions between women's groups and the limited range of feminist activities sometimes opened them to the charge that they spoke for middle-class rather than for all women, attitudes to women's issues themselves also revealed a lack of ideological agreement. On the important issue of venereal disease legislation, varieties of feminist response were evident. Feminist involvement in this question represented one of the major, long-term struggles of the movement and illustrates the debt that Australian feminism owed to international bodies such as the International Women's Suffrage Alliance, as well as to the League of Nations and the United Nations Status of Women Commission, which formulated a rigorous and coherent attack on this discriminatory legislation. Through organizations such as these, non-party feminists entered the arena of international politics. In Australia, however, women's groups did not present a united front on venereal disease legislation. One of the divisions documented here occurred between Edith Cowan, the first woman in Australia to be elected to parliament, and the Women's Service Guilds.[249] In this way, feminist divisions over venereal disease legislation look forward to later differences between women's organizations over "basic women's issues", such as the right to abortion.

The documents in this section, while raising a number of the problems confronting women in politics, also suggest ways in which women's political activity was influential. Acting as a reform lobby, early women's groups were quick to claim legislative changes in the area of welfare as a result of their influence. As long as welfare and civil-rights issues were considered to be peripheral to "real" politics, this contribution has tended to be trivialized. But the attempt to create a more humane and just society, while reflecting the basically moral response of women's groups, can be seen not only to look back to a Victorian concept of women as the moral guardians of the community and as the moral superiors to men — the temperance wowsers of the caricatures — but forward to a society in which government welfare policies, the civil rights of women, Aborigines and children would be seen as central rather than marginal political issues.

Notes

1.   Norman MacKenzie, *Women in Australia* (Melbourne: Cheshire, 1962); Sol Encel, Norman MacKenzie and Margaret Tebbutt, *Women and Society: An Australian Study* (Melbourne: Cheshire, 1974); Peter Biskup, "The Westralian Feminist Movement", *University Studies in Western Australian History* 3, no.3 (October 1959); Miriam Dixson, *The Real Matilda: Woman and Identity in Australia, 1788 to 1975* (Ringwood: Penguin, 1976); and Anne Summers, *Damned Whores and God's Police: The Colonization of Women in Australia* (Ringwood: Penguin, 1975).
2.   There is a discussion of this in Kay Daniels, Mary Murnane and Anne Picot (eds), *Women in Australia: An Annotated Guide to Records* (Canberra: A.G.P.S., 1977), vol.1, p. 109.

218. "An Amazon Named Walyer"

George Augustus Robinson described in his journal an Aboriginal woman named Walyer, who led her tribe against the white invaders.

22 June 1830

I busied myself in conversation with the two sealers, who told me of the amazon named Walyer [or TARE. REE. NORE] that headed a tribe and would stand on a hill and give orders to the natives when to attack the whites, calling them bad names and telling them to come out and they would spear them.

30 December 1830

Walyer returned with Parish and this I was heartily glad of. I was fearful this woman had escaped. . . A few hours after this woman returned she had thrown the whole of the natives into a state of alarm by telling them the white people intended shooting them, women and all. I keep this woman apart from the rest of the people, but notwithstanding she had put this report afloat. Turnbull [a sealer from Gun Carriage Island] informed me that Walyer had boasted to the other women how she had taught the blackfellows to load and fire off a musket, and instructed them how to kill plenty of white people; and that she has been wont to recount her exploits, how she used to tell the black fellows how to act when they used to rob a hut, and has said she liked a LUTE.TA.WIN, i.e. a white man, as she did a black snake. Turnbull said he overheard her propose to the women to kill him, but as they would not agree to it, she could not carry her designs into execution. If my boat had not gone, there is no doubt but the man would have been killed and the woman would have escaped to the main.

G.A. Robinson, Journal, 22 June and 30 December 1830.

219. Last Days

Another "chieftainess", Truganini, one of the last survivors among the full-blood Tasmanian Aborigines, ended her life as a curiosity. Visiting English social commentators Rosamond and Florence Hill saw her in this way when they visited her in Hobart, unaware of the political role she had played in the relations between the races.

. . . our dealings with the aborigines of Tasmania are a blot on our national character. The race is now extinct with the exception of one old woman, supposed by some persons to have been a chieftainess. She is well cared for at the expense of the colony, and lives in a family at Hobarton, who are paid, I heard, 60*l*, a year for her support. Her native name is Truganini, but she is equally well known by that of Lalla Rookh. We were in lodgings at Hobarton next door to where she lived, and as she often came into our landlady's kitchen we had the opportunity of making her acquaintance. She is a hale, healthy-looking old woman, short, and rather stout. A scarlet handkerchief tied round her head, leaving her grey locks partially visible, gave her quite a picturesque appearance; the rest of her attire was of prosaic European fashion. She spoke a little English, and accepted with apparently much gratification sixpence for the purchase of tobacco. I was advised to make my offering small, and perhaps even this sum would have been better withheld, as there was considerable danger of her spending it in drink. Our landlady said that on the occasion of one of Lalla Rookh's visits, when she (the landlady) had a black eye, the result of an accident, Truganini enquired if her husband had given it her. Answering in the negative, the landlady asked if Lalla Rookh's husband had ever given her black eyes? "Oh yes, a thousand," was the reply. I told the old woman I had come a very long way across the sea. She asked if I had come from Oyster Cove — about twenty-two miles distant. I believe this voyage had been her longest, and most probably her only sea experience. She had lately paid a visit to Government House, and when introduced to the Governor had poked him in the chest, saying at the same time, "Too much jacket, too much jacket," implying thereby that his Excellency was becoming too stout.

Rosamond and Florence Hill, *What We Saw in Australia* (1875).

220. "Services to Our People"

James Erskine Calder had been Surveyor-General of Tasmania and in 1875, his study of the "native tribes" of Tasmania was published. In this letter, he emphasizes the use that was made of Truganini by white authorities. His wish that she should be remembered by erecting a public memorial was not realized until 1976. Instead, her skeleton was put on display in the Tasmanian Museum, Hobart.

... I will here claim permission to say that something more than a slight interest will be long associated with the name and memory of this poor woman, not only as the last of her race, whom we have dispossessed and superseded, but from her personal history having been an eventful one; and her services to our people, at the time when her countrymen were still struggling — as they did to the last — for supremacy, having been of the highest value to the colonists.

To your predecessor I took occasion to give a faint outline of these too scantily requited services, which I will now repeat.

As the most active and fearless of the associates of the late Mr G. A. Robinson, she was largely concerned in the removal of all the aboriginal tribes from the mainland, who (particularly towards the close of their existence at large) were much more pugnacious and destructive than at any other period of their history, as the ample records preserved in your own office, and the public journals of the time, will convince anyone who will take the trouble to study them. To Mr Robinson himself, no doubt the merit is due of great perseverance in pursuit of them and devising the plans for their capture, but to others, and prominently to Truganini, it was, that he assigned the perilous task of opening every negotiation with them for their surrender; and she it was who once saved this most useful and energetic public servant from death in a savage onslaught made upon the lives of his party by a horde of blacks (called by him the Jackine or Sandy Cape tribe), who having separated these two from the rest, drove them into the Arthur River, then greatly swollen by recent rains, where he must have died, for he could not swim, but for her constancy and courage in the end she got him safely through the torrent, just in time to save him from his pursuers.

In his official accounts of this repulse, (29th. of July and 14th. of September, 1832) written doubtlessly in haste, and perhaps excitement, he speaks of this service as the work of "a woman", but without distinguishing her; but in his private conversations, he always named Truganini as his preserver.

To those who are unacquainted with the history of the surrender of the blacks, it may appear none too creditable in her and some others of her people, to have aided in their subjugation. But Robinson was no ordinary man, and those of them whom he had subdued to his will, held him in such reverential awe, as to induce the belief that they regarded him as something more than human.

His supremacy over them was too complete for opposition, and his will too potent to be withstood. Hence, he impelled them into perils, that others would have shrunk from in pure terror. In some of his Reports, he tells us, of his engaging them in embassies to the still unsubdued tribes, from which they expected nothing but death; but such was his ascendancy over them, that he gives but a solitary instance of any disobedience, which was in the case of a chief, whose fears of his wild brethren, so over-mastered every other faculty, that he fled from the camp rather than face them. Some of their escapes like his own, read more like romance than fact; and Truganini had a full share in these dangers, if not in the rewards and honors that followed them.

To the late Premier I proposed, while this woman's death was a subject of frequent conversation, to give his influence to a movement for an appropriate monument by subscription; but the time for any such organization, I fear has gone by; but as anything is better than the little mound, now almost level with the surface, that still indicates the grave, I would respectfully suggest that a substantial slab at least, be placed over it, while any trace of it remains; the trifling cost of which, even if made a charge on public funds, would assuredly evoke no other remark but one of general approbation; though for my own part, I still think it would be more to our credit, if something better than a plain tablet were raised to her memory by public subscription.

J.E. Calder to Thomas Reibey, Premier of Tasmania, Hobart, 6 February 1877.

221. Rights

In the second half of the nineteenth century, the Tasmanian Aborigines living on the Bass Strait islands, most of them descendants of white sealers and Aboriginal women, made numerous claims to the government in an attempt to secure tenure to the land and to protect the mutton-birds from stock run on the islands by white settlers. While their petitions appear to have been lost, this reply reveals the prominent role of women. Lucy A. Beedon's aunt had earlier pressed similar claims.

Ladies,

I have the honor to inform you that your Petition to His Excellency The Governor has been referred to me and I have now the pleasure of informing you that Chapple Island has long been reserved for the use of Sealers and Mutton Bird Catchers, and that Mr. Allan Smith [police constable] has been instructed not to allow stock to be run upon it.

I have the honour to be,
Ladies,
Your obedient Servant.

Nicholas J. Brown, Minister, Lands and Works Office, Hobart, to Misses Elizabeth Everett and Lucy A. Beedon, and others who signed the petition, Chapple Island, 11 June 1886.

222. The Superiority of Women

Caroline Emily Clark in South Australia and her cousins, Rosamond and Florence Hill in England, were well-known social reformers. Never a suffragist, Miss Clark, in this letter, explains her attitude to the franchise for women.

You ask me my ideas upon the extension of the franchise to women. I should be very glad for you to have the vote and perhaps about 20 or 30 of my acquaintance but I am afraid I know twice that number who would misuse the privilege. When I say misuse I mean give the vote for some other reason that the character of the person voted for. This is perhaps almost equally true of men, and my greatest objection is that I fear it will introduce a new subject for quarrelling and a new source of tyranny. The idea of women being brought into public notice and the turmoil of politics is so utterly repugnant to my feelings that I cannot judge fairly and only hope that nothing and nobody will ever give me such a right as my conscience would oblige me to use it. I suppose you know that female rate payers here have a vote for the corporation, but there are not many who use it. I do not want women to be put upon a level with men. I want them to be very much above them. I do not want them to be rival clocks trying to tick equally loud. I want them to be the little unseen escapement that checks the wheels when they are going too fast and regulates the whole machine. I think the moment women become independent sources of action they will lose the regulating power. It is one of the puzzles of the universe that there should be too many women in the world, I think that we are managing very badly in rearing such a preponderance of girls when the sexes are born in almost equal numbers. It is quite hopeless to argue with me, I cannot even say I am sorry to disagree with you for I would not agree with you for the world.

Caroline Emily Clark to Florence Hill, from Hazelwood, 27 August 1866.

223. Won to the Cause

In 1891, Dora Montefiore invited a group of people to her home in Darlinghurst Road, Sydney, to discuss forming an association to work for the suffrage. Among them were Rose Scott, Margaret Windeyer and Mrs Wolstenhome, and the result was the formation of the "Womanhood Suffrage League". In her autobiography, Dora Montefiore described her conversion to the women's movement.

My eldest brother was married and living in Australia. His wife was delicate, and he wrote to ask that one of his sisters should come out on a visit and help her with the children and the housekeeping. It was decided that I should be the one to undertake this duty, and I went out under the charge of a cousin to stay in my brother's house. This was how I first came to know Australia and Sydney. Sir Hercules Robinson was at that time Governor of New South Wales, and I had introductions to Lady Robinson and other friends out there. It was there I met my future husband, Mr. George Barrow Montefiore, but I returned home before marrying him, was introduced to his family and spent some months among my own people. Then in 1879 I went out again, was married, and we lived in Sydney, where my two children were born. In 1889 my husband died and I was left with a daughter of five and a son two years old.

It was after the death of my husband, when I had to go into business matters with trustees and lawyers that I had my initiation into what the real social position of a widow meant to a nineteenth-century woman. One lawyer remarked to me, when explaining the terms of the will: "As your late husband says nothing about the guardianship of the children, they will remain under your care." I restrained my anger at what appeared to me to be an officious and unnecessary remark and replied, "Naturally, my husband would never have thought of leaving anyone else as their guardian." "As there is a difference in your religions," he continued grimly, "he might very well have left someone of his own religion as their guardian." "What! *my* children, the children *I* bore, left to the guardianship of someone else! The idea would never have entered his mind, and what's more, I don't believe he could have done it, for children belong even more to a mother than to a father!" "Not in law," the men round the table interjected; while the lawyer who had first undertaken my enlightenment added dryly: "In law, the child of the married woman has only one parent, and that is the father." I suppose he saw symptoms of my rising anger, for he appeared to enjoy putting what he thought was a final extinguisher on my independence of thought; but I could hardly believe my ears, when this infamous statement of fact was made, and blazing with anger, I replied: "If that is the state of the law, a woman is much better off as a man's mistress than as his wife, as far as her children are concerned." "Hush," a more friendly man's voice near me remarked. "You must not say such things." "But I must and shall say them," I retorted. "You don't know how your horrible law is insulting all motherhood." And from that moment I was a suffragist (though I did not realise it at the time) and determined to alter the law.

Dora Montefiore, *From a Victorian to a Modern* (1927).

224. "Good Enough"

> The cause of women's suffrage received support from church groups and women's organizations such as the Women's Christian Temperance Union, which stressed women's moral role in the community and their opposition to the "iniquitous traffic" in liquor. South Australian women were the first to get the vote, in 1894.

The annual meetings of the Assembly of the Congregational Union were held in the Guild Hall of Stowe Church, Adelaide, in October. During their course the Rev. J.C. KIRBY moved — "That this meeting sympathises with the Women's Suffrage League in its efforts to secure the national franchise for women." He considered that if a woman was regarded as good enough to take part in the affairs of the Church she should also be thought good enough to share in the control of secular affairs. ("Too good.") He asked why they were so terribly afraid of their mothers and their wives as to be unwilling to grant them this privilege. If they were accorded the concession desired it would lead to the raising of the tone of Parliament to a proper conception of the true dignity of woman, would lessen war, and would greatly conduce to a better state of morals throughout the community. He referred to the success which had attended the granting of women's suffrage in the state of Wyoming, and said the giving of the right there had not led women to neglect their home duties. The movement in that state, he found, had been opposed by the whisky distillers, and that had led him to support it. The aid of the women in suppressing this iniquitous traffic would be very valuable. Women would never make laws to treat men as men had made laws to treat women. He trusted that the meeting would carry the motion. (Cheers.) The Rev. W.R. FLETCHER, M.A., seconded the proposition and contended that the question was certainly one which might be discussed by them, Mr. J. A. CHARTIER proposed the previous question, holding that the council should not be turned into a political association. He, however, found no supporter. The Rev. F. HASTINGS approved of the motion, although he was not certain that, as Mr. Kirby had stated, the influence of women would tend towards the lessening of war. He was not quite sure as to the effect of women's suffrage in the home, but he held that if a woman had a right to an opinion on religion she should also have a similar right with regard to politics. (Hear, hear.) Mr. J. A. CHARTIER moved as an amendment — "That the Parliamentary franchise be extended to unmarried women and widows who are taxpayers." He explained that he had no wish to be obstructive in moving the previous question, but he considered that their union should not be converted into a political society for the discussion of all sorts of questions. He thought that the modified form in which he had put the question was the more fitting one. The Rev. C. MANTHORPE seconded the amendment. Mr. J.M. DOWIE and the Rev. D. MILNE supported the motion. The Rev. T. HOPE pointed out that men who were not tax-payers had a right to vote. The Rev. J. McEWIN supported the motion, which was finally carried with a few dissentients.

The Dawn (Sydney), 5 November 1889.

225. Advantages of the Vote

This letter from a branch of the Women's Christian Temperance Union in Western Australia points out the electoral advantages for the present government if it were to give women the vote. The letter followed five years of W.C.T.U. agitation for the franchise in Western Australia.

Dear Sir John,
    At a public meeting held in Northam on 24 May, the following resolutions were carried unanimously and it has fallen to me as Sec. to forward them to you.
I.   That in the opinion of this meeting it is desirable that for the best interests of this Colony the Franchise be extended to Women.
II.   That a copy of this resolution be sent to the Premier.
    I will only add my ardent hope that you will recognise the justice of woman's claim to the Franchise and that on your government will devolve the high honor of bringing our desire to fruition.
    I am sure you have recognised that there are special reasons existing in this colony that render the concession of the franchise to women of the utmost import-ance to stable government. I need only mention the fact, of the great disparity between the sexes, to show that the addition of women to the electoral roll would go far to minimise the extravagant demands likely to result from a large *unsettled* male population, possessed of political power.
    I am confident that the women of our dear old colony would rejoice to owe the privilege they seek to yours instead of any succeeding government and you who are so generous and so high minded in other directions, I trust and hope will add to your laurels by granting our request. I assure you that although there may have been little

public agitation; there is a great earnest desire among women to be permitted by their vote to have a voice in the legislation of our common country.

It seems passing strange that while a woman is thought fit to rule an empire she should be denied a vote in a democratic country.

A ready affirmation to Woman's request would I earnestly believe be a most tactful act at this particular junction in our history.

Ada R. Throssell, Secretary, Northam branch of the Women's Christian Temperance Union, to the Premier of Western Australia, Sir John Forrest, 27 June 1898.

226. "It Has Cost Others Much"

Rose Scott described the strategy of the Womanhood Suffrage League in New South Wales in this way: "Our attitude from first to last was to avoid all Party Politics and to persuade Members of all Parties in the House to help us to attain our objects." With the vote granted, the League's work was over and it ceased to exist in October 1902. In September of that year, a celebration was held to thank Sir William Lyne, Acting Premier at the time the Act was passed, and Sir John See, the new Premier, for their advocacy of the women's cause. In her speech on that occasion, Rose Scott said:

Eleven years of life closely connected with political hopes and fears, letters, and interviews with all leading politicians, have taught me that in political life, as well as in any other life, all honour to the men who can recognise their duty and do it. What higher ideal is there in life? From the captain, who goes down with his sinking ship, to the engine-driver who rides to certain death upon his train! From the men who seek to save their fellow men in the Mt. Kembla mine; yes, even from all these up to the Minister of Home Affairs, and the Premier of New South Wales! Oh, how well I know how easy it would have been to postpone our enfranchisement indefinitely; to lay the blame on my "colleagues," "my supporters," or other "more important measures," "the time has not arrived," and all the rest of the political paraphernalia. There are some people who can recognise nothing till it is hall-marked and dished up in the musty old volumes of past history, and I deeply regret that in the national life it has become a cheap and degrading fashion, often, to abuse members of Parliament, and talk as if they can do nothing noble and nothing conscientious. Now, I look upon the obtaining of the vote for women as a direct contradiction to those libels! The natural man's prejudices whether as a politician or a pressman (and ought we not to thank the press also) are always in favour of the clinging ivy and oak business, and therefore it has been all the more noble of these leaders and their supporters to give women justice in the teeth of men's natural prejudices.

And oh! fellow women, you who have never worked for this vote! Prize it not too lightly, for if it has cost you nothing, it has cost others much. The price of freedom is always sacrifice. Hope deferred hath often made the heart sick. There have been days of despair, and hours of heartache, and, worse still, a knowledge of human nature one would rather have been without! But let us look above and beyond, and realise how wonderful is this flower of freedom which has blossomed for the women of Australia this year. Are we to rush round, like so many little children, crying out — one, "it is mine, I saw it first!" another, "it is mine, I touched it first!" Oh, foolish and blind! a thousand unseen influences have gone to develop that outward growth of form and colour! Let the "I," "I," fade upon our lips, for lo! we stand in the presence of Freedom, a part of the eternal and immortal, to obtain which men in all ages have lived and died and suffered martyrdom.

The hour came, and with it the men whom we have met here to strive to honour to-night. Their names will live when ours are forgotten, not only in the history of Australia, but in that of the world.

Make no mistake, accept no petty, local short-sighted interpretation of this double victory for women. Its impossibilities are for all nations and for all time, and its birth, at the beginning of the 20th century, heralds to a world oppressed with poverty, suffering and sin, the advent of the mother-woman's world — the wide, loving heart and sheltering arms.

Rose Scott, *Woman's Sphere*, 10 October 1902.

227. "Our Absolute Right"

Nellie Martel was a prominent member of the Pankhursts' Women's Social and Political Union in England, and during its campaign to win the vote, she published a penny pamphlet to show what the franchise had already accomplished for women in Australia. Mrs Martel describes her own involvement in the Australian struggle and, in this excerpt, one of the other "causes" that mobilized women at this time.

In the year 1891, I returned to Australia, and in May of that year a Woman's Suffrage Society was formed. I was one of its first members. We worked very hard to get the vote for women on the same terms as applied to men in the home of my adoption. We began with very small numbers, and worked on until we had many branches. I was made the Honorary Secretary for Petitions in this Society, and remained in that office until the time of the granting of the vote to women in 1902. Every petition that was presented to the Legislative Assembly consequently passed through my hands. I know the amount of labour that was put in the collecting of these signatures. The question was not popular. We were subjected to ridicule, contempt, abuse, and to anything but flattering cartoons. Not only the public had we to educate, but the Members of Parliament themselves. After eleven years of hard work we succeeded at last in getting political freedom. Words cannot describe the joy which fills one's heart at the realisation of one's life work. Could our legislators know they had the power to make women so thoroughly happy, I think they would no longer withhold from us that which is out absolute right.

During our eleven years of agitation we had worked for many removals from the Statute Books of laws which were a disgrace to any country. First and foremost we had asked for the raising of the "age of consent" for the protection of our girls. In New South Wales the girls were only protected by law until they were fourteen years of age. Any man could take advantage of a girl of fourteen years and a day to rob her of that which our great poet calls "the immediate jewel of the soul" — her good name. Should he succeed in coercing, intimidating, or bribing the child into saying she had consented to her own ruin, the law allowed that man to go free, even though he were a father of children of the age of his victim. I had spoken at fourteen deputations on this one question to protect our girls at least for two more years. The law protects the property of the rich girl until she is twenty-one; she is not considered wise enough to know how to dispose of her land or her property, yet she is supposed to be wise enough to understand the consequences of parting with that which is dearer to all women than property or land — chastity. The Women's Christian and Temperance Union had been fighting for twenty years without avail for the extension of years for the protection of girls. The women of New South Wales were enfranchised in August, 1902. Before the end of that year the girls of the State were protected up to sixteen years; since then to seventeen years of age.

Mrs Nellie Alma Martel, *The Women's Vote in Australia* (n.d.).

228. Support for the Suffragettes

Victorian women were the last to get the vote and the length of the struggle in that state contributed to the militancy of the movement there. This circular letter won only luke-warm support from the non-party organizations to whom it was sent and at least one group (in South Australia) proposed more moderate wording.

That we workers in the Women's Cause in the State of . . . most earnestly ask the Irish Delegates to make use of all their influence to urge the Members of Parliament for Ireland to strain every nerve to get the Conciliation Bill for Women's Suffrage passed within this present session, we having now for over ten years used the franchise in the Federal Commonwealth Elections and for over. . . years in the State Parliamentary Elections and are fully assured that no one would ever dream of taking away our franchise.

Victorian Women's Political Association, Melbourne, Resolution proposed and circulated by letter (1911).

229. Disgracing the Cause of Womanhood

This attack on the English militant suffragettes was not written by an anti-feminist but by the leader of the fight for the women's vote in New South Wales, Rose Scott. It is likely that the majority of the women who supported the franchise in Australia were suffragists who espoused the concept of "womanhood" elaborated here.

To the Editor.

In an article on Saturday "Epacris" in speaking of the suffragettes in England says that when I was interviewed on the subject I declared myself an anti-suffragette, and afterwards goes on to say "as politics are under discussion, perhaps it is permissible to say that the former lady sits on a rail." This evidently alludes to me, as I am the first person mentioned. My greeting to the woman suffrage conference in Amsterdam has already been published in your paper — besides the interview in which I declared myself opposed to the methods of the noisy and militant section of women in England, known as "suffragettes." Must it then be inferred that I have not the courage of my opinions because I have not declared them for the third time? Profoundly as I sympathise with women suffragists all over the world, I am, as I have always been, utterly opposed to the methods adopted by the law-breaking suffragettes in England. I consider they are doing infinite harm, not only to the cause they advocate, but also to a far greater, more important cause — and that is the dignity and beauty of true womanhood. I consider the adoption of physical force as a means to persuade, convince, or coerce human beings is absolutely barbaric, and supremely so when women are found using it to convince men. In no country in the world have women ever won the vote but through tact, and sympathy, and by appealing to man's intellectual and spiritual nature. All men, of whatever nationality, who have become representative of the interests of other men have in them a sense of justice — and although prejudice dies hard, where women are concerned, an appeal to this sense which men possess even in a greater degree than most women cannot fail in the end to convince, and lead to victory. The more conservative the country, the more patience and self-control the women need.

Sir James Stansfeld (who was called the woman's friend in England), and who was also the friend of Mazzini and John Stuart Mill, wrote to me as follows when, in 1891, we started the Woman Suffrage League of New South Wales. Speaking of the woman's vote he wrote: — "It will be the greatest of all revolutions, the greatest, and in my opinion, the most beneficent. It will preserve democracies from being selfish and savage, but I would always argue it from the loftiest standpoint, and I would do it in a manner to make it evident that true womanhood was all the more womanly for the assertion." This, I may say, was the ideal upon which we worked here and in New Zealand and other States. And I am quite convinced that if we had gone about breaking windows, defying laws, and inciting the mob to do so also we would have alienated the sympathy of men from our cause, and would have been as voteless today as we would have well deserved to be! Any man worth calling a man may be persuaded or convinced, but never coerced. Finally, I consider that the militant suffragettes of England are disgracing not only the cause but the womanhood of England.

Rose Scott, cutting from unidentified newspaper, 7 December 191 (?1).

230. Women and Unionism

The Dawn **was the first feminist newspaper in Australia and its editor, Louisa Lawson, a pioneer in the fight for the vote.** *The Dawn* **also supported the formation of unions among women workers, especially in the sweated trades such as tailoring, but were open to the claim that they employed non-union labour on the paper itself when the women compositors working on the paper were prevented from joining the male-dominated printers' union.**

The meeting [of the tailoresses] was held at the Temperance Hall, Pitt Street, and about 30 tailoresses were present; the president of the Trades' and Labour Council took the chair and many other officers of that body occupied the platform and spoke during the evening on the subject of the meeting. A president and secretary pro. tem. were appointed for the new union and most of the women present gave in their names as members.

So far so good; the union which was long ago suggested and which we have for sometime in many ways endeavoured to promote is now in a fair way towards firm establishment. The membership list though small is very encouraging for a start and doubtless it will soon expand to the dimensions of strength.

The success of the principle — which is the main thing — being thus assured, we may be permitted to refer, not in egotism but in self-defence, to the position of "The Dawn" in this matter.

Our representative who attended the meeting to report for our columns was treated with discourtesy and finally requested to leave the Hall on the ground that "The Dawn" being opposed to Trade Unionism the presence of any member of its staff was objectionable.

We can hardly allow such a statement of "Dawn" principles to remain un-contradicted; moreover it can be easily disproved.

The widening of the spheres of labour for those women who are compelled to earn their living by trade, and the protection of women workers by union is what we have consistently aimed at and urged. Twelve months ago we wrote to England and procured from the Secretary of the Women's Protective Union in London, copies of the rules of English associations and volumes of their reports. More recently we began in a small way the public agitation which has resulted in the adoption of the work of forming a Tailoresses Union by the Trades and Labour Council here.

When so much was done, we were only too glad to leave the matter in the hands of those who are more experienced in trade questions and who have particular facilities for the formation of trade associations. In those hands we are well content to leave the matter so long as the advantage of women-workers is thereby secured.

Trade Unionism in general as a method of protecting labour against the undue oppression of capital has also always had our support.

At the Sunday mass-meeting in the Domain held to express sympathy with the London Dock Labourers, the Editress (Mrs Lawson) was the first to contribute towards the funds, and Henry Lawson — already known to many by his songs of the people — lent his aid by writing some verses intended to speed the enthusiasm in favour of the London poor. The printing of "The Dawn" was, at that time stopped and the issue delayed in order that some thousands of copies of those verses — gratuitously printed and distributed — might be run off in time for the meeting.

At that public gathering, enthusiastic cheers were given for Mrs. Lawson and her son, in recognition of their services to the cause of labour; this scarcely looks as if there were any opposition to the interests of the workers on the part of "The Dawn."

The real cause of the intolerance and bitterness of some members of the Trades' Council must be looked for elsewhere. The cause is — as some of them practically admitted — that "The Dawn" employs and defends women compositors. Many of the chief union officials in Sydney are compositors themselves and their own interests so far predominate over their zeal for the cause of honest work generally, that the idea of women compositors creates at once in them a feeling of extreme rancour. The compositors in our office get higher wages than anyone of similar years of service could get in any Union house in Sydney, and as soon as they are numerous enough to form a Women's Union, they will have our aid in the effort.

The opposition of the Trades' and Labour Council is not made on the question of wages but on the point of the employment of women, whom they will not tolerate in the field of labour on any condition. This seems to us an injustifiable interference with honest workers and a piece of sheer tyranny which must be opposed.

The intolerance exhibited and the misstatements made by the other side are our justification for this explanation and these personal details.

The Dawn, (Sydney), 5 November, 1889.

231. Labour Church, Women's Crusade

The confluence of Christianity, socialism and feminism is expressed in this address given by Jean Beadle in Melbourne in 1899. Jean Beadle later established a "Women's Crusade" in Western Australia, as well as labour women's organizations in that state. The emphasis on equal pay at this time differentiated the Women's Social and Political Crusade from other women's organizations. The Reverend Turnbull and his wife were founders of the Labour Church and members of the Crusade, and the occasion of this address was an appeal for assistance to the Reverend Turnbull following his wife's death.

... [The Rev. Turnbull] has endeavoured for some time to establish a "Labour Church". A church based on the true spirit of Christianity where the workers could meet in a spirit of comradeship and ventilate their wrongs and there is no doubt that if the workers would rally around him many of the wrongs would be put right — but strange to say the workers are always divided instead of being one big united body of men and women, all bent on one object — the emancipation and the uplifting of suffering humanity. Unless this great combination of workers is a reality I fear we will continue to suffer the evils of the cruel system and peace and happiness will continue to be a long way off. Mr Turnbull is not only a good comrade in our great work but he and his late wife were the parents of the Women's P. & S. Crusade — the first meeting was held here in this Labour Church. So there are good reasons we think of offering him a helping hand. The other object we had in view was to remind you that the crusade still exists — we are now in the 2nd year and I have been requested to make an urgent appeal and to bring before you the aims and objects of our organisation. 1st we are a crusade of women against Social & Political & Industrial wrongs — you all must admit that a vast number of people are victims of our present system (women and children especially). Women are sweated and underpaid. I for one look forward to the time when men and women shall be equal in every trade and profession, when we can claim *equal pay for equal work*. I cannot understand why a woman is content to accept half the wage paid to a man for doing the same amount of work. If I could press equally as well as Mr Stephen Barker, prescribe for and attend patients *equally as well* as Dr Maloney why should I not be paid the same money — simply because I am a woman. What does it matter whether male or female perform the work (providing it is done well) the same rules of equality should apply to every kind of work male and female are engaged in. I look to the time when women will rise and remove for ever the stigma of *dragging down wages*: special attention given to the weak and helpless members of society — Factories legislation & proper administration under the Act — proper control of charitable institutions — the study of constitutional history and all legislative measures before Parliament — stimulation of democratic thoughts amongst women — All women should take the keenest interest in all things pertaining to the welfare of the present and future generations. It is often argued that her place is at home, that it is unladylike — if not immodest — for a woman to take any part in public affairs. I was told that by a friend of mine. She was so disappointed and expressed great sorrow that I had taken up this kind of work. It certainly was not ladylike. I too felt sorry for I could not resist from saying — well, if it is ladylike to recline on soft cushions with interesting books, attend amusements, wear fine clothes etc all purchased by the sweat and brains, nay out of the very life of sweated labour and to be content with such conditions, then I had no desire to be ladylike. I was most anxious, however, to be a woman full of love for her fellow women — for I believe that whatever sphere a woman may move or work, it is still possible for her to remain *a woman* — like man a woman's place is where duty lies . . . her duties extend beyond the home. A woman that finds no interest beyond that narrow sphere is dull. Our country is our home — every woman should take an interest in the welfare and management of her country and its citizens. Is it not my duty as a wife and mother to raise my voice against wrong conditions that my husband is forced to labour under. Is it not my duty as a mother to see that my children, who later will be compelled to work to live, are not turned into human machines for the purpose of piling up wealth for the Master. Is it not my duty to demand that they work under healthy and moral conditions and that the hours of labour be so arranged that they have time for recreation and study. In my opinion it is a woman's duty to do her very best to make this world an ideal place and its people a happy healthy human family. The Crusade strives for justice to all. Its aim is to labour for a higher moral life for all — believing that in the diffusion of love and justice we are fulfilling the true functions of human beings and serving the highest ideals of Christ and Humanity.

Jean Beadle, President of the Women's Social and Political Crusade, Melbourne, address given at the Labour Church, Melbourne, 1899.

232. Using the Vote

This short-lived attempt to set up an organization to educate women in the use of the vote followed the granting of female franchise in South Australia and involved prominent women such as Catherine Spence and her niece, Lucy Spence Morice. The last meeting of the Woman's League was held in 1897.

Mrs Morice proposed that a Woman's League be formed and read the objects which after some slight alterations were carried and stand . . .

I   To educate ourselves politically and socially that we may be capable of intelligently taking part in the politics of our country with the object of securing as our representatives men of good character and ability.
II To stand together as women apart from all considerations of class and party and to interest ourselves in questions relating to women and children.
III To try by all means in our power to interest other women in this movement and to try to awaken in them a sense of responsibility.

It was agreed that the entrance fee should be 1/- so that it might come within the reach of the poorer class of women and it was decided that members should in the case of the very poor have power to remit that fee.

. . . it was hoped the Working Women's Trade Union women would send a delegate.

Woman's League, Adelaide, Minutes of first meeting, 27 July 1895.

233. Inequalities

The fight for political equality, rather than restricting women's organizations to one issue, made many of them more aware of other, more subtle inequalities.

The inequality of sentences passed for assaults on the person continue to be a puzzle to the female mind.We suppose it is due to our natural inferiority of comprehension of which we sometimes hear; but at the same time we would be glad if some of the superior male intellects would condescend to explain for our benefit how it is possible to reconcile the sentences passed for brutal assaults in the two following cases. A man, aged 30, was charged at the Fitzroy Court last month with unlawfully assaulting his mother, aged 74. Sub-Inspector Oliver "swore that the assault was of a very brutal nature. Accused was a drunken loafer, and owing to his outrageous conduct, the police had been called to the house on many occasions beside the present. Accused had returned home drunk, deliberately knocked his feeble mother down, and then bumped her head against the wall." It was also in evidence that accused loafed on his aged parents, and had only done three weeks' work since last Christmas. Sentence — a fine of 40s. (which most probably his parents paid). In the second case, which also occurred last month, the accused had assaulted brutally another man, and bitten his nose. Sentence — five years' imprisonment, and 40 lashes. Possibly, there is an idea in the minds of some of our superior fellow-beings that women do not feel the effects of kicks and blows and head bumpings so acutely as men, and that, therefore, a brutal assault on a woman, even on a mother, does not matter so much as one on a man. We wait for further enlightenment.

Woman's Sphere, 10 October 1902.

234. The Servant Problem

While women's organizations concerned themselves with the problems of women workers, one such group presented difficulties that women's groups were unable to resolve. Servants were the only group of women workers whose conditions of work were clearly controlled by other women. The *absence* of suitable servants was a continual worry for middle-class women who wanted the free time to engage in public and political affairs. Frequently, when the hardships of servants were discussed, solutions acceptable in other categories of work were rejected because advantages to the servant were accompanied by disadvantages for her employer. And it was often "her employer" who was active in women's organizations. In this letter, "A Domestic Servant" attempted to draw the attention of the *Woman's Sphere* to the *servant's* problem. The *Sphere*'s response to the letter was to print both sides of the debate, showing the strength of some of the things that divided women.

DEAR SPHERE, — I want to enlist your sympathy and help for a class of women who are very much in need of assistance — viz., domestic servants.

Circumstances have recently forced me into their ranks, and while there I have had an opportunity of proving that "things seen are mightier than things heard" — how very real their grievances are. You are doubtless familiar, as we all are, even unto weariness of the mistresses views upon the domestic servant problem, but like every other problem there are more ways than one of viewing it, and I do think the view of the maids may assist its solution. Why domestic service, the most womanly of all occupations, should have sunk into such disrepute because of the conditions of that service is a disgrace to women, and demands reform, and as this is truly "woman's sphere," I appeal for your help.

While I admit there are many causes that make domestic service distasteful — causes that no law can ever remedy, save the divine law of "doing unto others as you would they should do unto you" — there is one cause that the law could and should remedy, and that is, the long and indefinite hours and Sunday work.

Men and women wax eloquent about girls being "sweated" in factories, while in their own homes girls are working twelve, fourteen and often eighteen hours daily, and that, too, for seven days weekly. It is an acknowledged fact that early closing would never have been conceded unless enforced by law, and why the only workers excluded from the benefits of that Act should be domestic workers is an unjustice. It is justice, liberty, that "servants" desire, and have a right to demand, but it will never be enjoyed by them until granted by law. While the law will better domestic service, there is much women themselves can do to raise its status, and as it is ever true, "All that we send into the lives of others, comes back into our own," so shall the whole domestic atmosphere of our country be better and brighter when its servants become so — Yours, etc.,

"Domestic Service" by "A Domestic Servant", *Woman's Sphere*, 10 July 1903.

235. The Age of Consent

Like later women's movement discussions of rape, the concern of the early feminist organizations with age-of-consent legislation was based on the realization that the law institutionalized a double standard of morality that tended to protect "the aggressor" rather than the victim. The *Woman's Voice* was the Journal of the Women's Reform League, founded by Mrs Hilma Molyneaux Parkes of the Women's Liberal League.

. . . The age of consent legislation seems to have been instituted in the interests of sensuality, for the interpretation of the law makes it protective of man rather than of woman. It implies that above the statutory age, her consent is taken for granted, unless her resistance be almost to the death. If the aggressor can prove the voluntary acquiescence of his victim, no matter how or when it was obtained, he need not make any attempt to deny the commission of the crime, for it is only held to be complete when it is committed by force, without the consent and against the wish of the woman. In a court of law it was decided that a girl must resist until exhausted or over-powered, for a jury to find it is against her wish — that resistance and dissent ought to have been continued to the last. No wonder that under this interpretation of the law by the judge and jury, the popular sentiment is that the age of consent means that the State consents to this criminal injustice — consents to legalize the destruction of virtue and protect the man at the expense of the woman. No wonder that earnest souls cry out that the age of consent laws should be blotted from our statute books, and girls and women placed under the protection of the law as long as they live.

"The Protection of Girls and Young Women", *Woman's Voice*, May 1905.

236. Women's Votes

Catherine Spence was the first female political candidate in Australia. Here, in a letter to Alice Henry, she comments on Vida Goldstein's decision to run for the

Senate in Victoria, a state in which women had the vote in federal but not state elections. The other woman mentioned, Elizabeth Webb Nicholls, was both state and national president of the Women's Christian Temperance Union.

. . . I am not at all sure that Vida Goldstein is wise in standing for the Senate. Women do not vote as women for women. If the S.A. women had done so I should have been elected to the Federal Convention — of the 7500 votes I had I feel sure that there were as many men's votes as women's.

When we had the franchise first in S.A. Mrs Nicholls and I were both approached to suggest canditature — No two women were better known all over S.A. than we but we knew that we had no chance of a majority in any district and we also thought it unwise in these early days to suggest our fitness for parliament — My candidature for the Convention was hopeless but it was a big advertisement for Effective Voting in S.A. — and therefore I have never regretted it.

Catherine Spence to Alice Henry, 15 August 1903.

237. A Vote for the Woman

We make a final appeal on the eve of the election to the women of Victoria for unity of action. On this great occasion, which we know is exciting keen attention throughout the English-speaking world, when for the first time in history the women of a nation have an equal voice with the men in selecting the governing body, we would ask all women to drop minor differences, and cast a united vote on the side of progress and reform. Only in this way can the woman vote have the effect which is its due. All women interested in social reform and improvement, in good and pure government, who are on the side of "righteousness," should go to the poll, and should record their votes. And they should endeavour to the best of their ability, to find out who amongst the candidates are honest and straightforward in their advocacy of reform and progress, and then vote for them. They should not be misled by the various organisations touting for certain "tickets," nor by the partisan lists of the daily press. Let them exercise their own judgment and boldly follow it. Let them, above all, sink all personal prejudices, all sectional jealousies, and all little matters that cannot affect the broad policy of a government. They have a chance of showing their disinterestedness, their superiority to pique, and their real devotion to the causes which thinking women have at heart. We fully recognise the fact that to many women this sudden plunge into the sea of politics is disconcerting, and to some even repugnant. But women in their hearts have as a rule a strong sense of duty, and when once they recognise that the gift of the franchise lays an important and momentous duty upon them, they will not shrink from going to the poll and doing that duty. If they would witness the triumph of the cause of women, and feel that they, too, had had a share in that triumph, they should record one of their four votes for the Senate in favour of the woman candidate. If they will do this with some degree of unity, the triumph is assured, and they will hereafter be proud that they had a share in it.

"Close Up the Ranks," *Woman's Sphere*, 5 December 1903.

238. "A Mere Tool"

With the granting of the franchise, the problem facing women's organizations was how to ensure that the best use was made of the vote. In this letter, Catherine Spence, firm advocate of the non-party principle, suggests that a women's organization associated with a political party could still retain enough independence to make it an effective voice for women.

... I was at Miss Scott's on Friday evening and met some nice people. She lent me Percy Roland's New Nation which I like very much. On the previous Saturday afternoon I met Mrs Barbara Baynton [an author] whom I did not like very much and I borrowed Miss Scott's presentation copy of Bush Studies which I liked less... Saturday afternoon I went to Mrs Hilma Parkes [founder of the Women's Liberal League] and met about fifteen progressive women. I think this league is doing more work than Miss Scott and is drawing to it other women's leagues. Working women come to their meetings but the payment of the shilling keeps them from being [illegible] members. There have been 40 Women's League meetings in the year well attended... They have Children's Protection and Courts on their programme also Effective Voting. I think Mrs Parkes is doing great work and although she works for the Liberal Party she will not amalgamate or sink into a mere tool of the men's organisation which is what Miss Scott says women will do if they take sides.

Catherine Spence to Alice Henry, undated letter.

239. Questionnaires for Candidates

The belief that not only were there particular "women's issues" but a shared view of those issues was enshrined in the concept of the questionnaire, in which potential candidates were asked their opinions on a variety of pieces of legislation.

Dear Sir,

In the event of your being returned to Parliament, my League desires to know whether you will undertake, regardless of Party, to support the following Bills:—

1. The Girls' Protection Bill, raising the age of protection to at least 17 years.
2. The Family Maintenance Act, which will not allow men to leave all their money, when they die, away from their widows and children.
3. The Enforcement of the Inebriates' Act.
4. The Guardianship of Children by both parents, on the lines of the English "Custody of Infants Act."
5. The Inspection and Registration of all Registry Offices.

Faithfully yours,
ROSE SCOTT
President.

Jersey Road,
        Paddington.

Questionnaire, Woman's Political Educational League, Sydney.

240. The "Non-Party" Concept

In keeping with the idea that women had a special moral role to play in the community, some groups suggested that women's choice of male candidates should be based on their "moral character". In this way, the Women's Liberal League of New South Wales was able to suggest that it was both "independent" of the political party with which it was associated and opposed to the idea (put forward by the Sphere) that women should vote for "reform".

"Do you mean to sink the woman politician in the philanthropist? Is the power of the vote to be directed exclusively to social reform?"

I answer, emphatically, that woman as a citizen is keenly interested in all that concerns the good government of her country, and that such questions as defence, finance, constitutional government and immigration are as vital to the woman as to the man. Loyalty to the Empire, patriotism, liberalism, are the watchwords of the League I have the honour to represent — and by means of speeches, leaflets, and articles in the *Monthly Record*, these aims have been clearly set before the women electors of N.S.W.

But it is in the selection of candidates that the woman's point of view makes itself felt. Our supreme test is CHARACTER. We must have clean, upright men! We will have them! We refuse to be represented by any others. . .

I desire to state most emphatically that the religion of a candidate and his opinions on such matters as vegetarianism, temperance, Sunday observance, and particular amusements should not influence our choice. If the candidate enjoys a good moral reputation, and is generally regarded as a worthy patriotic citizen, we have no right to enquire further. We do not wish to be represented by drunkards — but a rule to vote only for prohibitionists would have shut out Mr. Gladstone. We do not wish to be represented by blasphemers — but a man's creed is not our affair. If we see the fruit of a clean, upright life, we need not ask to see the root-principle. . .

To sum up—

"The principle of women's associations for women alone" is based on the fact that woman silent for long ages has at last found her voice, which she can only exercise clearly and forcefully by means of associations organised by women.

She is bringing into politics a new element, what the Baroness Gripenberg calls the "mother heart," and her influence upon the Nation will differ from that of the man — just as in the home, the influence of the mother differs from that of the father. It is in order to give the political world the full benefit of this precious new element that we maintain the principle of Woman's Associations — acting *with*, but not *under* the men — Associations free to make their own laws, think their own thoughts, and work out their own political salvation. We claim the right to exercise our own judgement, both in the choice of candidates, the selection by ballot, and on the trend of legislative action. Although firmly pledged to Liberal principle, we are not the blind supporters of any body of men.

The Principle of Women's Associations for Women Alone, paper read before the Commonwealth Conference, held in Brisbane in 1909, by Laura Bogue Luffman of the Women's Liberal League of New South Wales.

241. An Appeal to Queensland Women

After the granting of the vote to women in Queensland, the Queensland Women's Electoral League was formed. In its early hand-outs, it stressed the right of women to vote without coercion from any party and advised them to vote for "men of honour" who would be "independent of dictation from any party". It also asked women to support a set of proposals, none of which particularly related to women. Later electoral advice continued to appeal to women as a group with shared interests, but as this broadsheet shows, the pretence of a non-party position was dropped.

AN OPEN LETTER
TO EVERY
WOMAN IN QUEENSLAND.

DEAR MADAM,

On **WEDNESDAY, APRIL 13th,** it will be your right and your duty to once more record your vote for the Candidates who will represent you in the Federal Parliament — for the Lower House, **ONE REPRESENTATIVE** (for your Division) for three years; and for the Upper House, **THREE SENATORS** (for the whole of Queensland) for six years.

On the Candidates you help to return depends the good government, or otherwise, of Australia, and, therefore, that of **QUEENSLAND.**

In 1903 — the first Federal Election at which the Queensland women voted — 44,569 women electors voted. In 1906, 44,972 women electors voted.

There are now **115,944 WOMEN** entitled to vote **ON APRIL 13th.**

You are counted among that number, and in **THE HANDS OF WOMEN** lies the tremendous power of making Queensland either a **PROGRESSIVE LIBERAL STATE,** or a retrogressive Socialist one.

Which do you prefer?

If the former, then let nothing prevent you voting for the **LIBERAL POLICY.**

> Which is **OPPOSED** to the **FURTHER ENCROACHMENT** of **SOCIALISM.**
>
> Which will **SECURE THE FINANCIAL POSITION** of **THE STATES.**
>
> Which will **PREVENT UNIFICATION.**
>
> Which, if the Socialists had their way, would **WORK IRREPARABLE INJURY** to Queensland — a magnificent State only in the early stages of development.

Help Queensland by voting early on April 13th, and by voting for the **LIBERAL POLICY.**

> **BECAUSE** your homes are in Queensland.
>
> **BECAUSE,** therefore, all you and your children's real interests are there.
>
> **BECAUSE** on you and all the women of Queensland lies the responsibility of raising to a higher level the politics of your country.

Remember the **FINANCIAL AGREEMENT** — the blue ballot paper — **AND PUT A CROSS** before the word **YES** when voting on it. That is all that is required.

> **BECAUSE** the Financial Agreement will **SECURE FINANCIAL INDEPENDENCE TO QUEENSLAND** and the other States.

When the figures of the Federal Election of **APRIL 13th,** 1910, are out, let it be said that, to **THE WOMEN OF QUEENSLAND** belongs the credit of securing such a majority against Socialism as will leave the Federal Government in no doubt as to which policy the people of this State wish to see carried out.

We need the vote of every woman to bring this about, and we are fully confident that **YOU WILL DO YOUR PART,** and then help your friend to do hers.

QUEENSLAND WOMEN'S ELECTORAL LEAGUE,

27 KENT'S BUILDINGS,

ADELAIDE STREET, BRISBANE.

Election handout, Queensland Women's Electoral League, Brisbane, 1910.

242. "£iberal Organizer"

The early realization of the importance of attracting "the woman's vote" is shown in the appointment of a woman's organizer by the newly formed Liberal Party. In this letter to the Western Australian press, Mamie Swanton, who was active in the feminist and labour movements and an organizer among the tailoresses, expresses the opinion of women from the labour movement and her scorn at "the want of Australian knowledge displayed by the first lady organiser of the Liberal Party in her first attempt to educate the women of all classes". Conservative political groups were more confident than labour groups that they could appeal to women of all classes on specifically "women's" issues.

Sir, —

Being of a humorous turn of mind with a philosophical temperament, delightful amusement is afforded me in the perusal of the platform of the golden dollar efforts of the new Liberal party. On the men's side we find them catering "to ensure to everyone the peaceful enjoyment of the fruits of their labour." On the women's side Miss Jessie Ackerman, an American lady, who we are told is not even a British subject, engaged as organiser to educate Australian women of all classes, to teach us how to use our Australian vote on all Australian political subjects for Australian Parliaments. In her first lesson she tells us we have nothing to do with the men. The average Australian woman will object to that, for we have been their companions from the cradle, and that is why our men have gracefully laid the franchise at our feet, after a very slight request from us for it. . . This lady organiser further remarks that man still demands the woman's moral instinct should be higher than his own. To that I unhesitatingly give an unqualified denial on behalf of our Australian men, who have been educated up to a higher moral standard, and who desire their women to help them to live up to all that is best and truest in man.

Mamie Swanton, Press Book, clipping from unidentified newspaper (n.d.).

243. "Greater than Party"

In its first issue, the *Woman Voter* attempted to sort out the confusions between non-party and non-political by suggesting that for non-party organizations, some political differences could be tolerated because they did not interfere with a set of shared beliefs that cut across party. The paper itself became a casualty of that philosophy and its demise in 1919 was the result of the realization that women's politics could not be isolated from politics in general.

As the Women's Political Association is non-party we get no assistance from the party organs, the "Age" and the "Argus". They are always courteous to us, but naturally we cannot expect them to blow our trumpet as they blow the trumpets of the party organizations they respectively support. In order, therefore, that the general public may be able to form a fairly accurate idea of the scope of the Association's work we proposed to issue the *Woman Voter* as a monthly leaflet, which will give some details of our activities.

At the outset we desire to remove a false impression as to our non-party policy. By adopting such a policy it is not to be supposed that we are a body of gelatinous creatures, who have no definite political views. We have all got very decided views as to the merits of the various political parties — some of us are protectionists, some are free traders, some are single taxers, some are labourites, some are socialists, some are anti-socialists, but we differ from those organized on party lines in one important particular. We believe that questions affecting individual honour, private and public integrity and principle, the stability of the home, the welfare of children, the present salvation of the criminal and the depraved, the moral, social and economic injustice imposed on women — we believe that all these questions are greater than party, and that in 9 cases out of 10 they are sacrificed to party interests.

Woman Voter, August 1909.

244. "Housekeeping the State"

The second attempt to form a non-party association of women in South Australia was more successful that the first, which followed closely on the granting of the vote. The organization put on their platform the method of proportional representation, which had for so long been advocated by Catherine Spence and which was particularly appropriate to the anti-party approach to parliamentary representation supported by the women's group. The association was affiliated with the Victorian Women's Political Association and was founded after a visit by Vida Goldstein to Adelaide.

The 1st meeting was held in Bricknell's Rooms on Mondary evening July 19th. Miss Spence took the chair, and there were between 50 and 60 women present.

The Victorian Constitution was read and discussed. It was decided to adopt the Victorian constitution with a few modifications. Two planks were added to the platform, viz. The Hare-Spence System of Voting, and Prevention of Cruelty to Animals. The power to form sub-committees was given to the Council, and it was decided to hold the meetings on the 3rd Wednesday of every month. Miss Spence said that uniformity of marriage and divorce laws in all the states was most important, and pointed out the trouble caused in America through divergence in these laws. The vote in S.A. was not fully prized, because won too easily, and legislation in S.A. prior to women having the vote had been on the whole favourable to women. But the least the women here could do would be to send encouragement to those women struggling for the vote in England and America. She emphasised the need for a non-party association, for politics were degraded by being made the arena for party fights, when politics should mean the right government of the state. Women were much criticised when they essayed to enter the field of politics, but women may well take their share in housekeeping the state, without neglecting their own houses. The whole trend of society now is towards service, in the last century people spoke of rights, this century of duties. We should aim at raising the status of the domestic servant, and realise the importance of manual labour; for there is now too much charity in the world and too little justice.

Women's (Non-Party) Political Association of South Australia, Adelaide, Minutes of first meeting, 19 July 1909.

245. Women's Issues

The constitution of the Women's (Non-Party) Political Association of South Australia, which later became the League of Women Voters, in its platform, gives a summary of those issues that were thought to be of specific relevance to women.

II — OBJECTS.
The objects of the Association shall be —
  1. The protection of the interests of women, children and the home.
  2. The education of public opinion as to the value of non-party political action.
  3. The study and support of kindred movements throughout the world.

III — PLATFORM.
    To attain these objects the following shall be the platform of the Association, power being reserved to add such other planks as may from time to time seem desirable:—
  1. The removal of all existing inequalities in the law as between men and women.
  2. Uniformity of laws throughout the Commonwealth in regard to marriage, divorce, and parental rights over children.
  3. The opening of all offices and employments to men and women equally and payments for work done independent of sex.
  4. Election of women as —
    (a) Members of Parliament
    (b) Members of municipal and district councils.
  5. Appointment of women as —
    (a) Jurors
    (b) Police matrons
    (c) Sanitary inspectors
    (d) Truant officers
    (e) Inspectors of all public institutions.
  6. Increased numbers of women as —
    (a) Police.

   (b) Justices of the peace.
   (c) Inspectors of state schools.
   (d) Members of public boards.
  7. An equal moral standard of sex morality, and protection of young people against the vicious and depraved.
  8. Furtherance of child welfare.
  9. Provision of pure food and milk supply.
10. Education of public opinion on hygiene and food values.
11. Town planning and better housing.
12. Reform of the liquor traffic.
13. Penal reform.
14. Universal woman suffrage.
15. Proportional representation.
16. International peace and arbitration.

Women's (Non-Party) Political Association of South Australia, Adelaide, Constitution, as amended and adopted, 1919.

246. Equal Pay

Decisions made in the Arbitration Court that were based on assumptions about male and female responsibilities within the family led to the continuation of differentials between male and female wage rates and were condemned by feminist organizations in the period just prior to the First World War.

. . . The Judge saw clearly that, where a man and a woman did exactly the same work, the pay should be equal, but he failed to see the full significance of our demand when he inferred that a blacksmith and a nurse girl were not entitled to the same minimum wage, that women who had others dependent on them were the exception, and that there was a difference in the expenses of men and women for dress. The point is not whether a nurse girl's work is equal to a blacksmith's work (some would think it is of infinitely greater value to the community), but that a woman blacksmith who does the same work as a man blacksmith should get the same pay. It is a grave error to suppose that women wage earners are not responsible for the support of home and dependents. Given an equal number of men and women in a given trade it will be found that as a rule women have heavier responsibilities to their families than men have. Unmarried women contribute a far greater proportion to the support of the home than do unmarried men. Married women contribute all their earnings to the home while married men retain often a considerable share of their earnings for their exclusive use, for extras such as beer, tobacco, sport etc. In the matter of dress women workers do not usually spend as much as men, because the dress of men is made a first charge on their earnings; with women it is the last charge, and they scrimp and save making their own clothes, working late into the night, when men are free to take recreation or indulge in social intercourse in a more congenial atmosphere than a cramped home provides.

    This was the first occasion that the question of women's work had arisen in the Arbitration Court, and Mr. Justice Higgins said frankly that his ideas were open to revision. We know that his whole desire is for justice between employer and employee, between men and women. He has always been a good friend to women, and, when the position of women as industrial workers has been considered in all its bearings by the Court, we are sure that Mr. Justice Higgins will take a definite stand for a fundamental principle of justice without any of the bias of sex usually shown in industrial matters.

"Equal Pay for Equal Work", *Woman Voter*, 11 July 1912.

247. A "Special Representative"

The belief that one woman could represent in parliament the common interests of women is suggested in this open letter from one female candidate.

Dear Friends —

If I am returned as member for Kooyong in the House of Representatives, I shall consider myself not only the representative of the electors of Kooyong, but the special representative of the women of Australia. Therefore I ask you to pledge all candidates on the following questions, which are on my programme.

1. Federal Marriage and Divorce Law equal for men and women.
2. Raising the age of marriage which is now 14 for boys and 12 for girls.
3. Equal opportunities for men and women in the Federal Public Service.
4. Justice for semi-official postmistresses.
5. Retention of a woman's nationality on marriage with a foreigner.
6. Women inspectors under Maternity Allowance Act.
7. Protection of deserted wives and children.
8. Protection of women and girls against White Slave Traffic.
   Unity is strength.
                              Yours sincerely,

Vida Goldstein, President of the Women's Political Association, Melbourne, "Message to the Women of Australia", *Woman Voter*, 21 July 1914.

248. The Peace Movement

From the time of the South African war, leading feminists had also been prominent in the peace movement. (Rose Scott, in fact, was president of the New South Wales branch of the Peace Society.) With the outbreak of war in 1914, any proclamation of pacifism became a highly political statement. To many feminists of this period, pacifism was merely the logical extension of the application of morality to politics, and as such compatible with their non-party espousal of women's issues. In contrast, during the Second World War, women's non-party organizations defined women's issues less widely and did not see conscription as an issue to be debated.

The blank spaces in last week's issue of the *Woman Voter* show that our paper has come under the ban of the Military Censor. We had been informed by letter that the two previous issues contained matter that should not have been published. As we have only made a plea for the application of the teaching of Christianity to international disputes, and were not told what we might publish about war, we put a specific question to the Censor. In last week's issue, we published the correspondence, a brief appeal to mothers, and a quotation containing a statement by Ruskin as to the responsibility of women for war.

On 9th inst. an armed guard, with fixed bayonets, a commanding officer, a detective, and police, took charge of the establishment of our printers, Messrs. Fraser and Jenkinson, 343 Queen Street, seized the first prints of the *Woman Voter* and the correspondence etc. referred to above was destroyed.

We are told that we may publish anything that will "stimulate military enthusiasm" which is explained by the "Military Journal" as developing a "desire to kill." We shall continue to publish articles that plead for love instead of hatred, for arbitration instead of bloodshed, and for the observance of the commandment, "Thou shalt not kill".

Our civil liberty and the freedom of the press are in jeopardy, and we are prepared to fight for both. We ask you to stand by us. The new government will take office almost immediately, and we must appeal to them to safeguard the rights of the people. We shall ask them to receive a deputation, and we urge you to accompany us when we interview the Prime Minister and the Minister of Defence.

Much more, however, is necessary. The *Woman Voter* is the only paper that has even attempted to make a fight for civil liberty, and we urge you to help us in that fight. Take extra copies of this week's issue, distribute the paper widely, get new subscribers.

We are fighting for Civil Liberty and against Military Depotism in Australia. We may have to suffer in many ways and we appeal for moral and financial support, so that the Woman Movement may grow stronger because it has taken this stand for righteousness.

Vida Goldstein Editor
Cecilia John Business Manager

Woman Voter, 16 September 1914.

249. "A House Divided Against Itself"

Differences between women's groups over women's issues exposed those organizations to the criticism that such "squabbling" would divide the "women's vote" and render ineffective their attempts to get women into parliament. This demand for consensus (seldom extended to the male electorate) echoed ideas put forward by feminists. The following two documents reveal the basis of disagreement.

Western Australia was the first State of the Commonwealth in which a woman succeeded in making her way into Parliament, and is still the only State in which a member of the fair sex graces the halls of the legislature. Mrs Cowan's success has, there is reason for saying, fired the ambition of quite a bevy of her sisters to emulate her hardihood. It is rumoured that at least half a dozen women will be found on the hustings at the general election, which, in the ordinary course of events, will be held in March or April next. That Mrs Cowan, if she herself is re-elected, will be appreciably reinforced as a consequence is, however, highly improbable, not because of any strongly-rooted objection in the constituencies to female representation, but because the women form a house divided against itself. The National Council of Women and the Women's Service Guild will furnish candidates enough, but they are more likely to neutralise each other than to make common cause. The leading protagonists representing these organisations — now frankly rival organisations — are Mrs Cowan, M.L.A., and Mrs Rischbieth, who, besides being the soul of the Women's Service Guild, is President of the Australian Federation of Women's Societies, which is linked up with the International Women's Suffrage Alliance, whose congress has lately been sitting in Rome and in which seven Australian delegates, including Mrs Rischbieth, participated. The breach between the two organisations, which had its origins in strongly divergent views over the compulsory registration clauses in the Health Act having to do with venereal disease, has grown deeper and wider since, until today the emnity of the two bodies is open and unashamed. Anything and everything done in one camp is anathema in the other. To the detached observer, who realises the good work to be done by the National Council and by the Guild, each in its own sphere, the present vendetta is deplored, but in those quarters where women's entry into the political arena finds no favours, it is a matter for either scoffing or rejoicing. Certainly, unless peace be proclaimed before the next election, the chances of more women winning seats in the Legislature are extremely remote. Indeed, it will surprise very few, supposing the feud to be continued, if even Mrs Cowan herself is excluded. This would be matter for regret, since such influence as she has been able to exercise in the Assembly has, generally, been wholesome and stimulating.

Australasian, 16 June 1923.

250. In Every Other Respect Equal

Edith Cowan, at the time President of the National Council of Women, was more concerned with the heath provisions of the Western Australian Health Amendment Act, which was designed to control the spread of venereal disease, than with the civil liberties of the women involved. In contrast, the Women's Service Guild maintained that these provisions, especially the informant's clause, discriminated against women. Venereal disease legislation continued to raise problems for women's organizations.

We women rightly object to such drastic power being given to one man, and many of us realise that to give women a protective and beneficient voice on a mixed board would be the most progressive remedy yet suggested, for the Act is, in every other respect but that, equal between men and women.

Edith Cowan, Letter to the Editor, *Western Woman*, March 1918.

As a safeguard against malicious actions in the cases where compulsory action is contemplated against women, it is recommended that the Commissioner shall seek and act upon the advice of a board, to be composed of 2 women, the Commissioner himself and one man — such committee to be appointed by the Governor-in-Council.
But this safeguard against any likely abuse of power on the part of the Commissioner does not in the slightest particular alter the principle underlying the proposed Bill, for the Commissioner and the Committee are both contemplating taking action on anonymous information received from sources that are under no necessity of producing proof for making any such statement.
Women and mothers awake! Let us realise in time that to frame an Act on such

a bad foundation can bear no good fruit, and would inevitably lead to grave injustice and indignities.

Statement from the Women's Service Guild, ibid.

251. Achievements of the Vote

Nellie Martel's pamphlet, *The Women's Vote in Australia*, produced by the suffragettes in England, attempted to show what women in Australia had achieved since winning the franchise. This article from *The Dawn* makes similar claims by listing legislative reforms gained in Western Australia after women had gained the vote.

SOCIAL LEGISLATION IN W.A.

Acts Passed since Granting of Women's Franchise under Electoral Act, 1899

Elementary Education Act, 1899, No. 3. — Deals with school fees, attendance at school, employment of children, census, etc.

Slander of Women Act, 1900, No. 36. — Words imputing unchastity or adultery to be actionable without special damage.

Indecent Publications Act, 1902, No. 14. — An Act to suppress indecent and obscene publications. Works of recognised literary merit and bona fide medical treatises are excepted.

Police Act Amendment Act, 1902, No. 31 (Sunday Entertainments) — Provides for statutory authority in writing from Colonial Secretary to keep, open, or use premises for public entertainment or amusement on any Sunday, or during any part of any Sunday, in respect of which any charge is made for admission.

Prostitution. — Summary proceedings against persons connected with prostitution.

Lunacy Act, 1903, No. 15. — Relates to habitual drunkards, and empowers the Court to make an order for compulsory detention in any hospital for the insane (but in a ward or division in which lunatics are not detained), or in a licensed house, for a period not exceeding twelve months. (Part IV.)

State Children Act, 1907, No. 31. — A consolidating measure to make better provision for the protection, control, maintenance and reformation of neglected and destitute children. It follows the lines of legislation in the other States in making provision for the constitution of a State Children's Department, special courts for the trial of offences committed by children, and the licensing of children engaged in street trading. The Amending Act of 1921, No. 14, provides penalty for publishing conviction.

Legitimation Act, 1909, No. 44. — Provides for Legitimation of illegitimate children on registration after marriage of parents.

Health Act, 1911. — Deals with the following:— Sanitary Provisions, Sewers and Drains, Scavenging, Cleansing etc., Public Buildings, Nuisances and Offensive Trades, Food Inspection Milk and Dairy Produce, Sale of Food and Drugs, Infectious Diseases, notification of disease, Hospitals, Protection of Life, Midwives.

Interstate Destitute Persons Relief Act, 1912, No. 30. — Provides for Summons for maintenance against person in another State. Reciprocity is established by proclamation. Enforcing order for maintenance made in another State.

Parliament (Qualification of Women), 1920, No. 7. — Provides that a woman shall not be disqualified by sex or marriage for being elected to or sitting and voting as a member of the Legislative Council or the Legislative Assembly.

Guardianship of Infants Act, 1920, No. 15. — This Act relates to the guardianship and custory of infants, and to assure to the widow and widower and family of a testator an adequate maintenance from the estate of such testator.

Factories and Shops Act, 1920, No. 44. Relates to registrations of factories.

Restrictions regarding persons not of full age. Health, sanitation and safety. Special provision for certain trades. The closing of shops. Employment of assistants in shops. Working hours for women and boys.

Reciprocal Enforcement of Maintenance Orders Act, 1921, No. 27. — This Act facilitates the enforcement in Western Australia of Maintenance Orders made in other parts of His Majesty's Dominions and Protectorates and vice versa.

Nurses Registration Act, 1922, No. 7. Provides that persons attaining the age of twenty-one years holding a certificate of not less than three years' training as a nurse in a hospital or training establishment, is entitled to registration.

Married Women's Protection Act, 1922, No. 28. — This Act provides that any married woman whose husband shall have been guilty of cruelty to her or any of her children, adultery, desertion or wilful neglect to provide reasonable maintenance for her or any of her children, may apply for summary protection.

Women's Legal Status Act, 1923, No. 56. — Relates to removal of disqualification on grounds of sex. Any person may be appointed to or hold any civil or judicial office or post and may be admitted and entitled to practise as a practitioner within the meaning of that term in the Legal Practitioners Act, 1893.

The Dawn (Perth), 14 December 1925.

252. Aboriginal Women

The continued concern of women's groups such as the Women's Service Guilds with the conditions of Aboriginal women in Western Australia is shown by demands such as those reproduced below. In the period after 1908, the issue was frequently kept before the public only because of the actions of women's organizations.

Will you affirm the right of the aboriginal woman to the sanctity of her person, and ask for definite reforms for her protection — two of these reforms should be the appointment of married protectors of high character and qualifications and of a doctor as a travelling protector.

Dorothea Cass, State Secretary, Women's Service Guilds, letter to the Honorary Secretary, Country Women's Association, Western Australia, 1932.

253. "Give Women a Chance"

This election handout argues that the woman candidate should be voted for solely because she is a woman.

SOMETHING YOU DON'T KNOW

1. Up to date a Parliament of 90 men have ruled New South Wales without the interference or help of women. Are you satisfied with the way they have done it?
2. Men and women together make up the human race. Justice will prevail when they rule together. Take this opportunity of electing a woman to Parliament.
3. The best conditions in the *home* are produced by the *joint control* of the *mother* and *father*. The best conditions in the *State* will be produced by the *joint control* of *men* and *women*.
4. *Men's* training tends to direct their interest to business (which covers trade, commerce, industry, work, wages, profits). *Women's* training tends to direct their interest to *Social Welfare* (which covers health, food, housing, care of children, care of sick, care of poor, preservation of family and home life). *To take care of the Social Welfare, women must be in Parliament.*
5. The evils of to-day are greed, selfishness, love of money, love of power, dishonesty, bribery. They must be replaced by justice, honesty, sympathy and understanding of the needs of all.
6. Women have greater sympathy and understanding.
    Women are not easily tempted to bribes.
    Women are free from the domination of party or business interests.
    Women are practical and economical.
    Women's domestic training has taught them to live within their means.
7. Women have made a success of every new opportunity. Give them the opportunity to help govern.
8. Women believe that most of the crime and disease and suffering are the results of the bad conditions under which many people live. Give women a chance to alter these conditions.
9. A higher moral standard has always been expected of women. Let them help you now.

These are nine unanswerable reasons why you should vote I for your woman candidate.

Please remember these most important points.
IT DEPENDS ON YOU WHAT HAPPENS ON THE 11th JUNE.

YOU MUST VOTE FOR ALL THE CANDIDATES OR YOUR VOTE WILL BE INFORMAL. BUT
VOTE I FOR THE WOMAN.

Voting handout, N.S.W. state elections, (?)1932.

254. The Role of Women

The *Pioneers*, the organ of the Australian Women's Guild of Empire, was founded and edited by Adela Pankhurst Walsh. This leading article, entitled "Our Demand", reveals the way that a feminist belief in the special moral role of women could be extended to the point where women were seen as defenders of the *status quo*.

In all Warfare, Industrial and International, women are the chief sufferers. They know the price of human life and their chief business is to care for it. If women controlled the destiny of the Nations, there would be No More War. If women were given the right to vote in the Trade Unions, there would be No More Strikes. On the coal fields today the homes of women and the health, happiness, and future of children are at stake. We demand that the wives of miners shall be given the right to vote in a Secret Ballot as to whether the stoppage shall continue.

Adela Pankhurst Walsh, "Our Demand", *Pioneers*, December 1929.

255. Class Struggle

The Militant Women's Group of the Communist Party of Australia appealed to working-class women to "take part in the struggles of their class".

From Domestic Slavery to Communism

An Appeal to Australian Working-class Women to Take Part in the Struggles of Their Class

This pamphlet is addressed to women of the Australian working-class whose lives are spent in the ceaseless nerve-wracking routine of factory life where they eke out a precarious existence on wages barely sufficient to provide the simplest necessities of life, while their employers amass huge fortunes and spend their useless lives in idleness and luxury.

Not only to the industrial women workers do we appeal, but to those whose lives are spent in the dull monotony of domestic duties in the crowded and insanitary dwellings of the slums; to those wives of workers who carry out their toil in houses devoid of the wonderful labor-saving appliances which labor and science have devised; where an insufficient income and the fear of unemployment are ever-present — to these women workers we send out the message that their lot is a striking indictment of the present system of capitalism.

Drastic and fundamental changes are necessary both to improve present conditions and to achieve a different basis of society, and they can only be obtained by both sections of the workers — men and women — agitating and organising for a saner and more scientific form of society in which ownership and control of the means of production will be in the hands of the world's workers and wherein the economic dependence of one human being upon another will be impossible.

Militant Women's Group, *Women's Path to Freedom* (1927).

256. "A Real Solidarity"

Adela Pankhurst Walsh's right-wing women's organization, the Women's Guild of Empire, maintained that the Guild was both non-party in its orientation and anti-communist in its politics.

Our Guild exists to bring about among women a deeper realization of the value of their British citizenship and to awaken them to their responsibilities as members of the community for the well being of the whole.

Though we are a non-party organization, we are opposed both to Communism and class government, recognizing that equal rights for all people must be the foundation of a free nation. As there is a real solidarity of interest between capitalists, employers and employees, we wish to bring about co-operation between these three elements.

Empire Gazette, December 1930.

257. The Results of Class War

The *Empire Gazette*, edited by Adela Pankhurst Walsh, maintained an anti-communist stance and encouraged women to oppose strikes. Supported by a number of large businesses, the paper frequently printed photographs of women who worked in these factories.

GUILD OF EMPIRE.

The EMPIRE GAZETTE

NON-SECTARIAN	INDUSTRIAL PEACE	NON-PARTY

No. 41.—Issued Monthly.   OCTOBER 30, 1933. Registered at the G.P.O., Sydney, for transmission by post as a newspaper. Price 1d.

Russian Sovietised Women only work. They are not encouraged to cultivate the womenly graces. Only the "High Up" Communist Women like Mesdames Litvinoff and Stalin are "dressy." Here are some of Australia's working girls at play. It is co-operation in industry which gives these lovely girls their pretty frockings. Class warfare would reduce them to rags.

DEBUTANTES AT "LUSTRE" HOCKEY BALL.

Back Row. Mr. J. M. Forsythe (Director), Miss Jean Charlesworth, Miss Dot Appleby, Miss Ivy Mitchell, Miss Lily Cranny, Miss Mollie Clark, Miss Thelma Jones, Miss Ruby Allen, Miss Connie Larson, Mr. W. G. Forsythe (Director).
Front Row. Miss Lorna Cox, Miss Joyce Cole, Miss Percival, Dr. Marie Hamilton (President Hockey Assoc.), Mrs. F. J. Davey (Secretary Hockey Assoc.), Miss Beryl Russell, Miss Marjorie Brown, Miss Pamela Tucker.

258. Unemployed Workers' Wives

The organization of workers' wives, not to oppose strikes but to improve the conditions of the unemployed and their dependents, is shown in this excerpt from the minutes of an Adelaide relief organization during the Depression.

The Chairman reported that the representatives of the Peterhead Unemployed Workers' Wives Committee had called on him on the previous day, and had brought under notice the following matters:—

1. They stated that the Waterside Workers Mothers' Social Club, the Rosewater Ladies' Social Club, and the Port Adelaide Girls' Social Club were openly soliciting money and goods from shops and houses in any district.

The council resolved that the Commissioner of Police be requested to have enquiries made as to the accuracy of this statement and to see what action can be taken to prevent infringement of the Collection for Unemployment Act.

2. Difficulty in obtaining rail orders to enable them to attend Adelaide Hospital.

Mr Macgowan said he was making enquiries in this matter and would report to Council later.

3. More and better nutritious food for Mothers.

The Chairman had informed them that this was receiving attention in connection with a request made by a previous Deputation.

4. Increased children's rations during school holidays.

They had been informed that this could not be recommended.

5. They complained that Mr Evans, land agent, Semaphore, insisted on his tenants performing work when they were not able to pay rent. In one case a man earned £9 and was given 10/- in cash, the balance being credited against his rent.

The council resolved that the Minister be asked what action he desired to be taken in this matter.

6. They asked that a special grant be made to them similar to last year to enable them to purchase material, etc. as they found it almost impossible to collect funds now.

Deferred until reply is received from the Minister regarding special amount of £1,000 to be expended by the Council in special cases.

Unemployed Relief Council, Adelaide, Minutes of meeting held 25 May 1932.

259. Politicization

In this article in the Working Woman, *the politicization of working-class women during the Depression is attributed to the propaganda of the Australian Communist Party.*

WOMEN PARTICIPATE IN PT. ADELAIDE STRUGGLE
REPRESENTED ON STRIKE COMMITTEE
POLITICAL AWAKENING

PORT ADELAIDE, 6th September, — In the tremendous struggle of the workers of Port Adelaide against the maintenance of the scabs on the waterfront and against the police terror, the working women have played an unprecedented role.

Back in 1928, when the ship-owners made their drive to smash the waterside workers, the women also participated in demonstrations. But today the movement of the women is marked by greater political understanding and a greater estimation of their importance by the men workers.

One of the most powerful factors in arousing the Port women of the situation has been the propaganda of the Communist Party. The Party speakers have drawn attention to the terrible plight of woman under capitalism. They have shown the drab nature of woman's lot — shut in by the four walls of some suburban slum dwelling. The widespread unemployment among women has been explained as one of the main factors in driving so many girls to prostitution. The Party has also shown that women have been politically segregated by the politicians and Trade Union bureaucrats.

Against women's sordid life under capitalism — chained to the pots and pans; sweated in the factories — the Communist Party points out the emancipation of women in the Soviet Union. The revolutionizing of women's life under workers' rule has been dealt with at length by the Party lecturers.

SIDE BY SIDE WITH THE MEN

In the organization of the unemployed the Communist Party has from the beginning raised the importance of having women upon the Unemployed Committee.

Today the Port women have their own Unemployed Committee. About 150 women attend the meetings. It is in clear-cut opposition to the reactionary Women's Committee of Mrs Jonas, wife of a "Labour" politician, and to all "bumming institutions". Most of the women comrades are enthusiastic about the "Working Woman".

IN THE STRIKE

As soon as the Central Rank and File Strike Council was formed to conduct the general strike at Port Adelaide, the call was made for women to sit on the Council with the men. Comrades Mullin and Davies were the two delegates appointed by the militant women.

It may be pointed out that a great many of the women are free from the dope which has been drummed into the men by the "Labor" parliamentary tricksters. Nor are they so easily hoodwinked by the treacherous Trade Union officials.

PICKETING

After one of the meetings of the Women's Unemployed Committee, over a hundred women pursued a scab, and only the police saved him from disaster.

Many other instances could be listed of attacks upon the scabs by women pickets.

The capitalist press versions of the behaviour of the women pickets are worded for the purpose of prejudicing opinion against women getting into the fight. In one case, a woman picket was described as "jumping on the back" of a scab, "bearing him to the ground, scratching and screaming."

CLASS BIAS AGAINST CHILDREN

In some of the worker's demonstrations a number of working-class children have marched.

This did not suit one of the teachers at the Port Adelaide Central School, and she forced some of the children to "stop in" and write 500 words each for using the term "scab", etc.

In order to put this vindictive bosses's woman in her place, several hundred women comrades marched towards the school in protest, but were stopped by [Labor Premier] Lionel Hill's police thugs. However, a deputation was allowed to see the Headmaster and we think there will be less of this class bias against the children in the future.

Towards Communism

The Port women were pleased to get fraternal greetings from Communist women in Sydney and Melbourne.

At the present time the fight is on. Whatever the outcome, there will be no turning back in the march of the Port women towards emancipation. One thing in particular we have learned in this strike, and that is the Social-Fascist nature of the "Labor" Government. Our women comrades who have been trampled on by the troopers' horses, hit by batons, will never forget the scabbiness of Hill & Co.

> Long live the Rank and File control!
> Long live the Soviet Republic!
> Against Capitalism and its "Labor" lackeys.

Forward to Communism and the emancipation of the working class, which alone can bring about the emancipation of working women.

Working Woman, 15 September 1930.

260. Police

Communist Party descriptions of events at Port Adelaide in this period emphasize the role of the police. Less obvious police activities included reporting on the behaviour of organizations of the unemployed (as in this case) and "keeping an eye" on the way workers on relief spent their money. The minutes of the Unemployment Relief Council contain references to both kinds of reporting.

1. That the conduct of the Port Adelaide Unemployed Workers' Wives Committee is at times very unruly and both Police Constables and Women Police have been called.
2. It is not an unusual thing for some of the members to have a fight.
3. A disturbance took place about a week ago between Mrs Mullins (President) and Mrs Renton, and the language of Mrs Mullins was reported to be disgusting.
4. They have been refused the use of the Oddfellows Hall owing to the disturbances.
5. It is common knowledge that some of the Committee have been helping themselves very freely to the goods given them for distribution, leaving only a small quantity for the wives of the unemployed.
6. Three of the Members of the Committee are believed to have a good many communistic ideas.
7. In the opinion of the Police Officer, the Committee were not fit and proper

persons to have the handling of moneys and goods contributed by the Unemployment Relief Council or any other source.

Police report transcribed in Minutes of the Unemployed Relief Council, Adelaide, 27 November 1931.

261. Undone

Jean Devanny's novel *Sugar Heaven* breaks new ground in political fiction in Australia, in its exploration of the role of women. The novel was based on the North Queensland cane-cutters' strike of 1935 and Devanny dedicated a later edition to the wives of the strikers. In this excerpt, Dulcie has difficulty in getting her husband to take her political ideas seriously. In the second excerpt, the women have organized themselves.

But now that her time had come Dulcie's courage almost failed her. "Hefty. I—I want to tell you something."

"Hey?" He looked at her with mild inquiry which changed into concern. "What's up?"

"There's——. Something has happened to me."

"Something's happened to you! Begod! You've fallen in!" Consternation mingled with husbandly love. "That's stiff luck." He made to put his arms around her but she pushed him back with shrill laughter.

"No, no! Not that!" She ceased laughing. "Yes, you would think that, wouldn't you? That's the only thing you *would* think could happen to a woman. But it's not what's happened to me!" Her tone grew acrimonious. Her fear left her.

Hefty ran a hand over his hair and sat on the table beside her. "What has happened to you, then? Why all the mystery?"

"What's happened to me is that I want to do something——. About this strike——. About the women's part in it."

"God's truth!" He thrust his hands into his pockets and stared. Dulcie flushed deeply now and trembled. He was not taking it as she had expected. "What do you want to do?" Blankly.

"I dont know!" She almost shouted it at him. "I dont know what to do! You know that! All you men, who can talk and talk and — and do nothing but lose strikes!" Her voice broke on the inevitable note of revolutionary hysteria. More than anything else in the world she wanted to be calm. Instinct warned her that Hefty would judge her constructive capacities by her bearing now, and tears of sheer fury that he should be such a fool scalded her cheeks. She knew she was undone by the flux of revolution; by the very shame of her woman's dependence on him; by her need to propitiate and solicit, by the interweaving of her most elementary rights with his will.

Hefty became prodigiously uncomfortable. He cleared his throat. "Yer know—— You're letting the strike run away with you, Kid. That's the trouble with women: no balance. Swing from one extreme to the other. You dont have to worry about the strike. We can cop it. It's all to the good——." He stopped, for she had turned her eyes on him and Hefty read hatred in them. "What the hell's the matter with you?" he burst out.

"The wives of the strikers should rise up and tear you to pieces! No balance! These women who are stuck in their miserable homes! These women who are feeding families — families! — on the relief! These women who laugh at their privations because they are loyal to their men! These women who are dying to help their men in the strike and are kept back by such as you——!''

They sat there, then, looking at each other as deadly combatants might have looked. But not many seconds went by before Hefty found that this roused, fighting Dulcie stirred him to an extent that the old personality had never done. The anger which had risen swiftly from his sense of the injustice of her barbs dissolved into admiration. Still staring at her he muttered "Hey, I'm a sick man, dont forget. I'm supposed to keep my blood quiet.''

"I dont care if your blood is quiet or not.''

"You dont care! Aw, Dulce, what's biting yer?''

"You've forgotten what I said to you, haven't you? Forgotten already. You want to make love to me now. I know. Love! Well, I dont want to make love to you. I want to talk like men, d'ye hear? I want to make love at the proper time and at other times I want to be exactly like a man!''

Hefty began to laugh, immoderately. His mirth became uncontrollable. He lurched towards her and forcibly took her in his arms. "Like a man, ay? You like a man! Begod, but a man would be stiff! You're my wife. Dont struggle, little bird. You cant get away from me.''

"If you kiss me I'll—I'll call Mrs. Linn.''

"Call the whole world! Begod, but I never knew the daisy I was gettin'.''

So Dulcie's new-found politics were settled that way, for the time.

Jean Devanny, *Sugar Heaven* (1936).

Inspired neophytes, they planned and drafted. What could women do? Eileen Lee's display of natural organising ability humbled and excited Dulcie in turns. "Organisation is for the purpose of developing the latent talents of the women. See how we live! Nothing uplifting about our lives, is there? We're got no objective. We live and breed and die. Life isn't meant to be like that. Life is meant for joy and expansion and objective living. I think it's the job of women to rear a race of young who will live better lives than we live; who will be able to create a better world than we, their elders, have been able to create. It's not a question of what women can do; it is what cant they do? We've got to bring the women closer to the men, to an understanding of the men's work problems. Look at the Country Women's Association! It's everywhere in the north. There's its big hall in the next street. But does it benefit the working women? What part has it played in this strike? As an organisation it has been utterly opposed to the strike. We should have been working in that——.

"All sorts of social activities are our objective, I think; with educational work on mother and child welfare. Our doctors will lecture for us when they see we are in earnest. Red Cross work, relief for the very poor — goodness knows there is plenty of scope among the big families — sewing circles, reading circles, lectures by specialists on subjects connected with our men's jobs. If we had had an organisation like this during this strike we could have run lectures for the wives on the cause of the strike. We could have canvassed the homes and encouraged and helped the women. It's being alone——. We could have marched with our men, organised public functions and deputations to authorities. Oh, there's no end to it!'' Her eyes turned inwards and her tone became pregnant with weighty realisation.

"There will be rows, naturally,'' Eileen was merely sensible again. "But if we are going to start the thing we shall have to resolve to bear the brunt. The most advanced women must be prepared to carry the blame for trouble. But the men will help us there. I'm sure.

Ibid.

262. Humiliation

For some women, the experience of the 1930s Depression revealed to them the nature of the society in which they lived and led to a life-time involvement in politics.

For the young marrieds it [the Depression] was absolutely disastrous. You know, one week you'd be working and the next week you'd be out of work and at that time you didn't immediately get dole. I know that we had to wait three months before we even got 24 shillings from our union because my husband was a paid up member of the printers union and he got, after three months, 24 shillings a week until we got the dole money, which I think was 27/6 a week. But then they had to do a day or two's work for that on the roads to get this. It was a most terrible time, very humiliating for young people who were good workers. And you know professional people were out of work; it wasn't just the ordinary labourer, it was people in all walks of life . . . My little boy was born when we were on rations. We got a ration docket for so many goods that we could get — like necessary goods — you weren't allowed to have any luxuries on it, it had to be potatoes and these sorts of things. Just before I was married I was working on the counter of the B[risbane] C[ash &] C[arry] and people came in with their ration dockets. They were only allowed this, that, that, you know, like milk or potatoes, sugar, tea — these things, and I never ever thought it would happen to me. I was in a job. And they'd come in with them and they'd want a little bit of extra, a tin of cream or something like this. Well, we all used to fake up the dockets. We would let them take the amount of money that was specified, whatever they were allowed to have (I think it was 15 shillings) and we would just write "potatoes", "onions", "flour" and this and that, and we'd say go and get your goods to the amount whatever. But when it happened to us — the humiliation of having to go with a docket to get goods to feed your child. It was the most humiliating experience and one that you never forgot and one that determined your politics, I think. You knew that the unplanned economy was wrong, where people wanted to work there wasn't work for them. And yet you still had these people in high income brackets. You still had millionaires and so on. So I think the worst part of it for young people was the humiliation.

Interview with Jenny Prohaska, a member of the Union of Australian Women, Brisbane, 1975.

263. Unemployed Women

Many women who were unemployed felt that their position was being neglected both by the government and by working-class men as well. Descriptions of the position of unemployed women at this time frequently contain references to the increase in prostitution.

Though there is an increase in the numbers of unemployed, and in the misery and poverty of our class, the U.W.M. [Unemployed Workers' Movement] seems to overlook the fact that the woman worker is suffering from unemployment and short time. It may be that so far women are not so much in evidence at the Labour Bureau and in the demonstrations. However, they appear in greater numbers on the city streets and even the ancient profession is overcrowded; only the young and attractive have a chance.

In the Brisbane parks women and girls camp out, and are harrassed by the police. Two young girls were arrested recently for sleeping out and wearing the clothes of men. While the pampered dolls of the boss are waited on by domestics, the unemployed woman is driven to desperate measures in the struggle for the means of life.

INSURANCE SWINDLE

There is unemployed insurance in Queensland for women who work under an award, but domestics are not covered. Recently the government, which was returned on a promise to find £2,000,000 and 10,000 jobs, cut the dole by 1/- per week, because the enormous army of unemployed has depleted the fund.

Men must give more attention to the conditions of working women, and we women must realize that our fight is a class fight, with the menfolk against the capitalist class.

"Misery of Women Unemployed", by "D.P.", *Working Woman*, August 1930.

264. Demands for Working Women

This report of the discussion at the New South Wales Conference of the Unemployed Workers' Movement gives a clear picture of the problems of unemployed women and formulates a series of demands.

One outstanding feature of the State Conference of the Unemployed Workers' Movement held in Sydney during 26th, 27th and 28th July, was the discussion and resolution adopted on the question of unemployed working women.

On this conference, which was a huge success, were a number of women workers and working men's wives who have only come into the movement recently. It was decided at the conference to organise a woman's section of the U.W.M. which will concentrate on the work of organising unemployed working women and drawing them, along with employed women workers, into active participation in the unemployed movement. Comrade Mrs Cook was elected to the State Executive Committee, and also Comrade Grace Peebles as representative of the Women's Section.

The resolution on women adopted by the Conference contains the special demands for women workers, and reads as follows:

It is impossible adequately to deal with the unemployed without considering the special question of the unemployed working women. Previously the labor movement has shut its eyes to the conditions of working women and has followed the bourgeois illusion about "women's places in the home".

Instead of understanding that women have a permanent place in industry, the labor movement has heretofore regarded women as only temporarily in industry. With rationalisation their number is increasing precisely because of the fact that they are forced to accept low wages because of their disorganised condition. During the war years, when women first entered industry in large numbers, the official trade union bureaucracy made no attempts to organise them. The excuse was put forward that as soon as the abnormal situation was over, women would leave industry for "the home".

Instead of leaving industry, the number of women workers has increased until today there are no less than 400,000 women in Australia dependent upon industry for a livelihood; of these not less than 80,000 are today in the ranks of the unemployed.

Rations, given to unemployed women workers, are not sufficient to maintain any sort of living standard. These, long refused, are now granted only after the most degrading examination by arrogant bureaucratic officials of the various governments. When unemployed women workers act in behalf of their class interests in the unemployed workers' movement, or in the labor movement generally, they are victimised by the police who charge them with vagrancy (the charge registered against common prostitutes who are not in good standing with the police).

The Unemployed Workers' Movement denounces all labor organisations denying working women their rightful place and proclaims as its policy the energetic struggle to unite the unemployed women workers in this movement. Women must be on all committees, participate in demonstrations, marches, etc.

Also we must organise along with the men and unemployed working women and youth, the wives and daughters of the unemployed for a militant struggle for our demands.

We must demand:—

(1) Unemployed women receive wages for the period they are out of work, the fund to be raised by a special tax on industry and administered by workers' committees, including men and women.
(2) Equal pay for equal work.
(3) Seven-hour day.
(4) Five-day week.
(5) Two weeks' vacation with pay every year.
(6) Abolition of night work for women.

"The Unemployed Workers' Movement and Working Women", *Working Woman*, August 1930.

265. Hunger Strikers

Police assault, arrest, gaol, the hunger strike are all associated with the activities of the English suffragettes. They were also part of the experience of militant Australian women who protested about the policies of Depression governments. One of the women gaoled on this occasion was Jean Devanny, novelist and political activist.

BASHED AND JAILED BY LANG'S POLICE
WORKING WOMEN HUNGER STRIKE

The offensive of capitalism against the working class is being carried on more vigorously by the Lang "Labor" Government than any of its predecessors. Particularly in its attacks against the unemployed workers the Lang Administration has exposed a brutality and viciousness that it would be hard to equal.

The framing up and gaoling of some 82 members of the working-class — militant workers and members of the Communist Party, who are prepared to lead the struggles of the workers at all times, has been carried out since the return of Lang to power in an endeavour to suppress the growing militancy of the workers, but actually results in more and more workers coming in to the revolutionary movement.

Our contention that capitalism does not differentiate between men and women

workers has been amply borne out in the brutal assault and batoning of workers —
men and women — that has taken place in Sydney during the last five or six weeks.

The women workers have also proved their willingness and ability to take the
lead and fight the police when they attack workers' demonstrations.

Convicted on various charges, despite their protests that it was because they
were members and sympathisers of the Communist Party that they were being sent to
gaol and that there was no justice in the bosses' courts for workers, six of our women
comrades went to gaol, where, in conjunction with the men comrades who were also
convicted, they conducted a hunger strike — the only means of protest against the
framing up of workers in the Clovelly case.

Their sentences having terminated, our women comrades are now free and
although weak from the long spell without food, are rapidly recovering and are more
determined than ever to participate in the struggles of the workers for the right to
live.

Comrades Jean Devaney [sic] and Mrs Saul (who is active in the Unemployed
Workers' Movement) are both sympathisers of the Communist Party.

Comrade Pat Devaney [sic] (17 years), a member of the Y.C.L., who put up a
plucky fight against the police in the Unemployed Women's Demonstration on the
14th November, is writing a statement for the Y.C.L. column of the "Workers'
Weekly" . . .

Lindsay Mountjoy [one of the Communist women gaoled]: " . . . I myself was
attacked by several thugs, who at first tried to knock me out by throwing me on the
pavement, and while down kicked me; other workers were being treated in the same
manner. The result that twelve of us were arrested upon various charges. I had three,
riotous behaviour, assault and damaging a constable's watch . . . The most terrible
part of gaol is the long confinement in the cells, which is 16½ hours out of 24.

We were not allowed to associate with the other prisoners and were kept locked
in an asphalt yard on our own during the day. Should any prisoner stop to enquire
how we were (we were hunger-striking in protest at the sentences of the twenty-one
innocent men who are still in gaol), they were instantly called away by the wardress.

*Perhaps the authorities were afraid we would start a general strike for better
conditions and better food in gaol — there is plenty of room for improvement.*"

Joy Barrington: ". . . Some of the unfortunate women at Long Bay asked us why
we were put in and when we told them we were arrested for going down to see Mr
Lang to demand the right to live they were amazed. *Yes, even those women out there
who can tell some very poignant stories of how they are hounded down by the armed thugs
of capitalism were actually surprised to hear that unemployed girls were set on by the
police in such a savage fashion . . .*"

Working Woman, 15 December 1930.

266. Indignation

There was a tremendous number of unemployed, single women and they were
getting a very, very small dole. Some of them weren't getting any. They used any
excuse for stopping single women getting the dole. You had to go through all kinds of

questions. Personal things: "Why don't you work?" It's obvious why you can't work. "Do you want to leave home?" You had to go where you were put. Textile workers could be shoved anywhere. You could send a young kid of 16 out picking apples hundreds of miles away from her family. And you had to sit in their ghastly drab offices down there by Millers Point. The impertinence of the people behind the counter was unbelievable. "Sit down you", they'd say, and it was extremely rude — they'd keep you waiting for hours and there was no queue system organised. You could be refused the dole if you said, "Don't speak to me like that." Well, you wouldn't get the dole. You were "impertinent". You "won't work". We got sustenance chits, for tea, sugar. You weren't allowed to get any luxuries like cocoa or anything; it was tea, sugar, some butter, bread, potatoes, onions. And then your meat ration was separate. It was rations really, it wasn't money. A very restricted diet.

So we called this fantastic meeting in the Lower Town Hall. And that was my debut as a speaker, in front of all these hundreds of unemployed women.

We decided we'd have a march up to Parliament House and present a deputation to the Minister for Labour. So we all got outside the Town Hall and we all marched. We got as far as Castlereagh Street and this huge big police inspector with all his policemen standing across the roadway called upon us to stop and read us the Riot Act, I mean literally read the Riot Act, and then asked us to desist and go home. None of us would do it. Some women lay down on tram lines. One woman started fighting a policeman with an umbrella and there was a great melee, oh a terrific fight. All these hundreds of women — the traffic was held up right back to the railway station.

I was standing there rather dumbfounded watching all this. Suddenly something slapped me on the wrist. I looked down. It was a handcuff. And as I was walking out with this policeman, this one slapped something on it. It was another handcuff on that one. Why he picked on me I don't know. I asked him, "What are you doing?" He said, "You're under arrest." And when I pulled the handcuffs they said, "Oi, you're resisting arrest. That's another charge." Then they started to drag me right down — (this is up in Castlereagh Street), right down to the Kent Street Police Station, right down near the Town Hall, dragged me through the streets of Sydney. And I got indignant. I wasn't frightened strangely enough. I got indignant and so I started to punch one of the blokes and hit him with the handcuffs. He said, "That's assaulting the police. That's another charge." I'm only 5 foot 2 and he's this great big policeman.

Well, I was literally dragged through the streets of Sydney and put into the Kent Street Police Station and then they took me from there up to the watchhouse, up in the Central Court there. There I was charged. Kept us in the cells all night with all these prostitutes and dope fiends and god knows what — dreadful. Then I got charged and found guilty and they put us in Long Bay Gaol. So we all decided to go on a hunger strike. There were a lot of us arrested on that day. And there were about ten framed eviction fighters. In some eviction battles a lot of property got damaged and the police arrested the wrong people. The wrong ones were arrested and they got very savage sentences — 6 or 9 months. These men had all decided to go on a hunger strike and the policy of the movement was, anyone else who gets arrested, you too go on a hunger strike to attract attention. It was an act of solidarity with these wrongly arrested anti-eviction fighters. Some of the women were so weak they had to be taken to hospital and forcibly fed at four days. I lasted the longest because I came from the strongest, better fed family I suppose. Joy Barrington, I think she went out on the sixth day. Lindsay Mountjoy went out on the fifth day. She was an organiser for the textile workers' union. I finished my eight days hunger strike. I was let out on the eighth day.

Interview with Patricia Hurd, Townsville, 1975.

267. Work at Any Price

During the Depression, women were frequently obliged to take work that was ill-paid and exploitative. At this meeting in Western Australia, presided over by Katharine Susannah Prichard, it was claimed that a relief organization headed by women had sent girls to such positions.

UNEMPLOYMENT.

MINISTER'S REPLY DISPLEASES

Girls' Complaints.

A resolution of protest against a reported reply by the Acting Premier (Mr. C. G. Latham) to a deputation of unemployed girls recently was passed by a largely attended meeting of unemployed women and girls at the Arundel Hall on Tuesday. Mr. Latham was reported to have said in the course of his reply, that if a position were found for a girl she must take it and stay there, unless she could secure a better position, but that any case of a girl who had no home would be taken in hand by the Unemployment Board. Mrs. Hugo Throssell presided at the meeting.

Miss Cecilia Shelley described the disabilities and hardships of unemployed women and girls, and declared that it was impossible for them to remain in many of the situations to which they were sent. A registry office had received a report from one woman that a man to whom she had been sent as a housekeeper had insulted her, so that she could not accept the position; but the office had sent another applicant subsequently. Such applicants had to pay registry office fees and return railway fares, for no benefit. Speakers declared that girls had to work from 80 to 90 hours a week in country hotels, or 15 hours a day (with two hours off a week) in homes. It was alleged that the Young Women's Christian Association had sent girls to positions at less than award rates, and a motion was passed urging the association not to do so.

The meeting decided to form an organisation to be called the Unemployed Girls' and Women's Defence Association, to protect working women and girls from unfair conditions of work which were being placed upon them. Arrangements were discussed for a deputation to the Premier (Sir James Mitchell) for the purpose of bringing before him certain immediate needs of unemployed girls and women in the metropolitan area.

West Australian, 22 July 1932.

268. Going Too Far

While during the Depression women's groups involved themselves in relief work, direct criticism of government policy from left-wing women brought accusations of political manipulation.

UNEMPLOYED GIRLS.

Minister's Reply to Allegations

When the Minister for Unemployment Relief (Mr. J. Scaddan) received a deputation yesterday from the Unemployed Women and Girls' Assocation, a heated argument developed between the Minister and Miss Cecilia Shelley. The two other members of the deputation present were Mrs. Hugo Throssell and Mrs.E. North.

The association, it was explained, was recently formed to protest against the statement of Mr. C.G. Latham (as Acting Premier) to the effect that if a situation was found for a girl she would have to stop in it or be refused sustenance. The deputation, however, alleged that it was morally impossible for self-respecting women to remain in certain of the upcountry positions to which they had been sent by registry offices, and they therefore asked that registry offices should be done away with, and that under no conditions should girls out of employment be refused sustenance.

In pointing out that no such assurance could be given, the Minister said that the principle upon which the Labour Bureau worked applied to men as well as to women. If a job was not suitable for the girl or the girl was not suitable for the job she was not sent, but some girls wanted to refuse to take a job of any sort, and some of them had been inclined to become cheeky recently because they thought the new association was going to support them if they refused work altogether. Mr. Latham had certainly no intention of suggesting that anyone should be sent to a position which was morally impossible. He asked why, if conditions were in certain isolated instances so bad as had been stated, the association had taken so long to bring facts to his notice. If specific cases could be brought to him of men battening (as was alleged) on un-employed women and girls, he would see that they were investigated by the police, but it was no use talking in generalities. The department had no knowledge of such incidents as those complained of and would not tolerate them in any circumstances. He hoped the aim of the association was not merely to cause discontent among girls looking for work. He thought that in trying to attack Mr. Latham over a statement which was obviously meant to contain the qualification of suitability they were trying to make a mountain out of a molehill. He hoped, too, that Miss Shelley's connection with the association was not more for publicity than with a real desire to help.

"If you want to be insulting, Miss Shelley, you can get out of this office. You are organising the girls for an entirely different purpose," Mr. Scaddan added on another occasion, rebutting a somewhat personal attack on the administration of the Labour Bureau.

West Australian, 30 July 1932.

269. Conscripted into Domestic Service

Women offered jobs in domestic service at lowered wages saw government policies on female unemployment as a threat to their living standards. Three of the women in this deputation were offered employment by the authorities to whom they protested. Another woman in the deputation described this as an attempt "to silence those of us who agitate" and suggested that mass demonstrations be substituted for small deputations.

FIFTEEN BOB A WEEK AND KEEP!

The N.S.W. Government has launched a special attack on the unemployed women in the form of appeals to prospective employers to place untrained domestic workers at 10/- a week, with a Government subsidy of 5/-, making a total wage of 15/- per week.

When the deputation of unemployed girls called on Mr Farrar last week we pointed out that this scheme was a definite smashing of our already inadequate living standard. Of course, Mr Farrar did not agree with this. "Not at all, not at all," says he; "it is only while this depression is with us."

If we once get put on to fifteen bob a week there we stick until we get together and decide with the rest of the workers to take some action for a living wage and also carry on the fight to throw the class of capitalists overboard.

Girls of the Labor Bureau, *don't be fooled into accepting these starvation conditions, because if you do you are only helping to lower the standard of living of all of us!*

Join in the unemployed committees which are being formed around the employment exchanges, and in the district where you live.

Letter from "One of the Deputation", *Working Woman*, 15 September 1930.

270. Finding a Scapegoat

Apart from their concern for the unemployed and their involvement in relief work and job training schemes during the Depression, middle-class feminist organizations, which had long advocated the entry of women into paid employment, were forced to cope with the allegation that such women caused unemployment amongst male workers. The dilemma of married women teachers highlighted this problem. In confronting it, these organizations moved towards an analysis of the competitive nature of society, which set worker against worker in the fight for jobs.

. . . As long as women did their work in the home and received payment only in keep and in kind, no objection was made, but the moment they became wage-earners and were paid for the work they did, the cry was raised that such work was not women's work. One is tempted to ask, is it no longer women's work because it is paid?

WOMEN'S RIGHTFUL OCCUPATIONS

Too long have women been unpaid workers, and the time has come when society must recognise the right of women to obtain payment for their labour. "The labourer is worthy of his hire" applies to women as well as to men. There is no rightful inheritance where jobs are concerned — it is only through custom that certain work has come to be recognised as man's or woman's.

Women workers can more justly blame men for causing unemployment among women, since men have definitely invaded occupations which are historically women's. Men bake the bread; men cure the hams; men work power sewing machines; men dispense medicines, and do cooking, waiting, cleaning, and other domestic duties. Men have invaded women's millinery, dressmaking, and dress designing spheres. So men have ousted women from work which has been theirs from time immemorial, and have left women unemployed in their own spheres.

INJUSTICE TO WOMEN

It is not the concern of this pamphlet to trace the causes of unemployment, but it is the business of this article to prove the fallacy of blaming women for the world depression and its widespread unemployment.

Unthinking men, anxious to find a scapegoat, and eager to grasp at any panacea, fall back on the age-long habit of blaming the women. This incites public opinion against women workers with the result that women find it difficult to secure employment, and then it becomes an easy matter to edge women already in work out of employment, in many cases leaving them destitute and hopeless. Such a position is bad for women as well as for men. When will it be grasped that such action does not relieve unemployment — it merely shifts the burden from one set of shoulders to another.

WOMEN'S RIGHT TO WORK

Finally we come to the justice of the question of the right to work. Women who are wage-earners have as a rule as many responsibilities as men wage-earners. Many women workers are single, but so are many men workers. Women workers have very often to support children, parents, nephews, nieces, young sisters, young brothers, invalids, etc. — who can gauge the extent of their responsibilities, and these cannot be met unless women can fully enter the wage-earning arena.

AN IDEAL: A JUST WORLD

"We must refuse to accept a jungle world in which men and women live in stupid destructive competition. We must build a lively society in which men and women cooperate. Healthy women, in common with healthy men, desire stability, security, beauty and dignity in their lives. These cannot be obtained unless their human needs for work and play are satisfied. Neither one of these needs can be violated without destroying the other. If their work life suffers, their emotional life does too. What a poignant tragedy it is that men learn so slowly that, unless women are allowed to choose their own work, they become poor things and wretched mates. Either we are going down together in this swampy jungle of sex antagonism, or through women's freedom we shall free both sexes. With both free, we may dare to contemplate building together a civilised community."

United Associations of Women, *Are Women Wage-earners Responsible for the Unemployment of Men?* (n.d.)

271. Questions for the Candidates

The use of the political questionnaire was a commonly used method of seeking to reveal candidates' views on issues relating to women and expresses the changing concerns and preoccupations of women's groups.

To the Candidates for the Senate, and for Fawkner.

Sir,

I shall be glad if you can find time to let me know whether, if elected, you will support the following:—

1. That complete freedom be given to Christian Scientists in the exercise of their religion, in relying on *Prayer* in sickness — provided always that they obey the

laws of the land in regard to contagious and infectious diseases. Yes.   No.

2. Reduction of the alcoholic content of all liquors, and drastic regulation of the drink traffic — as doing more than any one thing to demoralise our young men and girls.   Yes.   No.

3. Substitution of the correct term "mistresses" for "female dependents" in illegal partnerships between men of the Services and women — as being a complete degradation of marriage.   Yes.   No.

4. That if women who contract venereal disease are to be treated as criminals and gaoled, the men who are their paymasters shall be given the same punishment.
                                                                     Yes.   No.

5. That the need for drastic revision of our Protection Tariff and White Australia policy be held before the people as essential in furthering the ideals for which the war is being fought.   Yes.   No.

6. The establishment of an Australian system of Education, with safeguards for individual freedom and initiative in administration, based on a spiritual foundation, making the training of character the first essential.

7. The establishment of a Financial System which will make Money the Servant and not the Master of the people.

Vida Goldstein, Questionnaire, 12 August 1943.

272. Illusions

Feminist organizations tended to believe that once the truth about discrimination and inequality was revealed and documented, humane men would implement reforms regardless of party interest. For some, the 1930s Depression led to disillusion and a rejection of this approach.

"Why I stood in the Labor Party interests? Because I believe that the Labor Movement offers the best facilities for remedial measures.

"In my early years I was not interested in party politics. I believed, in my innocence, that all parties were only too anxious to rectify wrongs. I believed that their limitations lay in their ignorance and that if solutions of problems were revealed to them they would gladly put those solutions into effect.

"During the years of the depression, the appalling nature of which led me to study politics and economics, I was completely shorn of those illusions. Over that period it was impossible for any child even to fail to recognise that the opportunity to make profits and not to render service was the major concern of those who control our present social and economic system."

Jessie Street, interviewed by Jean Devanny, in *Bird of Paradise* (1945).

273. Voluntary Work

During both world wars, women's voluntary organizations lent patriotic support to the war effort or took over welfare and charity work. During the Second World War, the Women's Voluntary National Register, which was staffed by women from a variety of women's organizations, allocated women to war work both in the services and in industry. This voluntary organization was absorbed by the Department of Man Power and the unpaid workers became government employees. After Russia's entry into the war, no women's organizations remained opposed to the war effort.

Early in July last year, an official from the Staff of the Director General of Man Power came to Brisbane to enquire into the possibility of bringing all the Women's War Work Departments together in one building with a central Enquiry Office, at which women and girls could get information and advice about war work. Nothing further was heard of this project until September, when Mr. F.E. Walsh, Deputy Director General of Man Power, called a Conference to which were invited representatives of the Naval Service, the Australian Women's Army Service, the Women's Australian Auxiliary Air Force, the Women's Land Army, the Women's Industrial Office, the Women's Voluntary National Register, and officers of the Man Power Department. During the Conference, the Service Representatives expressed appreciation of the work done for them by the Women's Voluntary National Register and approval of the suggested scheme. After discussion, Mr. Walsh decided that, since the City Council was still willing to make the office in the Town Hall available, the Women's Voluntary National Register should remain there and continue for the time being to be the distributing medium for information about war work for women.

... The W.V.N.R. carried on its work in Room 40, Town Hall, and in December, Mr. Walsh arranged another Conference, to which the same representatives were invited. Here it was decided that the time had now come to bring together all the women's work. The Women's National Service Office, and the Australian Women's Land Army, already occupied adjacent offices on the 2nd Floor, of the Primary Building, in Creek Street, immediately beneath the Man Power Offices. Further space on this floor was made available, and a Central Enquiry Bureau was established with recruiting offices for the Women's Australian Auxiliary Air Force, the Australian Women's Army Service, and the Australian Army Medical Women's Service. The Enquiry Bureau was to embrace also the work of the Women's Voluntary National Register, and Miss Vera Catt, the organising secretary of the Women's Voluntary National Register was appointed by the Deputy Director General of Man Power as Information Officer in Charge of the Bureau. She took up her new duties at the beginning of the year, but Room 40 was kept open by voluntary helpers for a month longer. Too much cannot be said in appreciation of the splendid service rendered by the loyal band of women who came week after week to give information and advice to all those other women and girls seeking ways to help the war effort. As the war organisation has expanded most of these voluntary workers have been absorbed into paid employment, and many are now holding responsible positions. ...

Women's Auxiliary Services

It was not till November 1942 that the A.W.A.S. opened a Recruiting Centre outside the Post Office. Up till this time all applicants for the A.W.A.S. were interviewed at the W.V.N.R. and their completed applications sent to Victoria Barracks. From September on an officer from the Man Power Department attended at Room 40 to "man power" the applications...

An Austerity Cooking Campaign instigated by the Department of Information and carried out by the Education Department was organised by the W.V.N.R. In Brisbane and throughout Queensland, 62 demonstrations were given in halls and schools to enthusiastic audiences by Domestic Science teachers.

Emergency Services: (Mrs. W. G. Hamilton, Section Officer)

Over a period of nine months, a group of women averaging 80 per day, did more than three and half million square feet of camouflage garnishing for the Allied Forces. Later they ungarnished 1,000,000 square feet of nets. The group, many of whom had made camouflage garnishing their special war effort, disbanded regretfully in February when the work came to an end.

Entertainment Section: Mrs. R. G. Allen (Section Officer)

The Concert Party formed by the Section Officer for Entertainment is extremely popular. Fifty six concerts have been given in Military Camps in and round Brisbane during the past twelve months. . . .

Since the Department of Defence has organised Women's Auxiliaries for every Branch of its service, it is fitting that the Women's Voluntary National Register should now find itself part of the Department of Labour and National Service. This has become the distributing agent for women's work, with a staff of qualified advisers.

During the early war years, the burden was borne by voluntary workers who gave service of inestimable value. Much honour is due to these women who have done and still are doing such untiring, selfless voluntary work.

"Summary of the Work of the Women's Voluntary National Register, July 1st, 1942 to June 30th, 1943 (Queensland)."

274. Divisions

Jessie Street's increasing radicalization, which is suggested in this popular article, attracted attention during the war. In the post-war period, with her formation of the Australian Women's Charter Movement, fear of communist influence led to attacks on Jessie Street from inside the women's movement. Anti-communism, heightened by the atmosphere of the cold war, created divisions inside and between middle-class women's organizations.

Why this woman came to like the Russians

Aboard an Australian-bound ship in the Indian Ocean 46 years ago a little girl aged 7 wanted to climb the rigging as some boys were doing, but she was not allowed, although she thought she was just as good a climber as they were.

Today that little girl is one of Australia's foremost Feminists and political radicals, Mrs. Jessie Street, wife of Mr. Justice Street, mother of two grown-up sons and two daughters.

If you go to the Sydney Domain this afternoon to join with those celebrating the Anglo-Soviet Treaty and Russia's magnificent year of war you will hear her speak from the platform as vigorously and enthusiastically as anybody there.

She went to Russia in 1938, came back to Australia anxious to tell everybody all about it, but people didn't seem to want to know what she had seen there.

"Some didn't believe me, others didn't want to," she tells you. "Some said I was a Communist. I didn't know anything about Communism, so I said I would find out, and when I read some books the ideas seemed to me to be simply an expression of the ideas at the base of Christianity — equality, brotherly love, treating your neighbor as your brother."

If you ask her, as an interviewer did this week, just how "red" she really is, she laughs and says:

"Some people think I am very red, but all I do is believe warmly in justice and an equal chance for all people whether men or women, rich or poor."

Sex was unimportant

Then, in case you should believe that's too red, she adds: "I am a member of the Official Labor Party."

All she is now politically she attributes to that early prohibition aboard ship and to other prohibitions imposed on her (she believes unjustifiably and simply because of her sex) as she grew up.

As a girl at school in England she came under the influence of the suffragettes, including Mrs. Pankhurst and Mrs. Pethick-Lawrence, at a time when Mrs. Pankhurst was going to jail again and again for women's rights.

It was Mrs. Street's Feminist interests that took her to Russia — not an interest in Bolshevism, Socialism or any political creeds, but a desire to see for herself what the position of women was there.

Then the Bolshies showed her the whole works — what they were doing to help the sick, the aged, the babies, to encourage cultural development, to organise agricultural and industrial development — and she came away convinced they were out to give every man and woman there the training that would develop their capabilities.

"It seemed to be immaterial whether a person were a man or a woman," she says with undimmed enthusiasm. "It is the only time I have lived in an atmosphere where sex is unimportant, where men and women have equal opportunities and equal pay for the work they do."

And now in Australia?

At 53, active in the United Associations of Women, chairman of the Russian Medical Aid Committee, she is a dynamo of energy, answering telephones, attending meetings, giving speeches.

Political snobbery

Her interests are not confined to Feminism, but she finds herself fighting the same fight for women's rights, kicking against political conventions, believing that in Australia —

● Although everybody is calling out for a 100 per cent. war effort, we have only a 50 per cent. effort because the boards which control policy and administer the war effort are marked FOR MEN ONLY and the brains, initiative, and driving force of women are not being used — they are allowed only to do the lower grades of work at the lowest pay.

● There is more political snobbery here than in England or America.

She found out about the snobbery after joining the Labor Party. She smiles a little wearily when she recalls that some people wouldn't introduce her to their wives because she joined it, says some people think it a sign of social superiority to belong to the U.A.P. or the U.C.P.

They told her the policy of the Labor Party was against her own personal interests, that she must have only wanted publicity joining it.

"But my belief," says she, "was that the policy of the other parties all over the world would eventually lead to war, that if the policies of the Labor parties were followed war could be prevented, and I had no personal interest so great as maintaining peace."

Well, war came, and she believes that Russia's entry into it turned the scales in our favor.

"The whole civilised world is indebted to the Russians for the way they have held the Nazis," she says. "We are entitled to ask now. If Russia hadn't come in, would there be an England, would there be an Australia . . .?"

Sunday Telegraph, 21 June 1942.

275. Women's Views

> In the same way that the war and the cold war led to political divisions between feminists, the question of morals and venereal disease, which was reasserted in the war-time situation, revealed divisions between women's organizations. No groups, however, argued for greater sexual freedom for women.

Carefully shielded from publicity, conference after conference has been held recently by responsible authorities on VD, to seek a common plan to control it. All have failed.

Within the next few days the Police Vice Squad, backed by information from its own activities and research, once more will seek additional powers.

They want them to deal with women who, they say, they cannot control at present.

There are three main groups of women concerned in the problem of VD:

- Girls under 18
- Women not in employment
- Those who, when caught in circumstances of promiscuity, can produce some soldiers' allotment card, or proof of some legitimate means of livelihood.

"The first two groups we can deal with, take them to court, return them to their homes, put them into jobs, and give them a chance of rehabilitation," said a Vice Squad officer.

"The extra powers are needed to cope with the third group.

"We need power to:

- "Arrest these women when they are detected in circumstances which reveal their promiscuity,
- To compel them to undergo treatment,
- And, if necessary, to segregate them.

"It is reasonable to assume that at least a fair percentage of them are infected, and a prolific source of infection for servicemen and others.

"But under existing laws, we can't take them before a court or a clinic. "Apparently, the authorities are lothe to bring in legislation which would clean up this scourge, even as a wartime measure."

With the extra power, the Vice Squad, he said, could go a long way towards effectively controlling VD.

To which Director of Social Hygiene, Dr. Cooper Booth, replies doubtfully, "Perhaps."

But Dr Cooper Booth himself confesses that control of VD has too many loose ends, that a solution has not yet been found, yet must be found.

His own suggestion was that women who contract VD more than once should have their heads shaved.

It aroused many people to protest. They regarded it as "too drastic," "barbaric," "medieval". A few, only a few, wanted to go still further.

They told Dr Cooper Booth that such women should be tattooed. Others would have them whipped, privately or publicly. The Social Hygiene Director repudiates such punishments in one word, "horrible". . . .

"The public's reaction to such a plan would be a most valuable guide," he said, "and, in particular, the reaction of the women's organisations."

Dr. Cooper Booth also believes that women's organisations, which have done wonders for girls in the Services, have failed to tackle the big job of caring for the girls in civil life.

Dr. Cooper Booth is hesitant on endorsing the police request for extra powers. He thinks such authority would cause a public outcry, that it is very wide power to give a police constable, "who is only human."

Views of women's organisations on the suggested extra powers are:

United Associations of Women President Mrs Jessie Street:

"The whole approach to this problem is wrong, for the police should have nothing to do with it. The official approach to promiscuous indulgence is to regard it as inevitable, and endeavour to make it as safe as possible for men, and to hold up to scorn and derision the women concerned. Until we cease to regard VD as a crime, hold men equally to blame with women and make a sincere attempt to eradicate promiscuity, we will never eradicate VD."

Housewive's Association President Mrs Glencross said:

"We are quite content to leave the problem of stamping out VD to the medical profession. I do, however, think it is disgraceful that while decent people are waiting for penicillin treatment, it is wasted on girls who contract the disease a second time. They should be segregated from the rest of the community."

NSW Racial Hygiene Association General Secretary Mrs Goodisson:

"Police should certainly be empowered to order any woman found in promiscuous circumstances to have treatment for VD if she has the disease, whether she is over 18, has a job or not. But education is needed to protect these girls from their own folly."

Feminist Club President Mrs Cameron:

"This problem has become so serious that the police should certainly have added power if they think it will help. But it has become wider than just a police problem, and any Government with the welfare of the nation at heart should review its authority to control not only the girls but the men concerned, and those living on the downfall of young people."

"Vice Squad Plea for Power to Check VD", *Sunday Sun and Guardian*, 6 August 1944.

276. History of a Women's Organization

In this article, novelist Katharine Susannah Prichard gives a full description of the life of a woman's organization of which she was a member.

When the State Executive of the A.L.P. resolved not to allow its women members to join the Council Against War and Fascism, I suggested, at a meeting of the Committee, that we should have a women's club where the members would be free to discuss any subject which concerned them. This was in 1938. The idea was agreed to by Mrs. Alice Kretchmar, a scientist of the University of Western Australia, and other members of the Movement against War and Fascism approved, including prominent Labour women who were members. Among others, Mrs. Jean Beadle, Mrs. Margaret Green and Mrs. Elizabeth Rogers.

After some discussion it was decided to go ahead with arrangements for this club, and several members offered to make an initial payment of two shillings a week towards the rent of a room for the purpose of club meetings. Within a week, a room was found on St. George's Terrace, and members agreed to furnish it by each donating some chairs, a table and other odds and ends. An electric kettle was bought for making afternoon teas, and regular meetings and discussions were arranged.

The first meeting was packed, and it was obvious after another, that the idea of this women's club for free discussion was so popular, larger premises would have to be found. Then we moved to the second floor of a building in Howard Street now occupied by the Adult Education Board. Before removal into these more spacious quarters, members did some spring cleaning — Vern and I scrubbed the lavatory. It was decided to purchase furniture at a cost of £50.0.0. Meetings were then held regularly every week, and the name Modern Women's Club was adopted. Membership increased, and we served cold lunches and light refreshments when there was an evening function. But this was done only by the enthusiastic co-operation of members who cleaned the premises, washed dishes, and generally kept the quarters supplied with food and flowers, although they had only an electric kettle to heat water.

Again, the premises got too small and inconvenient for the growing membership. I happened to be on friendly terms with the owner of a building further along St. George's Terrace. Its basement was used as a restaurant, and when the owner was dissatisfied with the way the restaurant was being run, I saw the possibility of the Club being able to use the basement. At least we would have more conveniences for preparing meals and obtaining hot water. I was able to arrange for the Club to move into this building at a nominal rent, on the understanding that at the end of the year, if the Club was in a flourishing condition, the owner might charge a higher rental.

Unfortunately, I was in Sydney when the end of the year came round, and other members overlooked this agreement between myself and the proprietor. So a row developed between him and the Club treasurer. This ended in the Club having notice to quit.

It established new quarters in Padbury House, at the corner of King Street & St. George's Terrace. Here we had the convenience of kitchen cooking arrangements in a basement that had another room adjoining the main dining room. For several years this was the headquarters of the Modern Women's Club, and marked on street maps of Perth at the time. We acquired a substantial library, crockery and furnishings. Lunches were served, and a speaker provided for each weekly meeting day.

After the business meeting later, donations to the peace movement were made by regular subscribers. These usually amounted to £4.0.0 a week. As well as the weekly midday meetings and talks on local and topical subjects with discussion following, there were evening meetings when talks and readings or debates and dramatic performances were arranged for by Club members. For instance, one evening would be given to discussion of Scottish poetry, songs and novels; another to Irish, or Welsh, English or Australian literature. On the Irish evening, Club members produced scenes from THE TINKERS WEDDING by Synge, and a one-act play which I wrote for the occasion, "GOOD MORNING."

The Club always sponsored the interests of aborigines. Mary Morden was an aboriginal member with all speaking and voting rights, and her friends came to Club functions and lunches free of charge. We assisted Sister Kate's Home, and every year gave a party for aboriginal children at the Bassendean camp. Also sponsored an aborigine girl in one of the Charity Queen competitions. Don McLeod's appeal for the aborigines who left the stations in the May Day strike was made at the Modern Women's Club. The Club made its quarters available free of charge to the peace movement.

During the war, there was a suggestion that a volunteer body of women should be formed to act as guardians of young girls who were behaving in a disorderly manner and drinking with soldiers on the streets. The Modern Women's Club called a meeting of representatives of women's organisations to oppose the idea of a volunteer organisation of untrained women undertaking this responsibility. As a result of the representations from several women's committees, the Commissioner of Police decided to appoint trained and paid women for this work.

The Modern Women's Club entertained many interesting overseas visitors, and for International Women's Day, one year, organised an exhibition of famous women of the world in photographs and newspaper cuttings.

Funds for the support of the Club were derived chiefly from an annual membership fee, a sale of work once a year, though there was an exhibition of women's work in the Town Hall on one occasion.

Many women gave time and energy to make a success of every phase of the Modern Women's Club. Among these as Presidents, Secretaries and Treasurers should be mentioned Helen McEntyre, Vern Roberts, Dorothy Irwin, Jean Wilbur, Alice Kretchmar, Bernice Ranford, Elsie McLeod, Betty Main, Dorothy Cameron, although officers received no remuneration.

A tribute must be specially paid to Mrs. Vern Roberts who devoted time and energy to every administrative function as chairman, cook, actress, entertainer and a friend in need to every member.

I think the Modern Women's Club should be regarded as a memorial to her active and always loving service.

Success of the Modern Women's Club was responsible for a request from Melbourne and Sydney that I should organise similar circles for free discussion in these two cities. Later, organisation of the Union of Australian Women in Melbourne and Sydney made this unnecessary. After twenty years, we realised that the U.A.W. was attracting and interesting younger women, and that no useful purpose was being served by two organisations of the same type in Perth. Therefore, as most of our members were becoming grey-heads, at a general meeting, although the Modern Women's Club was in a healthy condition financially, members decided that the Club should go out of existence. At the same time, all the assets of the Modern Women's Club were donated to the U.A.W. as the younger, more active and progressive organisation to carry on the purposes for which the Modern Women's Club was originally founded.

Katharine Susannah Prichard, "Notes on the Modern Women's Club" (n.d.).

277. Child-minding

Although the demand for creches and child-minding centres goes back to the beginning of the century, it assumed much greater significance during the Second World War, and in the post-war period radical women's groups made it part of their platforms.

"Mrs J.", called out Mrs S. over the back fence, "Will you mind Billy for me this morning? My sister's been rushed off to hospital and I have to go to town to get her some things."

"All right", I said resignedly, for this was the third time this week and Billy needs minding. Keeping him amused and out of mischief is a full time job and wears me out completely.

When my husband came home I wondered aloud to him what to do about it. "Why doesn't she send him to the Kindergarten?" he asked.

"Well, in the first place you have to have your name down for at least a year, so that's out now. In the second, when I suggested it when Billy was a baby, she was so angry with me that I dropped the subject. She told me that her husband thought, and she agreed with him, that mothers could and should mind their own children better than bits of girls who'd never had any. When I pointed out the advantages of having Billy play with children of his own age with suitable toys in the fresh air, and with the added attraction of music and freedom for her for a few hours, she gave the worn-out crack "My mother never sent us to a kindergarten and what's wrong with me?" I didn't want to quarrel so I dropped the matter.

However, she commits Billy to my untrained hands or, in fact sometimes to girls of 12, in the neighbourhood quite cheerfully.

Billy is a lonely little soul spending his energy in a small house and a smaller back yard — the tram line is at the front — wearing out his own, his mother's and my tempers by being naughty when he would be a happier, healthier and better little boy at the kindergarten.

One of our jobs as New Housewives is to show our neighbours the advantages of the local kindergarten.

"Be Good — Or Else", *Housewive's Guide*, May 1947.

278. "Feminism" — Meaning the Same Thing

By the end of the war, it was clear that not only were there political divisions between groups of feminists but also different ideas about how feminist goals should be pursued. Edith How Martyn, fighter for the suffragette cause in England, raised the problems in this letter to Jessie Street.

Dear Jessie, Thinking of what you were saying about Feminism and Feminists I see clearly we must define to each other what we mean by the words for I do not think we mean the same thing at all!

When we got the vote in 1918 the old national Union of Suff Soc. split on the policy of working for particular reforms or of working to get women into key positions & to help them when they were there — M.P.s, Councillors, Mayors, high up Civil Servants, Heads of Schools, Magistrates, Police women, Architects, Inspectors and so on. I was with the second group and measure the Feminist advance by numbers of above. In the 28 years since 1918 we have never had a British Parlt. without a woman . . .

Working for special reforms leaves me quite cold unless there are women to do the jobs like Eleanor Rathbone M.P. pegging away at children's allowances, though as a secondary aim let us work at them . . .

We have a long way to go. . .

Edith How Martyn to Jessie Street, 10 February 1946.

279. "For Women"

In looking back at early feminist organizations, including the Western Australia group, the Women's Service Guilds, of which she was a member, Irene Greenwood expresses both the nature and the dilemmas of the post-vote women's movement.

They [the Women's Service Guilds] believed in making the status of women's occupations higher. The thing they wished to do was raise the status of all women's work. They wanted to have payment made for all work that was done and they deplored to a great deal the tendency to voluntary work which women were expected to do as part of their contribution to society. (Although the women themselves never said to a woman who wished to do philanthropic work, do not do it.) ... they were asked to form the National Council of Women (in fact they were asked to *become* the National Council of Women), and they strenuously resisted this request by Lady Strickland, who was the wife of the governor of the day. They said — no, we wish to keep single mindedly to our objectives which are to raise the status of women and to improve the conditions of professionalism and pay for women, and this was the sole reason: to raise standards and to raise status. They saw the way to do that was not by having women's attempts syphoned off into philanthropic or other such work, necessary as it was for the community. They formed these other organisations. They called the first meeting from which the National Council of Women was formed and into that went a lot of their very good women, including Edith Cowan and Dr Roberta Jull, because it embraced all those other groups, the groups that were working for ministering children's needs, the church groups, the groups that were doing this kind of work. And the Women's Service Guilds went steadforward on their one tack. Frequently in their debates when contentious things came up they made a plea ... they pleaded not to be distracted with such issues. While they debated them within their own organisation on various occasions and doubtless with some heat at times and with a good deal of difference, they were unified in their single-minded objective ...

We've always adhered to our strictly non-party policy, though we have had the opinion of very strong Labor women within the organisation and we've had the opinion of very strong National Party women within the organisation too. But we've been allowed to join our parties and work with our parties outside ... Whenever a contentious issue was coming up we had on the same platform a speaker from one party and a speaker from the other party, and people asked questions of them ...

I never voted for a party per se in my life and I have never belonged to a party per se in my life. I have voted for women's issues and I believe they did. We always voted for a woman, irrespective of party, when a woman stood, so eager were we — although later on we came to the conclusion that party dichotomy made it necessary that a person advocating a certain platform should be voted for (especially when the party numbers grew so close) irrespective of whether they were a male or a female. But we were really and truly in that sense of the word "for women" because we believed that women had certain issues which they saw. Remember, that does not apply today. Nor do people today within the Guilds think that sort of thing, because most of their membership have drifted into party affiliations due to the polarisation of politics during and after 1972-1975. The non-party idea does not have the relevance it did for the early suffrage groups, valid in their day.

Interview with Irene Greenwood, Perth, 1976.

Location of Documents

Abbreviations

A.O.T.	Archives Office of Tasmania
BL	Battye Library, Perth
H.R.A.	*Historical Records of Australia*
LTL	La Trobe Library, Melbourne
ML	Mitchell Library, Sydney
NLA	National Library of Australia, Canberra
OL	Oxley Library, Brisbane
P.R.O.V.	Public Record Office of Victoria
Q.S.A.	Queensland State Archives
S.A.N.S.W.	State Archives of New South Wales
S.A.S.A.	State Archives of South Australia
S.A.W.A.	State Archives of Western Australia

Part 1   Outcasts of Society

1.   Rev. Samuel Marsden Papers, ML MSS 18.
2.   *H.R.A.*, Series 1, vol. x, pp. 689-90.
3.   Ibid., vol. xi, pp. 114-15.
4.   Ibid., vol. xiv, pp. 653-57.
5.   Colonial Secretary's Department, Correspondence Inwards, S.A.N.S.W. 4/2234.5.
6.   Ibid., S.A.N.S.W. 4/2317.2.
7.   Ibid., S.A.N.S.W. 4/2451.3.
8.   Ibid., S.A.N.S.W. 4/2317.2.
9.   Ibid.
10.   Transcripts of Missing Despatches from the Governor of New South Wales, 1833-38, pp. 880a, 882a, 882b, ML.
11.   Colonial Secretary's Department, Correspondence Inwards, S.A.N.S.W. 4/2359.1.
12.   Godfrey Charles Mundy, *Our Antipodes: or Residence and Rambles in the Australasian Colonies, with a Glimpse of the Gold Fields*, 3 vols (London: Bentley, 1852), vol. 1, pp. 136-38.
13.   Colonial Secretary's Office, "Report and Evidence of the Committee Inquiring into Female Convict Discipline, 1841-43", and Appendixes, A.O.T., CSO 22/50.
14.   *Colonial Times* (Hobart), 18 February 1840, A.O.T.
15.   Colonial Secretary's Office, "Report and Evidence of the Committee Inquiring into Female Convict Discipline, 1841-43", and Appendixes, A.O.T. CSO 22/50.
16.   Ibid.
17.   Ibid.
18.   Ibid.
19.   Female School of Industry, Sydney, *Annual Reports*, 1827-1926, ML.
20.   Rosamond and Florence Hill, *What We Saw in Australia* (London: Macmillan, 1875), pp. 282-87.
21.   Colonial Secretary's Department, Special Bundles, Biloela Industrial School: Administration and Investigations, 1871-75, S.A.N.S.W. 4/798.3.

22. Ibid.
23. Ibid.
24. Ibid.
25. Ibid.
26. Ibid.
27. Ibid.
28. Ibid.
29. Ibid.
30. Ibid.
31. N.S.W. Parliament, *Votes and Proceedings*, 1873-74, vol. 6, pp. 70-74.
32. Ibid., pp. 84-85.
33. Chief Secretary's Department, A.O.T. CSD 13/23/265.
34. Ibid.
35. Chief Secretary's Department, A.O.T. CSD 13/24/292.
36. Chief Secretary's Office, Letters Received, P.R.O.V. K8075, series 1189.
37. *Argus* (Melbourne), 2 August 1899.
38. Ibid.
39. Chief Secretary's Office, Letters Received, P.R.O.V. K8075, series 1189.
40. Rose Scott, Manuscript Journal, 1889-91, p. 79; Rose Scott Papers, ML MSS 38.
41. Parramatta Training School for Girls, Copies of Letters sent by Superintendent, S.A.N.S.W. 3432.
42. Girls Industrial School Parramatta Superintendent's *Report* 1908 (Sydney: Government Printer, 1910), p. 3.
43. Girls Industrial School Parramatta Superintendent's *Report* 1915 (Sydney: Government Printer, 1916), pp. 2, 4.
44. Colonial Secretary's Office, Official Forwarded Correspondence, S.A.W.A. CSO/561.
45. Ibid., S.A.W.A. CSO/541.
46. Ibid., S.A.W.A. CSO/561.
47. Ibid., S.A.W.A. CSO/541.
48. Ibid.
49. Ibid.
50. Ibid.
51. Premier's Department, A.O.T. PD 1/123/29.
52. Chief Secretary's Office, Charitable Institutions, Box 931, P.R.O.V.
53. *Proceedings of the First Australasian Conference on Charity*, convened by the Charity Organization Society of Melbourne (Melbourne: Government Printer, 1890), pp. 90-91.
54. *Proceedings of the Second Australasian Conference on Charity*, convened by the Charity Organization Society of Melbourne (Melbourne: Government Printer, 1891), p. 53.
55. Ibid., pp. 54-5.
56. George Washington Walker Papers, ML MSS 11.
57. Chief Secretary's Office, Charitable Institutions, Box 931, P.R.O.V.
58. *Proceedings of the First Australasian Conference on Charity*, op. cit., pp. 49-51.
59. Home Office, Benevolent Societies: Female Refuge and Infants' Home, Brisbane, Q.S.A. Col 291.
60. Ibid.
61. Woman's Crusade, *Our Erring Sisters: Being the Record of Work in the Lock-ups, Police Courts, Slums, Hospitals, Asylums, etc., etc.* (Sydney: Townsend, 1893), ML.
62. *Proceedings of the Second Australasian Conference on Charity*, op. cit., pp. 132-33.
63. Rose Scott Papers, ML MSS 38.
64. Premier's Office, Unemployment Box, 1930, P.R.O.V.
65. Lands Department, Minute of Books of the Unemployed Relief Council, Adelaide, S.A.S.A. GRG 35/64/1, pp. 9-10.
66. *West Australian* (Perth), 5 July 1935.
67. Ibid., 22 April 1932.
68. State Reformatory for Women, Long Bay, Copies of Letters Sent, S.A. N.S.W. 2276-77.
69. United Associations of Women Papers, ML MSS 2160.
70. Frank Johnson Papers, ML MSS 1214/3, 1214/22.

Part 2   Private Lives

71. N.J.B. Plomley (ed.), *Friendly Mission: The Tasmanian Journals and Papers of George Augustus Robinson, 1829-1834* (Hobart: Tasmanian Historical Research Association, 1966), pp. 256-57.
72. Ibid, p. 82.
73. George Augustus Robinson Papers, ML MSS A7066, vol. 45.
74. Colonial Secretary's Office, Daisy M. Bates, Personal File, S.A.W.A. 4875/1910.
75. Chief Secretary's Department, Aboriginals, S.A.W.A. 342/1925.
76. Ibid.
77. Ibid.
78. Department of the North West, S.A.W.A. 232/1925.
79. Chief Secretary's Department, Aboriginals, S.A.W.A. 166/1932; *West Australian* (Perth), 6 June 1932; ibid., 26 May 1932.
80. Chief Secretary's Department, Aboriginals, S.A.W.A. 166/1932.
81. Ibid.
82. Home Secretary's Office, Q.S.A. A/4732.
83. Department of the North West, S.A.W.A. 31/1924.
84. Registrar-General's Department, S.A.W.A. 144/1944.
85. Richard Penney, Memorial, 1842, S.A.S.A. A634/B9.
86. "One of Four" (pseud.), *Words to Women: A Plea for Certain Sufferers* (Hobart, 1858), pp. 8-9, Tasmanian Collection, State Library of Tasmania.
87. *The Woman's Voice* (Sydney), May 1905, ML.
88. Social Welfare Department, Cascades Contagious Diseases Hospital, A.O.T. SWD 58.
89. "Board of Inquiry into the General Management of the Gaols, Penal Establishments, and Lock-ups of the Colony of Queensland", *Journals of the Legislative Council of Queensland*, vol. xxxvii, pt. 1, 1887, p. 1345-46.
90. Home Secretary's Office, Lock Hospital, Q.S.A. COL 360.
91. Chief Secretary's Department, A.O.T. CSD 16/49/1574.
92. Ibid., CSD 22/29/7.
93. Rose Scott Papers, ML MSS 38.
94. *Progress Report from Select Committee on Prevention of Venereal Disease: Evidence and Appendices* (Sydney: N.S.W. Government Printer, 1916), p. 40.
95. *Transactions of the Australasian Medical Congress* (Sydney, 1929), p. 516.
96. United Associations of Women Papers, ML MSS 2160.
97. Police Department, S.A.W.A. 3833/1938.
98. *Daily Telegraph* (Sydney), 18 May 1943.
99. *Sydney Morning Herald*, 21 July 1944.
100. Kylie Tennant, *Tell Morning This* (Sydney: Angus & Robertson, 1967), p. 260.
101. Ada Bromham, *V.D. Legislation: How It Works*, prepared for the National Women's Christian Temperance Union of Australia (n.d., c. 1946).
102. United Associations of Women Papers, ML MSS 2160.
103. Ibid.
104. Phyllis Owen Crompton Papers, S.A.S.A. PRG 331.
105. *Matrimonial Chronicle* (Tumut, N.S.W.), selection from nos. 1-4, July-October 1879.
106. Miles Franklin Papers, ML MSS 364.
107. United Associations of Women, *Incomes for Wives: How Can It be Managed?* (Sydney: n.d., c. 1937).
108. Destitute Persons Department, S.A.S.A. GRG 28/28.
109. *Brisbane Courier*, 6, 8 March 1905.
110. *Proceedings of the First Australasian Conference on Charity*, pp. 88-90.
111. Crown Solicitor, Q.S.A. CRS 227.
112. Home Office, Q.S.A. COL 289.
113. Home Secretary's Office, Q.S.A. A/4730.
114. *Brisbane Courier*, 23 February 1923.
115. *Queensland Figaro* (Brisbane), 22 July 1922.
116. N.S.W. Parliament, *Debates*, vol. 110, 8 February 1927, pp. 1037-38.
117. *The Working Woman* (Sydney), 1 July 1932, ML.
118. Rose Scott, *Presidential Address to the Woman's Political Educational League* (Sydney, 1904).
119. *The Woman's Sphere* (Melbourne), 10 June 1903, ML.

120. Dr Roberta Jull Papers, BL 1643A.
121. *Argus* (Melbourne), 10 September 1935.
122. The Nation's Forum of the Air, *Population Unlimited*? (Sydney: Australian Broadcasting Commission, 1944).
123. United Associations of Women Papers, ML MSS 2160.
124. Ibid.
125. Tape-recorded interview, Brisbane, 1975; in possession of compilers.
126. Bessie Rischbieth Papers, N.L.A. MS 2004.
127. Piddington Papers, N.L.A. MS 1158.
128. United Associations of Women Papers, ML MSS 2160.
129. Racial Hygiene Association of New South Wales, *Annual Report* (Sydney, 1939), ML.
130. *Herself* (Sydney), April 1929, ML.
131. Education Department, Sex Education, P.R.O.V. 1106, series 892.
132. *The Working Woman* (Sydney), January 1932, ML.
133. Mrs. B. Smyth, *Limitation of Offspring: Being the Substance Delivered in the North Melbourne Town Hall and Elsewhere to Large Audiences* (Melbourne: Rae Bros., 1893), pp. 23-25.
134. Marie Stopes Papers, British Library, London, Add. MS 58573.
135. Ibid., Add. MS 58572.
136. Victoria. Parliament, *Debates*, vol. 198, 23 October 1935, p. 3762.
137. International Planned Parenthood Federation Library, London.
138. Norman Haire, *Sex Problems of Today* (Sydney: Angus & Robertson, 1942), pp. 26-27.
139. Bessie Rischbieth Papers, N.L.A. MS 2004.
140. Racial Hygiene Association of New South Wales, *Conference Papers* (Sydney, 1932), ML.
141. *The Working Woman* (Sydney), January 1932, ML.

Part 3   Working Women

142. Typescript copies of Margaret Catchpole Letters, held with Harold R. Lingwood's manuscript biography of Catchpole, Shelley Garner Papers, BL 1613A.
143. Plomley (ed.), *Friendly Mission*, p. 273.
144. Ibid., pp. 294-95.
145. *H.R.A.*, Series 1, vol. xviii, pp. 344-45.
146. Typescript copy, S.A.S.A. D5063(L).
147. NLA MS 3334.
148. *Proceedings of the First Australasian Conference on Charity*, pp. 52-56.
149. Department of Labour and Industry, Factories Letterbooks, vol. 2, 1898-1901, S.A.S.A. GRG 64/1/2.
150. Ibid.
151. Ibid.
152. *Journal of Agriculture*, February 1899.
153. Department of Labour and Industry, Factories Letterbooks, vol. 2, 1898-1901, S.A.S.A. GRG 64/1/2, manuscript copy or draft of prospectus.
154. Department of Labour and Industry, "Report on the Working of the Factories and Shops Act for 1898", N.S.W. Parliament, *Votes and Proceedings*, 2nd Session, 1899, p. 297.
155. *The Woman's Sphere* (Melbourne), 10 March 1902, ML.
156. Records of the Women's Organiser, Australian Labor Party Metropolitan Council Records, BL 1319A/211.
157. Ibid.
158. *Proceedings of the Third Australasian Catholic Congress Held at St Mary's Cathedral, Sydney 26th September-3rd October 1909* (Sydney: St Mary's Cathedral Book Depot, 1910), pp. 287-94.
159. *The Dawn* (Perth), 20 February 1929, BL.
160. Tape-recorded interviews, Adelaide, July 1976; in possession of compilers.
161. Department of Industries, Jubilee Appeal: Motherhood and Youth Welfare, file 25/35, S.A.W.A.
162. *The Working Woman* (Sydney), August 1930, ML.
163. Chief Secretary's Department, S.A.W.A. 166/1932.
164. Department of the North West, S.A.W.A. 325/1921.
165. F.W. Eggleston et al., *Australian Standards of Living* (Melbourne: Melbourne University Press, 1939), pp. 78-79.

166. Tape-recorded interview, Adelaide, July 1976; in possession of compilers.
167. Muriel Heagney Papers, LTL MS 9106.
168. Ibid.
169. Ibid.
170. Ibid.
171. Bussell Family Papers, typescript copy, BL 337A/16.
172. Penelope Belt Letters, typescript copy in possession of J.S. Horn, Sydney.
173. South Australia. Parliament, *Votes and Proceedings*, 1855-56, 1st Session, vol. 1.
174. Ibid.
175. Colonial Secretary's Office, Female Immigrants' Hiring Reports, S.A.S.A. 24/6/1855/2969.
176. South Australia. Parliament, *Votes and Proceedings*, 1855-56, 1st Session, vol. 1.
177. Ibid.
178. "Reports of the Select Committee of the Legislative Council of South Australia Appointed to Inquire into the Excessive Female Immigration; together with the Minutes of Evidence and Appendix", South Australia. Parliament, *Votes and Proceedings*, 1855-56, 1st Session, vol. 11.
179. Ibid.
180. Ibid.
181. Ibid.
182. *Proceedings of the Second Australasian Conference on Charity* op. cit., p. 68.
183. Colonial Secretary's Office, Immigration of Domestic Servants, S.A.W.A. 80/1895.
184. Ibid.
185. Ibid.
186. Ibid.
187. Immigration, Publicity and Tourist Bureau Department, Notebooks of Matrons Conducting Women Emigrants to South Australia, 1912-14, S.A.S.A. GRG 7/55.
188. Ibid.
189. Immigration, Publicity and Tourist Bureau Department, Applications by Women for Assisted Passages to South Australia, 1921-30, S.A.S.A. GRG 7/8.
190. Ibid.
191. Ibid.
192. Tape-recorded interview, Adelaide, July 1976; in possession of compilers.
193. United Associations of Women Papers, ML MSS 2160.
194. *H.R.A.*, Series 1, vol. xviii, pp. 788-89.
195. Women's Migration and Overseas Appointment Society Records, 1862-1901, ML FM4/2130. Originals held in Fawcett Library, London.
196. Board of Education, Letterbook of the Inspector-General, June 1860-31 March 1864, Q.S.A. EDB/1.
197. Queensland. Parliament, *Journals of the Legislative Council*, vol. xiii, pt. 1, 1875, p. 638, pp. 640-41.
198. Education Department, Special Case File 599, P.R.O.V., series 892.
199. Ibid., Special Case File 577.
200. Ibid., Special Case File 473.
201. *Englishwoman's Review*, October 1873, Fawcett Library, London.
202. Copy, Colonial Secretary's Department, Special Bundles, Engagement of Nurses at Sydney Hospital, 1866-68, S.A.N.S.W. 4/768.1.
203. Tasmania. Parliament, *Journals and Papers of Parliament*, 1887, vol. xii, paper 145.
204. Education Department, Special Case File 902, P.R.O.V., series 892.
205. Shirley School and Kindergarten Papers, ML MSS 35.
206. Education Department, Attendance File, Mia Moon, S.A.W.A., 2759/26.
207. Education Department, Special Case File 1215, P.R.O.V., series 892.
208. Ibid.
209. Nurses Board, Correspondence Files, S.A.S.A. GRG 14/1.
210. Ibid.
211. Ibid.
212. A. B. Piddington, K.C., *The Martyrdom of Women: Speech at the Bar of the Legislative Council of New South Wales: September 29, 1932, with Prefatory Notes and Order of Topics* (Sydney: Government Printer, 1932) p. 20.
213. United Associations of Women Papers, ML MSS 2160.
214. Ibid.
215. Ibid.
216. Ibid.
217. Kindergarten Union Records, BL 2308A.

Part 4   Women and Politics

218.   Plomley (ed.), *Friendly Mission*, pp. 182, 304.
219.   Hill, *What We Saw in Australia*, pp. 416-17.
220.   Colonial Secretary's Department, A.O.T. CSD 10/31/488.
221.   Tasmanian Aboriginal Centre, Hobart; copy, Lands and Works Department, General Letter Book, A.O.T. LSD 16/64.
222.   Typescript copy, Caroline Emily Clark Papers, in the Phyllis Owen Crompton Papers, S.A.S.A. PRG 331.
223.   Dora Montefiore, *From a Victorian to a Modern* (London: Archer, 1927), pp. 30-31.
224.   *The Dawn* (Sydney), 5 November 1889, ML.
225.   Premier's Department, S.A.W.A. 686/1898.
226.   *The Woman's Sphere* (Melbourne), 10 October 1902, ML.
227.   Mrs Nellie Alma Martel, *The Women's Vote in Australia* (London: The Woman's Press, n.d.), British Library, London.
228.   League of Women Voters of South Australia, Records, S.A.S.A. SRG 116.
229.   Rose Scott Papers, ML MSS 38.
230.   *The Dawn* (Sydney), 5 November 1889, ML.
231.   Manuscript in the possession of Mrs Evelyn Wood, Perth.
232.   Woman's League Papers, S.A.S.A. 570M.
233.   *The Woman's Sphere* (Melbourne), 10 October 1902, ML.
234.   Ibid., 10 July 1903, ML.
235.   *The Woman's Voice* (Sydney), May 1905.
236.   Catherine Spence, letters to Miss Alice Henry, S.A.S.A. D2475.
237.   *The Woman's Sphere* (Melbourne), 5 December 1903, ML.
238.   Catherine Spence, letters to Miss Alice Henry, S.A.S.A. D2475.
239.   Rose Scott Papers, ML MSS 38.
240.   Laura Bogue Luffman, *The Principle of Women's Associations for Women Alone*, Paper read before the Commonwealth Conference [of Women's Liberal Leagues] (Brisbane, 1909), ML.
241.   Queensland Women's Electoral League Records, OL OM71-47.
242.   Mamie Swanton Papers, ML MSS 1275X.
243.   *The Woman Voter* (Melbourne), August 1909, ML.
244.   League of Women Voters of South Australia, S.A.S.A. SRG 116.
245.   Ibid.
246.   *The Woman Voter* (Melbourne), 11 July 1912, ML.
247.   Ibid., 21 July 1914, ML.
248.   Ibid., 16 September 1914, ML.
249.   *Australasian* (Perth), 16 June 1923.
250.   *Western Woman* (Perth), March 1918, BL.
251.   *The Dawn* (Perth), 14 December 1925, BL.
252.   Chief Secretary's Department, S.A.W.A. 166/1932.
253.   United Associations of Women Papers, ML MSS 2160.
254.   *The Pioneers* (Sydney), December 1929, ML.
255.   Militant Women's Group, *Women's Path to Freedom* (Sydney: Proletarian Press, 1927), ML.
256.   Australian Women's Guild of Empire, *The Empire Gazette* (Sydney), December 1930, ML.
257.   Ibid., 30 October 1933, ML.
258.   Lands Department, Minute Books of Unemployed Relief Council, S.A.S.A. GRG 35/64/1, p. 399.
259.   *The Working Woman* (Sydney), 15 September 1930, ML.
260.   Lands Department, Minute Books of Unemployed Relief Council, S.A.S.A. GRG 35/64/1, p. 299.
261.   Jean Devanny, *Sugar Heaven* (Sydney: Modern Publishers, 1936), pp. 226-29, 246-47.
262.   Tape-recorded interview, Brisbane, 1975; in possession of compilers.
263.   *The Working Woman* (Sydney), August 1930, ML.
264.   Ibid.
265.   Ibid., 15 December 1930, ML.
266.   Tape-recorded interview, Townsville, 1975; in possession of compilers.
267.   *West Australian* (Perth), 22 July 1932.
268.   Ibid., 30 July 1932.

269. *The Working Woman* (Sydney), 15 September 1930, ML.
270. United Associations of Women, *Are Women Wage-earners Responsible for the Unemployment of Men?* (Sydney, n.d.).
271. United Associations of Women Papers, ML MSS 2160.
272. Jean Devanny, *Bird of Paradise* (Sydney: Frank Johnson, 1945), p. 283.
273. Typescript, Women's Voluntary National Register, Queensland State Council Records, OL OM72-57.
274. *Sunday Telegraph* (Sydney), 21 June 1942.
275. *Sunday Sun and Guardian* (Sydney), 6 August 1944.
276. Katharine Susannah Prichard, typescript "Notes on the Modern Women's Club", Union of Australian Women Papers, BL 1838A.
277. *Housewives' Guide* (Journal of the New Housewives' Association, Sydney), May 1947. ML.
278. United Associations of Women Papers, ML MSS 2160.
279. Tape-recorded interview, Perth, 1976; in possession of compilers.

Index